Merry Christmas &
With love and good wishes
Pretty Lady '1989'
xxx

IMPERIAL REARGUARD

Wars of Empire, 1919–85

Brassey's Defence Publishers

Editorial Advisory Board

Group Captain D Bolton
Director, Royal United Services Institute for Defence Studies

Lieutenant General Sir Robin Carnegie KCB OBE

Armande Cohen CBE
International Civil Servant and formerly with the
Assembly of Western European Union

Dr Christopher Coker
London School of Economics and Political Science

Professor L D Freedman
Department of War Studies, King's College, London

John Keegan
Defence Correspondent, *Daily Telegraph*

Lord Mulley
Former Secretary of State for Defence

Henry Stanhope
Foreign Policy Correspondent, *The Times*

John Terraine FRHistS
Hon. Fellow Keble College, Oxford

Brassey's titles of related interest

COKER
A Nation in Retreat: Britain's Defence Commitment

DANCHEV
Very Special Relationship: Field Marshal Sir John Dill
and the Anglo-American Alliance, 1941–44

DIETZ
Garrison: Ten British Military Towns

HARTCUP
The War of Invention: Science in the Great War

JACKSON
The Alternative Third World War, 1985–2035

LAFFIN
War Annual 2

SOKOLOV & ERICKSON
Main Front: Soviet Leaders Look Back on World War II

IMPERIAL REARGUARD

Wars of Empire, 1919–85

by

LAWRENCE JAMES

BRASSEY'S DEFENCE PUBLISHERS
(a member of the Pergamon Group)
LONDON · OXFORD · WASHINGTON · NEW YORK
BEIJING · FRANKFURT · SÃO PAULO · SYDNEY · TOKYO · TORONTO

U.K. (Editorial)	Brassey's Defence Publishers, 24 Gray's Inn Road, London WC1X 8HR
(Orders)	Brassey's Defence Publishers, Headington Hill Hall, Oxford OX3 0BW, England
U.S.A. (Editorial)	Pergamon-Brassey's International Defense Publishers, 8000 Westpark Drive, Fourth Floor, McLean, Virginia 22102, U.S.A.
(Orders)	Pergamon Press, Maxwell House, Fairview Park, Elmsford, New York 10523, U.S.A.
PEOPLE'S REPUBLIC OF CHINA	Pergamon Press, Room 4037, Qianmen Hotel, Beijing, People's Republic of China
FEDERAL REPUBLIC OF GERMANY	Pergamon Press, Hammerweg 6, D-6242 Kronberg, Federal Republic of Germany
BRAZIL	Pergamon Editora, Rua Eça de Queiros, 346, CEP 04011, Paraiso, São Paulo, Brazil
AUSTRALIA	Pergamon-Brassey's Defence Publishers, P.O. Box 544, Potts Point, N.S.W. 2011, Australia
JAPAN	Pergamon Press, 8th Floor, Matsuoka Central Building, 1-7-1 Nishishinjuku, Shinjuku-ku, Tokyo 160, Japan
CANADA	Pergamon Press Canada, Suite No. 271, 253 College Street, Toronto, Ontario, Canada M5T 1R5

Copyright © 1988 Brassey's Defence Publishers Ltd.

All Rights Reserved. No part of this publication may be reproduced, stored in a retrieval system or transmitted in any form or by any means: electronic, electrostatic, magnetic tape, mechanical, photocopying, recording or otherwise, without permission in writing from the publishers.

First edition 1988

Library of Congress Cataloging in Publication Data
James, Lawrence, 1943-
Imperial rearguard.
Bibliography: p.
Includes index.
1. Great Britain—Colonies—History. 2. Great Britain
—History, Military—20th century. 3. Great Britain—
Colonies—Defenses.   I. Title.
DA18.J35   1987   941.082   87-24227

British Library Cataloguing in Publication Data
James, Lawrence, *1943-*
Imperial rearguard: wars of empire
1919-1985.
1. Great Britain, Army—History—20th
century 2. Great Britain—History,
Military—20th century 3. Commonwealth
of Nations—History, Military
I. Title
909'.0971241082 DA16

ISBN 0-08-031215-2

Printed in Great Britain by A. Wheaton & Co. Ltd., Exeter

To A. V. Williams

Acknowledgements

I would like to thank the following for their generous assistance in the preparation of this book; Mr J. E. Deighton, formerly of the Royal Engineers; Captain Robert Fraser, formerly of the Royal Artillery; Surgeon Commander Carl Hallam, formerly of the Royal Marines; Brigadier Paul Hopkinson, formerly of the Indian Army; Mr F. Paice, formerly of the Royal Navy; Mr F. T. Rainey, formerly of the Royal Air Force; Mr Harry Roberts, formerly of the Royal Artillery; Mr W. S. Simms, formerly of the King's Own Yorkshire Light Infantry; Mr R. Weaver, formerly of the Royal Navy, and Mr Fred Wright, formerly of the Queen's Regiment. I am also indebted to the late Lieutenant General Sir Ouvry Roberts for information about the Indian Army. I must also extend my thanks to those who have given me information, but who have wished to remain anonymous.

My thanks are due to the following for permission to reproduce photographs: Dr Charles Kightly for plates 1 and 2; National Army Museum for plates 3, 4, 5 and 7; Imperial War Museum for plates 6, 12, 13, 15–20; Commanding Officer, Number 6 Squadron RAF for plates 8, 10 and 11; Controller of HM Stationery Office for plates 9, 14, 23 and 24; Alistair Campbell for plate 21, and British Aerospace plc for plate 22.

I am also grateful to Michael Ffinch, Martin Edmonds of Lancaster University, Dr Charles Kightly, Squadron Leader Graham Richardson, Dr Bill Sheils, Dr Martin Stephen and Percy Wood for their assistance and comments. I also wish to thank the staff of Harrogate Public Library, the National Army Museum, the Imperial War Museum, and the Public Record Office for their many kindnesses. Lastly, I must express my gratitude to Miss Jenny Shaw of Brassey's for her patience, good humour and help.

Crown copyright material appears by permission of the Controller of Her Majesty's Stationery Office. The extract from *The Mottled Lizard* by Elspeth Huxley is reproduced with the permission of Chatto and Windus, and the extract from *Officers and Gentlemen* by Evelyn Waugh is reproduced with the permission of Evelyn Waugh's Estate.

Contents

LIST OF ILLUSTRATIONS	ix
LIST OF MAPS	xi

1. **Introduction** — 1
   - *The Fighting Man's Empire* — 1
   - *The Façade Crumbles* — 9
   - *The Last Post* — 15

2. **The Raj Under Siege: India** — 29
   - *The Soldier's India, 1919–47* — 29
   - *Faqirs and Feuds, 1917–47* — 34
   - *Wapits over Waziristan: Frontier Pacification, 1919–46* — 40
   - *Passive Resistance and Partition, 1919–47* — 53

3. **An Empire Founded Upon Sand: The Middle East** — 67
   - *The Turkey's Carcass, 1918–20* — 67
   - *Mandates and Mayhem: Iraq, 1918–42* — 70
   - *Mandates and Mayhem: Palestine, 1919–47* — 83
   - *Oil and Troubled Waters: Egypt, South Arabia and the Gulf, 1919–79* — 101
   - *Curtain Call: Aden, 1962–67* — 117

4. **Wars of the Jungle: The Far East** — 129
   - *Prelude: Old Empires for New: the Far East, 1945–46* — 129
   - *Tuans and Terrorists: the Malayan Campaigns, 1948–60* — 136
   - *The Last Frontier: Brunei, Sarawak and North Borneo, 1963–66* — 157

5. **Winds of Change and Storms of War: Africa** — 164
   - *Chariots in the Sky: Somaliland and Sudan, 1919–29* — 164
   - *Black Terror: Kenya and the Mau Mau, 1952–63* — 172

6. **John Bull's Other Wars: Ireland** — 196
   - *The Rattle of a Thomson Gun: 1919–22* — 196
   - *The Old Cause: Northern Ireland, 1969–* — 208

7. With Moore to Port Stanley, or Regained for Britain: The Falklands War 222

NOTES 229

BIBLIOGRAPHY 236

INDEX 239

List of Illustrations

(Between pages 116 and 117)

PLATE 1 TRADITIONAL IMPERIAL SOLDIERING: Showing the flag; dismounted Kent Yeomanry with band, Egypt, c.1918.

PLATE 2 TRADITIONAL CHORES: Digging latrine trenches, Egypt, c.1918.

PLATE 3 FRONTIER POST: Razmak, Waziristan, c.1925.

PLATE 4 TRADITIONAL WARFARE: Column of Indian Infantry with mules marching along a military road in Waziristan, c.1925.

PLATE 5 TECHNICAL HITCH: An officer emerges from an armoured car which may have developed a fault, Waziristan, c.1925.

PLATE 6 THE NEW CUTTING EDGE OF EMPIRE: BE2c Aircraft about to take off for a bombing or reconnaissance mission from a newly levelled airstrip, North-West Frontier, 1917.

PLATE 7 RIOT: Peshawar, 22 April 1930.

PLATE 8 WINGS OVER EGYPT: Westland Wapiti bombers of No. 6 Squadron fly in formation over the Nile Delta.

PLATE 9 IMPERIAL CHASTISEMENT: RAF bombers attack Ghabaish, a village on the Tigris Delta, December 1924.

PLATE 10 GROUND SUPPORT: RAF Rolls Royce Armoured Car squadron on parade at Amman, Jordan, 1940.

PLATE 11 GUERRILLAS: Captured photograph of Arab nationalist commanders in Palestine, c.1938.

List of Illustrations

PLATE 12 MANDATE IN RUINS: Survivors are carried from the rubble of the Hotel David, Jerusalem, after its destruction by a bomb planted by Menachem Begin's Irgun terrorists, 1946.

PLATE 13 THE TUANS ARE BACK: Two youthful Indonesians are questioned about their nationalist sympathies, Java, 1945.

PLATE 14 THE EYES OF EMPIRE: Aerial view of pirate junks [centre] anchored on a creek of the Yangtse Delta, 1934.

PLATE 15 TERRORIST HUNTERS: An Aborigine tracker in gala dress poses in front of a light transport aircraft, Northern Malaya, 1954.

PLATE 16 THE EMPIRE HELPS OUT: Askaris of the King's African Rifles patrol the jungle in search of Communist guerrillas, 1950.

PLATE 17 AMBUSH: A patrol rests after a successful attack on a Mau Mau bush camp, Kenya, 1953.

PLATE 18 THE BRITISH ARE BACK: Landing craft and helicopters converge on Port Said during the Suez campaign, November 1956.

PLATE 19 SUSPECTS: British infantrymen stand guard over a batch of suspected IRA members rounded up in the Southern Irish countryside.

PLATE 20 OPERATIONAL DELAY: A motorised infantry patrol, held up after the mining of a bridge by the IRA, Southern Ireland, 1921.

PLATE 21 THE TROUBLES: A 40 Commando Royal Marine on night duty in Bessbrook, South Armagh, Northern Ireland, May 1983.

PLATE 22 THE EXCLUSION ZONE: Within the 150 mile limit around the Falklands, two Royal Navy Sea Harriers are about to land on a British aircraft carrier.

PLATE 23 CAPTURED: Argentinian soldiers taken prisoner at Goose Green, East Falkland, 2 June 1982.

PLATE 24 REGAINED FOR BRITAIN: Royal Marine Commandos raising the Union Flag over the Falklands again, 22 May 1982.

List of Maps

MAP 1	India and The North-West Frontier	42
MAP 2	The Middle East	102
MAP 3	South East Asia	159
MAP 4	East Africa	175

1

Introduction

The Fighting Man's Empire

One could scarcely believe that this tall, disciplined officer, master of several dozen supermen each twice as strong as any ordinary mortal, had so lately fawned upon a person of such meagre parts as Miss Cooper. He who had been a slave was now the centurion. I wondered if the askaris marching behind him had been seen off from Nairobi by wives and sweethearts with coiled wire bracelets and bead ear-rings even more copious than Miss Cooper's, and if they had noticed the same change. Perhaps some of them had seen their black warriors for the last time. The Northern Frontier was full of perils, and had bleached the bones of many soldiers and hunters in its time. 'I hope that he will remember to take his quinine regularly,' Miss Cooper said, as we walked back to the car. 'Men are so careless about these things. I remember my father, who was a military man just like Captain Dorsett — we are an old army family — was always forgetting hs quinine. He had served a lot in India, so I have the Empire in my blood, as you might say, and understand the sacrifices men like Raymond make to build and maintain it. A lot of people nowadays don't understand it, but I do. . . .'

Elspeth Huxley, *The Mottled Lizard*

The British Empire flowed through the arteries not only of individuals like Captain Dorsett, but through the common bloodstream of many of the British Army, Navy, and Air Force. Battle honours such as Quebec, Seringapatam, Chillianwala, Lucknow, Ulundi, Omdurman, and Paardeberg decorated regimental standards. Old sailors and some not so old wore medals with such bars as 'The Nile 1884–5' or 'Persian Gulf 1909–14'; not famous campaigns but still important in the process of conquest and pacification which extended and sustained the Empire. Moreover, many sailors spent much of their lives on foreign stations aboard men-o'-war which guarded the sea-lanes upon which the Empire depended. By 1919, the newest service, the Royal Air Force, had already had its first taste of Imperial duty, and during the next two decades its squadrons would see action in Africa, the Middle East, and India.

During the hundred years which had separated Waterloo from the outbreak of the First World War, the first duty of Britain's armed forces had been to protect the Empire, push back its boundaries, and impose the Imperial peace on its subjects. One imperial warrior, Major General Sir George Younghusband, whose services on the Empire's battlefields stretched back to 1878, wrote over forty years later, that his own and his brothers-in-arms' efforts were justified by the benefits which followed Imperial conquests,[1] Younghusband proudly claimed that thanks to the labours of Britain's soldiers, 'The sun never sets on the dominions of the King of England, and in righteousness and justice does he reign over half the world'. High-principled, selfless and ready to endure hardship, the archetypal Imperial warrior made war in the interests of progress and civilization. After the battle of Omdurman in 1898, *Punch* celebrated the victory with a drawing of Kitchener triumphant, faced with the vision of a new university which symbolized the coming of civilization to the Sudan. It was captioned 'Dreaming True'. In the film *The Drum*, which was made in 1936 and loosely based on the siege of the Chitral Residency forty years before, the hero, Captain Tony Carruthers, bravely faces a treacherous ambush by reminding his fellow officers that by risking his life he is furthering the ends of the Empire. The murder of a British officer was 'a not unusual preliminary to our establishing law and order', and in support of his case he cites, amongst others, Gordon at Khartum.

Gordon had preferred the path of honour to expediency and had taken duty to the point of self-sacrifice, choices which earned him a special place in the Pantheon of Imperial heroes. Their martial virtues had been popularized through the boys' tales of G. A. Henty, Captain Brereton and Percy Westerman. The moral and physical courage of the men who defended Britain's Empire was even more widely broadcast by the popular cinema. Tales of frontiers and wars were exploited during the 1920s and 1930s by British and American film-makers, and the resulting productions were littered with references to Britain's Imperial mission. In *Lives of the Bengal Lancers* (1935) the regimental adjutant, played by the physical embodiment of the older Imperial warrior, C. Aubrey-Smith, lectures newly-arrived subalterns about their duties. 'We are here to serve the King-Emperor', he insists, but points out that this means service to India and its peoples. The services approved of this sort of stuff and willingly co-operated with the film companies. Indian army units were loaned for the battle scenes in *The Drum*, and the Royal Navy provided an aircraft-carrier and a cruiser for the making of *Our Fighting Navy*, which appeared in 1937. Amongst the hype which preceded the film's release was the following statement:[2]

> There has always been a naval way of doing things and our film proves that the Navy way is the right way, a way that brings out the finest qualities in the men who had adopted the Navy as their one and only job in life. Truly the men of the Navy are sons of their fathers and possess more salt in their blood than any other race, resulting in the fact that we are the proud possessors of the finest navy in the world. The British Navy has not been used in the

picture as a background to some stirring love drama, but the story deals with the protection of these islands of ours and the far outposts of the Empire.

This was stirring stuff, and most reassuring six years after the mutiny of the Home Fleet at Invergordon. Careful censorship of scripts ensured that nothing appeared on the screens which was critical either of the Imperial system or those who ran it. Since a retired officer, Colonel J. C. Hanna, was vice president of the British Board of Film Censors during the 1930s, special care was taken that nothing was said or shown which harmed the army's public reputation.

Imperial films both extolled the integrity of the men who ruled the Empire and glamorized the duties of those who defended it. There was nothing new in this; from the 1870s onwards, the British public had been bombarded with vivid images of adventure and gallantry on Imperial frontiers created by journalists and war artists. The cinema continued in the same vein and fixed the Empire in the popular imagination as guarded by brave and dedicated men beset by native people who were either loyal and ingenuous like Gunga Din, or sly and cruel like the fanatic *khan* who vainly tried to overcome the *raj* in *The Drum*. It was a simple picture, but an influential one which coloured public attitudes towards the Empire, and encouraged the view that Imperial wars were an unavoidable burden for a nation like Britain, which had accepted the responsibilities of Empire.

The adventurous and exotic aspects of the Empire had long been recognized by the Services as a way to attract recruits. In the 1920s, a brightly-coloured RAF recruiting poster showed a smart and smiling airman against a background of the Pyramids. The simple appeal of adventure in distant and strange countries has always aroused restless young men, and this was as true between the wars as it had been earlier. Service in India, where forty-five battalions of the British army were always stationed, offered its own special enticements which included an abundance of whores and servants. Sexual adventures, told by his comrades when they returned to barracks, agitated Private Swindlehurst of the Lancashire Fusiliers in 1920. A serious-minded soldier, he took pleasure in learning about India and its people from a local photographer of whom he became a close friend.[3] Not all the men who served abroad during this period had joined up to pursue a life of excitement or to discover about foreign lands. As in the past, economic recession and a lack of jobs pushed men towards the regimental depots and recruiting offices.

It was very different for the officer class. Imperial service, whether in the British or Indian army offered wonderful opportunities for a rigorous, active life where duty and the pleasures of sport were happily mingled. 'The lure of sunlit days in the saddle, of nights under the stars, of big game and small, of care-free existence in a young country, is still irresistible to adventurous youth', claimed a correspondent to *The Cavalry Journal* of April 1926. He was advertising the joys of life in the Rhodesian Police whose ranks were filled by public-school men. Elsewhere in the same publication there was much to tempt men of like taste and temper. A team of polo players, from the 9th Lancers, who called themselves the 'Philistines' escaped 'the hot weather' of Palestine to win the Open Cup in Alexandria. The regiment's transfer from Palestine to Egypt soon afterwards was a disappointment since the polo teams missed the first part of the local season. Nevertheless, there had been compensations in the form of prizes for tent-pegging, won at the Palestine Police and *Gendarmerie* Shows. From India where many reports of polo contests and news that the officers of the 20th Lancers had already stuck forty-two pigs that season. Also out of India was an account of falconry, written by a cavalryman who had been introduced to it on the North-West Frontier. This was no mere diversion for, as the author pointed out, falconry 'employs the great principle of all true sport — namely, the employment of one animal for the capture of another, for the pleasure of man'. Other pieces list the placings of cavalrymen in point-to-point races and, were it not for a couple of articles on armoured cars and airships, the journal could easily have been compiled thirty or forty years earlier.

There was much about interwar service life which belonged to the world as it had been before 1914. The officer class by-and-large stayed true to that late-Victorian ethic which insisted that the able and versatile sportsman was also the best soldier and leader. Playing by the rules of the game and placing team before self lay at the heart of the moral code taught in public schools and in later life proclaimed the gentleman. Within society this precept still obtained, although after the First World War it was under increasing attack from intellectuals anxious to discredit the world of their grandfathers and poke fun at what was seen as the hypocrisy of the Victorians. The same groups veered towards pacifism which for a short time in the mid-1930s enjoyed a wide popular support. Adherence to pacifism went hand-in-hand with a rejection of militarism, which meant a tendency to condemn the armed forces and the attitudes of those in them. In such a climate, the officer could appear as either a hidebound martinet or a hearty oaf, and in both cases the possessor of outdated opinions. Sir David Low's Colonel Blimp is the most memorable stereotype of this breed, together with the overblown Brigadier Ritchie-Hook, whose 'blood on the bayonet', no-nonsense views enlivened the first and final parts of Evelyn Waugh's *Sword of Honour* trilogy. Ritchie-Hook had seen service in Africa, and like so many of his kind, real and imaginary, was never at a loss for a lurid anecdote based on his experiences.

> 'I've had fun in Africa too. After one of my periodic disagreements with the powers that be, I got seconded to the African Rifles. Good fellows if you keep at them with a stick but devilish scared of rhinos. One camp we had was by a lake and an old rhino used to come down for a drink every evening across the parade ground. Devilish cheek; I wanted to shoot him but the C.O. talked a

lot of rot about having to get a game licence. He was a stuffy fellow, the sort of chap,' he said as though defining a universally recognized and detestable type, 'the sort of chap who owns a dozen shirts'.

And so on through a tale which included an Askari spitted on the rhino's horn and the final demise of the beast at Ritchie-Hook's hands.

When war broke out in 1939, the War Office was less than pleased when many such figures, veterans of the Empire's wars, offered their services, as General Sir Aylmer Haldane discovered.[4]

> Many of them [retired officers] were fit and had served with distinction during the 1914–18 war, and these would have been valuable in helping to instil discipline — the absence of which was noticeable not only in the dress but in the behaviour of soldiers of that period . . . But youth and not experience were now regarded by the Army Council as principal requisites for the soldier who was to fight the Germans, and representations which I made on the subject were ineffectual.

Haldane's rebuff was much like that of General Wynne-Candy in the film *The Rise and Fall of Colonel Blimp* (1944). Wynne-Candy, like Haldane, had fought the Boers, and had also served in Somaliland but found that his experience and belief that war could still be waged according to some martial equivalent of the Marquess of Queensberry rules no longer qualified him for any kind of military responsibility.

Haldane's irritation with slackness in dress was understandable. Just as the interwar army fell back on some of the pre-war service values, so it made much of the routines of old service life with their emphasis on bull, parade smartness and doing things by the book. This concern manifested itself in all sorts of ways; one soldier, serving with the Queen's Regiment in India in 1939–40, recalled his Colonel's vexation whenever he found a sweaty chinstrap, a foible which continually forced men to buy new ones for a few *annas* each. Of course, fresh, neat uniforms together with precise drill were important when it came to 'showing the flag', that is showing colonial peoples the might and splendour of the British army.

Such public shows were an essential part of military duties between the wars. In August 1919, soon after the signing of the Treaty of Versailles had officially ended the First World War, the Cabinet laid down the future functions of Britain's armed services. It was agreed that there would be no war in Europe for the next ten years and so the 'principal functions of the Military and Air Force is to provide garrisons for Egypt, the new mandated territory [Iraq and Palestine] and all territory (other than self-governing) under British control'. It was the same for the Navy which had to maintain sizeable fleets in home waters and the Mediterranean, as well as smaller squadrons in the Caribbean, South Atlantic, Indian Ocean and China Sea. The thinking behind this disposition of men and warships was under attack by the RAF, which was anxious to defend its recently acquired independence and increase both its budget and influence. Its commander, Lord Trenchard, pressed for more and more RAF squadrons to be stationed not only at such strategic points as the Suez Canal but in regions where resistance to British rule persisted. Trenchard got his way, thanks in part to the backing of Churchill who was successively Secretary for War and for the Colonies between 1919 and 1922. As a result, the RAF was given responsibility for the 'policing' of Iraq and later Aden, an arrangement which was viewed with jealousy and suspicion by the other two services.

Soldiers, sailors and airmen serving in different parts of the Empire had one fundamental duty which was to show by their presence and their weaponry the hopelessness of resistance to Imperial government. Not long after a bout of violent unrest in Cyprus in 1929, *The Times* suggested that 'the Cypriots had been too little conscious . . . of their membership of the British Empire'. Their awareness would be heightened by 'permanent contact with Imperial forces and the constant presence of British aeroplanes and warships'. Displays of force were the usual way of not allowing the potentially restive to forget the power which was on hand to crush resistance. 'Showing the Flag' was the euphemism for what was, in effect, brandishing the cudgel and it lasted as long as the Empire. In September 1956, the civil authorities in Kenya were perturbed by the appearance of the subversive *Dini ya Msambwa* cult amongst the remote Suk tribesmen. In the aftermath of the Mau Mau uprising, no chances were taken, and so at the request of the local District Commissioner, a patrol of King's African Rifles with mules and Land Rovers proceeded through Suk territory. At various villages tribesmen were assembled and treated to displays of firepower. After one such exhibition, which included the cutting down of a tree by controlled rifle fire and the explosions of phosphorus grenades, the Company Commander, Major Stockwell, noted, 'I believe the lesson has sunk in'. This was indeed true. When the District Commissioner warned Suk and Turkana tribesmen that 'they must hand over any stranger who might enter the District to spread disaffection', he was assured by 'a splendid old Turkana' that interlopers 'would merely be killed and the District Commissioner need not think any more about it'.[5]

It was not always so easy as that. The lesson of British invincibility did not always sink in, and so the defiant had to feel as well as see the cutting edge of Imperial chastisement. In the Sudan, Somaliland, Aden and the North-West Frontier of India there were tribesmen who had not accepted British government and constantly spurned its regulations in favour of old, deeply-ingrained habits of feuding, plundering neighbours and travellers and rustling each other's stock. The same was true in Iraq, which had been acquired from Turkey in 1918 and included vast areas whose inhabitants had hitherto been untroubled by civil government, its law and taxes. Matters were made worse in these areas by the regular appearance of messianic Muslim holy men who found no difficulty in whipping up *jihads* (Holy Wars) against unwanted, infidel rulers.

The keeping of order in such conditions was a Sisyphean task for civilian administrators who were forced many times to invoke the army and air force. The result was a sequence of minor campaigns waged intermittently during the 1920s and 1930s in which Imperial forces always got the upper hand, at least for a time. There were risks in such operations but the deployment of technical novelties such as armoured cars, tanks (on the North-West Frontier after 1935), aircraft, and even poison gas (in Iraq in 1920) gave a permanent advantage to the British. As in late-Victorian and Edwardian wars of pacification, technology always triumphed, a fact which Major General Dunsterville acknowledged at the end of a spell of North-West Frontier fighting in 1917.[6]

> The Frontier tribes who in the previous year had made things quite lively for us, had been lulled to rest by various ingenuities of frightfulness that accompany modern war — aeroplanes and armoured cars having quite taken the heart out of them.

A great deal was changed by the coming of air power. From 1919 the RAF was sure that it possessed the *force majeure* which would bring the most stubborn tribesmen to their senses. 'Uncivilized tribes' would have no choice but submission according to one RAF officer who felt certain that aircraft would 'create in their mind the belief that they are confronted with a weapon against which they cannot retaliate'.[7] Other minds were unconvinced by such arguments or were made uneasy about the resort to bombing as a means to persuade men to accept the government of what was outwardly a benevolent Empire. Governments in London, whilst no doubt agreeing that the Empire was a benign institution, were impressed by the cheapness of air operations when set against the high costs of punitive actions by ground forces. Since the last word lay with the holders of the purse strings, what was called 'aerial policing' continued in spite of moral objections. The last air strike against recalcitrant tribesmen was made in 1948 on the borders of Aden and Yemen but, as in other similar raids, the details were not widely advertised to the public.[8]

The RAF contributed in other, less controversial ways to Imperial peacekeeping. After 1924, when Vickers Victoria transports carried a company of infantrymen from Baghdad to Kirkuk in Iraq, value of aircraft for swift troop movement was appreciated. It was a welcome discovery since past experience had taught British commanders and administrators that a fast response to unrest, however trivial, was vital. When the Imperial authorities either tolerated or turned their backs on signs of insubordination, they bruised their own prestige and opened the way for more trouble. Moving men by air meant that regions where the local forces were small could always be reinforced, as occurred in Palestine in 1929 and Aden in 1947. On both occasions the forces on hand were unable to cope with unexpected, large-scale disorders. The value of air transport was given a spectacular demonstration in 1928 when RAF transports evacuated the staff of the British Embassy in Kabul and other Europeans after they were threatened by political disorders. Another, even more daring mission was flown in April 1949 when the frigate *Amethyst* had been disabled by Chinese Communist gunfire whilst she was cruising on the Yangtze. Amongst those killed by the bombardment was the ship's doctor and his staff, and so the following day a RAF Sunderland flying-boat landed on the river under fire enabling a doctor to be put aboard. A further landing the next day was prevented by fire from the shore.[9]

This type of quick response in an emergency was made possible by the widespread use of wireless throughout the Empire. Its value, like that of aircraft was quickly recognized. A wireless signal from the embattled Government House during serious riots in Belize was picked up by the cruiser *Constant* which hove to a few hours later and landed sufficient bluejackets to restore order.[10] Naval landing parties helped keep civil order elsewhere in the West Indies during 1919–20, and again in Palestine in 1929 and 1936. They also appeared to assist the besieged Sheik of Kuwait in 1928 and lend support to the international force which protected the European quarter of Shanghai in 1927–8. There were other echoes of the old days off the China coast in June 1934, when Swordfish aircraft from the carrier *Eagle* joined in a hunt for pirate junks after some Europeans had been kidnapped from a steamer. The pilots discovered the pirate flotilla in a creek, photographed them, and when they were attacked by Chinese troops, assisted the assault with machine-gun fire and bombing.[11]

This was the stuff of *Boy's Own Paper*, adventure yarns of popular cinema scenarios, like so many other small wars fought by British forces keeping the Imperial peace. In retrospect, the imperial campaigns undertaken between 1919 and 1939 appear as an extension of those of the late nineteenth century to which modern weapons had been added. All the actions of this Indian Summer of Imperial warfare were small in scale and brief in duration. The end of the Boer War in 1902 had marked the conclusion of the massive Imperial wars of conquest and subjugation, so that British forces were left with mopping-up operations and keeping the lid on resistance in remote regions. By contrast, other colonial powers were still engaged in full-scale wars. Half a million French and Spanish troops supported by over 400 warplanes were committed to the Rif War in Morocco between 1921 and 1926, and an equally formidable muster of men and equipment was needed by Mussolini for the invasion and conquest of Abyssinia (Ethiopia) in 1935–6.

Introduction

The Façade Crumbles

The British flag has never flown over a more powerful and united empire . . . Never did our voice count more in the councils of nations; or in the determining of the future destinies of mankind.
Lord Curzon, 18 November 1918.

We are a world power and a world influence, or we are nothing.
Harold Wilson, 1964.

When Lord Curzon addressed the House of Lords in 1918, the British Empire was at the height of its power. Its former international rival, Germany, had been decisively beaten and British soldiers were already entering the Rhineland where they would remain for eleven years. Britain's other adversaries were also beaten and in disarray. Austria–Hungary's central European empire was breaking up, and the Middle Eastern provinces of the Turkish Empire had fallen to British conquest. Imperial troops held Baghdad, Damascus and Jerusalem, and for a short time occupied the Ottoman capital, Constantinople (Istanbul). Britain's former ally and one-time antagonist, Russia, had been dragged into chaos and civil war by the Bolshevik Revolution. Britain's other partners, France and Italy, had been cruelly debilitated by the efforts of waging total war, and would soon fall victim to internal dissensions. The United States, which had joined the Allies in 1917, soon withdrew into the shell of isolation. By contrast, the British Empire showed a brave face to the world, which glowed with vigour and health.

Before, during and after the First World War, Britain's accumulation of territories and peoples was the basis for her universal recognition as a world power. 'The British Empire is pre-eminently a great naval, Indian, and Colonial power' was the simple assertion of the Committee for Imperial Defence in its first report of 1904. Each part of this compound contributed to the Empire's survival and eventual victory in 1918. The Royal Navy kept open the seas which ensured, amongst other things, that the manpower of Britain, India, the white Dominions and the tropical colonies could be deployed in many theatres of war. World power and fighting a world war needed manpower. Between 1914 and 1918, India raised a million fighting men, most of whom served in the Middle East. The effort was even more prodigious during the Second World War, when in 1945, there were over 2.5 million men in arms, and a further 8 million otherwise engaged in the war effort. Other parts of the Empire answered the call for men during both world wars. East Africa provided a million soldiers, porters and labourers for the campaign which ended with the conquest of Tanganyika. The response was often astonishing; two-thirds of the adult male population of the small central African colony of Nyasaland came forward as soldiers and porters. African exertions were needed again during the Second World War. Two hundred thousand soldiers and labourers were recruited from West Africa for duties in non-European theatres of war, and by the end of 1943 there were 240,000 East African blacks doing the donkey work of the Allied forces in the Middle East and North Africa. More were needed so that during 1944 an intensive recruitment drive was in full swing to satisfy what Eisenhower called a 'heavy demand for labour'.[12]

These contingents of Africans not only toiled on such tasks as levelling airfields; they enabled white troops to be moved to Britain in readiness for the invasion of France. In an appeal for an additional 34,000 labourers made in October 1943, the War Office insisted that 'East Africans can not (repeat not) serve in Europe [but] they can release other troops for this purpose'.[13] This distribution of men and allocation of duties followed the pattern established by 1917 when over 250,000 locally-contracted labourers from Egypt, South Africa, India and China were imported into northern France for employment in docks and along lines of communication. Some of this drudgery had been given to volunteer infantrymen from the West Indies, much to their anger for they claimed to have joined up to fight the Empire's foes. Ill-usage led to rancour and some unrest, which made the War Office rather chary about bringing West Indian volunteers to Britain in 1940 despite the men's zeal to get to grips with the enemy.[14]

The part played by men from the white Dominions in both world wars has been overshadowed by the contributions made by the tropical colonies. Together with India, they gave Britain the sinews and muscle with which to defend itself and the Empire. Most important of all, in both peace and war, was the Indian army whose role in the preservation of the Empire and the maintenance of Britain's position as a world power was equal to that of the Royal Navy. During the First World War Indians fought Germans in France, Turks in the Middle East, and Bolsheviks in Central Asia and northern Persia. During the Second, Indians served in Hong Kong, Malaya, Burma, Iraq, Palestine, Egypt, North Africa and Italy. There were enough Indian troops in Italy in 1945 for British diplomats to demand the admission of India to the Allied conference called to determine Italy's future. At the end of the war, Indian troops formed the bulk of the contingents despatched to Java and Indo-China for the restoration of Dutch and French colonial rule. Indian troops were invaluable to Britain in peacetime. They had been transported to Malta in 1877 in anticipation of a war with Russia in South-East Europe, took part in the invasion of Egypt in 1882, the subsequent campaigns in the Sudan and smaller operations in East Africa in the 1890s. After 1919, Indian troops formed garrisons in Palestine, Iraq, the Persian Gulf sheikdoms, Aden, Malaya and Hong Kong.

Control of the Indian army provided other benefits. Britain was able to man her Imperial outposts without resort to peacetime domestic conscription, a measure which ran against libertarian traditions. A further bonus was that before 1933 the cost of Indian forces deployed outside the sub-continent was met by the Indian taxpayer, who also paid the expenses of the British forces

Introduction 11

stationed in his own country. Wartime financial arrangements were more complicated and did not always operate in Britain's favour. During the First World War, charges beyond the normal peacetime budget were reimbursed by Britain, although the Indian Treasury donated £100 million to the Imperial war chest. A similar accommodation was made at the beginning of the Second World War when it was mistakenly imagined that few Indian troops would be sent abroad. Unlooked for developments in the Middle East, followed by Japan's offensive in South-East Asia multiplied the demands made on Indian forces and Britain's coffers. By April 1943, India's sterling balance was over £400 million which led Churchill to wonder whether at the end of the war Britain would not only be expelled from India but left heavily in debt to its new government. He comforted himself with the thought that Britain might present its own account for the monies spent on the Imperial forces which had defended India from the Japanese.

On the whole Britain did well out of the bargain despite occasional hints that the former reliability of India's fighting men could no longer be taken for granted. Whilst many recruits from the accepted 'martial' races were, by temperament, disinclined to follow nationalist leaders drawn from the predominantly Hindu intelligentsia, many servicemen sympathized with the movement for self-government. Investigations which followed a mutiny by over eighty Sikh artillerymen in Hong Kong in December 1940 revealed that they had been swayed by pro-Japanese and Communist agents, who had also picked up converts among the colony's Sikh police force.[15] This was just a straw in the wind, but it was followed by more alarming signs that customary loyalty to the King Emperor was no longer unquestioned and universal. A small number of Indian POWs taken in North Africa defected to the Germans and during 1942 as many as 20,000 Indians who had been captured in Malaya and Burma joined the Japanese-backed Indian National Army. Turncoats also quitted their posts in Java in 1946 and joined the Indonesian nationalists.* Graver still were the mutinies by ratings of the Royal Indian Navy which involved 20,000 in violent, nationalist demonstrations at the end of February 1946. Accounts of the suppression are contradictory with nationalist sources alleging that Baluchi infantry refused to storm the corvette *Hindustan* in Karachi harbour. In Bombay, mutineers called to Mahratta infantrymen 'You are Indian, so are we. Why do you want to shoot us?'[16]

The great mass of Indian servicemen, whatever their political views, condemned the perfidy of their comrades who had broken faith, but there was still anxious speculation in Delhi as to what might happen if a crisis occurred in which the fealty of Indian troops was put to the test. In the event such questions about the future trustworthiness of Indian soldiers were academic. India and Pakistan became independent in August 1947, and control of the Indian army passed from Britain's hands. A vital limb had been amputated and

* See page 134.

the consequences for Britain as a world power were far-reaching, as the Chief of the Imperial General Staff (the title would soon be redundant), Field Marshal Alexander, realized.

> With the loss of India and Burma the keystone of our Commonwealth Defence was lost. Without the central strategic reserve of Indian troops able to operate either east or west, we were impotent.

There was a paradox here. For nearly the whole of its existence, this 'central strategic reserve' had been used to keep order inside India and guard the string of Imperial bases which had been originally occupied in order to secure the sea passage from Britain to India. In both World Wars the main job of the Indian army had been to keep open Imperial communications, to which end it had been concentrated in the Middle East, supported by units from the Dominions and tropical colonies. Imperial strategy had not altered since the 1870s, either in its objectives or methods. The manhood of the Empire was mustered for one purpose, the perpetuation of British supremacy in India. In the meantime British forces, augmented by Dominion units, waged war in Europe. There were sideshows which soaked up some Imperial manpower, such as the conquest of German East Africa between 1914 and 1919, and the expulsion of the Italians from Ethiopia, Eritrea and Somalia between 1940 and 1942, all of which incidentally added to the territory of the British Empire. It was not surprising that Roosevelt remarked: 'The British would take land anywhere in the world, even if it were only a rock or a sand-bar'.[17] This appeared true enough even during the Second World War, yet always the fixation with India was uppermost. By the end of 1940, the greatest weight of men and material from Britain, the Dominions, and India had been concentrated in the Middle East, first to wage war against Italy's North Africa colonies and scotch Mussolini's schemes for supremacy in the Mediterranean and then, as the course of the struggle changed, to defend Egypt and the Suez Canal from Axis attack. There were just enough resources for the task, but other strategic considerations had to be overlooked. The defences of Hong Kong and Malaya were therefore left in disarray and unable to withstand the Japanese onslaught in 1942.

The sombre debacle at Singapore in February 1942 and the subsequent collapse of British power throughout South-East Asia and the Pacific did more than just shatter the façade of British Imperial power; the essential weaknesses in the structure of the edifice were revealed. For over a century the façade had been well maintained. Haggling with other powers over spheres of influence, bribing, badgering and sometimes browbeating weaker governments, moving men-o'war and reinforcing garrisons at the right moment were all skills which Britain's rulers had learned to use for the preservation and enlargement of the Empire. At times, the diplomatic and military balancing act took on an air of allure and romance, as Duff Cooper noted in his diary in December 1916:

Introduction 13

I was almost shown into the dining-room, where Edwin, the Prime Minister and Reading were waiting for Lord Crewe. I stopped the servant in time and went up to the drawing-room, where I found, sitting on cushions round the fire, Venetia, Lady Wimbourne and Lady Goonie. They were all looking very pretty and beautifully dressed. I liked the scene — lovely women warming themselves at the fire this bitter night while under their feet the fate of the Empire was being decided.

The diaries of those who directed the Empire were less sanguine about their own and their charges' capability. During 1919 and 1920, Field Marshal Sir Henry Wilson, the Chief of the Imperial General Staff, was constantly troubled by fears that Britain's 'far flung battleline' had been stretched too taut by over many commitments.

There were good grounds for his misgivings. In Ireland, Egypt, Iraq and Northern India Imperial forces struggled to keep the lid on local nationalist movements. At the same time ships, men, and aircraft were deployed in North Russia, the Baltic, the Black Sea, Persia, Turkey, and the Rhineland in furtherance of the ambitious foreign policies of the Lloyd-George coalition. Matters were made worse by an Afghan invasion of India which, although rather spiritless, managed to trigger a large-scale tribal uprising on the North-West Frontier. When, in February 1919, the deputy-governor of Jamaica asked for a battalion of British infantry in anticipation of local rioting, he was informed by the War Office that none could possibly be spared.[18] Wartime helpmates seemed indifferent to Britain's predicament. The Dominions refused to lend troops for policing Iraq and distanced themselves from Britain's belligerent policy in Turkey. There was murmuring as well in India. The Viceroy, Lord Chelmsford, queried the wisdom of pulling British and Indian battalions out of a country convulsed by violent disorder in order to crush an insurrection in Iraq. His objections were overruled, but it was found necessary to offer bounties to tempt discharged Indian soldiers back to the battalions earmarked for Iraq. In Britain, too, similar devices were needed to recruit special corps of ex-servicemen for duty in Ireland (where they formed the 'Auxis' and Black and Tans) and North Russia. Such expedients had been required after widespread expressions of discontent by soldiers and sailors who, having joined up to fight the Germans, discovered themselves kept in uniform to wage wars in Russia and on India's frontiers.

The crises of 1919–22 passed, but they were a worrying reminder that Britain could overreach herself. To outsiders and many of the Empire's subjects, the Imperial façade appeared impressive, even fearsome. Those in charge of the day-to-day running of the Empire too often recognized weakness and bluff, and were all too aware that Britain's pretensions could easily run beyond her abilities. The gulf between what could be done and what should be done yawned large during 1935. The problem was how to give substances to the sanctions imposed against Italy by the League of Nations on the eve of the invasion of Abyssinia. The service chiefs advised Baldwin that sanctions would lead to a sea war against Italy which the Mediterranean Fleet could not win without heavy reinforcements. Even so, the naval planners concluded, Malta 'must be considered untenable as the air menace could not be accurately estimated', and so a Greek sea base might have to be obtained. The Home Fleet steamed to Gibraltar at the end of August and further units were ordered from the Far East, where the depletion of the British squadron aroused much Japanese interest.[19]

The trouble was, quite simply, a shortage of money. After 1919 the burden of being strong everywhere was more than Britain's exchequer could bear. The economy continued to suffer from the symptoms of paralysis which had been evident before 1914, and it soon fell victim to new, debilitating distempers. Productivity sagged and after the 1929 slump, Britain's old stand-by, overseas earnings, dwindled. An enfeebled economy meant that less and less was available for Britain's war chest. The recession made new, unprecedented demands on public expenditure. In 1933–4, social service payments, which included the dole, totalled £272,500,000; over double the allocation for the three armed services. This was at the end of fourteen years of unavoidable Treasury penny-pinching which had cut the service budgets and reduced personnel and equipment. The political support for the extension of 'air control' during the early 1920s had been a side-product of this overall obsession with retrenchment. Another was the Washington Naval Treaty of 1922 in which Britain accepted that in the future the Royal Navy would maintain parity with the United States Navy. What was, in effect, the throwing overboard of the 'two power' principle which, since the nineteenth century, had set the size of the Royal Navy at twice that of its strongest rivals, was greeted with dismay by many senior officers. An indirect beneficiary in this shift of policy was the RAF. In 1921, the Chief of Air Staff, in a memorandum to the Imperial Conference, claimed that the Navy was no longer the chief guarantor of the Empire's safety.[20] Its place had been taken by the RAF. The point was well understood so that in 1925, when plans were drawn up for a trial of strength against Turkey, and ten years later when preparations were made for a show-down with Italy, special emphasis was laid on aerial operations. The grim prospect on an air war closer to home led to the grants for the RAF to overtake those for the Navy after 1938.

By this date, rearmament was underway in anticipation of a European war which, for Britain, would mean a struggle to retain control over its Empire. Churchill saw the contest in Imperial terms. During its most crucial stage, he extolled the gallantry and sacrifice of the RAF pilots during the Battle of Britain in terms of an Imperial victory which would remain in the collective memory of an Empire which might last for 'a thousand years'. It was a theme which Churchill returned to many times during the war, and reflected a personal faith not only in the Empire but in its future durability. This was ironic for by the end of the war in 1945 Britain had been grievously weakened and was ready to shed the burden of an Empire which it had defended and held together during six years of struggle. In the Far East the strain had proved too much for, whilst Anglo-Indian forces had recovered Burma unaided, Britain's scattered pacific islands and atolls had been retaken by Americans, Australians and New Zealanders. Borneo, Sarawak and the profitable colony of Malaya were only reoccupied after a Japanese surrender induced by atomic bombs. In spite of the valour of its many individual parts, the Imperial battle line had snapped.

The British Empire had survivied the test of global war. Yet the experience had exposed many of its contradictions and weaknesses and so opened the way for its unmaking. The exertions of total war had stretched Britain to her limits and left her less able to fulfil her former obligations or reassert her old influence. Still, her Imperial will seemed as strong as ever, as American diplomats noticed when they observed Britain's serpentine manoeuvres to create new spheres of influence in the Balkans during 1944. What was lacking were the resources. Britain's financial and industrial resources had been drained and she entered the period of post-war reconstruction as the world's largest debtor nation. In stark terms of treasure and military might, Britain in 1945 lagged far behind the United States and Russia, the two 'superpowers' which now shared an uneasy world paramountcy. During and after the war, both had admitted Britain to their counsels and heeded her leaders' views, but there was no advantage to be gained for either from the preservation of Britain's Empire. Both in fact had much to gain from the falling apart of the old European world empires.

The Last Post

The Army, the Navy and the Air Force,
Are all we need to make the blighters see
It still belongs to you, the old red, white and blue

Those bits of red still on the map
We won't give up without a scrap.

What we've got left back

We'll keep — and blow you, Jack.
                    Archie Rice's song in *The Entertainer* by John Osborne.

Combative jingoism was part and parcel of the British music hall tradition. Raucous songs which celebrated the triumphs of British arms across the globe had served as a chorus to Victorian Imperial wars and a reminder that the lower-middle and working classes relished such adventures. When it was first heard, in April 1957, John Osborne's pastiche struck a jarring and mocking chord. It was less than six months after the Suez fiasco and the middle of a period in which the old Empire was falling apart. 'People seem to be able to do what they like to us. Just what they like', was the comment of Archie Rice's father, expressing a commonly-shared bewilderment and dismay. The retreat from Empire after 1945 stirred up much residual patriotism within Britain, where generations had grown up in the belief that the Empire was a source of national pride and strength. It rankled that now its inhabitants, once considered as backward natives, were coming forward and dictating terms to Britain. At the same time, Britain was counting for less and less in the world. It seems incomprehensible that after the exertions and sacrifices of the Second World War, victorious Britain and her Empire passed so swiftly into decline and dissolution. It was perhaps a consolation that her postwar rulers, Attlee, Bevin, Eden, Macmillan and Wilson, still believed and acted as if Britain was a great world power and sometimes said so.

Great power status had always depended upon possession of the Empire and the wherewithal to keep and defend it. The loss of the Indian army had been a blow, but Britain was cushioned from its effects by the National Service Act of 1947 which extended conscription until the late 1950s. Eighteen-year-old National Servicemen soon found themselves busy with the chores of Empire which did not always mean the dog days of service routine and off-duty lassitude which made up Imperial garrison duty. In Palestine, Malaya, Kenya and Cyprus, national servicemen found themselves fighting wars against local insurgents who wished to accelerate the end of British rule. 'Happy, hot, perspiring, and tired every evening', was how one national serviceman, serving with the Royal West Kents in Malaya, described himself and his comrades. Their daily life included timeless irritations of colonial service, insects and diarrhoea as well as road ambushes by Communist guerrillas.[21] There was also danger.[22]

> One bright morning moving through a rubber estate a young national service soldier behind me was hit through the chest and neck. It was only one bullet and it went fairly high in the chest. I had him in my arms and bright red frothy blood was pouring from his mouth and his face was going purple through suffocation. I had one hand on a pulse and one hand with a handkerchief scooping the blood from his mouth and holding his head down, desperately trying to get the blood to pour out. But in seconds the pulse weakened, a few moments later it flickered, and then it stopped for good. What a waste.

The involvement of national servicemen in the rump of Britain's Imperial campaigns may have been a factor which encouraged widespread reporting of these wars. War correspondents rarely appeared on campaign during the small wars in the 1920s and 1930s, although general accounts were published in newspapers. Details of the progress of the struggle against the Faqir of Ipi between 1936 and 1939 were included in BBC news bulletins, which were listened to by British servicemen anxious to discover exactly what was happening. Post-war Imperial wars were, by contrast, often front page news, reported by on-the-spot correspondents. The Right-wing press fell back on the type of strident jingoism which had marked coverage of imperial wars fifty years before, a style of journalism which again broke surface in 1983 during the Falklands campaign. On the Left, editors and politicians were always uncomfortable about colonial campaigns. They shared the opinion of Cleon 'that a democracy is incapable of empire' on the grounds that imperial rule often involved the abandonment of principles of justice and equality which were taken for granted in Britain. Whenever and in whatever circumstances, instruments of political and military coercion were applied in the colonies and, however sparingly, certain men of liberal conscience felt obliged to protest. In the 1880s and 1890s radical MPs voiced their reservations about the behaviour of Imperial troops in the Sudan and Rhodesia, and during the 1950s Labour members like Tom Driberg and Maurice Edelman badgered ministers for precise details of the treatment of suspects in Kenya or Cyprus. Often such interrogation was a result of newspaper reporting. In July 1953 a report in the *Daily Express* attributed thirty-three 'kills' to Sidney 'Davo' Davidson, an Assistant Labour Officer, then serving with British forces in Kenya. This prompted a number of critical questions from Labour MPs already perturbed by accounts of the death toll in the campaign against the Mau Mau; they were told by Oliver Lyttelton, the Colonial Secretary, that Davidson's prowess had been exaggerated and that he had actually accounted for just three murder suspects.

It was not easy for the soldiers involved in these operations, whether regulars or national servicemen. During the winter of 1946–7, the Adjutant General's Morale Committee was told that amongst soldiers in Palestine 'feeling against the Jews increases with outrages committed by thugs who obviously suffer no interference from the Jewish general public'.[23] There was 'friendly indifference towards the Arab' even through his pilfering habits inflicted extra guard duties on many men. This was a period in which large numbers of servicemen were kicking their heels as they waited for demobilization and felt that what was officially described as an 'absence of any purpose' in their being detained abroad. Lord Louis Mountbatten was 'seriously concerned' by what he described as the 'very low standard of discipline' which he discovered in Singapore at the end of 1945. Amongst its manifestations were slovenly saluting, a lack of 'manners towards civilians', and too much crime, including looting.[24] During 1946 and 1947 there were isolated protests from men on foreign service in Egypt and India, but they were trivial when compared to the disorders in 1919.[25] With the arrival of new waves of national servicemen, this immediate postwar *ennui* evaporated, although the newcomers showed signs that they were not willing to submit uncomplainingly to what they considered as unnecessary hardships on foreign service. Exasperated paratroopers demonstrated against disgraceful camp conditions in Malaya in 1946 and, in February

1947, 200 men walked off a troopship at Kure in Japan in protest against poor conditions aboard.[26]

In retrospect such incidents were signs of a new mood within Britain, where the Labour Government had been elected in the summer of 1945 with a programme for extensive social and economic change. Yet, whilst the way ahead was clear for Britain, the future path of its Empire still seemed obscure. Labour's Imperial policy had always been ambivalent. The party embraced working-class patriotism, like that of A. V. Alexander, one of the delegation which visited India in 1946. The Viceroy, Lord Wavell, warmed to his 'John Bull' attitude towards Gandhi's demands and noted approvingly that he was 'all for firm handling, equally so with the Jews in Palestine'.[27] On the other hand there was amongst middle-class Labour supporters a strong, intellectual feeling that the Empire was somehow a denial of the fundamental right of men to choose how and by whom they were to be ruled. Empires were at heart the exploitation of the weak by the strong and an extension of aggressive capitalism. Nevertheless the British Empire was a fact of life which the intellectual Left had to live with. It was possible for socialists to find common ground with conservative imperialists since both envisaged membership of the British Empire as a means by which backward, uneducated and often wayward people could be taught new and better ways. Just as the British working-class could be put in the way of moral and physical improvement, so could the peoples of the Empire.

This paternalist concept had long been current in Britain and was preached at every level. The Empire 'liberated' men and women from ignorance and oppression. 'The down-trodden peoples, in Turkey, in Palestine, and in Mesopotamia breathed freely after years of subjection' wrote Captain Brereton in *With Allenby in Palestine* published in 1919. His young readers were encouraged to see the recent war in the Middle East as a crusade on behalf of civilization, and the benefits of enlightened colonialism were set down for youth in *The Boy's Own Paper Annual* of 1923. An article described the work of improvement then in hand among the Kikuyu of Kenya, 'a simple people whom Fate had brought under our care'. It was the duty of young men to prepare themselves to help such people throughout the Empire. 'Let us see to it that we do not disappoint them; let us train ourselves so that we, in our turn, may be able to assist them in their development'. What could be achieved was outlined in the *Empire Review* of August 1924 which lauded the new irrigation schemes initiated in the Sudan. Here the 'wise and benevolent rule' of dedicated British officials brought 'peace, prosperity and happiness' to natives who had in the past known 'massacres, disease, famine and misery'. Such stories of progress were set before the British public for as long as the Empire lasted. In May 1952 Basil Davidson reported in the *New Statesman* that the Gold Coast (Ghana) and Nigeria 'are happy places where people feel that the doors are open to a better future', a fact which should be a cause of 'pride and satisfaction' for all British people.

When this was written, plans were underway to give both colonies self-government. In July 1920, T. E. Lawrence wrote in a letter to *The Times* that, 'I shall be told that the idea of brown Dominions in the British Empire is grotesque'. For many it was and continued to be for over thirty years. The arguments against any measure of self-government for Indian and the tropical colonies always boiled down to a matter of timetables. It was widely accepted that many of Britain's colonial subjects were unready for any kind of responsibility on grounds of backwardness and ignorance. This view was often held by those who believed that they knew the people concerned intimately and were therefore in the best position to judge their maturity. The 'liberal idea' at bottom spells rape and loot to the negroid tribes, concluded Captain Phillips, who had got to know some of them as an army intelligence officer in Uganda during the First World War.[28] After one of his young district officers had been speared to death by Guer tribesmen in 1927, the local governor praised him as 'one of our solitary workers in that morass of ignorance where we progress slowly'.[29] The 1959 Training Manual for the King's African Rifles reminded officers that in Kenya's northern provinces tribal war and caravan raiding had only been eliminated fifty years before, and 'any breakdown of law and order would encourage their revival'. In many other remote regions of the Empire, the picture was the same. The veneer of civilized, lawful behaviour was thin and the primitive savage was always just below the surface ready to break out. Generations of firm government and contact with civilization would be needed before such people had shaken off their past and were ready to govern themselves.

So ran the conventional arguments and the evidence to support them was plentiful. From Northern Rhodesia (Zambia) came the story of how Lever Brothers had, in 1953, promoted Lifebuoy soap by way of free samples. The promotion went awry for the recipients imagined that the bars of soap might induce rashes or even sterility. Some suspected a Government trick at a time when a debate was raging over the colony's future and alleged that the soap 'was capable of cleansing people from anti-Federation sentiments'.[30] More serious and compelling were the repeated claims that in many areas British rule alone kept the peace between implacably hostile racial and religious groups. This was certainly so in India where local forces held the fragile line between Hindus and Muslims and tried to hold in check the religious pogroms which recurred with baleful regularity during the 1920s and 1930s. Sporadic affrays between Sinhalese and Tamils in Ceylon (Sri Lanka), Malays and Chinese in Malaya, and Jewish settlers and Arabs in Palestine added to this burden of peace-keeping and so arguments in favour of the continuance of colonial rule.

Another shot in the locker of those who called for a slow and measured pace towards self-government in India and the tropical empire was the vulnerability of their simple inhabitants to self-seeking and guileful local politicians. Just and disinterested British administration would be uprooted, and in its place would follow a regime directed by an educated élite indifferent to the wishes of the rest of their people or representative of sectional or tribal interests. In the early 1950s, Sir Ralph Furse, a veteran Colonial Office official, was wary of the claims of generations of African political leaders who said they spoke for their people.[31]

> Because African crowds shout slogans at the behest of such leaders it does not follow that they understand what those slogans mean. In any country a good demagogue can rouse a rabble. This was true of Athens in her prime: it is easier when the rabble are uneducated — and intimidation, thanks to fear of witchcraft, is doubly effective . . . I am not questioning the sincerity of African political leaders, only the reliability of their utterances as interpreting the private, spontaneous throughts and aspirations of the African masses.

What mattered was that Indians in the 1930s and 1940s believed that the replacement of a British administration with one chosen by themselves offered a way to happiness and self-fulfilment and Africans in the 1950s felt the same way, so '*uhuru*' (freedom) became a talismatic word offering hopes of a new, better future. The words and phrases advanced by the educated Indians and Africans to support claims for responsible government also struck chords which were recognized within Britain. They were, after all, expressions of political doctrines such as underpinned Britain's own system of government and law. Since the mid-nineteenth century, successive British governments had conceded the rights of those colonies settled by British emigrants to govern themselves. By the beginning of the twentieth century, Canada, New Zealand, Australia, and South Africa all possessed their own governments based upon British ideals and practices. In acknowledgement of India's efforts in the war, she too was promised Dominion status in 1917 although no time limit was set for its introduction. Having admitted the principle of a 'brown Dominion', Britain then shrank from its implementation. The impatience of Indian leaders in turn led to nearly thirty years of agitation.

The pattern of Indian popular agitation for home rule was repeated elsewhere. Such activity posed a serious problem for local administrators, and for British Governments. In 1920 T. E. Lawrence had suggested that the only alternative to concessions was 'conquest, which the ordinary Englishman does not want and cannot afford'. The British Empire was based on consent and when it became clear that its subjects would no longer tolerate its government it could either bow to the force of opinion or fall back on naked coercion. The latter alternative led to the hideous wars of repression fought by the French in Algeria and Indo-China or, on a smaller scale, by the Portuguese in Angola and Mozambique. Both cost the colonial powers involved dearly and ended with vast domestic upheavals. It is doubtful whether the most bombastic adherent of the British Empire would have wished to pay that sort of price for the postponement of its collapse.

Introduction   21

Attitudes in Britain and the Empire had been changed by the experiences of the two World Wars. In both, the Empire's subjects had been exposed to different worlds from that of their towns and villages. 'The killing of white by black as illustrated before their eyes' had disturbed the minds of many ex-Askaris, warned an official in East Africa in 1918. South African blacks were amazed by the lack of colour prejudice outside their own country, but West Indians were distressed by it in Britain. 'The white class does not appreciate the altered tone of the black man', noted a Colonial Official to the governor of Barbados, where there had been restlessness among discharged servicemen during 1919. A new tone was evident in Africa. Former Askaris, disillusioned with 'the white men's religion', turned towards Islam or the 'Africa for the Africans' churches which were springing up under the guidance of black American missionaries. A generation later, in 1943, Sir Charles Dundas, the Governor of Uganda, was far from hopeful about the chances of drawing more recruits from the colony. 'Hardships and losses of the last campaign [1914–18] are vividly recalled and the feeling that we broke faith still lingers'. It was the same in Tanganyika.[32]

It was much harder for Britain to 'break faith' in 1945 than it had been in 1918. For six years she had been fighting for the 'Four Freedoms', the Anglo-American ideals which, it was hoped, would form the foundation of a new postwar world. Whether the victory of these principles implied an end to the old colonial system was not clear. *The Times* suspected that changes were overdue. In an Editorial in March 1942, it wondered whether the old Imperial order had become ossified since 'it had retained too much of that "stratified" spirit of inequality and discrimination whose last strongholds are now being rapidly attacked and eliminated in our contemporary society'. Given that the year before Indian commissioned officers had been banned from the swimming pools of European clubs in Malaya, the observation was justified. For many years after, colonial society was commonly seen as hierarchical and stuffy. On his return to Britain in the 1960s, one ex-colonial official was dismayed to discover that, 'we were viewed at home as a lot of rather superior beings who'd come along via the Somerset Maugham route, living in luxury and drinking gins in large clubs and flying their flags in large cars as they passed through their districts'.[33] While affirming his own faith in the 'Four Freedoms', Churchill quibbled about their application to the British Empire, but the new world power-broker, America, had no reservations about their universality. 'In the Middle East, as elsewhere, the objective of the United States is to make certain that all nations are accorded equality of opportunity', wrote Roosevelt. 'Special privileges', he added, 'have little place in the type of world for which this war is being fought'.[34] As that war ended, historical forces were gathering which would hasten the dissolution of Britain's empire.

Roosevelt's mistrust of Britain was based on wartime experience which had suggested to him and his advisers that once the war was over, Britain would make a bid to resuscitate her former Imperial and global pretensions. He was not entirely mistaken. As they oversaw the dismantlement of the Empire, successive Labour and Conservative Governments initiated policies designed to salvage as much of Britain's former international prestige as possible. On a political level much was made of the Commonwealth. Its existence satisfied the strong internationalist feeling which had always existed on the Left, and at the same time offered Britain the chance to pose as the leader of an influential block of countries. The Commonwealth grew quickly. India, Pakistan, and Ceylon joined when they became independent and between 1956 and 1964 were followed by Ghana, Nigeria, Sierra Leone, Tanganyika, Kenya, Zambia, Malawi, Malaysia, and Singapore. When he visited Nigeria in March 1964, Sir Alec Douglas-Home, the Prime Minister, announced that 'the evolution of the old Empire into the new Commonwealth is almost completed. For us, colonialism, is dead'. In place of an Empire which partly rested on coercion was a new institution based on consent.

In hard political terms, the nominal leadership of the Commonwealth did not endow Britain with the same international status she had enjoyed as the master of a world Empire. While it was commonly described as a 'family of nations', the precise nature of the familial ties were very hard to discern, let alone describe. Commonwealth states were not always willing to accommodate Britain over military matters. In 1962, Nigeria refused to concede Britain a staging base on her territory, reflecting a widely-shared view amongst the governments of newly independent nations, jealous of their new sovereignty and reluctant to commit themselves to either the Eastern or Western blocs. The terms of Cyprus's independence in 1957 allowed Britain to maintain two military establishments on the island, and Britain retained bases at Singapore and in Kenya. In the latter cases, the arrangement buttressed the internal security of the host country.

The Commonwealth was never of one political mind. There was widespread dismay among Commonwealth states after the Anglo-French invasion of Egypt in November 1956, when only Australia backed the action. There were further rows over Southern Rhodesia, for which Britain was nominally responsible, at least until its white settlers took matters into their hands and declared independence. 'All the platitudes on the role of the Commonwealth will count for nothing', remarked the *Ghanaian Times* in April 1964, unless Britain stopped shilly-shallying over Southern Rhodesia. There was more sour wrangling during the summer of 1986 over Britain's policy towards a former Commonwealth member, South Africa. This in turn led some commentators in Britain to call into question the value of the Commonwealth. Yet for all its puzzling contradictions and strange bedfellows (in 1975 Idi Amin of Uganda threatened to discountenance the London Commonwealth Conference by making an appearance), the Commonwealth has stayed alive.

The new Commonwealth grew up in a world dominated by the United States and the Soviet Union, both nations publicly committed to bringing an end to 'colonialism' everywhere. Antipathy towards 'colonialism' was most intense amongst countries which had recently escaped its clutches, and which, by the early 1960s were well on the way to becoming a majority within the United Nations. All were intensely concerned about speeding up the end of colonial government and were always ready to jump on what they considered as the crimes of the Imperial powers. Colonial difficulties and the dismantlement of Britain's Empire had become an international issue, and so policies had to be concocted and carried out with an eye to international opinion.

This was nothing new. During the 1930s German propagandists exposed what they considered humbug by making contrasts between British censure of Nazi brutality and Britain's waging war with tanks and aircraft against primitive tribesmen in India. They went further and offered covert assistance to Arab insurgents in Palestine.[35] After the war, the Communists took up the same line. On 2 November 1952, the Polish newspaper *Zycie Warszawy* printed a photograph of a pair of Mau Mau suspects flanked by two Kenyan policemen. Beneath was the caption: 'Here are two members of the "Mau Mau" organization, manacled like slaves, standing between two colonial policemen. They fought to liberate Kenya from the imperialist yoke and for this, they were regarded as bandits'. Under the headline 'The Colonists are on the rampage', *Komosomol Pravda* of 30 May 1953 reported that: 'The soldiers and police are cruelly persecuting the Negro population of the country. News of mass murders of Negroes arrive each week from Kenya'. The piece ended by quoting the British Communist newspaper, *Daily Worker*, which alleged: 'Terror reigns in Kenya which can be compared in brutality only with the occupation regime introduced by Nazi SS units'.

International sympathy and support was a bonus for the leaders of colonial independence movements. It was not, however, a new feature of such struggles. Before 1939, the Grand Mufti of Jerusalem had attempted to win German support for the Arab movement in Palestine, and in 1942 Nehru tried to persuade America to put pressure on Britain to grant immediate Indian self-government. More successful were David Ben Gurion and other leaders of the Jewish settlers in Palestine who, through the mobilization of American Jewish opinion, swung President Truman behind their cause. After 1945 the opportunities increased as the pace quickened. 'We had to get outside support for our liberation struggle and if we could not get it from the West, we should have to ask for it from the East', recalled Joshua Nkomo, one of the leaders of the Zapu nationalist faction in Southern Rhodesia.[36] As an exile in Britain, like so many others of his kind and in his position, he was generously received by Labour MPs. In Egypt, Nasser was sympathetic, and in New York he had the opportunity to lay his people's plight before the United Nations committee which was investigating colonialism. In June 1962, Nkomo approached the Casablanca Group of African states who had pledged to assist colonial liberation movements. It secured a stack of arms, including two dozen Kalashnikov rifles, which Nkomo smuggled aboard an *Air France* flight to Dar-es-Salaam. With the secret help of government ministers in Tanganyika and Zambia, this embryonic arsenal was smuggled into Southern Rhodesia.

The fortunes of Joshua Nkomo illustrated the new problems which faced administrators and commanders who found themselves having to fight colonial wars. Not only were their opponents likely to be in receipt of international support, but they had access to modern arms and in some cases safe areas in which to equip, train and rest their fighting men. Like other colonial powers, Britain suffered from these new circumstances. After 1945, Jewish terrorist groups in Palestine were able to procure arms through sympathizers abroad, and in the Suez Canal Zone, Arab terrorists had the goodwill of the Egyptian Government. More formidable was the help offered by Egypt and the Yemen to guerrillas in Aden, and the insurgents in Dhofar not only possessed a base in South Yemen, but were equipped with modern Russian weaponry, including small guided missiles which constituted an extra hazard to aerial operations.

For Britain, the postwar dismantlement of her Empire was always a complicated and sometimes a tricky process. Governments could not contemplate a helter-skelter flight from old responsibilities, a path which would have been morally and politically undesirable even in a world where the climate was hostile to empires. Imperialism may have been discredited as an idea, but Imperial duties could not be shrugged off. Britain was morally bound to do all within her power to ease her colonies along the road to self-government towards an orderly transfer of authority. Britain's own interests and her wider international obligations had to be taken care of. Wherever possible, Britain tried to arrange matters in such a way that the successor governments of her colonies were broadly aligned to the capitalist West rather than the Communist East. In Malaya, this was achieved after a twelve-year jungle war against Communist insurgents. Here, independence did not terminate military commitment. In 1963, British units defended the Malaysian provinces of Borneo and Sarawak from Indonesian incursions, and stationed V-bombers at Singapore in readiness for a full-scale war with Indonesia. When Turkish forces menaced Nicosia in June 1974, a squadron of Phantom fighters was ordered to Cyprus as a way of showing the Turks that Britain would not tolerate a complete takeover of the island. Post-Imperial responsibilities to Belize, persistently troubled by Guatemala's territorial claim to the colony, led to the retention of a small garrison there.

Former colonies were a trifle wary of invoking their former rulers' military assistance. From afar and sometimes from within the countries themselves, such help looked like a return to the old days. In January 1964, a mutiny by Askaris at the Colito barracks, just outside Dar-es-Salaam, forced the Tanganyikan Government to ask for British aid. Over 600 marines came ashore from HMS *Centaur* and dealt with the mutineers. Immediately afterwards, the Tanganyikans asked for Nigerian troops to fly in and keep order until the situation calmed down. Likewise Iranian and Saudi Arabian forces took over from a British contingent which had been rushed to Kuwait in 1961. The likelihood that there would be a recurrence of this sort of emergency has since led to the creation by the United States, Britain, and France of specially trained units which are on permanent stand-by for a swift descent on a distant trouble spot.

Imperial disengagement inevitably involved strategic issues. They dominated official thinking when it came to the Middle East, where Britain was faced by insurmountable political hurdles. Arab nationalism was affronted by the presence of alien military bases, which Britain insisted on maintaining. The result of this clash of wills was a strange game of military hopscotch in which Britain's major base in the region jumped from the Suez Canal Zone to Cyprus, from Cyprus to Aden, and from Aden to Bahrain. By 1967, the Labour Government concluded that the game was no longer worth playing and announced the end of military deployment east of Suez. The Conservatives, still hankering after old glories and conscious of political pledges made to rulers in Malaysia and the Persian Gulf, reversed the decision. As a result bases, manned by small units, were kept open at Bahrain and Singapore, together with a jungle training school in Johore. Another staging post was kept open at Nairobi where British forces have regularly trained ever since.

The trouble in the Middle East revolved around oil which, after the loss of India, became Britain's justification for clinging on in the area. A complete disengagement would leave such loyal British clients as Jordan and the Persian Gulf sheikhdoms vulnerable, and would create a political vacuum which might tempt Russia. Middle Eastern bases also played a part in Britain's nuclear defence system which was being developed during the 1950s. When some of the details of that programme were revealed by an Australian inquiry in 1985, it appeared that Britain's defence chiefs anticipated that Russian forces would overrun the region, capturing its oil resources. To fight back effectively Britain would, like the United States, have to employ nuclear weapons, some of which would be carried by V-Bombers based at airfields in the Middle East. The creation of the Baghdad Pact in 1954 brought Turkey, Iraq, Iran, and Pakistan into the Western Camp and, given that these countries were armed by Britain and America, created an apparently strong and stable bulwark in the region. These calculations ignored the force of local, Arab nationalism and its historical antipathy towards foreign domination. The Suez adventure in 1956 was a timely reminder to Arabs that Britain had not shed its old ways.

Sir Anthony Eden and the other architects of the Suez campaign laid their plans, convinced that Britain was still a world power capable of asserting its traditional paramountcy in the Middle East. They also believed that since the war, Britain enjoyed a 'special relationship' with the United States. This was true to a limited extent for the concert only really obtained when both countries were facing up to Soviet Russia. The 'special relationship' was never, at least for the Americans, intended to provide Britain with a *carte blanche* to behave as she liked in the Middle East or anywhere else. Eisenhower wholeheartedly condemned the Suez adventure.

Since before 1945 American governments had been embarrassed by

Britain's ambitions. The United States had already edged Britain from its former global authority and, what was more, possessed the wherewithal to act as a world power itself. In the Middle East, America had nudged British influence out of Saudi Arabia and by 1953 had found in Shah Reza Pahlevi of Iran what Dr Kissinger later described as 'a friend of our country and a pillar of stability in a turbulent and vital region'. As Britain's power crumbled, so America's grew. Britain's former clients realized what was happening and increasingly turned towards the United States, which did not disappoint them. There was still a small place left for Britain. British 'advisers' were helping the Omani army in operations against the Communist-backed insurgents in Dhofar, where they fought alongside Iranian and Jordanian units.

As America picked up the threads of Britain's former world influence, it hoped that Britain might find a new part to play in Europe. In 1960, President Kennedy remarked of Britain that 'we are in Europe but not of it', and he and his successors pressed British Governments to involve themselves more closely in Europe. There was, in fact, nowhere else for Britain to go by the late 1960s. Claims to world influence looked threadbare; Rhodesia was defiant and British mediation in the Nigerian civil war and the Indo-Pakistan conflict came to nothing. A course was set towards the Common Market and wranglings about groceries. De Gaulle, the arbiter of British admission, suspected that Britain, like France, still yearned for dominance somewhere in the world. He likened Europe to a farmyard where one but not two cockerels could rule the roost of ten hens.

Britain's armed services had already 'entered' Europe. They had been there since 1945 and their presence was confirmed in 1949 when Britain joined NATO. For over ten years the forces combined the task of guarding western Europe with residual Imperial peace-keeping. It was a formidable burden in terms of cash and manpower. The Defence budget rose from £724 million in 1950–1 to £1,230 million in 1955–6 with much of the increase being spent on the atomic and hydrogen bomb programmes and V-Bombers. Total service manpower stood at 900,000 at the beginning of the decade, a third of them national servicemen. In the next few years many were kept busy with operations in Malaya, Kenya and Cyprus as well as the war in Korea. These campaigns against guerrillas were all very labour-intensive. The insurgents were based in inaccessible areas or else moved amongst a civilian population which was either sympathetic or benevolently neutral, circumstances which demanded large numbers of men for tracking, cordons, searches and guard-duties. Certain units of specialists created during the Second World War adapted themselves to this kind of warfare and, like the SAS and Commandos, were able to perpetuate their élite status and reputation.

In Kenya and Malaya, specially recruited and trained native formations performed many useful tasks, and helped solve manpower problems. Such units were not always easy to handle. Sudanese infantrymen stationed in the former Italian colony of Eritrea quarrelled with the townsfolk of Asmara in

August 1946 and were stoned by a small mob. The enraged soldiers escaped back to their barracks where they obtained rifles and Bren guns from emergency stores. About eighty armed men swarmed on to trucks and drove back to the town where they attacked all the Asmarans they could find. Thirty-eight townsfolk were murdered and over seventy injured during two hours of mayhem.[37] Three Sudanese infantrymen were killed before British officers restored order and later a battalion of the Warwickshires was called in. As more and more colonies approached independence, native forces had to be transformed into national armies which was often a daunting task for their British officers. 'We looked along the ranks of soldiers', one recalled, and wondered 'who the hell are going to be the officers'.[38] Amongst those surveyed by this officer was Idi Amin, who like many others was picked for crash training courses at Sandhurst and Mons.

The Indian army, in 1947, had its own officer cadre, but there was no equivalent in the King's African Rifles so that British officers stayed on after the East African colonies received independence. The arrangement displeased many Askaris and there were mutinies in Uganda, Kenya, and Tanganyika in January 1964, all put down by British forces called in by alarmed governments. A Ugandan minister, Felix Onama, was locked in a guard room by mutineers and forced to lend his support for higher pay and the removal of British officers. Lieutenant Colonel Hamilton, the Commanding Officer, feared that compliance with these demands would sap discipline. Within a year his position had been taken by Colonel Amin and Ugandan army discipline deteriorated further. The army was becoming a Praetorian guard which gave notice of its new function by joining in the *coup* which dethroned the Kabaka of Buganda. Here and elsewhere in Africa, events uncannily mirrored those which had followed the departure of the Roman legions from Britain, with army commanders using their forces as a means to exert political power.

There was nothing which Britain could have done to prevent this increasingly common phenomenon. Her Imperial responsibilities had been relinquished, and her legions had been called back from their outposts. They returned to a country whose people, unlike Imperial Rome, had been outwardly little affected by the abandonment of its Empire. It had long been the habit of British servicemen to accept political control unquestioningly, so that whilst individuals may privately have regretted the handing over of the Empire, the duty of withdrawal was carried out without cavilling. Paradoxically, the army's return home was quickly followed by its embroilment in Britain's oldest Imperial problem, for in 1969, British troops were drafted to Northern Ireland to forestall a revival of the struggle between the Gaelic, Catholic Irish and the descendants of the seventeenth century Protestant settlers. A large garrison is still needed to maintain stability and there are no signs that it will be pulled out. This was not all. In the spring of 1983, Argentinian forces invaded and occupied the Falkland Islands, from which they were ejected by a formidable expeditionary force two months later. 'The

Empire strikes back' was how some American commentators described this amazing campaign which aroused in Britain the sort of excitement which had not been experienced since the heyday of Victorian Imperial wars. The physical links with the old Empire may have been sundered, but the emotional ties were still strong beneath the surface.

2
The Raj Under Siege: India

What you do not realize is that your empire is a dictatorship exercised over subjects who do not like it and who are always plotting against you; you will not make them obey you by injuring your own interests in order to do them a favour; your leadership depends on superior strength and not on any goodwill of theirs.
                    CLEON (From Thucydides, *Peloponnesian War*)

The Soldier's India

In February 1920 the Lancashire Fusiliers got ready to take ship for India. Old sweats were excited by the prospect of a tour of duty and entranced the younger men with lurid tales of the East and its people. Such men probably had little time for the official lecture in which the battalion was warned of the perils of sunstroke, too much alcohol and too many whores for later a young soldier, Private Swindlehurst, recalled how they came to barracks at night and told anyone who would listen about their recent sexual adventures. This was in the future however, and as they got ready to embark, Swindlehurst and his fellow greenhorns read Kipling's *The Young British Soldier* which seemed to have an uncomfortable relevance for them. 'The last verse sounds a bit ghastly, especially when we are bound for the frontier station of Quetta somewhere in Afghanistan, inhabited by a warlike tribe of Afghans called Wazirs, reputed to be wonderful shots with a rifle; they never take any prisoners, leaving them for their women to have a bit of fun with'.[1]

Swindlehurst's anxiety was unnecessary; when his battalion came ashore in India the Wazirs had been pacified, at least for a time. The Fusiliers were moved into the Punjab where they were called on to back up the local police who were trying to contain political and communal riots. It was less nerve-racking work than fighting Wazirs, but not without danger. 'Most of us bore traces of the marksmanship of the throwers of cow dung', after a march from Lahore station, and following a day of street patrols the medical officer faced many cases of bruised heads and sunstroke.

Private Swindlehurst was one of just over 50,000 British soldiers who were permanently stationed in India. In 1921 there were about 150,000 Europeans (including Armenians) living in India, guarding, serving and ruling a native population of 250 million. British soldiers made up at least a third of the Europeans in India, and together were a formidable buttress for that awesome edifice, the British *raj*. Outwardly impressive with its magnificent state pageantry, the *raj* was in reality a hotchpotch of different administrations directed by the Viceroy and the Secretary of State for India who ruled from a desk in London. There were ten provinces, regions under the direct administration of Delhi and 680 princely states which were more or less protectorates run by native rulers under British guidance. Few Indians ever saw a British soldier or, for that matter, a British official, but they knew that the army was there, as a last resort, to uphold the authority of Delhi. Over the past two hundred years India had been conquered either by direct force of arms or the threat of it, and a few years before Swindlehurst arrived there were old soldiers alive who were veterans of the Sikh Wars of the 1840s. Others, still living in the 1920s, were veterans of the Indian Mutiny of 1857-8, memories of which had been recently awakened by the unrest in the Punjab. The Mutiny had been a dreadful lesson in the dangers of over-confidence and carelessness. As an insurance against its repetition, the garrison of India was fixed at one battalion of British to three of native troops.

Together, British and native troops made up the Indian Army which had its own Commander-in-Chief, who sat on the Viceroy's council, and four subsidiary commands. The deployment of troops in India was dictated by two basic requirements, defence against invasion and internal security. A screen of twelve battalions covered the North-West Frontier, placed there to act as a tripwire to stem either Afghan or Russian incursions whilst the Field Army mustered and moved to support it. At the same time, other forces took over the protection of the 4,000 miles of designated strategic railways upon which the frontier forces depended. With its own arms and ammunition factories, many built during the First World War, India possessed a degree of strategic self-sufficiency. From 1919 onwards, the 'reserves' were increasingly used as support for the police who were facing more and more demonstrations by supporters of Indian self-government. By 1938, twenty-eight British battalions were stationed in various regions for these duties, a political necessity which weakened the strategic reserve.

In purely military terms the major threat to Indian security was concentrated on the North-West Frontier. It took the form of the volatile Pushtun tribes and clans who refused to live by rules set by the government in Delhi. Beyond the tribal areas was Afghanistan, an independent kingdom, which, in May 1919, had launched a rather half-hearted invasion of India. Further north was Russia, where the new Communist government was officially suspected of having inherited the Czarist taste for Asian aggrandizement and meddling on the borders of India. After the palace *coup* by the pro-British Nadir Shah, in which he made himself *Amir* of Afghanistan, the likelihood of trouble from this quarter receded, although Moscow continued to stir up Indian discontent through revolutionary propaganda. Even when, after 1941, Russia was

Britain's ally, Indian Military Intelligence kept an eye open for the activities of Russians close to the Indian–Persian border, and was suspicious about their motives.[2]

The 'Great Game' of the Frontier was traditional, and was the basis for active soldiering in India as well as the justification for the concentrations of troops and aircraft on the North-West Frontier. The region was never tranquil, and at one stage, during the late 1930s, over 40,000 British and Indian troops, supported by several RAF squadrons, were drawn into one area to bring its inhabitants to heel.

When they were not pacifying the frontier tribes or standing ready to support the police, British soldiers in India followed the commonplace routines and rituals of peacetime service life. The actual military value of Indian service was sometimes questioned by staff officers in Britain on the grounds that the battle experience of frontier campaigns had virtually nothing in common with what might be expected in the event of a European war. There was much that was anachronistic about frontier campaigns where many of the methods of waging war had changed little for a hundred years. A single column, operating in Waziristan, in 1919, needed 4,000 camels and mules for its transport, and there had been a cavalry charge during the Tochi Valley operations in November 1936.[3] Frontier soldiers did appreciate the novelties of modern war, especially where they gave them advantages of firepower and mobility. Aircraft and armoured cars had been used on the frontier since 1917, and, two years after, a battalion of the Somerset Light Infantry had been moved up to a forward post by motor lorries. Under pressure from the War Office, tanks had been introduced to India in 1932 and were soon used in action against the Mohmands. They were an unwelcome innovation, both to the Mohmands, who complained about them to Political Officers, and to old frontier hands who were sceptical about their effectiveness. The lack of motor transport was a worry on the frontier; staff planners, devising a strategy for a swift advance to Kabul in the event of Afghan hostility, were dismayed to find that India did not possess sufficient lorries for such an operation. Matters were put right, and a few years later, in 1936, ten light tanks, ten armoured cars, and nearly 100 lorries took the replacement garrison to Chitral in the far north of the frontier zone.[4] The despatch of such a formidable convoy was an exercise in prestige for it showed what sort of backing the *raj* could provide for its local client, the Mehtar of Chitral. Still some tribesmen were unimpressed and sniped at the vehicles.

For an officer, the frontier offered the rare opportunity to see action and perhaps make himself a reputation. One later summed it up as 'an exhilarating life' where the excitement was heightened by 'a good deal of scattered fighting'. Another called to mind memories of 'brown, hard lean faces' seen by the light of a hurricane lamp, as he and his brothers-in-arms exchanged yarns in their tent. They had been enthused by the peculiar *Boy's Own Paper* quality of the frontier campaigns which, even during the last days of the *raj*, still belonged to the world of Kipling, Newbolt and G. A. Henty. For this reason they were attractive to film-makers, both in Hollywood, whence the frontier resembled the Wild West, and Britain. *The Drum*, shot on location at Chitral in 1936, made use of the local garrison for its battle sequences, for which a fee of £3,000 was paid. The film was set in the 1920s to judge from Valerie Hobson's dresses, but the fighting belonged to a period twenty years earlier. While mountain and machine-guns appear, armoured cars and aircraft do not. The same is true of other frontier films which were set in a Victorian limbo, where the British did not have too many overwhelming technical advantages and there was room for personal pluck. In moral terms, the British stood for fair-dealing and civilization, their adversaries for deceit and cruelty; in *The Drum*, the villainous *khan* (Raymond Massey) received help from an unnamed power — a nice contemporary touch.

The frontier campaigns were not all high adventure and derring-do. 'Defending India' gave a soldier 'less freedom, leisure and a much harder life than the average prisoner in Britain today' was the recent recollection of a signaller, Private Deighton, who served on the frontier in the late 1930s. War was waged in an unkind landscape where rocks, cacti and camel thorn tore at the unprotected parts of the legs. Soldiers who served in Waziristan during the 1917 campaign experienced a twenty to thirty degree variation between day and night temperatures. Over half the British involved, nearly all of whom were unacclimatized, fell sick from sandfly fever, dysentery or diarrhoea. Troops at Dakka in June 1919 endured daytime temperatures of 125°F, which dropped at night to just under 100°F. They wore a standard uniform which changed little over the next twenty years. On the head was a pith helmet with a neck curtain and the groin and backbone were protected by quilted pads — spinal fluids were believed to get overheated. A greyish-black wool and cotton shirt was worn with long, baggy shorts, and the legs were covered with woollen hose, cotton and wool socks, ankle-length puttees and heavy boots. To prevent irritation from prickly heat, shirts were worn outside shorts, and eye-strain was reduced by glare-glasses. Drinking water was heavily chlorinated after a cholera epidemic amongst Indian bearers but it offered little relief to thirst because it boiled in the iron storage tanks.

Soldiers survived these discomforts and flourished. 'We were a credit to our country', Private Deighton remembered with pride. Fred Wright, who served with the Queen's Regiment on the frontier in 1941 found the area 'an ideal training ground for troops', where the lessons learned 'stood us in tremendous stead in Burma'.[5] A few years earlier, a young soldier with the Northampton-shires prized the Kiplingesque element of frontier fighting. 'Razmak to me was as soldiering should be, a tough soul-stirring experience, something that I, as an eager NCO, really enjoyed, each and every column a story unto itself'. A part of this soldiering was the apprenticeship in frontier warfare in which newly-arrived British battalions understudied more experienced Indian units. It was not always an easy process, and some did not care to learn the ropes. A junior British officer, serving with a Punjabi regiment during the 1937 campaign, was dismayed by the casualness of one British private, whom he found propped up against a Vickers gun, scanning the sporting news of the *Pink 'Un*, oblivious to the dangers from unseen snipers. 'The British soldier simply would not take things seriously and got into unnecessary scrapes', regretted the officer.[6]

By contrast the Indian soldier knew his business for, in the eyes of his British officers, he was a natural warrior drawn from races that prided themselves in warlike skills. There was always a *frisson* between regular British officers and their counterparts who commanded native troops. Both were Sandhurst-trained, and every officer destined for an Indian regiment spent a year attached to a British battalion. Many were snubbed, victims of a spiteful snobbery based on the knowledge that they had chosen Indian service because they lacked the private resources to keep their heads above water in a British Mess. John Masters both suffered the slights and the deeper hostility to Indians. 'I did not like hearing Indians spoken of as "niggers", "wogs", "Hindoos", or even "black-bellied bastards" — the standard terms of the British soldier and often the British Service officer. To me already, from the evenings I had spent in the Messes of Indian regiments in Razmak and on column, they were Dogras, Bengalis, Afridis, Kokani Mahrattas'.[7] It would be unfair and mistaken to extend the prejudices heard by Masters to every British soldier and officer in India, but given the imperial traditions of the British army, its part in the conquest of India and its role in sustaining the *raj*, it was all too easy for all ranks to see themselves as masters over the country and its people.

The foes of the *raj*, at least those who lived on the frontier, sometimes drew respect. The Pushtun tribesman, for all his reputation for cruelty, was often portrayed as a noble savage who, like the British, saw war as a game. 'We liked their hail-fellow-well-met, open manners and manliness and they were given to much reminiscence about the fighting, almost as if talking about some hard-fought cricket match', observed one officer for whom sport and war were obviously inseparable. The Pushtun gave evidence that he could think along the same lines, even to the point of toleration for the British sportsman. 'When the Peshawar Vale Hunt, in hot pursuit of a jackal, used to cross into tribal territory they held their fire', recalled Brigadier Prendergast. Such goodwill was not universal for, in 1928, two Highland officers who were shooting game were themselves ambushed and shot dead close to the Khyber Pass. Around Razmak and Datta Khel other tribesmen were intolerant of cricketers and footballers, and picquets had to be sent into the foothills to clear them of snipers who would otherwise have taken shots at the players. When not on the look-out for a soccer or cricket team, tribesmen close to Razmak enjoyed themselves by taking shots at the cast-iron screen which shielded the latrine trench, and made a loud, satisfying clang when hit, much to the vexation of the users. For all this, the Pushtun was still considered by some as a worthy opponent. Harry Roberts, who served with the artillery in the 1930s, remembered that when his unit was withdrawn from the frontier, their last march through the streets of Peshawar was watched by local tribesmen, some with illicit rifles.[8] He wondered then and later whether these former adversaries had come to see him and his comrades off. He thinks that they had, and is probably not mistaken.

Faqirs and Feuds

Seven tribes and many smaller clans of Pushtuns inhabited the North-West Frontier. According to *Imperial Military Geography*, an army text book of 1929, they could muster, if united, nearly 150,000 riflemen. Another estimate of tribal strength, made by military intelligence in 1940, calculated that in the turbulent region of Waziristan there were 400,000 tribesmen armed with a quarter of a million rifles, many of them the standard .303 British Lee Enfield. For the government in Delhi, the governor of the North-West Frontier Province and the army, these tribesmen were a permanent problem.

At the centre of the frontier problem was the intractability of the Pushtun tribesmen, who would not be tamed to appreciate the benefits of stability and order under the *raj*. In ethical terms the British Empire was a force for moral good; it brought the ungovernable to heel and made them forsake such habits as raiding and feuding which appeared, in both London and Delhi, the stumbling blocks to social, economic and political progress. An ill-defined frontier peopled by recalcitrant and belligerent tribesmen was an affront to soldiers and administrators. To bring order and tranquility to such a region was a high duty which was undertaken cheerfully by soldiers, not least because frontier wars offered the chance for making a reputation and so gaining advancement. Wars of pacification were costly and in the past they had had unlooked-for and unwelcome results. Opinions often differed about military solutions to the frontier problem, and politicians and administrators were wary of army men who wished to find excuses for a war; everyone knew what had happened in Zululand in 1879 and, a few years later, in the Sudan.

The frontier commander was less troubled by fears of suffering some setback. He stood by his experience and often arcane knowledge of the people with whom he had to deal, which always made him keenly aware of the need to uphold and advance prestige. Prestige was all-important when handling tribesmen, particularly warlike ones, who always needed periodic displays of military might to remind them of what the Government could and would do if pressed too far. Prestige demanded aggressiveness, for any action which could be interpreted as withdrawal was likely to encourage the frontier tribes. This canon of frontier policy ruled out any solution which involved the evacuation of British forces to the Indus. In the nineteenth century the steady advance of British power into the foothills of the Himalayas had been followed by treaties in which some tribesmen had submitted to British control. Such people looked to Britain for protection from their defiant and armed neighbours, as did the Indians of the plains on whom the hill tribes had traditionally preyed. Delhi was therefore wedded to what was called a 'forward' policy, and this had been pursued since the early 1890s and would be until 1947. In action, the 'forward' policy meant the military and political penetration of the tribal territories right up to the border with Afghanistan and the Hindu Kush.

There were sound strategic reasons for the 'forward' policy. The North-West Frontier was crossed by five passes, of which the Khyber was the largest and best known, and all were routes into India from Afghanistan and Russia. Governments in London and Delhi had, from the 1830s onwards, suffered sporadic nervous spasms about these passes, which were seen as conduits down which the Russian hordes might suddenly pour. Whether or not the Czars' armies could have ever mounted an operation to occupy Afghanistan and invade India is open to question, although practical considerations did not stop Russian Generals from dreaming and devising plans. What mattered was that generations of British statesmen, politicians and Generals believed that the Russians could have attacked India and would have done so, given the opportunity. After the revolution of 1917, Russia still seemed a threat to India but now Russian ideas rather than Russian soldiers were the danger. The new regime in Moscow had pledged its support for all colonial liberation movements in Asia, and offered open house for Indian Communists and revolutionaries. 'The gravest military menace which faces the British Empire today', was how the Chief of the Imperial General Staff described Communist subversion in 1927. His fear was based upon a report which outlined some of the mischief the Russians were up to, including offers of succour to anti-British fanatics from India. There were Communist cells in Afghanistan, and the Russians had established arms dumps, propaganda centres and wireless listening-posts along the frontier. The British too had listening posts which monitored Russian radio messages.[9]

Technology and revolutionary politics were new counters in the Great Game, even though its objective remained much the same. The ostensible object of British and Russian interest were the Pushtun tribesmen who lived in a highland region which stretched for over a thousand miles from Baluchistan to the headwaters of the Oxus. Across this belt of tribal territory ran the Durand Line, a neat piece of late Victorian map-making which officially divided India from Afghanistan. It meant next to nothing to the Pushtuns, who passed to and from India when they had to, usually towards Afghanistan where they were safe from imperial retribution. The painful experience of two invasions of Afghanistan in 1839 and 1878 made the British chary of direct intervention in this buffer state.

The Pushtun tribesmen were Muslims (there were thought to be about fifteen million of them in 1947 when they came under the new Government of Pakistan) and they were divided into tribes and clans which were usually hostile to one another. Farming was done by the women and children which left the men free to prey on each other, pursue vendettas and plunder their lowland neighbours. Armed plundering raids were essential to the Pushtun economy, but from the plains they appeared to be an enterprise which looked very much like banditry. This was the view of soldiers and administrators, for whom the Pushtuns were a race of defiant reivers who spurned the imperial peace and needed chastisement. The frontier tribes and clans saw no value whatsoever in submission to the rules of the British which, if complied with, would beggar them, and end a way of life which they enjoyed.

The Pushtuns resisted the *raj*, not only in defence of their customs but in defence of their faith. The wars waged on the frontier from the 1890s onwards were invariably *jihads*, holy wars against the infidels. The columns of imperial soldiers, the forts they built and the roads which supplied the forts and armies seemed to the tribesmen the outward signs of approaching infidel rule which would, in time, extinguish their faith. Like other Muslims in Asia and the Middle East, the Pushtuns were aware of a wider conflict in which European Christian nations were overcoming what had once been Muslim states and communities. Just before the frontier uprisings in 1917, a *mullah* had crossed the region with encouraging tales of Turkish victories over the British, news which made many Wazirs keen to join the struggle for Islam. Such stories were 'mendacious' according to the British Government, although it was hard to justify such an adjective in the light of Kut and Gallipoli.[10] The final defeat of Turkey in 1918, and rumours that the Allies were set on dethroning the Turkish Sultan, who as Caliph claimed spiritual leadership over Muslims, incensed many tribes. Wazirs were furious when they heard tales which alleged that British soldiers defiled Muslim shrines, including the Kabaa at Mecca.[11]

Tribesmen who normally feuded with each other could be united by the rallying call that Islam was in danger. Even an outwardly trivial incident could spark off widespread alarm and agitation. The elopement of a Hindu girl from Bannu with her Wazir lover in 1936 led to her conversion, and demands from the Hindu community for her return. The British authorities intervened and the girl was taken back to her family. This was a contumelious insult by the British to Islam, and the incident led to over ten years of intermittent warfare on the frontier. During a relatively quiet period in 1941, frontier hearsay claimed that the British and their Russian allies intended to invade Afghanistan, and other fictitious reports told of an uprising against the Russians by the Muslims in Turkestan. Such talk was enough to trigger a revival of Wazir unrest which culminated in an attack on, and determined siege of, the fort at Datta Khel in the following year.[12]

In common with earlier wars of Pushtun resistance, those in the late 1930s owed much to the intervention of Holy Men who transformed local religious apprehension into the cause for a *jihad*. It was the duty of Muslim ascetics and teachers to warn the faithful when their faith seemed in danger, and to show them how they could defend it. Congregations were exhorted to turn their back on sin and rediscover the zeal and purity of faith which they would need for

fighting a holy war. The preachers of the *jihad* were always Holy Men who enjoyed a high standing amongst their people. As prophets of war they quickly assumed all powerful, messianic and charismatic powers with which they fortified their adherents. The *mullah* Maslan (called 'the Mad Faqir of Swat') proclaimed that he could turn bullets into water, feed the masses from one tiny pot of rice, and promised that heavenly hosts would join his warriors in battle.*
In May 1919, a *mullah* at Miramshah, who boasted that his spells could bring down aircraft, gained brief credibility after one 'plane crashed. Soon afterwards he was exorcized, as it were, by a bombing raid on his adherents.[12] Immunity from bombs was assured by another Holy Man in the Peshawar district in 1930 when his followers attacked a police station. Several were killed in a bombing raid, and the survivors gave the Holy Man a rough handling.

Mirza Ali Khan who, like other Pushtun religious leaders had made the pilgrimage to Mecca and acquired a reputation as an ascetic, united the Wazirs after the Bannu abduction of 1936. His powers as a miracle-worker were attested by one of his adherents.[14]

> [He] told us that if we threw a stone into the air it would turn into a hailstorm killing British and Hindus; and slivers of wood from an olive tree would turn into rifles. Once we started the hailstorm the enemy would not be able to escape, not even in England. We killed many *feringhis* [Europeans] and made many women widows.

This was the magic of the man whom the British knew as the Faqir of Ipi, and who, after their departure in 1947, led the movement for an independent Pushtun state, separate from Pakistan. He died in 1960 when *The Times'* obituary writer praised him as a man of 'principle and saintliness' — but this was now how he appeared to the British in the 1930s and 1940s.

Such zealots were a puzzle and a nuisance for Britain and its administrators. Uneasy about any kind of religious enthusiasm themselves, the British were and are suspicious of it in others, sometimes with good reason. Prophets and magicians like the Faqir of Ipi were highly dangerous for they refused to compromise. In other parts of India, and the Empire as a whole, British officials liked to do business with men who, outwardly at least, possessed some kind of political authority. Secular rulers were more open to persuasion and could be made to understand where their best interests lay. Such men could be induced, through bribes and menaces, to co-operate with the British, and as reward they were allowed to keep some of their former authority. Indian princes, Malay sultans and African chiefs relinquished some of their sovereignty in the face of the Imperial *force majeure*, but kept external power as

---

* All Holy Men who encouraged resistance were, by definition, insane according to the British. A few years later, in 1914, the imagination of the British public was caught by a tale of ghostly Agincourt bowmen who intervened in the retreat from Mons. In one development of the story, the archers became angels.

the clients of Britain. This ploy made some headway on the North-West Frontier where the Wali of Swat and the Mehtar of Chitral both ran their small states with the backing of British funds and troops. Elsewhere in the region, tribal and clan *maliks*, war-leaders and headmen who spoke for their people at tribal gatherings of *jirgas*, seemed susceptible to this sort of treatment. The usual concoction of bribery and coercion had a measured success, but British political officers tended to inflate the authority of the *maliks*, and underestimated their propensity for double-dealing. Major General Lewis found them contemptible. After coming across several at a *jirga* during the Waziristan campaign of 1920, he summed them up as 'awful scallywags in dirty white rags'. He went on: 'It seems wonderful that they are the leaders of a people who make us exert ourselves'.[15]

In search of an explanation for Waziri stubbornness, Lewis wondered whether it was encouraged by the hidden hand of Russia or, as he put it, 'the Bolshevik menace'. At the time covert Bolshevik activity was widely regarded as being behind every kind of unrest in Britain and the Empire, but a dozen or so years later Italian and German agents had replaced Russians as the imagined instigators of trouble. Between 1937 and 1939, there was some Press speculation about the possibility that the Faqir of Ipi was having secret help from the Germans and the Italians. The Germans certainly exploited the current bout of fighting on the North-West Frontier to blacken Britain and expose British moral pretensions as a sham. In November 1938, when the Germans were a little raw after the way in which British newspapers had reacted to the barbarism of the *Krystallnacht*, the Nazi mouthpiece, *Volkische Beobachter* retorted with an editorial.[16]

> The mountain people in Waziristan have felt the severity of British punitive measures when it tried to gain its independence. The English colonial authorities sent tanks and aeroplanes into rebel territory and killed thousands of women and children with bombs and shells.

The Italians were prepared to go beyond mere words of condemnation. The Italian minister in Kabul, forgetful perhaps of Mussolini's recent 'civilizing' of Libya and Abyssinia, called for the frontier tribesmen to rise up against Britain in 1939. Nothing came of this, but the outbreak of war soon afterwards concentrated German and Italian interest on the frontier and the mischief-making potential of the Faqir of Ipi.

Several schemes were devised to enlist the help of the Faqir, but all foundered. As the British had already found, the Faqir was a hard man to track down and when, after much difficulty, he was approached by Axis agents, he proved hard to please. The saga of German and Italian efforts to secure the co-operation of the Faqir of Ipi resembled a Kiplingesque episode in the 'Great Game' of eighty or so years earlier. The Axis moves were hamstrung by Anglo-Russian pressure on the Afghan government, which was obliged to expel the

German envoy from Kabul in November 1941, before he had made contact with the Faqir. The Italians were luckier, for their men actually reached the Faqir, but were dismayed by the high price he set on his ability to raise the frontier. His demands for a subsidy of £12,500 a month, machine-guns and a radio with which to communicate with Rome were all revealed to the British by a captured Italian agent. German military intelligence compiled a plan for a frontier uprising which was code-named 'Operation Tiger'. It needed the Faqir's help, and agents were sent to find and bargain with him. The one who finally met the Faqir (his fellows had been slain by Afghans) was disappointed for, like the Italian, he was faced with a series of amazing demands which included vast amounts of gold and artillery, to be flown to him by the *Luftwaffe*. At the end of 1942 with German forces in retreat in the Caucasus, this was an impossibility.

By some means never discovered by British military intelligence, the Faqir had obtained, by March 1941, some machine-guns, cannon and shells, all of which were used in his attack on Datta Khel. Soon afterwards, the Faqir put out feelers towards the Congress movement in India to whom he sent six agents with requests for money. They were arrested by the frontier authorities, but it is not likely that they would have had much success, given the widening breach between Hindu and Muslim nationalists.

The North-West Frontier tribesmen were not immune from the political ideas which were in circulation throughout the rest of India. Abdul Ghaffar Khan, the educated son of a well-to-do Pushtun family, had in the 1920s formed a political group which he hoped would fuse traditional resistance to British rule with newer ideas about political responsibility. These would require the Pushtun people to regenerate themselves, a process which would have to include the repudiation of such backward customs as blood-feuds. Ghaffar Khan's Red Shirt movement (his followers wore a distinctive shirt, variously described as of plum or russet colour) had attracted over 50,000 followers by 1930, and had forged links with Gandhi's Congress movement. Gandhi's doctrines of non-violence at first appealed to Ghaffar Khan, but his experience of arrest and imprisonment by the British drove him towards more forceful protest. His followers, inflamed by his treatment, rioted in Peshawar in 1930. To their political protests were added a number of raids by local Afridi tribesmen, encouraged both by political agitation and the knowledge that the British authorities had their hands full keeping order in the city. As a result, other areas became agitated and the army had to mount a number of expeditions to restore order.

Calls for Western political freedoms were a novelty on the frontier, and it is doubtful whether many of the tribesmen active during the 1930 uprising were motivated by anything more than a desire to loot. Pushtun society was conservative, which largely explains the prolonged resistance to the extension of Imperial control during the 1920s and 1930s. The will to defend the *status quo* was intensified by messianic Muslim clerics whose doctrine of *jihad* united the fissiparous tribes and clans. The concentration of stolen or home-made arms gave the tribesmen the means to wage guerrilla warfare which, it was hoped, would wear down the British and force them to reconsider their 'forward' policy. The British would have found such a course repugnant and injurious to prestige, so the army and the RAF were left with the task of teaching the tribesmen the folly of defiance and mischief-making.

Wapitis over Waziristan: Frontier Pacification, 1919–46.

Military operations on the North-West Frontier between 1919 and 1946 followed a pattern which had been laid down over the past forty years. With variations, it formed the basis for future operations undertaken by British forces against tribal opponents or guerrillas in other remote regions. Fighting was intermittent with scarcely a year passing without the need for some sort of demonstration of force of the bombing of a village which housed recalcitrant tribesmen. Soldiers marching beween bases and convoys of lorries were sniped at as a matter of course. Minor outrages had to be avenged by a small mounted patrol, which would enter tribal territory to track down the culprits. There was always the need for forces to show that they could come and go as they wished, and that no part of the region was closed to British influence. Official and usually large-scale campaigns were recognized by a bar for the Indian General Service medal. Nine were sanctioned for frontier operations between 1919 and 1939; they were for duty in the Afghan War of 1919, in Waziristan between 1919–21 and again in 1921–4 and 1925, for service in 1930–1, against the Mohmands in 1933, and for general operations in 1935, 1936–7, and 1937–9.

The Afghan War of 1919 was an exception to the general run of these campaigns since it involved fighting against a regular army which possessed some modern weapons. The Afghan invasion of May 1919 was not pressed with much zeal, and so was easily contained by the reinforced frontier army. What was of greater concern to the British was the effect of the Afghan incursion against local tribes, already agitated by rumours which followed the defeat of Turkey. The disruption caused by the invasion encouraged a series of tribal uprisings which flickered on until 1925.

The Afghans crossed the frontier on five counts. The most formidable advance was made at the western end of the Khyber Pass, where an assault on the post at Landi Kotal was deflected, and followed by a counter-attack. The government was justifiably apprehensive about the effect of the war on local tribes and, to impress them, an advance towards Dakka was sanctioned. Successes here were not enough to preserve British prestige and tribal rebellion became endemic. A disturbing feature of this tribal reaction was a spate of desertions by Muslims serving with the frontier army. Men from the Khyber Rifles went over to their fellow tribesmen, and mass desertions were common in Waziristan where the local crisis was exploited by the Afghan commander, Nadir Khan, who laid siege to the fort at Thal. It was relieved by Brigadier

General Dyer on 3 June, shortly before a general armistice was agreed between the British and the Afghans. Efforts by the Afghans to create a diversion in Chitral failed, thanks in part to the staunchness of its ruler, the Mehtar. The last Afghan offensive, in northern Baluchistan, ran out of steam leaving the local British forces kicking their heels, angry that they had not been allowed to make a counter-attack of any weight.

This restraint, which maddened aggressive commanders on other fronts, was imposed by Delhi. The Afghan invasion was an embarrassment, particularly at a time when there were still signs of the widespread unrest which a month before had convulsed the Punjab. Internal security was precarious, and a rightly nervous government did not want to do anything which might prolong fighting on the frontier and draw in more men from an already depleted Indian garrison. So, on 29 May, the commander on the Khyber front was told to call off a planned march on Jallabad which might have jeopardized the peace settlement which the *Amir* of Afghanistan was known to want. The bombing of Kabul on 24 May had nudged him towards an agreement, which was finally made in August when Britain conceded the Afghan government the right to make its own foreign policy.

Nearly everyone concerned was satisfied with this outcome. A few fire-eaters felt cheated that they had been denied the chance to take offensive action, but intelligence reports that the Afghans were getting aircraft from Russia indicated that they might not have had everything their own way. In any case, the memories of the excursions in 1839 and 1878 ought to have caused second thoughts in anyone who believed that the invasion of Afghanistan would have been a walk-over. There were, however, troubles enough on the frontier which kept the army busy for several years.

The simpler a war's objectives, the greater were its chances of being won, argued von Clausewitz. His dictum did not apply on the frontier where soldiers found themselves faced with many objectives, some of them seemingly contradictory. The Government in Delhi and its servants, the courageous local Political Officers, hoped in time to coax the tribesmen, through their *maliks*, into a state of mind where they would accept British overlordship, and all the rules and regulations that went with it. At the same time, the government could not stand by and permit British authority to be flouted, and so offenders had to be chastized. This was the army's job, but the government did not want the reproof to be too harsh for fear of creating bitterness which would make a political settlement more difficult. Army commanders were unconvinced. They argued that in turbulent Waziristan, the best and most lasting pacification would follow swamping the area with forts, roads and soldiers. To do this would mean thinning out garrisons elsewhere, which would inevitably tempt the Mohmands or the Afridis to rashness. In fairness to the Wazirs, it was pointed out that a concerted effort to disarm them would leave them defenceless against their neighbours over the border in Afghanistan. The British army would therefore have to commit untold men and resources to holding the

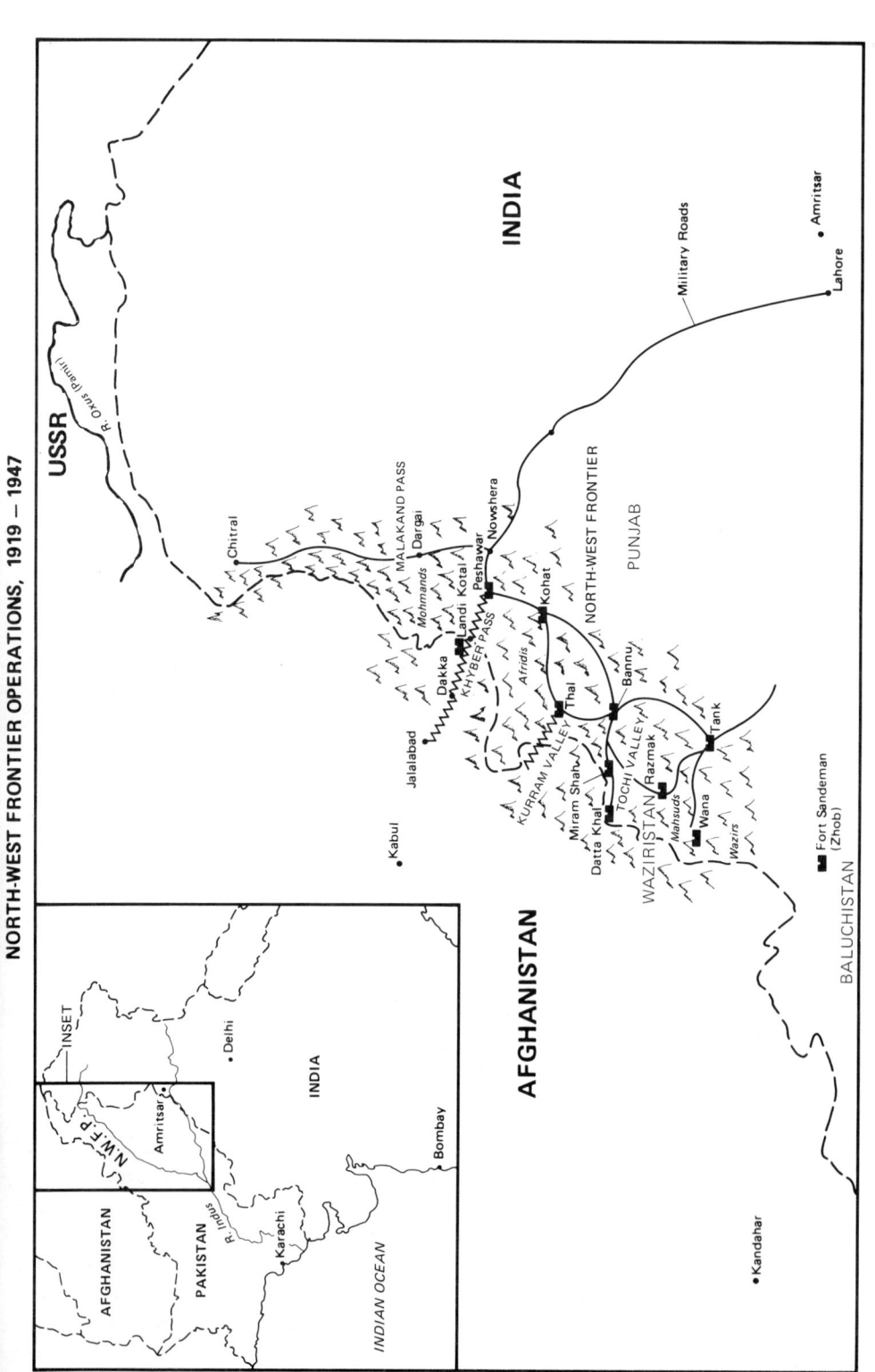

MAP 1 India and The North-West Frontier

Durand Line, which it was not willing to do. The very closeness of the Afghan border created its own problems for the Government was anxious to avoid any frontier infringements by British troops which would mean sour relations with Kabul.

This mesh of political and practical considerations placed all kinds of official restrictions on local army commanders, which they would have gladly done without. They had to restore and maintain tranquillity by methods which were politically acceptable. To all intents and purposes the army had to rely on limited force only. John Masters, who served in Waziristan between 1936 and 1939, voiced the frustration of many serving officers.[17]

> In the warming-up days of a Frontier campaign the rules and regulations governing our actions were irksome in the extreme. The troubled area was delimited and called the 'proscribed area'. Outside the proscribed area we might not take any action at all until shot at. Inside it we might not fire at any band of less than ten men unless they were (a) armed and (b) off a path. These were dangerous conditions in a country where arms can be concealed close to flowing clothes, and where paths are tracks invisible from a hundred yards.

Such restraints were circumvented. Masters continued to recall how a tribesman, legally walking along a goat track away from a place where there had just been some fighting, was found to possess a rifle. He was released after interrogation, but not before the barrel of his gun had been secretly and indetectably bent in an armourer's vice so that, when next fired, its barrel would blow up. This rough justice was more attractive than handing the man over to the local Political Officer, since Masters and his brother officers 'were not sure which side the politicals were on'. Yet if such men were to remain credible with the tribesmen, they had to appear impartial.

Resentment against what seemed the unreasonable straitjacket imposed by civilians was nowhere more acutely felt by soldiers than when they wished to take vengeance for the mutilation of the dead, or the torture of the wounded, by tribesmen. These loathsome customs left fighting men with a mixture of fear (it was 'a matter of honour' to bring in all wounded men) and fury. After operations near Dakka during May 1919, British troops came across the foully disfigured corpses of some King's Dragoon Guards troopers who had been killed during a charge against tribesmen. Those responsible lived in a nearby village which was visited, ten days later, by British soldiers bent on vengeance. The guilty villagers had fled, and so the men were able to booby-trap their houses with hand-grenades and wires. 'We kept the plan secret for fear it might be stopped by Political Officers', claimed one officer, and a subsequent trip to the village revealed 'ample evidence' that the stratagem had worked.[18] In Waziristan a story circulated that a regiment, whose members had suffered at the hands of tribal torturers, left *chappatties* laced with strychnine behind in their camp. Tribal retaliation was legendary; an outraged *malik* purchased an infected whore whom he left to ply her trade close by the regimental picquet line and so cause a minor epidemic. John Masters remembered that after one British officer had been found tortured, another devised a grotesque and excruciating death for a prisoner.[19] Pushtun cruelty was infamous, but after a year fighting them, Fred Wright thought that his next adversaries, the Japanese, were worse.

In setting somewhat unrealistic rules for frontier war, the Political Officers hoped that military action would lead to pacification rather than provocation. The army was called in when there was an emergency which was too serious for effective handling by local, loyalist forces. Forts scattered across the tribal territories were held by small groups of tribesmen under British officers. The forts, which reminded many who saw them of Zinderneuf in the film of *Beau Geste*, guarded roads, and were the first line of British defence, as well as bases from which small units of mounted man could sally out to seek troublemakers. This system of raising local levies had first been put into action in 1899, and its subsequent history was wayward. The worst hitches had occurred in May 1919 when large numbers of local militiamen ran off, taking arms and ammunition with them. Not all were half-hearted soldiers whose real loyalties were to their tribes and faith. One defector, Subadar Pat, had served in the First World War and won the Indian Order of Merit and the *Croix de Guerre*. All this was an unexpected bonus for the tribesmen, whom Major-General Lewis found 'cock-a-hoop' with the machine-guns, rifles and ammunition which fell into their hands.[20]

Official faith in the system of employing local levies was not shaken by the 1919 desertions. During the 1920s, the *khassadar* system was developed, under which main *maliks* controlled local policemen (the *khassadars*) who kept watch over roads. In return the *maliks* received payment from the Government which, by 1940, was dispensing over a million rupees for this form of security. Soldiers were sceptical of the value and the sympathies of the *khassadars*, too many of whom appeared to be old men and boys. Such doubts were given substance when seventeen of them, all deserters and 'desperate characters', were rounded up after an attack on a Wazir village in November 1937.

Not all local militiamen were likely to 'turn-a-cat-in-pan' and betray their employers. The Kurram Valley militia, over 3,000 strong and well armed with Lee Enfield rifles, put up a stiff resistance against Afridi reivers during 1930 with occasional assistance from RAF bombers. Once the Afridi threat had passed, the local administrator thanked the tribesmen and rewarded their efforts with a year's remission of the land tax.[21] Of course the interests of the militiamen, who were defending their property against plunderers, and the British government were the same. This confluence of interests, together with the cheapness of using local part-time forces, made such schemes attractive to the authorities in India and elsewhere. Later 'winning hearts and minds' policies had their roots on the frontier.

Local forces in disturbed regions were always under the command of a British officer, about one for every 100 tribesmen. This type of work was highly attractive to young officers with a taste for the exotic and adenturous. Such commands were a test of leadership, which often justified the claim that even the wildest tribesmen anywhere could learn to respect and follow a British officer because of his spirit and courage. This was a romantic kind of duty, a chance to share in the world of Gordon or T. E. Lawrence. Their exploits, and the Imperial yarns of writers like Henty, had given rise to a common belief that a special empathy could exist between wild, simple and fierce tribesmen and the plain-dealing, manly British officer. The young British officer, a sportsman and a gentleman, winning the admiration and devotion of untamed tribal warriors was a microcosm of the whole British Empire. Such a phenomenon showed how the British won respect, and with it the right to govern.

Small tribal units had many advantages on the frontier. The British officer could muster his little force at a moment's notice and they were moved swiftly across country on their ponies. Pushtun and Englishman were indistinguishable in khaki shirts, turbans and loose trousers, and all carried light, basic rations of flour, onions, tea and sugar. The small *gasht*, the gallop across rough hillsides and valleys, was an initial response to a local crisis. If it, or the garrisons of the outposts, were unable to cope, regular British and Indian troops were called in.

Regular forces and RAF squadrons were held in readiness in their frontier bases; there were four — Razmak, Bannu, Mirali and Wana — in Waziristan which were linked by road with each other and the smaller outposts. From these bases columns moved along roads between temporary camps where they spent the night, very much like the Roman Legions. 'Surrounded by a dry stone wall perimeter and surrounding that, barbed wire, with empty cans fastened to it', these camps gave the British and Indian troops mobility and a degree of security. Roads were the chains which held down a region. The tribesmen knew this, and did all that they could to hamper their laying. The Faqir of Ipi exhorted the *maliks* of the Khaisora Valley to refuse the government subsidy offered them for permission to allow a road to pass across their lands. When built, such roads were the targets for tribal raids and ingenious efforts to destroy them. On one occasion, an unexploded RAF bomb was carried to a road and laid in a culvert. It was then surrounded with brushwood which was set alight, exploding the bomb and damaging the road.

Extensive road-building changed frontier warfare after 1919. The new network of military roads meant that soldiers and supplies could be moved by lorry. Armoured cars could guard convoys and, after 1919, were a commonly used asset on the frontier. 'It was most reassuring', remembered Brigadier Paul Hopkinson, 'when returning from a patrol or from road protection to see armoured cars were out covering one back to camp', especially when under close pressure from the enemy.[22] Bullet-proof and armed with heavy machine-guns, the armoured cars offered valuable covering fire for units in difficulties, and were also useful as ambulances and ammunition carriers. One chased a lorry which, in 1941, had been highjacked by tribesmen who were forced to abandon it. By this time forces on the frontier could call upon thirty-two armoured cars, fifty-four armoured lorries and thirty-seven light tanks. The tribesmen watched all this with interest, and some purchased their own wagons which they used to carry passengers and goods making use of the military roads. It was hoped, rather optimistically, that greater communication with the outside world would generate economic change and with it the transformation of Pushtun society.

Side by side with the growing reliance on metalled roads and motor transport, the frontier army employed the older methods of column warfare with long trails of baggage animals. Ground tactics had been developed over the past forty years, and represented the accumulated experience of many actions. As the column moved forward into hostile territory, the advance guard detached picquets which fanned out to occupy the high ground on either side of the valley. Screened and therefore theoretically safe from ambush, the main column could advance. When it had passed, the picquets would be pulled back, their retirement covered by mountain and machine-guns. This manoeuvre was always fraught with difficulty, especially when it had to be undertaken in the twilight. Small parties of men falling back were vulnerable to a sudden rush from tribesmen armed with knives who had hidden themselves in the rocks and brush. Concealment was one of the tribesman's most effective weapons, and British officers learned to play special attention to fieldcraft. 'Strange signs such as a raven rising in alarm' assumed special significance on a frontier hillside, where they might give warning of an ambush.

The tribesmen knew the land and therefore had an edge over their adversaries. In their dun-coloured clothing they merged with the landscape, and hidden they always had the choice of when and where to attack. They were 'most formidable fighting men. . . ruthless, cunning, good marksmen' was the judgement of one officer, and most others would have concurred. As soldiers they were even set alongside the professionals of Germany and Japan by frontier soldiers who later fought in the Second World War. Their deviousness became legendary, for Private Deighton remembered how a tribesman 'had been known to crawl up among a flock of sheep or goats, with a sheep-skin over him, in order to get to a vantage point, out of reach of hand grenades and protected from rifle and machine gun fire, then snipe away to his heart's content; it usually took a section of Gurkhas to shift him'.[23] Such warriors travelled light, moving where they wished, unfettered by the supply columns which tied British forces to the valleys. The land in which the tribesmen fought and moved was barren, and so his fighting units, the *lashkars*, were subject to frequent depletions as men moved off to gather food.

The British could not match the stealth and swiftness of their adversaries. They could, however, cut them off from the means of their livelihood by the destruction of crops and livestock. This was a weapon held in reserve for markedly obstinate tribesmen, and it was one which Political Officers were reluctant to use too freely. Wazir and Mahsud stubbornness during 1919, and their slowness to surrender rifles, forced local forces to bring the campaign to a conclusion by a systematic destruction of villages, crops and food stocks. Major General Lewis watched the process. 'I am afraid that they will undergo most awful hardships this and next year, until they have got their crops going again'.[24] Without such an artificially-induced famine, the tribesmen would be ready for further mischief and the army would face 'another show in the near future'. Reprisals were often selective with sappers demolishing village watchtowers and the dwellings of men known to have been in arms. Sometimes a *malik* was given the task of firing the charge which brought down his own house, a bizarre joke which appears to have been thought funny both by the army and the *malik*'s fellow tribesmen. This warfare of retaliation and attrition was far from glamorous, and so did not form a subject for filmmakers nor, for that matter, find its way into the British Press where it might have caused disquiet.

Good intelligence and diligent planning were essential in frontier warfare. Both sides possessed their own intelligence services and the tribesmen were always quick to take advantage of misjudgement and indecision on the battlefield. A surprise raid, planned by the Bannu brigade, was revealed to local tribesmen who rightly interpreted the cancellation of a Saturday dance and orders for ice-creams as signs that the British garrison might be otherwise engaged. For their part the British had to be up to the mark with reconnaissance and map-making. Shortcomings in both areas led to two parties of the Guides being caught in an exposed position during operations against the Mohmands in 1935. Enfiladed, the Guides were driven back with heavy losses from what was called, from the map reference, Point 4080, and one of their officers, Captain Godfrey Meynell, was killed in hand-to-hand fighting as he rallied his men. He was awarded the last Victoria Cross to be won on the frontier.

There were other warnings that, for all their technical advantages and the courage of their troops, the British might not have everything their own way. Towards the end of November 1936 a demonstration in force was ordered to bring the Tori Khel Wazirs to their senses, and frustrate the efforts of the Faqir of Ipi, who was busy enkindling a *jihad*. British intelligence suggested that two columns would not meet any resistance. Two columns were formed; the larger, 'Razcol', would leave Razmak and proceed to Biche Kashkai on the Khaisora River where it would join the smaller force, 'Tocol', which had marched sixteen miles from Mirali. 'Razcol' faced no opposition, beyond the almost customary sniping. 'Tocol' soon found itself in trouble, for it was ambushed soon after it had crossed the Tochi River, misled by a pair of treacherous *malik* guides. The fighting began when a cavalry patrol was fired on and to the disgust of the column commander, Brigadier Maynard, the 'remainder of the squadron did threes about and disappeared. They missed a golden opportunity for a charge'. They were brought back, having galloped a couple of miles, by a staff officer. Maynard's infantry consisted of two Indian infantry battalions, one of which, 'Dogras', was new to this kind of fighting and soon found itself in difficulties. Several of their officers were killed, and they became confused. There was muddle also about orders, for which Maynard would later take the blame, but as night approached the situation improved thanks to a cavalry charge supported by machine-gun fire. Maynard was in a hurry to get on, and he ordered a night march, even though he was running short of ammunition. The column made its rendezvous, and was able to fight its way back to Mirali with the backing of light tanks. It was a tale which was quickly picked up by the newspapers — the *Daily Sketch* headline for 27 November 1936 ran 'British Column Ambushed'. Below the story began of how the column, 'lured by treachery into a valley', had been ambushed and suffered heavy losses; in fact seventeen men were killed. This was high for a frontier action, and there were official doubts about Maynard's conduct which led to his being 'kicked upstairs', much to his annoyance.[25]

'Razcol' and 'Tocol' were both able to call on RAF bombers during their march, although, for some reason, 'Tocol' did not have a wireless unit. Aircraft had made their debut on the frontier in 1917, when BE 2C fighters, based at Tank, had taken photographs for the forces operating in Waziristan. It was an ill-mapped area and so the aerial pictures were invaluable to column commanders. In June, the fighters had been used to bomb Mahsud villages in the Kaniguram Valley in order to show their inhabitants that isolation did not give immunity from Imperial retribution.[26]

Aircraft really came into their own in 1919, when they were extensively employed in sorties against the Afghans and Wazirs. Their appearance on the frontier provoked much controversy on military and moral grounds. At first the RAF's success rate seemed impressive, leading the air command at Miramshah to boast that the Afghans and their tribal supporters lived 'in dread' of aeroplanes. Such fear was well-based. Bombing raids against Afghan troop concentrations at Jallabad had inflicted heavy losses, and waves of attacks on Dakka on 17 May had left over 600 casualties, including two elephants.[27] On Empire Day (24 May), a Handley Page twin-engined bomber flew to Kabul where it bombed the *Amir*'s palace (terrifying his harem) and other targets, causing damage and panic. The *Amir* was indignant and pointed out that not long ago the British had been enraged after German air raids on London, which were vilified as 'Hun beastliness'. The British had short memories over such matters for, soon after the raid, an anonymous patriot made a present of £1,000 to the bomber's crew. (The aircraft was called 'Old Carthusian', for its pilot had been at Charterhouse School.)

The aerial operations during May 1919 seemed a great success. The continued warfare in Waziristan offered further opportunities for the RAF to prove its value and justify the claims of its godfather, Lord Trenchard, that it was the modern, effective and cheap way to bring truculent tribesmen to heel. Thirty aircraft, more than half of them Bristol Fighters, were concentrated at landing grounds at Tank and Bannu, from where they flew increasingly savage sorties against Wazir and Mahsud villages. An average of 10,000 bombs fell daily on Mahsud villages between 25–29 November 1919. The results were disappointing for, according to the official report, 'at no time did it appear possible that the Mahsuds would submit from the effect of air operations'. Major General Lewis had a ringside seat, but remained sceptical. 'About five tons of bombs are being dropped daily on the Mahsuds and a good deal of damage has been done, but I doubt if bombing will ever finish the show'.[28]

To make life more difficult for the tribesmen, delayed action fuses and incendiary bombs were added to the RAF's armoury towards the end of 1919, and the latter 'created a considerable sensation among the tribesmen' when they were first dropped. By this time the Mahsuds had discovered the aircraft's vulnerability for three were shot down by rifle fire during May and two more were brought low by fire the following January. In all cases the crews escaped the perils of capture; then and later, airmen carried messages which promised large rewards to any tribesman who found a grounded airman and returned him 'intact' to British units. As an insurance system, its success was variable. One airman, whose craft had been forced to land because of a mechanical fault, was saved by three Mahsuds who, luckily for him, were retained by British intelligence; others were less fortunate. Not only were the victims of bombing learning to shoot back at the aircraft; they also devised rudimentary air raid precautions. Families left their villages and took to the hills where caves provided excellent shelters, as the Faqir of Ipi discovered when his hideaway at Arsal Kot was bombed in 1938. Large herds of grazing stock, a common RAF target, were broken up, an action which pleased advocates of bombing who argued that smaller flocks required more shepherds and goatherds, thus keeping men away from the raiding *lashkars*. Some tribesmen even attempted to damage the aircraft on the ground; there was an attack on the aircraft hangars at an aerodrome five miles from Bannu in July 1919, which was beaten off by Rajput guards. Not long afterwards, Lord Trenchard assured the government in London that the Mahsuds, far from displayng malevolence towards the RAF, 'showed marked respect for RAF officers, based on admiration for the work they do'.[29]

This strange statement was made by Trenchard soon after the end of the Waziristan operations, to justify RAF actions. There was unease in army circles, and among civilians, about the morality of dropping bombs on native villages. Trenchard had no time for such humanitarian scruples. 'Unscrupulous savages, who will give no quarter and who mutilate the dead' were getting no more than they deserved, he argued. In the recent war, munition factories manned by civilians and lines of communication had been considered legitimate targets for bombing. In Trenchard's mind no line could be drawn separating the tribal warrior from 'his womenkind who murder the wounded and mutilate the dead'.[30] Air Vice Marshal Sir John Salmond returned from a tour of inspection of India well pleased with the achievements of 'air control'. He had noted that the destruction of food stocks and combustible fodder had been particularly useful as an economic blow against the tribesmen.[31]

Not everyone on the frontier endorsed the views of Trenchard and Salmond. At a conference held on 5 June 1923, the GOC in Waziristan was uneasy about the high civilian casualties during raids, and wondered whether the tribesmen's habit of seeking cover in caves might reduce the effect of such raids. Major Humphreys, the Minister in Kabul, was disturbed by the inhumanity of air control and voiced the criticisms of many other of the doubters, then and later. 'Much needless cruelty is necessarily inflicted, which, in many cases will not cow the tribesmen, but implant in them undying hatred and desire for revenge'.[32] This was a curiously accurate prophecy which would be fulfilled twenty years later when German bombing of British towns and cities and the Allied counter-offensive did not produce demoralization and panic, but instead stiffened resentment and resolve. Inside India nationalist politicians, like Nehru, exploited the frontier bombing as a means to challenge the assertion that British rule was 'civilized'. Closer to the depredations of the tribesmen, Hindus living on the frontier applauded the air attacks.

In the face of such censure, restrictions were placed on the application of air control. Prior to raids, warning leaflets were dropped on village targets (though there is little evidence of this practice in 1919). Bombing had been developed into an instrument of precise vengeance, for carefully gridded maps had been drawn making it possible for pilots to bomb just the houses of men who were known to be against the authorities, leaving those of the compliant undamaged. Air strikes were used in 1930 against Afridi *lashkars*, but a year later the Tribal Control and Defence Committee agreed to place less reliance on air control on the frontier, for fear that its continued use would antagonize the tribesmen. What stuck in the craws of many officers was the proven fact that bombing was indiscriminate. 'In order that 2,000 or 3,000 young ruffians should be discouraged from their activities, dozens of villages inhabited by many thousand women, children and old men, to say nothing of many who have refused to join the *lashkars*, should be bombed', commented Sir Philip Chetwode, Commander in Chief of the Indian Army in 1935.[33] This, coming from a soldier, was humbug, since in the past the army had punished without discrimination when it demolished buildings and despoiled food stocks and crops. The moral question about the use of the RAF was here and elsewhere fudged by the army's unease that its role as Imperial policeman was being usurped.

Churchill was one who had no doubts about the efficacy of bombing. He had suggested in 1919 that stocks of poison gas should be made available to forces on the frontier for use against the Afghans and tribesmen. Delhi was repelled by the idea, even though Churchill had considered non-lethal gas as best suited for dispersion among tribesmen. The question of whether or not to use gas broke surface again in 1938, but the Secretary of State for India, the Marquess of Zetland, and the Army Council turned down the suggestion that tear-gas bombs might be used by the RAF on the frontier. 'Hostile propaganda' and misinterpretation of the measure were the reasons given.[34]

What was euphemistically termed 'aerial proscription' continued to be used, with safeguards, on the frontier during the 1930s and 1940s. Areas where troublemakers congregated or were given succour were warned of the measures to be taken. If threats produced no results aircraft would drop warnings, and then undertake raids designed to disrupt economic life. Indications of a recrudescence of lawlessness, directed by the Faqir of Ipi, led to a number of sorties during 1942 and 1943. On 30 July 1942 a dozen aircraft bombed designated targets close to the Afghan border where the Faqir was known to be active. One flight of three Blenheims mistook the Afghan village of Narezai for their target, Raghzai Killi, and bombed it, killing eight, including four children. Flying conditions were the cause of the error, for which the government apologized to Kabul, and paid compensation.[35]

Whilst there was debate on moral and practical grounds about the value of strategic bombing on the frontier, there was general agreement about the enormous tactical value of air support for forces on the ground. Troops on service in Waziristan between 1936 and 1939 carried squared maps of their areas of operation, and by pigeon or wireless (which was less efficient, according to Brigadier Hopkinson) could summon up close air support when needed. Ground-to-air messages passed by way of the Popham Panel. 'This was a black canvas affair which had white flaps to convey such messages as 'Being attacked from area > III'. This meant hostile fire approximately three hundred yards. Strips of white cloth were sometimes placed on the ground to point the pilots in the direction from which enemy fire was coming. A white letter T indicated that a ground unit was in danger of being overrun and that an air attack was urgently needed, whilst an X signified that all was well. Occasionally, a hook was slung beneath an aircraft to pick messages in packets. It looked 'highly dangerous' to Brigadier Hopkinson, and for leading Aircraftman F. T. Rainey, who flew in the rear cockpit of a Wapiti, picking up such messages 'could be quite exciting'.[36]

When ground forces were out in hostile country, aircraft were always fuelled and armed in readiness for an emergency call. Mr Rainey recalled one such summons during April 1938 when his squadron of Wapitis was stationed at Miramshah.

We had been very busy at Miramshah and had been given a Sunday off. We were all on the tennis court when a call came from the South Waziristan Scouts. A patrol had been ambushed and cut off . . . We were airborne quite quickly, three aircraft in this particular sortie. We found the Scouts on a hilltop with signs out indicating hostile fire from three sides. We just flew round and round that hilltop for over three hours making the tribesmen keep their heads down.

On another occasion, Rainey's Wapiti was called on to give close support close to Razmak which had a small landing-strip.

> The aerodrome was small and had a fairly steep slope. On landing we were informed that some tribesmen had cut a water pipe line above the camp — the Gurkhas were engaged and artillery (one small gun) was firing from the camp over our head. We took off and went in to drop some 20lb bombs and spray the area with fire from the rear gun, but I saw very little movement. We took off and landed several times during the day. In the early evening the troops were falling back with the tribesmen following up. We took off and flew up and down the area while the troops came back through the wire and into camp. My chief worry on the last occasion was that the aircraft was difficult to start and it was no time to be teaching soldiers how to swing a propellor!

Eight years later, British forces withdrew from the frontier forever, leaving the region to the newly-created Pakistani army and the local *gendarmerie*. The final period of British occupation of the frontier had been comparatively quiet. In 1941 there had been fears that the Germans, after their successes in the Caucasus, might attack India and tank traps were set up in the Khyber Pass. Soon afterwards the news of the fall of Singapore caused more anxiety, for the local population's reaction was 'one of disdain that so grave a reverse should have been suffered at the hands of such foes'.[37] Local intelligence officers warned Delhi that: 'This blow to prestige may be expected to have adverse consequences'. They were wrong, and in May 1944 the Commander in Chief, General Auchinleck, felt the region to be sufficiently tranquil to justify the removal of three battalions for service against the Japanese. With forty-two battalions, the North-West Frontier forces were far below the usual minimum of fifty, but they were well supported by aircraft of the Royal Indian Air Force.[38] These were in action during the summer of 1946 after miscreant Mahsuds had refused to hand back a subsidy and surrender rifles.

A few months later, the *raj* had come to an end and it was fitting that one of its final acts of war was against frontier tribesmen. What had been achieved? Not very much, thought Lord Wavell, the Viceroy, who after a discussion about frontier affairs in October 1945, recorded in his diary: 'So the old seesaw of frontier policy goes on, much as it has done for the past 100 years, without getting any nearer to a permanent solution'.[39] Most of those present at the meeting had urged that only social and economic change would bring complete disarmament of the tribesmen. Chastisement, cajolery and bribes, together with the work of the Political Officers, had produced some tranquility.

From 1919 onwards the *raj* was on the political defensive against growing popular demands for self-government to which it eventually acquiesced. Yet this period of wane was also one in which the most determined efforts were made to enforce the Imperial will on a wild and backward region, perhaps because its rulers felt a special need to show that they were still strong. Uncertainty about the *raj*'s future made it more than ever determined not to forfeit military prestige, especially when signs of retrenchment might have encouraged further disorder. Success was difficult to measure for at no one time was every tribesman at peace with the government; but then the very nature of Pushtun society and its need to survive economically made such a goal unobtainable. British forces did well enough, trouble was contained and neighbouring regions were kept free from the attentions of the tribesmen, who, after independence, made forays into Kashmir, both to save it for Islam and to pick up loot.

In the long-term the British army found the frontier a valuable training ground, where innovations such as aircraft, armoured cars and tanks, conceived for European battlegrounds, were tested as instruments of colonial control. As with the French and Spanish in Morocco and the Italians in Ethiopia, it was discovered, on the North-West Frontier, that technical superiority did not automatically lead to cheap victory. There was another, more important lesson, and that concerned the nature of the army's duties. The army of India was the servant of the Indian government and had to abide by its strictures, even if they were hard to stomach. Imperial government in India and elsewhere justified itself on the grounds that it was benevolent and beneficial, existing to promote the welfare of those whom it ruled. For such a government to need constant recourse to force in order to get its way was contradictory. Military men, to whom military solutions so often appeared simple, had to acknowledge restraints which sometimes seemed to undermine their efforts. The same would be true for the other wars of pacification waged in Palestine, Malaya, Kenya and Aden. If India taught soldiers lessons in subordination to politicians and proconsuls, the experience of frontier warfare also offered a practical curriculum of fighting in remote regions against determined guerrillas.

Passive Resistance and Partition, 1919–1947

For twentieth century statesmen, many of whom were Victorian by birth and upbringing, as well as soldiers, possession of India was essential for Britain. Its loss was seen as a disaster for Britain, its prestige and its standing as a world power. Winston Churchill, who had served in India as a cavalry subaltern in the 1890s, spoke for all who dreaded its surrender. According to his physician, Lord Moran, Churchill's India 'was the land he knew as a subaltern. He could not conceive of India without the British. How often on our travels did he come back in his talk to the religious massacres which he felt must happen when we left the country'. 'Keep a bit of India', Churchill wrote to Lord Wavell in August 1945, even when it was clear that the newly-elected Labour government would soon agree Indian independence. Much later, after India had gained self-government, he reconsidered the matter, and told Lord Moran, 'When you learn to think of a race as inferior beings it is difficult to get rid of that way of thinking; when I was a subaltern the Indian did not seem to me equal to the white man'.

Yet, even when Churchill had been a subaltern, many of those who ruled India shared Lord Macaulay's opinion that British administration was merely the means of making the Indians ready to rule themselves. The benefits of British justice, commerce and education would, in time, spread an enlightenment throughout the sub-continent whose inhabitants would then be qualified to govern themselves. This uplifting of India and Indians appeared a Herculean task which to those engaged on it often seemed unending. From 1919 onwards, an élite of Indians, educated in Britain and soaked in British liberal ideas, claimed that their people were ready for responsible government and that British tutelage, maintained in the teeth of such demands, was no more than an alien tyranny. The right of such native politicians to speak for their countrymen was roundly questioned by opponents of self-government. 'A narrow oligarchy of high-caste Hindus under the domination of the seditious Congress' had a mind to set up a 'tyrannical Hindu *raj* in place of the King-Emperor's impartial and beneficient rule', warned Sir Michael O'Dwyer in 1931.[40] O'Dwyer had been governor of the Punjab and, whilst he always claimed that he had ruled in the interests of its people, his enemies, even in the British administration, throught him inflexible and over-zealous in the maintenance of order. O'Dwyer was contemptuous of educated Indians, including Gandhi, whom he characterized as greedy, ambitious charlatans who misled the peasant masses. Another 'old India hand', General Sir James Willcocks, whose service stretched back to the 1870s, shared O'Dwyer's views for like many soldiers he cherished the Indian peasant. For him, in 1925, they were the men 'who still wish nothing better than to be friends with the British. The school of experience affords a better elementary education than all the claptrap of their modern colleges; and the warrior classes respect soldiers more than agitators'.[41]

When Willcocks was expressing his distaste for 'agitators', they were already attracting a mass following for the Congress movement. Its leader, was Gandhi who, after his emergence in 1919, quickly stamped the independence movement with his own mystic doctrines. 'An Englishman', he wrote, 'is afraid of nothing physical, but he is mortally afraid of his own conscience if ever you appeal to it, and show him to be in the wrong'. The British were wrong, argued Gandhi, in thinking that their government was wanted by the Indian people. Their error would be brought to their attention by *satygraha* ('soul force') with which his followers would spiritually arm themselves for a campaign of passive resistance and civil disobedience. The sophistication of such arguments was often lost on Indians or rejected by others, and so nationalist demonstrations invariably ended with violence and disorder. Officials, policemen and soldiers on the streets of Amritsar in 1919 or Peshawar in 1930 might easily have been forgiven for thinking that the crowds which attacked and pelted them were not appealing to their consciences. In consequence Gandhi's enemies, like O'Dwyer, constantly rated him as a hypocrite.

The riots which followed in the wake of Gandhi's challenge to the *raj* were not just the consequences of most Indians' inability to appreciate or understand their leader's mysticism. Many nationalists were impatient and local grievances against the government often spurred men and women to violence, once it seemed that authority was on the defensive or losing control. There were also Indians, living on the margins of society, for whom any breakdown in civil order offered an opportunity for revenge or profit. The duty of the civil authorities was to contain and suppress such disorder, whatever its source. On the streets of India, the *raj* had no choice but to adopt a repressive policy or stand accused of failing to govern.

In terms of wider policy, repression alternated with concession. The legislation passed in London between 1919 and 1935 admitted more and more Indians into the civil service, army and policy-making, and allowed them to elect members for local assemblies. In 1940, dominion status was promised after the war, but the pledge could not have rung true, given Churchill's record of opposition to the independence movement and the known hostility to Indian self-government shown by the Viceroy, Lord Linlithgow. At the time, both men felt confident that the nationalist movement would suffer as a consequence of the deepening rift between the Hindu-dominated Congress and the Muslim League, which was already pressing for partition. In the past, champions of the *raj* pointed out how impartial British government kept Hindus and Muslims from killing each other; now, Churchill admitted, racial tension would prove a 'bulwark' for the *raj*.

The other bulwark for the *raj* was its army of British and Indian soldiers. When the civil police were unable to contain or suppress disorders, the army was called in to quell riots and guard property. As the national movement became increasingly impatient more and more troops had to be committed to duties supporting the civil government. It was a type of duty which soldiers disliked, for they entered, literally, the political arena, unfamiliar territory where they faced all kinds of difficulties. By custom and inclination, the British and Indian armies were apolitical. Officers and men held political opinions in private but when ordered to uphold the civil power such views had to be suppressed. Such disinterest was not always easy, for soldiers could be subject to all kinds of pressures which might lead them to have misgivings about playing a part in politics. Lord Wavell was aware of this when he wrote to Churchill in October 1944, on the possibilities of holding India down by force alone.[42] 'A comparatively small amount of force, ruthlessly used, might be sufficient for the task', but it was unlikely that British and world opinion would approve of such a policy. 'Nor', he added, 'will British soldiers wish to stay here in large numbers after the war to hold the country down'. There had been unrest among conscripted and volunteer soldiers, many hastily drafted from Mesopotamia during 1919, when they had been ordered to take part in the war against Afghanistan and help police the Punjab, which had come very close to mutiny. As it was, British troops had been willing to take part in the suppression of disorders during 1946, even though the Morale Committee at the War Office had been informed that the general mood was one of wanting to get back to Britain and peace-time reconstruction, which seemed more important than propping up the *raj* in India.[43]

The political views of Indian soldiers were another matter. In December 1945, Lord Wavell was unhappy about which way the army would jump in a crisis, and he warned London that 'it would not be wise to try the Indian army too highly in the suppression of their own people'. Confidence in the Indian army had been shaken by the events of 1942, when over 20,000 Indian prisoners-of-war succumbed to Japanese blandishments and joined the renegade Indian National Army, which was designed to fight alongside the Japanese army and 'liberate' India. In Burma, the Japanese encountered 'no difficulty' when they asked for recruits to join an anti-British army of Burmese, which included many policemen who wanted 'to free their country'.[44] This was not surprising given pre-war nationalism in both India and Burma and the dismal showing of Britain in the war in Malaya. The dismay and disorientation of Indian forces played their part in turning many soldiers against Britain, especially when her prestige had been damaged by the surrender of Singapore. Worse followed, at least from the point of view in the Indian authorities, in February 1946 when there was a large-scale mutiny of sailors of the Royal Indian Navy, which sparked off nationalist riots in Bombay and Calcutta.

Incidents such as this worried the Congress leadership which distanced itself from the naval mutineers, even though it had led a campaign to forestall the trial of the wartime defectors for treason. The nationalist movement had been civilian and had never made any serious efforts to subvert soldiers. There were, of course, many nationalists in the Indian army but their political views had never interfered with their duties, even the suppression of nationalist demonstrations. By 1946, when Indian independence was assured, Congress had no wish to become entangled in mutiny and violence. The new state of India would need its army intact and in good order, especially when it became clear that partition was unavoidable. As independence approached, the proto-rulers of India and Pakistan appreciated the need for apolitical, loyal and disciplined forces, still attached to traditions cultivated under the British. In deference to the opinions of officers of the Indian army, Nehru was forced to reject demands to show favours to the former renegades who had taken up arms for the Japanese, much to the irritation of many nationalists.

British forces in India had no domestic, cultural or political affinities with the native Indians. They were never isolated from the people with whom they mixed freely when off-duty. Friendships could develop and did; Private Swindlehurst noted in his diary that he often visited an Indian photographer in Lahore from whom he learned much about the country and its customs. Yet, as Harry Roberts remembers, 'you were living in two worlds, them and us',[45] and in retrospect he regretted that the relations between the races could not have been relaxed. Nevertheless, he doubted whether complete equality could have been achieved or whether it would have been desirable. Every British army camp had an abundance of native servants who undertook day-to-day chores; men were shaved in their beds as they lay asleep, their uniforms were pressed and boots shined. The many contacts between British soldiers and Indians made it axiomatic that when they were called upon to uphold civil order, they should not actually come to grips with rioters. Not only might they lose their rifles, but they could be identified and perhaps suffer rough usage at some later time when they were off-duty.

This advice was offered by a former commandant of the Staff College, Camberley, Major General Sir Charles Gwynn, who after his retirement compiled *Imperial Policing*, a text book for professional and non-professional readers. It appeared in 1934, and gave an officer some indication of the kind of situation he might have to face when called on to give assistance to colonial governments faced with civil unrest. In drawing up his guidelines, Gwynn offered examples of incidents in different parts of the Empire. They span the years 1919 to 1931 and two were Indian scenarios, the Amritsar riots of 1919 and those at Peshawar in 1930. In these and other cases, Gwynn offered analyses of the army's response, although he was reluctant to set any hard and fast rules for the future.

'Traditional doctrines, discipline and its own common sense' were the qualities on which an officer had to rely when faced with this kind of duty. There were pitfalls and Gwynn gave them much attention. Civilians were always uneasy when soldiers were called upon to act as policemen, for 'suspicions of ruthlessness' were aroused. The 'weapon of propaganda ... has made the task of the Army harder', which meant that officers had always to bear in mind the possible effect on public opinion of their actions. Reports of shootings and casualties did not make agreeable newspaper reading, and were difficult for politicians to explain and justify. After all, Imperial encomiasts were always saying that the Empire was benevolent and this assertion could appear indefensible when rioters were shot down, irrespective of the circumstances. News of such happenings always stirred up political passions, especially on the Left, where a strong belief persisted that the Empire, established by force of arms, was in fact kept in being by coercion. 'The *lathi*, the stick, and after the *lathi*, the rifle and after the rifle the machine gun' would become the sole props of the *raj* if the enemies of Indian self-government got their way, argued a Labour Member of Parliament, William Wedgwood-Benn, in 1931. Others, on the Conservative Right, were not troubled by qualms of conscience over such matters. Sir William Joynson-Hicks, Home Secretary between 1924 and 1929, proclaimed that the Empire had been conquered by the sword and would be held by it, and that was that. It was very bewildering for the soldier; on one hand he was the agent of the brutal repression and on the other he was pussyfooting if he did not use enough force.

Gwynn tried to offer some consolation, in that he made it his business to explain how military force could keep the Imperial peace firmly without excessive or disturbing bloodshed. Calm judgement was essential, together with a clear idea of what had to be done. A measured response ensured that delinquents were deterred, the neutral shown the folly of resistance, and those loyal to the Government were assured of its determination to guard them and their property. Inaction encouraged the spread of disorder as more and more men and women saw what they could get away with, but excessive and random use of force created bitterness and could even stiffen defiance. In abstraction, the army was a *force majeure* which appeared on the streets, acted decisively and dispassionately, and then withdrew.

There were many ways in which this could be achieved. True to his upbringing in the Victorian army, Gwynn had faith in the bayonet: 'The sight of cold steel has a calming effect'. An advance by bayonet-armed infantrymen was frightening but if the men actually closed with the crowd and became involved in brawls then they were vulnerable. Rifle fire was, inevitably, the best way to bring matters to a head, even though it was a final resort. Gwynn guardedly suggested that machine-guns could also be used, creating a killing zone which rioters would not dare to enter, or else terrifying by their noise. Here was the heart of the unpleasant business; soldiers assisted the civil powers because they could not cope with disorder and, unlike policemen, soldiers were armed and expected to kill. In theory their appearance marked that stage in a disturbance when the authorities were both frightened and determined to show that they would reimpose order, whatever the costs. To this extent, the deployment of soldiers was a warning and a bluff which the rioters might call. Then there was no choice but to fire. This was what was known as the 'moral effect' of the army's presence in support of the civil power. When, in 1938, a proposal to equip soldiers in India with tear gas was rejected by the Secretary of State, Lord Zetland, and the Army Council, it was argued that the effect of using soldiers would be lost. They entered the fray when disorders 'got beyond the control of the humanitarian weapons of the police,' and were there to shoot when necessary.[46]

For the soldier in the midst of disorders, such abstractions were puzzling. 'It's such a poor game — broken bottles if you don't shoot and execrations if you do — heads they win, tails we lose', wrote a Dragoon officer after several days of brushes with strikers in Johannesburg in 1913.[47] His words were echoed later by many others in similar situations. When they were in support of the civil power, all soldiers were on active duty and, according to the letter of the law, were allowed to treat their adversaries as enemies for as long as they resisted. Public order was legally the responsibility of the colonial government and its officers, and it was from them that the army had to take its orders. If they lost their heads or were not available, the officer could act on his own judgement. He could even take the initiative although the civil authority was giving directions to the contrary. Matters were less fudged when the civil authority abdicated its powers and permitted the declaration of martial law. Then the soldiers took over the police, and more important, their resources for gathering intelligence about trouble-makers, made the rules, and accelerated justice by bringing suspects before courts-martial. Further powers had been conferred on the armed forces by the Emergency Powers Act of 1920. Under its terms, soldiers could be ordered to take on duties 'for the securing and regulating the supply of food, water, fuel, light, and other necessities, for maintaining the means of transport or locomotion, and for any other purposes essential to the public safety and life of the community'. This had been laid down in anticipation of a syndicalist challenge to the British Government, but its provisions extended to India.[48] There the authority of the Government and the safety of the state were sufficient justification for using troops to break strikes, according to the Judge-Advocate.

Looming over the complex legal and practical arguments about how troops could best be used and the level of force most suited to the restoration of public order were the events in Amritsar in April 1919. The firing on demonstrators in the Jallianwala Bagh, the casualties suffered and the subsequent rumpus in India and Britain had a profound effect on the British army and its officers. Gwynn spent much time analyzing what had happened, and concluded by censuring Dyer, although he was less than happy about the way he had been treated by the authorities. Not everyone was appalled by the catastrophe at the Jallianwala Bagh, for many in Britain hailed Dyer as the 'saviour of India', whose incisiveness at a crucial moment had forestalled a second Indian Mutiny. Like the controversy which followed the suppression of the Jamaican uprising by Governor Eyre in 1865, the Amritsar affair caused a scandal of the sort specially relished by the British since it involved issues of moral right and wrong. It was a minor crisis of Imperial confidence since Dyer's behaviour called into question the ethical justification for the Empire. What sort of system was it that had to shoot down hundreds of men and women in order to survive? The circumstances in which these Indians died and the furore which followed are tales which have been told many times, usually with much emotion, and so all that is needed here are the bare bones of the story.

At the beginning of 1919, the energies of the Congress movement were channelled into a programme of nationwide civil disobedience which Gandhi hoped would reflect massive popular dismay at the Anarchical and Revolutionary Crimes Act. Indian nationalists had good reason to resent and fear this piece of legislation, which had been framed to give the authorities extensive powers to frustrate sedition. Free to arrest at will, detain and bring to summary trial anyone suspected of subversion, the authorities were in a position to impede or break any kind of opposition, and make political protest all but impossible, even though the act was directed towards terrorism. The new law imperilled the Congress movement and its organizers, whose work might easily appear as seditious and conducive to unrest. The chosen means by which Indians were to express their opposition to the new law was the *hartal*, a day in which all work and commerce ceased, and the protestors devoted themselves to fasting and prayer. To be effective, the *hartal* had to have the appearance of universal support and despite Gandhi's insistence that it was a gesture of moral force, many of his supporters browbeat those of their countrymen who were either lukewarm or hostile.

Disorder was worst in the Punjab, where many of the Muslim population were already disturbed by news of the Allied dismemberment of Turkey and the proposed abolition of the Caliphate. The region had been disturbed in 1915 by the efforts of the Sikh Ghardrite movement to foment an uprising and a mutiny amongst Indian troops. This had been checked by the swift action of the Lieutenant Governor, Sir Michael O'Dwyer who, then and later, made no effort to disguise his disdain for any form of Indian opposition to the *raj*. O'Dwyer's particular malevolence was directed towards those Indians whom, he believed, postured as men of peaceful protest, but were in fact the puppet-masters of riot and the destruction of property. Such attitudes were confirmed by the behaviour of extremist nationalists who saw the *hartal* as the opportunity for insurrection. Their propaganda added to official alarm. Lieutenant Colonel Morgan, who commanded the 124th Baluchis at Lahore in April 1919, recalled efforts to subvert soldiers. 'My own subadar-major brought me a letter from rebels saying that the time had come to murder all British officers'.[49]

Intelligence such as this, the known shortage of experienced troops caused by post-war demobilization, the demands of the frontier and the need to keep a garrison in Iraq, together with the disturbances which followed the *hartal*, made the Punjab authorities jumpy. In official quarters the belief soon became current that the region was on the verge of a major revolt. Symptoms of nervousness began to appear. O'Dwyer sanctioned the use of aircraft to bomb a Sikh school at Khalsa, a known hive of disaffection, and two villages close to Amritsar. When on 11 April, General Beynon, the local commander, ordered Lieutenant Colonel Morgan to proceed to Amritsar, his words revealed panic: 'Amritsar is in the hands of the rebels. It's your job to get it back'.[50]

Events at Amritsar certainly suggested that the local authorities had lost control. The second *hartal* in the city of 15,000 on 6 April had triggered off several days of rioting in which Europeans had been murdered, buildings were looted and burned, and the police lost all control. Lacking sufficient police and without adequate troops, the civil authorities had called for reinforcements and a commander who was prepared to act decisively. That man was Dyer, who reached Amritsar by train from Lahore, and soon became convinced that he was witnessing the first stage of a massive insurrection. His previous record had been impressive and the army authorities believed that 'his knowledge of the Oriental was profound'. Dyer and his wife and recently been accosted by truculent demonstrators, and he had been deeply angered by the news of how an English missionary, Miss Sherwood, had been murderously attacked in the streets of Amritsar. The psychological effect of this assault was probably far greater than is realized today. A few years later in 1923 the Ellis case, in which a woman was murdered and her daughter kidnapped by frontier tribesmen, deeply disturbed the British community in India. Air Vice Marshal Salmond argued that outrages against European women were indicative of the fact that Indians no longer feared British power, and there is no reason to think that Dyer or others in the Punjab would have disagreed.[51] Dyer was certainly troubled by police intelligence reports suggesting that agitators in Amritsar were sowing doubts about the loyalty of Indian troops. One rumour alleged that 'no British Officer would dare to fire on us and if they gave the order, Indian soldiers would not obey'.[52] Such an assertion, whether popularly believed or not, invited a trial of strength. Dyer looked for one, and his ban on public meetings gave him the opportunity he was seeking.

It is not known how many of those who attended the meeting at the Jallianwala Bagh on 13 April were aware that they were defying Dyer's ban, although those who organized the demonstration certainly did. One participant was nervous for he recalled that shortly before Dyer arrived an aircraft passed over the open space. He decided to leave, perhaps calling to mind the recent bombings elsewhere in the Punjab. Affronted by what he saw as a challenge to his authority, Dyer entered the city with a column of ninety *Indian* troops [my italics] backed by two armoured cars which could not enter the narrow gateway to the *bagh*. He formed up his men and ordered the fifty Gurkhas and Baluchis who were armed with rifles to fire into the crowd which, unwarned, at first believed the shots were blanks. Dyer directed the fire which lasted for about five minutes. Some 1,650 bullets were fired and most seem to have found targets, for the casualties were said to have been over 1,500, of whom at least 400 were killed outright or died later from their wounds. No exact figure exists for the numbers present at the demonstration nor of the dead and wounded. Dyer insisted that the curfew was kept and that only civilian medical help was made available for the wounded, many of whom lay where they fell throughout the night.

Dyer returned from the shooting to the supporting units he had left outside the city. They had waited there with orders to come to his rescue if needed. This instruction, his opening fire, and the employment of Indian troops left little doubt that he was convinced that he was dealing with a rebellion within the city. He had showed the Government's will to crush rebellion, and given the lie to assumptions that Indian troops might not be loyal. In the next few days he offered further evidence of his determination to show that the *raj* was still in the saddle. On the street where Miss Sherwood had been attacked, men were flogged and Dyer ordered that all Indians passing along that way must crawl. Among those subject to this degradation may have been some who lived on the street and had helped Miss Sherwood to escape. Such nice distinctions were not for Dyer, nor for other officials and officers in the Punjab where for some weeks various forms of humiliating punishment became the rule. As Dyer's advocates were quick to point out, the shooting was a prelude to the restoration of order, first in Amritsar and later in the rest of the Punjab.

Dyer's action was approved by his commander, Beynon, and by O'Dwyer, who thereafter remained staunch in his support. The details of what had happened in Amritsar and the rest of the Punjab filtered slowly back to Britain. As they became known, they caused disquiet which, together with the enraged clamour of Indian nationalists, forced the government to form a Commission of Enquiry. The Commission, chaired by a Scottish Judge, included British and Indian members and its warrant extended to a full investigation of events in the Punjab during April 1919. Dyer proved a bad witness, especially when under hostile cross-examination by Indian lawyers who were out for his blood. Whatever private doubts he may have had about the rightness of his action, he appeared callous and he was censured by the majority report of the Commission, which was kinder to O'Dwyer. The minority Indian report was predictably uncompromising in its censure of Dyer and all who had been concerned with the suppression of disorder in the Punjab.

The Hunter Commission report of 1920 began the debate about Amritsar. In London, the Secretary of State for India, Edwin Montagu, who had at first blurred the news of what has happening in the Punjab and assured the Commons that the region was menaced by a rebellion, changed his tack. In fairness to the unremarkable Montagu, he had already entertained doubts about O'Dwyer and his rigorous methods, and the Hunter Report confirmed his fears. Chelmsford, the Viceroy, dithered, first backing O'Dwyer and Dyer and then, sniffing scandal, he trimmed his sails and censured him. This fudging was to the credit of neither man, and intensified resentment against them from the military, who believed that they had first supported Dyer and then dropped him to appease Indian politicians. This was how it appeared to Lieutenant Colonel Morgan, who had been with Dyer at the Jallianwala Bagh and remained his stout supporter. 'They let those sweltering down in the plains to do the dirty work and then censure them for doing it', was his judgement on Montagu and Chelmsford.

Dyer, whose health was poor, had been ordered home by the Commander in Chief, and on his arrival heard his actions fiercely debated in Parliament. Those who had taken up the cudgels for him presented Dyer as the man who had saved India by his resoluteness, and was then thrown to the wolves by politicians too feeble to stand by him. This view was taken in Parliament where the debate turned into a witchhunt against Montagu, which he and the Ministry survived. Outside, a public fund was opened for Dyer which quickly reached £26,000, and to which Rudyard Kipling contributed £10. Other sums from rich and poor, in Britain and India, suggested that there was much public sympathy for Dyer's action and anger at his treatment. He died in 1927.

All those involved in the aftermath of the Amritsar affair had gained something from it, save Dyer who had lost his job. Indian nationalists had an example providing beyond doubt that the velvet glove of the supposedly humane and beneficient *raj* was the outer covering for an iron fist which had been callously used at Amritsar. The shootings had exposed Britain's moral pretensions as a sham, and nationalist agitation for an end to the *raj* intensified. For their part, O'Dwyer and the Dyer faction stood by a man whose steadfastness, they believed, had pulled India back from the brink of revolution and anarchy, and thereby saved its people from civil war. For officers in India and elsewhere who were called upon to use their forces to uphold the civil power, the fate of Dyer was a warning. A moral limit clearly existed to the scope of their action, and they could not take for granted the backing of their superiors.

The Amritsar affair had occurred in the middle of a wider Imperial crisis. In 1919 Britain's armed forces were stretched to the limit by global commitments, and one consequence of this was that the rulers of India lacked the resources to handle the disturbances in April. The troops available were, in many cases, inexperienced or anxious for demobilization, and many of them were earmarked for service on the frontier, already imperilled by signs of Afghan hostility. The men in the Punjab, with their vivid sense of history, must have known that matters had stood like this in 1857, on the eve of the Mutiny. They were fearful of another Mutiny, and obsessed with the belief that the disorders around them were part of a secret, revolutionary conspiracy to overthrow the *raj*. Fears of deep, secret and subversive plots had, for the moment, become an everyday feature of political life in Britain and Europe. The Bolshevik Revolution of 1917 had made the British government nervous, and politicians came to imagine the hidden hand of Communist agitation, working to foment unrest everywhere. This was the period in which the *Protocols of the Elders of Zion*, the fairy tale of a Jewish global conspiracy, was published and gained temporary credibility from many who ought to have known better. When the rulers of the Punjab faced examination by the Hunter Committee, they covered themselves and their actions by citing local intelligence which pointed to a massive conspiracy to disrupt and overthrow the Government of India with Congress connivance. The upheavals faced by Dyer and others were part of a postwar, world-wide phenomenon of restlessness, in which the existing order was called into question. The defenders of that order often felt bewildered and under pressure, and interpreted opposition to them and their ideals as manifestations of some shadowy conspiracy.

Many soldiers were dismayed by the treatment handed out to Dyer, which seemed grossly unfair. He 'did the only thing in the circumstances', thought Private Swindlehurst, 'But there are greater things at stake of which we know little'. There was sympathy for Dyer among the soldiers of the King's Own Yorkshire Light Infantry where Corporal Simms remembered 'most of the troops did not agree with it [Dyer's treatment], but they had no say in it'. Brigadier General Smyth, who had been involved in the suppression of other unrest in the Punjab, thought that whilst Dyer had been mistaken in firing so many rounds his decision to fire was correct. 'The Dyer incident would probably have faded into obscurity', had it not been for the Hunter Commission, thought Smyth, who was later to be caught in the thick of the riots in 1930 at Peshawar where he was City Commandant.[53]

Peshawar had been the target of prolonged political agitation by Congress and Abdul Ghaffar Khan's 'Redshirt' movement during 1929. The most serious trouble broke out at the end of April 1930 in response to the local authorities' decision to arrest leading agitators. The arrests and movement of the prisoners on 23 April created disturbances, prompting the Deputy Commissioner to call for armoured cars, which he hoped would cower the crowds. They were greeted with stone-throwing, and one of the motor-cyclist outriders was murdered by the mob, which then tried to set alight one of the four cars. The crew escaped, using their revolvers, and the crowd was finally broken up by machine-gun fire from the other cars. The armoured cars had made matters worse not only by their appearance, but because several rioters were knocked down when they crashed. Forty-five minutes later reinforcements from the King's Own Yorkshire Light Infantry arrived. Their passage through the streets was opposed by men throwing bricks from rooftops who were fired on. Thirty demonstrators were killed and thirty-three wounded by 130 rounds of fire. The next day, troops were taken out of the city, whilst the civil authorities tried to patch matters up through discussions with local leaders. This was seen as weakness; more disturbances followed and the troops were brought back to occupy strategic points. The situation was further complicated when the news of these troubles spread to neighbouring Afridi tribesmen and 'Redshirts' who converged on the city. When this news penetrated the Tirah it seemed, to some, to presage the collapse of the *raj*, an illusion which was soon after shattered by thirty-two aircraft over-flying the region.

There was more trouble inside Peshawar which was now jointly controlled by Smyth and the local magistrate, Olaf Caroe. It was 'that most unpleasant of all jobs for a soldier', in what Smyth remembers as 'a very unpleasant place'. Trouble got worse after an incident when a Yorkshire Light Infantryman's rifle was accidentally fired. The bullet narrowly missed Smyth, who was inspecting the detachment, and killed an Indian woman and her two small children. This provoked serious rioting for, understandably perhaps, the Indians did not see the incident as a mishap. Smyth and his men, reinforced by two companies of Sikhs, came under bombardment from bricks and bottles. Such a pelting, Smyth thought, 'encourages the rioters, leads to loss of morale on the part of the troops and nearly always ends in the situation getting out of hand'. Determined to prevent this, Smyth chose men who were good shots and when an officer was stunned by a brick, he ordered the thrower to be shot. 'The effect was electric. All the way down the street you could see people on the rooftops putting down their bricks and bottles and going inside'. The disorder subsided and the town became quiet.[54]

For the man on patrol in such a situation, it was often terrifying. Corporal Simms remembered such duty during the 1920s:[55]

> They came like a plague of locusts from nowhere. It was very frightening facing them, but we were soldiers, paid to do these kind of jobs. We were under iron discipline. The method used to deal with them was by firing over their heads. Most of the time it was exciting seeing them running away for their lives.

Such men and such methods were the sheet anchor of the *raj* and ensured that it kept control and maintained order until its dissolution. The most sustained effort at civil disobedience, Gandhi's 'Quit India' campaign of the summer of 1942, although widespread, never for a moment came close to its purpose of overthrowing British administration. Sufficient police and troops were available to contain unrest and guard the railways, which were targets for sabotage. The 70th Division undertook railway protection in Bihar, a seriously disturbed area, and six Indian battalions and one of Cameronians in the south of India. Lord Linlithgow, the Viceroy, had also made it clear that aircraft patrolling railway-lines would machine-gun any saboteurs. A further sign that the government meant business were the bomber patrols over disaffected regions.[56]

In spite of the *raj*'s success in countering the 'Quit India' movement, the possibility of a further campaign on this scale at the end of 1945 disturbed Wavell and his military advisors. The task of holding on seemed immense, and would have involved 'a considerable force of British troops' enforcing martial law, detention without trial and the indefinite suspension of Congress. Faced with such a problem, Alanbrooke's first reaction was to comment that he 'had no idea where the troops would come from if we wanted them'.[57] They were not, in fact, required; Congress had no need for a campaign of disobedience for its energies were devoted to the drawing up of a timetable for taking power and, briefly, thwarting suggestions for partition.

The heart-searching and political wrangling which preceded partition and independence do not lie within the scope of this book, nor does Lord Mountbatten's political mission as the last Viceroy. Whatever else may be said of his performance of this duty, it was accomplished without the loss of a single soldier's life. British troops pulled back from their garrisons and cantonments and the Indian army took over. Some 2,800 respected British officers of the Indian army remained for a time, a rearguard too small to do much to prevent the massacres which occurred across Northern India as Muslims fled to Pakistan and Hindus to India. During July and August 1947 Brigadier Bristow, one of the rearguard, was a witness of the baleful events in the Punjab and was able once to scare off a Sikh murder gang with a Gurkha patrol.[58]

'No one in India ever worshipped the setting sun, only the rising one, and that was now Congress', Muhammed Usman sorrowfully informed Lord Wavell in 1945.[59] From 1919, the *raj*'s sun had been setting and in its twilight the British army fought the last of its campaigns of pacification on the North-West Frontier, and the first of its new campaigns of policing throughout India. The British army, which had paved the way for the establishment of Imperial government, had found a new role — that of preserving the peace of the Empire whilst its rulers planned its dismemberment.

3
An Empire Founded upon Sand: The Middle East

The Arabs rebelled against the Turks during the war not because the Turk Government was notably bad, but because they wanted independence. They did not risk their lives in battle to change masters, to become British subjects or French citizens, but to win a show of their own. Whether they are fit for independence or not remains to be tried. Merit is no qualification for freedom. Freedom is enjoyed when you are so well armed, or so turbulent, or inhabit a country so thorny that the expense of your neighbour's occupying you is greater than the profit.

T. E. Lawrence, letter to *The Times*, 22 July 1920

The Turkey's Carcass

'I contended vehemently that a bird in the military hand was worth many in the diplomatic bush'; which was why Colonel A. T. Wilson supported a hurried push towards Mosul and its hinterland during the last weeks of the First World War.[1] The advance was also encouraged by Lloyd-George, for whom it mattered little that the region had already been earmarked for inclusion in the future sphere of French influence by the secret Sykes-Picot treaty of 1916. At that stage in the war the eventual defeat of Turkey was by no means a certainty, although this had not hindered Allied plans for the future partition of its Middle Eastern Empire.

Before 1914 the Turkish Empire had been an impotent and pliant buffer state between Europe and India. Its outlying provinces had been whittled away by France, Italy, the Balkan states and Britain. Britain's gains had directly reflected her commercial and strategic interests. Cyprus, Egypt, the Sudan and Aden had been obtained to guard the sea route to India. A squadron of British warships, based on Bushire, kept the peace between the semi-independent rulers of the Persian Gulf states and taught them to fear Britain rather than their Turkish overlords. Since 1836, British gunboats had steamed up and down the Tigris and Euphrates, watching over British subjects and their property, and keeping an eye on the behaviour of the local Turkish authorities. At the beginning of the twentieth century, the opening of the Persian oilfields deepened Britain's interest in the region. Wartime needs raised local production from thirty-eight to over 300 million tons a year, and customers included the Royal Navy. There were thought to be oil deposits around Mosul, which, as the war came to a close, gave Britain a further motive for obtaining as much of Mesopotamia as was possible.

The growth of Turco-German friendship just before the outbreak of war had disturbed Britain for it had seemed to point the way towards a stronger, more independent and therefore less tractable Turkey. In November 1914, the Turks had thrown in their lot with Germany, not least because her rulers realized that an Allied victory would mean the dismemberment of their empire and Russian occupation of Constantinople (Istanbul). Some kind of Turkish challenge to Britain had been expected for some years, and in 1906 the Committee for Imperial Defence had discussed how best to use force to make the Turks see sense. The conclusion, based on the best Imperial traditions of making war against non-Europeans, had been in favour of taking an immediate offensive. This was needed if British prestige was to be upheld and so, at the end of 1914, Anglo-Indian forces landed in Mesopotamia and pushed northwards towards Baghdad; and soon afterwards, Allied land and naval forces attacked the Straits. Success proved elusive; the Gallipoli landings went awry and ended with an ignominious withdrawal at the beginning of 1916, whilst at Kut, British and Indian forces had been forced to surrender. Elsewhere, the Turks and their supporters had made life awkward for the British. The Sanusi had attacked Egypt from Libya, Ali Dinar led a pro-Turkish revolt in the Sudan, Aden was under pressure from local Turkish forces, and the Suez Canal was menaced by a Turkish army based in Palestine. Counter-offensives followed, in which many of the forces previously fighting in Gallipoli invaded Palestine, and, under General Allenby, took Jerusalem in December 1917. Things also looked better in Mesopotamia where Baghdad had fallen in March 1917.

Local Arab populations contributed to this revival of the Allied cause. Shortly before the outbreak of the war, Lord Kitchener, then High Commissioner in Egypt, had sensed the advantage of listening to requests for British backing from Hussein, the *Sharif* of Hejaz, who was anxious to free himself from Turkish sovereignty. The coming of war made such a proposition attractive to the authorities in Cairo who opened negotiations with the *Sharif*. The unimpressive Allied showing in the Middle East made him initially chary of open commitment. In October 1915, Cairo's envoy, Sir Henry Macmahon, made vague offers of an independent Arabia, whose boundaries included western Syria, and Muslim control of the holy cities of Mecca and Medina as the price for an insurrection against the Turks. *Sharif* Hussein took the plunge in October 1916 when his irregulars, led by his sons, Abdullah and Feisal, took the field under the guidance of T. E. Lawrence. As the rebellion proceeded, many Arabs believed that they were fighting to liberate their country and the British naturally encouraged this view. In 1920, after the Arab-Jewish riots in

Jerusalem, the official report commented: 'As late as June 1918 active recruiting was carried on in Palestine for the *Sharifian* army, our allies, the recruits being given to understand that they were fighting in a national cause and to liberate their country from the Turks'.[2]

Later events did much to disabuse the Arabs. As was well-known to the agents of Cairo, including Lawrence, Sir Mark Sykes of the Foreign Office had agreed a treaty with Georges Picot at the beginning of 1916 which outlined a future partition of the Turkish Empire between Britain and France. Britain was to be satisfied with southern Mesopotamia and the ports of Haifa and Acre, both good harbours for warships and conveniently close to the Suez Canal; Palestine would be ruled by an international commission which would take account of Arab views; and France would be given control over the Lebanon and Syria whose borders enclosed much of what had been promised to the *Sharif*. The Foreign Secretary, Sir Edward Grey, planned to secure Jewish American backing for the Allies through a gesture towards the Zionist lobby which might also, it was thought later, encourage Russian Jews to support the precarious Provisional Government of Kerensky. Grey's successor, Arthur Balfour, accordingly issued the Balfour Declaration which announced British support for a Jewish homeland in Palestine in November 1917.

With the war over, the British government had to secure from this often obscure and contradictory bundle of agreements a lasting settlement which would guarantee Britain's future paramountcy in the Middle East. This was imperative for the political and strategic security of India, and meant not only safe lines of communication but keeping the lid down on Pan-Islamic movements which could disturb India's ninety million Muslims. The consolidation of Britain's Middle Eastern power was the responsibility of Lloyd-George and Britain's other representatives at the Peace Conferences during 1919 and 1920, where the victorious nations re-ordered the world and its peoples. There were plenty of experts on hand to offer suggestions but their advice was often contradictory. Sir Percy Cox and his Oriental Secretary, the traveller, Gertrude Bell, were both sympathetic to the *Sharifian* cause and wanted the British to place Feisal on the Iraqi throne where, they hoped, he would take care of British interests. His father, Hussein, had been declared King of Hejaz, and his brother, Abdullah, would be given the throne of Transjordan. T. E. Lawrence was also anxious to promote the *Sharifian* interests and dreamed of the proposed Arab states as 'our first brown dominions and not our last brown colony'. More down to earth, Colonel A. T. Wilson, until 1920 Commissioner in Mesopotamia, was convinced that the province and its people needed firm, uplifting government along Indian lines. Non-British interests also had to be taken care of, for France, who wanted more from victory than Alsace and Lorraine, was keen to get control of Lebanon and Syria, as promised by the Sykes-Picot treaty. In support of such claims, the French offered a ragbag of reasons which included, unbelievably, historical connections from the time of the Crusades. These were treated seriously by the British and with dismay by the Arabs.

France was dismissive of Feisal's claim to Damascus where he had been declared King. Syria's elected national congress responded, in May 1920, by declaring Syria an independent kingdom, whose frontiers included Palestine. This was too much for the Allies, who were unwilling to allow the Arabs the same national rights as they had the Finns, Czechs and Poles. At San Remo, Britain and France awarded themselves Palestine and the Lebanon and Syria as mandates. The mandate was a new and convenient formula which gave both countries the right to govern their new territories as trustees of the newly-formed League of Nations. In the Lebanon, General Girouad, true in spirit to France's antique Crusading traditions, gathered an army of Moroccans and Senegalese, who, with tanks and artillery, destroyed the Syrian government and sent Feisal packing.

Mandates and Mayhem — Iraq

The end of the war saw Mesopotamia, soon to be Iraq, under the thumb of an Anglo-Indian army of occupation which had just driven out the Turks. In the first flush of victory, the British had promised the region a 'national Government and Administration drawing their authority from the initiative and true choice of the native population'. This was soon seen as impossible by the British Commissioner, Colonel A. T. Wilson, since the Iraqis were for the most part illiterate and riven by tribal and religious feuds. The region was hopelessly backward, and to conquer it the British had had to raise 130,000 labourers, including 8,000 criminals from Indian gaols, to build roads and handle communications. 'Our supreme need in a country predominantly tribal was tranquillity', concluded one of the new political officers, recruited by Wilson from former army officers and Indian officials. They were given the job of putting into practice Wilson's vision of Iraq governed along Indian lines, so that people 'antagonistic to the aims of settled government' would, like the Indians, come to appreciate its benefits.

The Turks thought differently. To uphold their rule, they had encouraged feuding, which kept their more volatile subjects busy and disunited. This policy had been popular in some quarters, and one of the first tasks of the British was to stamp out the old ways. 'Anarchy and bloodshed' were too common amongst the Marsh Arabs, some of whom showed little inclination to accept the new regulations of the British. Sheikh Badr, who had joined the Turkish *jihad* aainst the British in 1915, was among the first to pay the price of continued defiance. Two gunboats shelled his village on the Lower Euphrates, near An-Nasiriya but he was unchastened. Soon afterwards, in May 1918, a punitive force of 400 Indian troops, infantry and cavalry, backed by two gunboats and three aircraft, attacked the village neighbouring hamlets. The use of aircraft was seen as a *coup de théatre*, for they had been moved in secret and attacked without warning to secure the maximum of surprise and terror, although two badly aimed bombs killed four Indian cavalry *sowars*. The shock did the trick, although one British officer wondered whether the use of aircraft had been 'unsporting'. It may well have been, at least to those for whom punitive expeditions were like away fixtures, but Political Officers soon got into the habit of summoning up machines when faced with Arab hostility or disobedience.[3]

There was more sustained resistance to British occupation in the northern part of Iraq, where the Kurds' joy at liberation from the Turks turned to anger after they realized that they had lost one yoke only to gain another. Wilson blamed their attitude on the Balfour Declaration, although he in fact meant President Wilson's 'Fourteen Points', which embraced Allied pledges of self-determination for subject peoples. Knowing this, the Kurds had welcomed the arrival of the British in Mosul at the end of 1918. Sheikh Mahmud warmly received Major Noel, a British Political Officer, in Sulaimaniya. The Major replied to his hospitality by assuring Mahmud and the Kurds that Britain had 'no intention of imposing on them an administration foreign to their habits and desires'.[4] One of these desires was the creation of an independent Kurdish state under British protection. This was not part of Colonel Wilson's scheme of things. He mistrusted Mahmud, whom he found possessed of too much 'natural cunning', and he wanted the Kurds to settle down in an Arab state, for, on their own, they were neither politically or economically viable.

Mahmud understood British intentions for in May 1919, he took over Sulaimaniya, declared himself ruler of Kurdistan, issued his own postage stamps and locked up the local British officials. He had taken the local authorities by surprise, and the military forces available at Kirkuk, 100 miles away, were not up to the task of driving him out of his stronghold. A battalion of infantry, backed by armoured cars, came to grief in a mountain pass a dozen miles from Sulaimaniya. Four armoured cars and twelve Ford lorries had to be left behind as the force fell back. Stronger measures were needed so, in June, Major General Sir Theodore Fraser, a veteran of four North-West Frontier campaigns and therefore used to his kind of work, moved towards Sulaimaniya with two infantry brigades, cavalry and armoured cars. RAF aircraft were extensively used to bomb and strafe villages and parties of Kurdish rebels. Amongst Fraser's forces were Kachins, hillmen from Burma, who managed to take the Baziyan Pass, opening up the road to Sulaimaniya. Cavalry from the 32nd Indian Lancers moved off, took the town, and rescued the British prisoners before the Kurds realized that the pass had been forced.

Mahmud had been wounded in the battle and was taken prisoner. He was tried before a court-martial, found guilty and sentenced to death. The British had no authority for this, he asserted, and to prove his point he produced a copy of the Anglo-French declaration of a year before with its promises of self-rule, which he had kept in an amulet on his arm. The authorities did not shoot him, but kept him in prison until 1921, when he was banished. But they had not heard the last of him, or the Kurds. Resistance continued in southern Kurdistan for several months; Political Officers were assassinated, columns were ambushed and villages were bombed. The Indian government thought all this unpleasantly familiar; for it seemed that a new North-West Frontier was being created by their proto-administration in Baghdad. It was therefore decided that the region around Ruwandiz was to be abandoned for the time being, so that the energies of the imposers of order could be concentrated on southern Kurdistan.

The upheavals amongst the Marsh Arabs, and the more formidable revolt of the Kurds, had been handled by forces which formed part of the army of occupation. In response to the need for War Office economies and the wish of soldiers for demobilization, this force of over 200,000 was progressively reduced during 1919. The Iraq garrison had been pruned to 4,200 British and 30,000 Indian troops by the beginning of 1920, some of whom had to be diverted to Persia to lend weight to Britain's anti-Bolshevik stance there. The short-fall had been partly made up by 2,000 locally recruited levies, drawn from the 30,000 Assyrian refugees who fled southwards from Turkish massacres during the war. The new force had a tough reputation, and was little liked by Iraq's Muslim majority.

Local resentment against British rule was increasing during 1920, along with fears that it was going to prove permanent. Muslim traditionalists were unhappy about some of the recent innovations, in particular schemes which pointed the way towards the education of women. The new apparatus of the state and its servants all had to be paid for, and Iraqis therefore found themselves faced with the disagreeable novelty of taxation: 666 million *rupees* was the annual price of the government and a quarter of this sum came from a land tax. External events also troubled the Iraqis, especially the Allies' bad faith in not honouring promises made to the *Sharif*'s family during the war. By thte early summer of 1920, nationalists believed that the chance had come to rise up and throw out the British, and there were hopes that the revolt would meet only token resistance. 'The British nation is weary of wars and will make no more sacrifices', one nationalist confidently informed Colonel Wilson. Political Officers' reports of rifle buying by tribesmen (some were 'mortgaged' by policemen for £30 each) made Wilson apprehensive and although he later censured the local army commander, General Sir Aylmer Haldane, for complacency, there seems little doubt that the civil administration, like the army, was taken by surprise when the Iraqi revolt began in May 1920.

Two separate incidents sparked off the uprising. The first, at Tall Afar in the north, involved the successful ambush of an armoured car and infantry patrol, which was followed by a severe punitive attack on the area. The second, in the south, was the outcome of what Haldane described as the 'tactlessness and overbearing manner' of a Political Officer, Captain Hyatt, who had been sent to Rumaitha to sequester the property of a sheikh for a £100 tax debt. Both incidents were spontaneous, but there were signs in the north of the involvement of *Sharifian* enthusiasts and former Turkish officers. From the start the rebels' motives were mixed and there was little cohesion between different areas. Action was limited to attacks on centres of British administration, many of which came under siege, and attempts to disrupt the rail network and ambush relief columns.

Haldane was, at first, embarrassed and hindered by a lack of men. The blockhouses which guarded Basra and Baghdad had to be manned by Indian labourers, who kept their spirits up at night by firing into the dark. There were about 6,000 men, most of them Indian soldiers, available for punitive columns at the onset of the revolt. Haldane likened his job to holding down a piece of parchment which, whenever pressure was removed, rose up. All over the country the British were on the defensive, in spite of the widespread use of aircraft to drop supplies and harass the rebels. A relief column from Hilla, on the Euphrates, marching to Dimaniya, came under heavy attack, and had to fall back after losses of 180 dead and 160 captured. The prisoners included seventy-nine British soldiers, mostly from the 3rd Manchesters, who were taken to An-Najaf where they were well treated, thanks to the intervention of Agha Hamid Khan, a cousin of the Aga Khan. Another prisoner who joined them was Jasdit Rai of 1/10 Gurkhas, who had been amongst the defenders of a derailed train. He had surrendered after defending the wreck for two days and had his *kukri* taken from him, along with his rifle. He was released with the other prisoners in September.

Others were less lucky. The crew of the gunboat HMS *Greenfly*, which had been stranded on the Euphrates above Khizr, had to surrender after all attempts at relief had failed, and were killed by their captors. A special vindictiveness was reserved for the wives of Assyrian levies, who were publicly raped, and their children, who were roughly handled; both activities characteristically were encouraged by former Turkish officers. As Colonel Wilson noted, the Arabs did not torture their prisoners.

In the first stage of the war, during June, July and August, inadequate numbers of British troops did their best to counter outbreaks and defend the railways. The task was beyond them and, on 15 July, Haldane wired London for an Indian division 'for it was essential to give the Arabs on the Lower Euphrates a good lesson'. Churchill and the Cabinet were not so sure but their hand was forced on 2 August, when Haldane warned that Baghdad was threatened.[5] Nerves were beginning to crack as the extent of the unrest became known, and Colonel Wilson, who had now left his post, proposed capitulation by suggesting that an Arab government, headed by Feisal, should be offered to the Iraqis. The Cabinet did not demur but for the moment concentrated on action. 'Concessions made in the moment of defeat never improved any situation' went its argument, and it was therefore necessary to 'teach the turbulent tribes a sharp lesson'.[6] Resolution had to be translated into action and this was not easy. The Indian Government, facing internal unrest and trouble in Waziristan, was unhappy about sending reliable Gurkha and British troops, and the latter were anyway needed in Ireland and Constantinople. The 'far flung battleline' was stretched dangerously thin, and Churchill at the War Office and Sir Henry Wilson, Chief of the Imperial General Staff, both feared that it might snap.

Relief forces were found from India during August and September but it was a difficult job. The 15th Sikhs were brought up to strength by tempting back demobilized men with 100 *rupee* bonuses.[7] This and other units were shipped to Basra, where they moved north along the Euphrates to carry out the pacification of the region. The relief of towns under siege, and the repair and protection of railways were the first priorities. As they moved, the columns exacted retribution from areas which had supported the revolt and disarmed tribesmen. The East Yorkshires were engaged throughout October in the Hilla district. They moved across country, flanked by Indian Lancers, building blockhouses and burning villages. Tribesmen who tried to interfere with their work were driven off by machine-gun fire. The battalion suffered two casualties, off-duty men wounded by a bomb from a RAF 'plane.[8] Further north, the 15th Sikhs went about reopening the railway at Baquba which had been abandoned in July. They were attacked by 700 tribesmen at Baquba on 17 August, but drove them off with grenades and Lewis gun fire for, with sufficient numbers at their disposal, British commanders were always assured of overwhelming fire-power. Shellfire and burning villages made a 'wonderful sight at night', as Colonel Bousett, a medical officer with Royal Artillery, noted in his diary. He was with his unit on the Euphrates during October, and he also recorded how the troops plundered the villages they passed through; he got some eggs at one place, and found time to shoot red partridge.[9]

By such means, the reinforcements were able to contain and then overcome the insurrection. It was a slow process, for in December the 8th Rajputs were still rounding up men, sheep and horses, and burning houses to make the Fatlah tribesmen hand over their rifles.[10] Other rebels may well have suffered worse treatment. In the face of continued resistance Haldane had, on 28 September, asked the War Office for poisoned gas shells as the only means of getting at the elusive Marsh Arabs. Colonel Wilson liked the idea, as did Churchill, The Secretary for War, and orders were issued to send 60,000 non-lethal gas shells to Iraq. They did not prove as effective as Haldane would have wished for a year later, when asked to comment on the use of gas against the Kurds, he answered; 'In the hilly country of the Kurds gas would be far more effective than in the hot plains where the gas is very volatile'.[11]

For some years before the Iraqi rebellion, Churchill and the War Office staff had been seriously considering the use of poisoned gas against natives. The concept was repugnant to many, including the Indian authorities in Delhi who did not use the stocks which had been sent to the Afghan frontier in 1919. Churchill was not much troubled by such feelings, and in a memorandum of March 1919 condemned 'squeamishness' over the use of gas, which irritated the eyes and was no more brutal than shellfire which tore the flesh of its victims. 'I am strongly in favour of using poisoned gas against uncivilized tribes . . . gases can be used which cause great inconvenience and would spread a lively terror' without killing. Two days before he wrote this, Churchill had conceded a request for poisoned gas from 31 Wing of the RAF, which had had the blessing of the Baghdad Government, although Air Officer Commanding in the Middle East, Sir John Salmond, believed that the gas would not be needed.[12] His objections were ignored, for Churchill agreed that 300 bombs, filled with lethal and non-lethal gas, should be sent to Iraq. A hitch soon occurred, for it was discovered that the technology for putting gas in aerial bombs had not been developed. The matter surfaced again during the Iraq rebellion, for on 29 August 1920, Churchill instructed Trenchard to get on with the work needed to produce mustard and other gas bombs which could be dropped from aircraft. These devices would, in Churchill's chilling words, 'inflict grave punishment upon recalcitrant natives without inflicting grave injury on them'.[13] What he may have had in mind was the novel DM gas which, it was said, knocked its victims out for forty-eight hours.[14] It is likely that such a gas, with new, highly toxic varieties, had already been used by British forces in North Russia in 1919.[15]

The question of using gas, this time against the Kurds in northern Iraq, was raised again in August 1921 when Churchill was anxious to get Cabinet approval for a gas bombardment.[16] That he and many others, in Baghdad as well as London, were thinking about the use of gas, lethal or not, to crush resistance to Imperial government, gives a remarkable insight into the minds of those responsible for the Empire at the time. As the Iraq revolt of 1920 confirmed, Britain had bitten off more than she could chew, let alone digest. Her armed forces, backing Imperial administrations and Imperial policies, were on active service in India, Persia, Iraq, Palestine, Egypt and Ireland. They were just not sufficient to do their job well. The imbalance between pretensions and means to uphold them could only be corrected by a resort to the weapons of mass killing used in the First World War. Alternatively, the British government could adjust its policies and seek to impose hegemony on the Middle East by means other than repression. So far, this policy had not worked well and was costing too much.

The Iraqi revolt and its pacification, which was officially over by February 1921, marked a turning point in Britain's Middle Eastern policy. This had been anticipated by an optimistic and far-sighted Iraqi nationalist on the eve of the uprising. He had told Colonel Wilson that, since 1919, the British had made concessions to the Afghan government and to Egyptian nationalist leaders. In both cases, the British had secured a military advantage but were not willing or able to press it too severely. The same proved true in Iraq. Its future was decided at the Cairo Conference in March 1921, which Churchill attended as Colonial Secretary. He was able to lay the foundations of British hegemony in the Middle East without, in the words of his admirer, T. E. Lawrence, 'sacrificing any interest of our Empire'. A British client state of the

Transjordan was created under the Amir Abdullah and his brother, Feisal, was made King of Iraq. The new Kingdom was tied to Britain by a series of treaties which permitted British air bases there. To all intents and purposes, and even after Iraqi 'independence' in 1930, the Kingdom remained under Britain's thumb.

Those hitherto responsible for Iraq did not fare too well. Colonel Wilson passed into civilian life, where his knowledge secured him employment by the Anglo-Persian Oil Company. Haldane, whose policy of not taking the offensive until he had reinforcements earned him Churchill's displeasure, returned to Britain (much annoyed by noisy children and gramophones on his ship) to find himself under a cloud. Unlike other Imperial generals who had 'broached rebellion', Haldane was not offered the customary honours. Instead, he was placed on the retired list, from which he emerged in 1940 to be rudely snubbed by the War Office, which made it plain that there were no opportunities for men who had once waged war against Boers and tribesmen.[17]

The strategic arrangements for policing the new kingdom of Iraq had been devised by Churchill and Trenchard. Their genesis had been the curbs on War Office spending, imposed in March 1919, which set a limit of £110 million on Churchill's budget. It was Churchill's task to find ways in which the high costs of Imperial garrisons could be reduced without damage to prestige or local security. Armoured cars and aircraft were his answer. The idea of 'smaller forces with machine-guns in armoured cars which are very mobile and which can move into streets and villages, and push across deserts', appealed to Churchill's imagination.[18] They would be supported by modern, swift-moving artillery — in other words, aircraft carrying bombs, which had already shown their value in the remote campaigns in the Sudan, on the North-West Frontier and Somaliland. Trenchard, the RAF commander, was also enthusiastic, for the concept of 'air control' offered a justification for his new service's independence from its rivals, as well as an argument for preference from the Treasury. There was hostility from the army, in particular Sir Henry Wilson, Chief of the Imperial General Staff, who feared that the traditional, imperial functions of his service might be superseded by the RAF. His objections were overturned, as were those of others who were nervous about the inhumanity of using bombs against tribesmen. To the satisfaction of Churchill, Trenchard, Gertrude Bell and T. E. Lawrence, already fascinated by the RAF, the scheme was approved and Iraq was to be its first proving ground.

'Air Control' was officially introduced to Iraq in 1922 and not long after it was offered to Abdullah of Transjordan, who was given RAF aircraft for intimidating his more unruly subjects. The entire internal security of Iraq rested with the RAF which had its Headquarters at Baghdad. Eight squadrons of fighter-bombers were distributed among three airfields, each of which had its own cantonment and defensive perimeter, guarded by Assyrian levies under British officers. The RAF also possessed armoured car squadrons and some gunboats for duties on the Tigris and Euphrates. The purpose of this self-contained Imperial police force was to assist Feisal's government in the task of bringing order and stability to remote regions. The whole business was summed up by Squadron Leader Keith, who served with the RAF in Iraq from 1926 onwards.[19]

> 'Air Control' is a marvellous means of bringing these wild mountain tribes 'to heel'. It is swift, economic and humane, as we always drop warning messages some hours before we start to 'lay eggs' on their villages so that they can clear out . . . an eastern mind forgets quickly, and if he is not punished for his misdeeds straight away, he has forgotten all about them, and feels his punishment is not merited if it is delayed.

Such procedures were not new; air raids against intractable tribesmen had been going on in Iraq since 1917 and, as Keith admitted, it took some time for the message to sink in.[20]

> It takes a long time to fathom the mentality of these people. They best understand a .303 bullet. The Turk beat them at their own games, and the German brought them to heel in his orthodox manner. They are rather apt to regard our leniency and straight dealing as a sign of weakness.

This is just the sort of conclusions to which Trenchard had come, for he insisted, 'when punishment is intended, the punishment must be severe, continuous and even prolonged'.[21]

The area most requiring such chastisement was Kurdistan, where old habits of tribal warfare died hard, and there were sporadic nationalist revolts. The situation was made worse, at least in 1922-3, by Turkish assistance to the Kurds. Kemal Ataturk, after his successful confrontation with the British on the shores of the Straits at Chanak, laid claim to Mosul which was threatened by a Turco-Kurdish force. The thrust towards Mosul had been encouraged by a temporary British withdrawal from the Ruwanduz region shortly before. This loss of face made the new Commander in Iraq, Air Vice Marshal Sir John Salmond, anxious to pursue a forward policy, in spite of calls for restraint from Bonar Law's Government in London which did not want a war with Turkey. The Turco-Kurdish offensive ran out of steam, and was easily deflected by two columns of 10,000 British and Indian troops in February 1923. Five months later Kemal's government dropped its claims to Mosul, but the British were unconvinced. The Committee for Imperial Defence discussed policy in the event of a fresh threat against Mosul in 1925-6, and decided that it would not be countered by the RAF. Instead, the Royal Navy was to blockade the Straits, and undertake operations against the Turks there, backed by carrier aircraft.[22] Traditional beliefs that the offensive was always the best way to handle Orientals lingered on, and the lessons of Gallipoli had already been forgotten.

No Turkish threat to Mosul ever materialized. Four years later the Turkish Government was having trouble of its own from the Kurds. Following the precedent established by Britain, the Turkish authorities turned to aircraft as the best means of bringing the rebels under control.[23] By this time the RAF's system in Iraq had been operational for eight years and had enjoyed much success. Aircraft had obvious advantages in a region where distances were vast and roads and railways scarce. Clashes between Assyrian levies and Muslims in Kirkuk led, in May 1924, to a call for British troops, since they were considered to be religiously impartial. Sixty-six men from the Royal Inniskillings, then garrisoned in Baghdad, were flown to Kirkuk in the holds of Vernons and Victorias, RAF transport planes. The air journey lasted eight hours, half the time it would have taken to move the men by train and foot.[24] A further eighty endured the bumpy ride in the transports (each seated 22) after which the local RAF authorities suggested that soldiers should in future be issued with cardboard sick-boxes of the sort handed out by cross-Channel ferry companies. Whatever miseries may have been suffered by the soldiers, this airlift pointed the way to a new form of Imperial military response by which forces could be moved by air to trouble spots. In the field RAF pilots and technicians were developing techniques for dropping arms, ammunition and supplies by parachute to ambushed columns or beleaguered garrisons. As a method of keeping the Imperial peace, the success of direct air control was hard to evaluate. It was most commonly applied in the mountain districts in the north of Iraq where Kurdish resistance was always simmering. In March 1931, Sheikh Mahmud, back from exile, was up in arms against the government. Aircraft were called in to rescue ambushed police columns, and attack parties of rebel horsemen in the open. Later, they co-operated with local Iraqi ground forces in an operation designed to cordon off an area and force the trapped rebels into a corner. The airforce also provided support for Iraqi troops and police during prolonged operations against Sheikh Ahmed of Barzan. From the summer of 1931 he had been at war with a neighbouring state and, after a particularly massive raid, his house was destroyed by the Iraqi army which had been called in to keep the peace. The ground forces were not strong enough to secure Ahmed's submission so, as a final resort, the RAF attacked his base at Barzan, driving him and his adherents into the mountains.

Ahmed submitted, claiming that he had not been the cause of the tribal war, but in April 1932 he was leading a rebellion against the government. Again, the RAF were called in. Sorties were flown against rebel villages, the planes dropping 112,250-pound and 520-pound high explosive bombs, the latter with light casings and therefore greater blast, proving the most effective against mud and stone buildings. On one occasion, fighters flew low over an embattled Iraqi column to raise the morale of the troops, who through default of their own officers, had to be commanded by the British 'advisors' attached to the unit. There was retaliation from the tribesmen, who had learned how to shoot back at aircraft. One returned to base with both its fuel tanks punctured.[25] As on the North-West Frontier of India, the pilot who was shot down, or whose machine was grounded through a fault, faced an unpleasant fate. 'Out here we always fly with "blood chits", which promise, in Arabic, Syrian and Kurdish, that if we are returned to the nearest British post, a ransom of Rs 3,000 will be paid'. This was all very well but, as Squadron-Leader Keith also pointed out, when the Arabs did not want the money, 'they turn you over to the attention of their women-folk'.[26]

In this kind of warfare, the RAF pilots always hoped to catch their enemies in open country. One party of 400 of so offered an 'excellent target and were soon on the run, with aircraft inflicting heavy casualties upon them'. In this 'concentrated bombing', a hundred rebels were killed or wounded, but Ahmed still refused to surrender. At the end of April 1932 the RAF turned to new tactics, designed to cut the rebels off from local support and supplies, and to make life so unbearable that submission was their only option. A local police inspector broadcast warnings in the Barzani dialect, from a Victoria transport which had been rigged up with loud-speakers. A booming voice from the clouds was thought preferable to the usual leaflet, which could hardly have been efficacious in a country with 98% illiteracy.[27]

What the rebellious Kurds heard was a call to leave their villages, and a warning that those who stayed faced bombardment. All movement by day and night was forbidden, delayed-action bombs would be dropped on villages by day as a deterrent and, if lights were seen at night, ordinary bombs would be dropped. By June, this aerial blockade was creating shortages and, under pressure from his people, Ahmed left the area with his followers and some livestock, crossing into Turkey. The success of the operation was measured by the establishment of police posts in the region soon afterwards, suggesting that stable government had arrived.

In the light of these and many similar experiences, the Kurds called aircraft 'the roaring lions of the air', a description which seems to have pleased RAF officers.[28] The roar and, for that matter, the bite of the lion were not to be heard or felt too often. This was Churchill's opinion, given in 1921, after Sir Percy Cox had complained about the deployment of aircraft to frighten Marsh Arabs into paying their taxes. In spite of Churchill's assurance that RAF aircraft would not be used for trivial purposes, they were later enlisted to assist the collection of government levies. In 1931, hints that Jaf nomads might be less than willing to render dues to a new government led to a series of flights over their territory. Pilots spotted tents and flocks, information which would prove useful in future operations. An RAF Intelligence Officer, escorted by armoured cars, visited the area, and quizzed 'friendlies' about the behaviour of the Jafs, who must have been left in no doubt about the consequences of refusal to pay their taxes.[29]

'Armoureds were greatly respected everywhere', was the comment of one of their crewmen, L. A. Simmons, who had served with the RAF in Iraq since 1926. The armoured car squadrons formed the ground support for RAF operations. Armoured cars guarded airfields, undertook scouting duties, fought alongside police or Iraqi army columns, and showed the flag in those areas where respect for it might be on the wane. They also kept watch over the deep ploughed line from Amman to Rutbah which, in the absence of reliable maps of the desert, guided pilots.

Simmons's section was typical. It consisted of four Rolls Royce armoured cars (named like warships, eg HM Armoured Car *Terror*), one wireless vehicle and four Model T Ford trucks, each carrying a Lewis Gun. Each car had a crew of four, commanded by a corporal, and in action the unit moved as a column, and set up camps with the Rolls Royce parked at the four corners as bastions. In emergencies, the cars and their crews could be moved by train to a convenient point from which to begin patrols. This is what happened to Simmons and his colleagues in January 1928, when they were ordered from Baghdad to Ur. 'We knew little of what was going to happen and where we were going', remembered Simmons; but it was a common practice for guardians of the Imperial peace to be in ignorance about just what they were doing. 'Cuttings from *The Times*', sent by Simmons's mother gave him and his fellows the first indication of what had been happening in Kuwait, to which they called during a threatened *ikwan* invasion of the Sheikdom in 1929.

After reaching Ur, chilled by overnight travel in open wagons, Simmons joined a patrol which moved westwards towards the Nejd, looking for *ikhwan* raiders. In terms of firepower, it was an impressive force with six Rolls Royces and eight armoured 'Tin Lizzies'. Its job was to discover the whereabouts of the tribesmen and send the information by wireless to 84 Squadron, which was flying sorties against the Wahhabis. On 22 January tents and camels were spotted, and two DH9As were called up. 'Some camels were observed to fall and bombs were seen to burst among the tents', noted Simmons. Soft sand made it inadvisable for the armoured cars to get too close to the encampment, so they were unable to fire their Vickers machine-guns. The remainder of this desert patrol was humdrum, the routine broken by stops for tea, making camp, mechanical breakdowns and, once, rescuing a car which had rolled down a hillside.[30]

The overall success of air control was hard to assess. Trenchard and Churchill, the originators of the scheme, were naturally full of its praises. Given that cheeseparing was the official order of the day for governments in the 1920s, the cheapness of air control was a powerful argument in its favour. In Aden and Iraq, the RAF and its locally-recruited, and therefore cheap, levies, saved money. But were air operations a deterrent? The RAF believed so and listed examples of restless tribes which had bowed to governments as a result of air control, but *The Times* in an editorial of 23 September 1932 wondered whether 'bitterness' remained amongst the tribesmen.

Against all the practical and cost-effective arguments in favour of air control were charges that it was inhumane and unjust. Trenchard dismissed such sentiments, and retorted that in the past army commanders had not waged war against primitively-armed tribesmen with blowpipes and boomerangs. In those days, columns, which had destroyed crops and livestock, brought famine in their wake; thousands had died in Somaliland in 1904 after one such expedition.[31] Nevertheless, one former column commander, Lord Plumer, who had helped put down the Matabele in 1896, wondered whether aerial control could ever show the natives 'the integrity, justice and humanity of British rule', which, in his youth, had been achieved through daily contact with the officers and men of British forces. He had voiced his feelings during a House of Lords debate in April 1930, during which many other Imperial veterans had had their say, mostly against air control.[32] There were good reasons for such misgivings. Group Captain Amyas Borton reported from Iraq that a raid on a Kurdish village near Rowanduz had killed eight men and many horses, sheep and cows, even though the attack had been intended only to frighten the villagers.

Another raid in 1921, carried out by eight aircraft from An-Nasiriya against Marsh Arabs was even more horrific: 'The tribesmen and their families were put to confusion; many of them ran into the lake, making good targets for the machine-guns'. Churchill was 'extremely shocked' after reading this and wondered why those responsible had not been brought before a court-martial. The reverberations of the Amritsar incident were still in the air, and Churchill made sure that such grisly details were kept secret: had they been made public they 'would ruin the air project'.[33] Trenchard made his own enquiries and discovered from Borton that the blame lay with Political Officers, who had insisted that this particularly obdurate tribe needed condign punishment. The buck was then passed to Sir Percy Cox, no enthusiast for air control, who admonished his men not to employ it too often. Such admonitions did not seem to change much; in June 1922 Borton reported that one village, 'a hot bed of malcontents', had been completely razed by 100 bombs.[34] He gave no hint of the number of the casualties, a subject on which the RAF often preferred to remain quiet. One senior officer, Air Commodore L. E. O. Charlton, found the Iraq policy utterly distasteful and dissociated himself from it, demanding a public investigation. Trenchard refused, and made sure that Charlton was kept away from the Middle East.[35]

The advocates of air control had their way. Trenchard seems to have had no difficulty in convincing the new Labour Prime Minister, Ramsay MacDonald, that it was a policy worth retaining and it was consequently followed by Labour as well as Conservative Governments. Save for murmurs from the backbenches and rumblings from the Lords, aerial control never became a subject of political controversy. It was already employed by France, Italy (which used mustard gas and phosgene in its war against Ethiopia) and Spain against their colonial subjects. The United States found it a useful means of punishment for Solomon Islanders during January 1943, when four villages were bombed for pro-Japanese activities.[36] The action was undertaken without consultation with the local British colonial authorities, who were worried about the random bombing of friendly villages. As one official lamented, 'young officers are sometimes too ready to bomb'. Past experience in other parts of the world had shown the same to be true of older ones as well.

As one counter to the moral argument against air control, its advocates had always emphasized its effectiveness. On a tactical level this was indisputable, for strafing and bombing were invaluable on the colonial battle field, and helped release many columns from ambushes or save them from being overwhelmed by their adversaries. Strategic bombing, which which areas were 'punished' or made to endure a blockade by aircraft, was another matter. Natives were quick to learn preventive measures and in Iraq, as on the North-West Frontier, many tribes devised their own air-raid precautions and shelters. A method of warfare which aimed to disrupt economic and social life, terrify and bring famine could never serve as an advertisement for the 'civilization' which its users claimed to possess and wished to share. Nor were its results always impressive. The Kurds, one of the first people to get a taste of air control, were not permanently cowed; their nationalist movement is still active today and is fighting Turkish, Iraqi and Iranian forces.[37]

In Iraq itself, air control was a temporary measure. In 1930 the government agreed to an alliance with Britain which permitted British forces free use of Iraqi ports, waterways and airfields for the movement of troops in wartime. Seven years later, the last British troops left the country, and the protection of the oil pipelines which ran westwards to Haifa and Tripoli was left to the Iraqi army. Britain also retained two air bases, at Shaibah, near Basra, and Habbaniya, which lay astride the route from India to the Middle East. In political terms, Iraq was safe in the hands of a puppet government which had conceded Britain the means to fulfil her Middle Eastern strategy of deploying Indian forces to defend the Suez Canal and Egypt.

After the outbreak of the Second World War, Germany and Italy attempted to upset this arrangement, with the assistance of the Mufti of Jerusalem, and the connivance of the Iraqi Prime Minister, Rashid Ali. For the Axis powers, meddling in Iraq offered an opportunity to sever British oil supplies, a possibility of which the War Cabinet had been aware since October 1940. Evidence of pro-Axis, anti-British activities in Baghdad mounted during the next few months until 31 March 1941, when the pro-British regent, Abdul Illah, fled Baghdad for the protection of a British gunboat. On 6 April, the day of the German invasion of Greece, Rashid Ali took power, backed by a group of army and air force officers. Unsure of whether he would take an anti-British line, the British government insisted on its treaty rights to move troops into Iraq as a wartime measure. Under pressure from nationalist army and air force officers, who were anxious to secure ties with Germany, Rashid Ali precipitated a crisis by sending his army and air force to lay siege to Habbaniyah. It appeared a good time to call the Imperial bluff, for British forces were distracted in North Africa and Greece, and their new commander, Lord Wavell, was unwilling to detach men for direct intervention in Iraq.

The determination of the Habbaniya garrison, which took the offensive in the air and on the ground, frustrated Rashid Ali. Reinforced by eight Wellington bombers, the obsolescent aircraft used by the RAF for training, took on the Iraqi air force and, by 12 May, it had been eliminated. The besieging forces had fallen back from Habbiniya on 6 May and Rashid Ali became importunate in his appeals for German help. This came in the form of *Luftwaffe* fighters, flown from Mosul on 14 May, but they were insufficient to swing the balance, although some heart was put into Iraqi resistance. The seriousness of the German threat had convinced the Chiefs of Staff to create 'Habforce', which was to cross from Palestine, relieve Habbaniya, and take Baghdad. This it did, leaving Rashid Ali no alternative but to flee with his chief adherents to Iran on 30 May. The regent was restored, in spite of rioting in Baghdad, and a government compliant with British interests was installed. A small force, with a squadron of RAF armoured cars, was allowed to garrison Mosul, and keep an eye on the oilfields. Towards the end of 1943, this force, together with the reliable Assyrian levies, was called out to deal with a local Kurdish leader, Mustafa Mullah. His messianic appeal was so strong that numbers of Iraqi soldiers and policemen had deserted and joined him.[38]

There had been other signs that Arab troops were becoming less willing to fight on behalf of Britain and its nominees. Units from the Transjordan Frontier Force refused to join with the Arab Legion and give assistance to 'Habforce' in Iraq. The catalyst for the growth of anti-British feeling among the Arabs had been British policy in Palestine which seemed, to the wider Arab world, partisan and indifferent to the rights of the Palestinian Arabs. Rashid Ali and his confederates had given notice of a new mood abroad in the Middle East which challenged the assumption that British interests were paramount in the region. Although Rashid Ali's efforts to break free from British control had failed, thanks to determined and overwhelming military intervention, he had pointed the way to the future by seeking succour from Britain's enemies.

Mandates and Mayhem — Palestine, 1919–47

'As long as we persist in our Zionist policy, we have got to maintain all our present forces in Palestine to enforce a policy hateful to the great majority — a majority which means to fight and continue to fight and has right on its side'. This bleak prediction was written by the local commander in Palestine, General Sir Walter Congreve, on 16 June 1921, the first year of the British mandate. He knew that his opinion would not be welcomed by the recipient of his letter, Winston Churchill, the Colonial Secretary, so he added: 'Don't label us all anti-Zionists; we only endeavour to see the truth and show it to you. You get the other side very fully I don't doubt'. Churchill, who supported the Zionists, needed little persuasion from 'the other side', then or later. He had, however, been warned in April 1921 by the High Commissioner in Palestine, Sir Herbert Samuel, that many army officers stationed in Palestine were unsympathetic to Zionism since they took their views from the newspaper *Morning Post*, apparently their favourite reading. Colonel Meinertzhagen was blunter: 'I believe that most Englishmen have inherited a dislike of the Jew . . . I do not think any normal body of British officers could hold the scales equally between Jew and Muslim'.[39]

These exchanges, during the first year of the British mandate in Palestine, indicated that army officers had already recognized that the enforcement of British policy there imposed a thankless task on them and their men. From 1920 until 1947, the British army and the Royal Navy were repeatedly forced to hold the ring in a contest between two irreconcilable antagonists, the Palestinian Arabs and the Jewish settlers. Both were infected with a form of rectitudinal fever whose symptoms were malevolence, ruthlessness and indifference to human suffering. In the face of this struggle for supremacy in Palestine, the British Government staggered unhappily between policies of repression and compromise. The latter, given the bitterness of Arab–Jewish animosity, was hopeless. A military solution was impossible for when British Governments turned to coercion the measures taken were circumscribed because of anxieties about international opinion, especially in the United States, where there was a formidable Zionist lobby, and in the neighbouring Arab states. Inside successive British Cabinets, decisions were shaped under pressure from pro-Zionist ministers [like Churchill], the demands of strategists obsessed with the Suez Canal, and Arabists, anxious not to offend Muslim opinion in India and the Middle East. In essence, the Zionists won the day, for in 1922 the Balfour Declaration was confirmed as British policy, and successive governments were left with the task of squaring commitment to a Jewish national homeland in Palestine with the wishes of the native population which had never been consulted in the matter, and which, throughout the 1920s and 1930s made clear its antipathy towards Jewish immigration.

Imperialists were not perturbed by this hostility. In the early days of the mandate, Colonel Meinertzhagen looked forward to a time when a Jewish-colonized Palestine would come of age as 'a healthy state and cornerstone of the British Commonwealth'. This was a pleasing prospect in strategic terms. Next to the defence of Britain, the Mediterranean and the Middle East were the major concerns of Imperial strategists, always haunted by spectres of insecure or broken communications with India and the Far East. In their minds Palestine assumed a vital importance for it lay on the eastern flank of the Suez Canal, The awakening of Egyptian nationalism, and with it a growing resentment of British military occupation and political tutelage, concentrated military and naval minds on Palestine as a seemingly reliable region upon which to base the defence of the Canal. Italy's bid for parity, it not superiority in the Mediterranean reinforced this view. The crisis which followed Mussolini's attack on Ethiopia in 1935–6 and the League of Nation's attempts to impose punitive sanctions forced the British Navy to face up to the prospect of a struggle for control of the Mediterranean. Operational plans drawn up to

An Empire Founded upon Sand: The Middle East

meet this contingency concluded that since Malta, vulnerable to air attacks from the Italian mainland, might well be untenable, the Navy would have to concentrate its forces in the Eastern Mediterranean and fight back from there. Alexandria was proposed as a major base, with Haifa playing a subsidiary role. The policy of facing up to Italy began with bluster and ended with a whimper when, in July 1936, sanctions were abandoned. French tepidity, European tension after Hitler's *coup* in the Rhineland, and the acknowledgement that waving the naval big stick in the Mediterranean involved the weakening of units in Home waters and the Far East made a show-down with Italy too risky.

War plans concocted during 1938 further emphasized the importance of Palestine in the defence of the Eastern Mediterranean and the Middle East. With Egypt under the threat of an Italian thrust from Libya, Palestine was designated the base for a reserve force earmarked for defence of the Suez Canal. The same force would also defend the land passage of Indian divisions landed at Basra, which were intended to reinforce the army in Egypt. This movement of troops from Iraq was a measure to frustrate any Italian plans for a blockade of the Red Sea. To be workable, these plans required a stable Palestine and the benevolent neutrality of the surrounding Arab states.

When these schemes were being devised, Britain had all but lost the goodwill of the Palestinian Arab majority. Indeed the first task of the Middle East brigade, which arrived in Palestine during 1938, was to lend a hand in crushing the two-year-old Arab revolt. Since 1918, the Palestinian Arabs had become increasingly anxious about their future under the mandate. They were apprehensive about Jewish immigration which, if unchecked, would result in their being edged out of their lands and reduced to the status of helots. The pattern was familiar from other Arab countries. It had been followed in Algeria, where French and Spanish settlers had secured the best lands, and in Libya, where Mussolini was introducing thousands of Italian colonists. In Palestine, Arab landlords, many of them absentees, were glad to sell their estates to Jewish immigrants with plenty of money in their pockets donated by well-willers in Europe and the United States. The *fellahin* peasant farmers were consequently evicted and, since the Jewish colonists wished to employ labourers of their own race, and had no choice but to drift to the coastal towns like Jaffa and Haifa. Here the landless labourers congregated in shanty towns on the outskirts and tried their luck in the local labour market. The prospects were discouraging, especially after 1930 when Palestine began to suffer from the effects of the world slump. It was inevitable that racial and religious tension was increased by the struggles of the labour market. Another factor which added to the ill-feeling was noted by the High Commissioner, Sir Arthur Wauchope, in 1937 when he reported that 'the Jewish standard of living', geared to European habits, required a daily wage twice that allowed to Arabs.[40]

The breakdown of the Arab rural economy and the straitened economic conditions of the early 1930s coincided with a sharp surge in the numbers of Jewish immigrants. Their numbers had risen soon after the Balfour Declaration, but had fallen to under 5,000 by 1930–31. This trend changed after Hitler's assumption of power in Germany in 1933 and the start of a vicious and vindictive persecution of the German Jewish community. In the wake of Nazi state-sponsored anti-Semitism, Jews in Austria, Poland and Rumania began to suffer ill-usage. The upsurge in Central European anti-Semitism triggered a new wave of immigration into Palestine which had now become a sanctuary as well as a homeland. Here Jewish thinking was turning towards the idea of Palestine as a Jewish state in its own right, peopled not by settlers but men and women returning to their natural home after an enforced absence of over 1,800 years. This concept of the Jewish, historical state was, needless to say, upheld by a mass of evidence from the Old Testament, which came to be invoked as a justification for a future, independent nation.

This vision was rejected by the indigenous Arabs who had set their sights on the creation of an Arab state in Palestine. The fulfilment of this ambition required the British government to abandon the Balfour Declaration and pledge that the Jews would remain a minority. The first signs of a struggle for local dominance had been seen in November 1918 when there were clashes between Jews and Arabs in Ramleh and Jaffa.[41] Two years later there were widespread attacks on Jews and their property in Jerusalem. The authorities took coercive measures, and did what they could to calm the Arabs with predictions that immigration and settlement would generate prosperity. The Arabs were unconvinced and there were riots in Haifa during 1921.

Until 1922, the internal security of Palestine rested in three battalions of Imperial troops which were scheduled to be withdrawn as part of the wider programme of retrenchment. They were replaced by a *gendarmerie*, recruited from former Black and Tans who were available as a result of the signing of the Anglo-Irish treaty of 1922. Colonel Meinertzhagan saw them training in Devonshire and was impressed, although Sir Herbert Samuel had doubts about their suitability for Palestine. 'Their reputation, as a corps, has not been savoury', he confided to Churchill. They were backed up by the RAF squadrons and armoured car detachments based in the Transjordan and were supplemented by locally-recruited Arab and Jewish police.

This system of security in Palestine collapsed during the summer of 1929 when the authorities faced widespread communal disturbances sparked off by a fracas between Arabs and Jews at the Wailing Wall in Jerusalem. Inundated with reports of murderous attacks on Jews by Arab gangs throughout the province, the authorities lacked the manpower to maintain order. Urgent calls for help were sent to Egypt and London on 24 August. The response was remarkable; two platoons of South Wales Borderers were flown from Heliopolis at $1\frac{1}{2}$ hours notice and were in Jerusalem within five hours. Reinforcements from the same regiment, together with companies of Green Howards, arrived at Lydda by train. During the next two days, the battleship *Barham* and the heavy cruiser *Sussex* hove to off Jaffa and Haifa and put landing parties ashore; they were followed by the aircraft-carrier *Courageous* which carried a battalion of the Staffords from Malta. Cars, lorries and motor buses were commandeered and troops and sailors were swiftly deployed into the countryside where they were used to guard settlements. Once the first outburst had died down, the bluejackets and troops assisted the police in searching villages and arresting Arab miscreants.

The British had been rather lucky. Undistracted by commitments elsewhere, they had been able to move adequate forces quickly to put down what was a rural and urban *jacquerie*, spontaneous and ill-organized. It was, however, clear that the political goal of the Palestinians was a self-governing, independent, Arab nation. The first political step in this direction was taken towards the end of 1935, when the Arab Higher Committee asked for an elected assembly, an end to Jewish immigration and no further land sales to Jews. The High Commissioner spurned these requests, which would have made a nonsense of the pledges given to the Jews. A few months later, in April 1936, the Arabs turned to force in the hope that by making the province ungovernable, they would get what they wanted.

The call for a general strike which marked the start of the Arab uprising was made by Haj Amin al-Husseini, the Grand Mufti of Jerusalem and President of the Supreme Muslim Council. The Mufti saw himself as a national leader of the Palestinian Arabs and threw his religious authority into the war by the proclamation of a *jihad* against the British and the Jews. He was also shrewd enough to realize that alone the Palestinians could not beat the British, and so he enlisted the goodwill of neighbouring Arab states in the knowledge that Britain could not afford to ignore their feeling. By the autumn of 1936, the Mufti had invited Kings Ibn Saud of Saudi Arabia, Ghazi of Iraq, and Abdullah of the Transjordan to act as mediators, which ensured that the Palestinian revolt would become an important issue in Britain's future relations with the Arab world.

Throughout the revolt and after, the Mufti's aim was a Palestinian state. His followers were less single-minded. By the end of 1937, and soon after the Mufti had left Jerusalem to begin a life of wandering exile, there were signs that his leadership was being questioned by many of his countrymen. For generations, Palestine had been dominated by two local families, the Nashashibis and the al-Husseinis, and in the early days of the revolt, the Nashasibis had accepted the Mufti's leadership of the national movement. With the guerrilla war proving unwinnable, the Nashashibi clan felt inclined to cut their losses and take up Britain's offer of partition, made at the end of 1937. The Mufti rejected partition out of hand. In 1946 he observed to the British 'put yourself in the Arab's place. Remember yourselves in 1940. Did you ever think of offering the Germans part of Britain on condition that they let you alone in the rest?' It was not only the Mufti's all-or-nothing line which split him from other Palestinians; many were repelled by his increasing resort to terror as a means of disciplining waverers and his reliance on extortion, robbery and murder as ways to stock his war chest. The fragmentation of the national movement during 1937–8 and the Mufti's attempts to assert his leadership led to a war within a war, a civil war between Arab and Arab, between those for and against the Mufti. This development was a welcome bonus for the British, whose police and troops found themselves fighting alongside former adversaries. In the Jenin district, Fahkri Abdul Hadr, who had been a prominent rebel commander in 1936, was, two years later, the leader of a band fighting against the Mufti's guerrillas.[42]

The Mufti, backed by his staff, directed the various groups of insurgents making up the Palestinian forces. These guerrilla bands, thought by military intelligence to number about 5,000 men, enjoyed considerable success in the two years before the imposition of martial law in October 1938. Their achievement was not so much the consequence of skill in arms or weight of numbers, but rather was a measure of British shilly-shallying. Still, at no time during the three-and-a-half years of the rebellion did the guerrillas come close to toppling the government, and when they fought skirmishes with British troops they invariably come off worst. This did not matter, for the guerrillas' success lay in their ability to spread disorder and force the civil authorities to abandon control of the large areas of the province. Like all such insurgent armies, they forced their opponents to deploy large numbers of soldiers at considerable cost.

From the start, the rebels had concentrated their forces in the inaccessible, upland countryside of southern Judea, Samaria and the frontier with Syria. For some time they were able to bring arms over the Syrian border with little hindrance, and gain influence over sizeable enclaves, forcing the government to shut Post Offices, courts and police stations. From these secure bases, the protean guerrilla bands waged hit-and-run warfare. Jewish settlements were harried, telephone and telegraph lines were cut down, railway tracks ripped up, convoys ambushed, roads mined, police stations raided and the guerrillas' enemies, Jewish, Arab and British, murdered. The rebels knew the countryside and could call upon the local population for help. Support for the uprising had been universal and where it was not, the lukewarm were threatened. As a result, the guerrillas could rely on food and shelter in villages, where they were often able to store arms. In emergencies the villages also yielded part-time partisans who joined the guerrillas and after the raid slipped back to their homes. The urban Arab communities of Jerusalem, Haifa and Jaffa also offered havens for the guerrillas and permitted them to set up an urban underground which waged war with bombs.

There were two answers to the revolt. The first was for the Government to give a free hand to the local armed forces and let them break the resistance through martial law and its attendant astringencies. The other was to keep a leash on the military authorities, and confine the armed forces to limited operations which would prop up the local prestige of the government, but would not further antagonize the Arabs. In the meantime, moves for a political solution would be taken. The local commander, Air Vice Marshal Sir Richard

Peirse, had demanded an immediate declaration of martial law, a view coloured by his experiences during May 1936.[43] As he toured the disaffected Nablus district, his car had been stopped by an Arab mob, and he had only escaped by driving at them and firing a Verey pistol. Passing along the road between Nablus and Tulkarem with an armoured car escort, he was ambushed, but had managed to collar three of the snipers. Worse followed for on 1 June the Arab police at Nablus mutinied and their example was followed by detachments in Jerusalem. In two days the local authorities had lost the services of 1,500 men, who were either frightened of reprisals against themselves and their families or were covertly in accord with the rebels. Yet, in spite of these developments and the spread of anarchy in his province, the High Commissioner, Sir Arthur Wauchope, shrank from surrendering his powers to the military, arguing that martial law would alienate the Arab community. From then on, many in the civil administration convinced themselves that they were merely witnessing an eruption of banditry and not a national uprising.

The Government in London was inclined towards Wauchope's views. It drafted reinforcements into Palestine, but refused to sanction martial law. The iron fist was clearly there, but first the Arabs would be offered the velvet glove of conciliation in the form of a Royal Commission under Lord Peel. As a further token of Britain's willingness to come to an understanding with the Arabs, there was some tinkering with the quotas for Jewish immigrants. 'Pandering to rebels' was the irritated response of Major General Sir Robert Haining, the local GOC in 1938–9, who echoed the frustration and annoyance of his predecessors, Lieutenant General Sir John Dill and Major General Sir Archibald Wavell. Their superiors were divided about a military solution, for the Chiefs of Staff pressed for concessions to the Arabs which would throw them and their friends behind the British in the event of a war. The Chief of the Imperial General Staff disagreed, and urged an accommodation with the local Jews which would secure their active help in the defence of the Middle East. For the Labour MP, Colonel Wedgwood, such dithering reeked of appeasement and a month after the Munich agreement he charged the government with cowardice. 'Our troops in Palestine who were well able to do the job, and were being hamstrung and held back by a pusillanimous government which dared not face a government like Iraq, which was very largely in the hands of Germany'.

Chamberlain's government could not have afforded such a Palmerstonian approach, even if they possessed the instinct for it. The India Office dreaded Muslim agitation if the Palestinians were betrayed or crushed, and the Foreign Office was worried that the rigours of martial law imposed on Arabs might set off hostile reverberations across the Middle East. The safety of the Canal and the oil pipelines which crossed from Iraq were at stake, which added up to more than the internal tranquillity of Palestine. The government therefore put its faith in compromise, which was proffered to the Arabs by the Peel Commission's recommendation for partition. Jews and Arabs would have their own states, and Britain would keep military control of the border with Egypt, and of Haifa, Jerusalem and Aqaba. The actual drawing of the lines was placed in the hands of a second Royal Commission under a former Indian civil servant, Sir John Woodhead, which got down to its work during 1938.

There was not much here for the Jews, who were fearful that Britain might wriggle out of its obligations to them in order to placate the Arab states of the Middle East. They were facing a crisis of their own as more and more Jews from Germany and Austria were pressing to come to Palestine to escape persecution. Their future, and that of the Jews already in Palestine, looked bleak as the British government haggled over immigration quotas, and so Weizmann and Ben Gurion began to court the United States. For their part, the Arabs were not enthusiastic about partition, although some were won over. However ingenious the actual division might be, there would be Jews under Arab rule and vice versa, which would have meant further trouble. 'The Arabs are treacherous and untrustworthy, the Jews greedy and, when freed from persecution, aggressive ... I am convinced that the Arabs cannot be trusted to govern the Jews any more than the Jews can be trusted to govern the Arabs', was the conclusion of the Right Honourable William Ormsby-Gore. He had spent two years as Colonial Secretary enmeshed in the entanglement of Palestine. His successor, Malcolm MacDonald, was more optimistic. He quietly shelved partition and put his faith in a scheme for a federated Palestinian state, in which minority rights would be specially protected. This was the gist of the White Paper of March 1939 which also set Jewish immigration at 25,000 a year until 1944.

With a political answer to the Palestine problem in hand, the Government turned to pacification. What were designated 'extremists', in other words followers of the Mufti who still wanted an Arab-dominated Palestine, had to be defeated. The process was delayed by the Czechoslovak crisis, which had concentrated minds on the possibility of a war in Europe and kept troops in Britain. General Haining's request for extra men to foil an Arab guerrilla *coup* in Jerusalem was turned down by the Cabinet on 31 August 1938 since they might be needed elsewhere. The Munich settlement on 29 September removed the immediate chance of a war and freed men for Palestine. Moreover exigency plans for the defence of the Middle East required a reserve to be stationed in Palestine, and so a stable countryside had to be secured.

A week after Munich, the Cabinet gave MacDonald authority to impose martial law. Within four weeks the army got what it had been wanting and the war against the guerrillas entered its final phase. Palestine came under martial law, its inhabitants were issued with identity cards, the local Press was censored (to cut the Mufti off from his audience), five members of the Higher Committee were packed off to exile in the Seychelles, and army officers took over the jobs of Assistant and District Commissioners. Courts martial were empowered to try suspects and pass death sentences on those found guilty of bearing arms or taking part in terrorist attacks. There were now 18,500 men in

Palestine and on 24 November MacDonald assured the House of Commons that 'powerful forces' were 'steadily and surely re-establishing order' in the province. Peace, he added, would follow, presumably once the Palestinians had accepted the political formula which was being concocted.

Before and after the stepping up of operations, the pattern of the struggle against the guerrillas was the same. Victory depended upon the ability of the army and the police to deny the rebels assistance from the Arab population. Isolated, the small guerrilla bands could be engaged by mobile forces supported by the RAF. The form of fighting guerrillas had been first established during the Boer War and its tactics resembled those of a grouse shoot. The operations were called 'cordon and search'; a village and its environs would be surrounded by a tight cordon of armed troops with orders to shoot fugitives, and then smaller forces would converge on the village to flush out rebels and search for stocks of arms. The villagers would be segregated, the women being sent to the mosque where they might be searched by policewomen, and the men herded together, often in the communal threshing barn, and questioned individually. There were variations on this procedure. Captain Norman, who had been seconded from HMS *Cyclops* with a searchlight and a 'pom-pom' mounted on a lorry, watched a 'correction' of one village in September 1936 in which the adult male population was forced to undergo an hour of strenuous PT under the eyes of a correction squad.[44] During the cordon and search of Halhoul in April 1939 eight Arabs died from heat exhaustion; their families were given £P2,065 in compensation.[45]

The success of such operations rested on surprise and so speed was essential. In January 1939 a detachment of the Queen's Regiment moved by night in motor buses to a village where, the battalion CO had heard, a guerrilla was hiding. All went smoothly but as the men moved into position dogs were aroused and their barking gave the wanted man the chance to slip away. Even if some escaped the net, the searches often revealed arms and explosives, and the army's right to detain suspects eroded the guerrillas' source of recruits. The second part of operations consisted of finding and engaging guerrilla parties. This had been made easier by a programme of military road-building which removed from the guerrillas the protective isolation they had hitherto enjoyed. New roads opened up the Carmel Hills, the Syrian marches (ending gun-running) and the Judean Hills. This strategy owed much to experience on the North-West Frontier of India and a few other Indian experiences were also exploited by commanders in Palestine, including collective fines on villages and the demolition of houses where arms had been hidden or were the homes of known insurgents. In Jerusalem, forces entered the Arab quarter and the previously inviolate Muslim holy place, the *Haram-esh-sharif*, where the guerrillas had set up a base.

In the early stage of the struggle, there had been a reluctance to use aircraft against rebel villages which was quickly appreciated by the Arabs. On 3 September 1936 a Hawker Hart of 6 Squadron was shot down by rifle fire from the rooftop of a house in a village on the Nablus-Tulkarem road, and two others had been forced to land.[46] Wauchope agreed that pilots could machine-gun villages housing rebels but refused to approve bombing. The Cabinet hedged, and agreed that pin-point bombing might be permitted against identifiable houses.[47] Aircraft were invaluable in detecting and attacking rebel bands; they killed fifteen guerrillas out of a band of one hundred which ambushed a convoy near Haifa in February 1938. Later that year, rations were dropped by parachute to ground units operating in the remoter parts of Samaria.

As in other parts of the Empire, technology, as always, tipped the balance and by the spring of 1939 the back of the Arab revolt had been broken. Much credit must go to the servicemen whose duties were routine and, luckily for them, not interrupted by ambush or assassination. Many knew little about the elaborate convolutions of the policies they were trying to enforce. Like Ronald Weaver, then an Ordinary Seaman on board the battlecruiser, *Repulse*, they 'did not know of the problems in Germany, and all we knew was that many more Jews than was allowed were trying to enter Palestine, and it was our job to stop this'.[48] Twice parties from the *Repulse* were put ashore at Jaffa to patrol the port and assist the local police. They found the local population friendly, and Mr Weaver recollected that he 'went on foot patrol without any fear and never felt in danger'. Maybe this was because the navy, unlike the army, had 'a reputation for being a soft touch'. Like many other servicemen in Palestine, Weaver was horrified by the results of the civil war between Arabs and Jews. 'There were some terrible things done by both Jews and Arabs on what seemed to us at the time to be innocent civilians . . . horribly mutilated bodies of both men and women. I myself saw a male who had been mutilated'.

During the three years of the rebellion the local Jewish population had thrown in its lot with the British, for they had everything to lose from any kind of Arab victory. Jewish supernumary police filled the gaps left by Arab mutineers in 1936, and Captain Charles Orde Wingate busied himself with the founding of *Haganah*, the Jewish volunteer defence force, which defended Jewish settlements. It quickly developed into a counter-terror force, taking the war to the Arabs in a series of nocturnal raids. *Haganah* gave the Arabs what was euphemistically called 'a dose of their own medicine', and during 1938 was fighting alongside British forces. Menachim Begin later noted that during the Jewish revolt the Arabs were no longer a force to be reckoned with, and that they were scared of the Jews which may be a testimonial to the effectiveness of *Haganah* before 1939. Still, in 1944, Begin's brothers-in-arms thought it worth their while to print pamphlets in Arabic warning the Arabs to keep out of what was simply a struggle between the Jews and the British.

The suppression of the Arab revolt was overshadowed by the outbreak of war in September 1939 and, with hindsight, it could be likened to clearing the decks before a major battle. From 1939 to 1945, Palestine's decks needed to be clean and tidy as it was a major training ground and resting area for British forces deployed in Egypt and the Western Desert. The Jewish population was, by-and-large, pro-British and Ben Gurion offered the British 130,000 *Haganah* fighters. Of course a Nazi victory would have been calamitous for the Jews in Palestine, as could be seen from events in Central and Eastern Europe. There was, however, deep resentment of the March 1939 White Paper which seemed to set a limit on the expansion of Jewish settlement which, after 1944, would be subject to Arab approval. Not all British soldiers were therefore welcomed, as John Verney recalled:[49]

> Tin-hatted and armed, we lined the streets of Hadar-le-Zion while a procession of Jewish youths 'demonstrated' against the recent British White Paper restricting their purchase of land from the Arabs. The youths booed and jeered at us standing silently along their route and we ourselves, though we had only the faintest understanding of the reasons for their resentment, became restive and angry.

These demonstrators satisfied themselves by breaking the windows of the Officers' Mess, but there were others in Palestine who were preparing for a war against the British. The moderate Ben Gurion had admitted that the Jews 'obey a higher moral, which overrides the authority of Britain when she acts contrary thereto'. The higher moral was the ideal of Jewish nationhood which was expressed in the widespread wish to create a historic Jewish state in Palestine. The possibility of a refounding of Biblical Israel had been reduced by the British Government's insistence on a Palestine in which Jews remained a minority. Britain had made herself the target of small guerrilla cells which looked towards terrorism and rebellion as the only way to secure Israel. The groups drew on a hotchpotch of philosophies and Biblical prophecies to support their aims and methods. From the Old Testament came the vision of a land promised by God and inspiring tales of testing times when the Jews had suffered under alien rulers. From Russia came the Jewish experience of underground resistance and terrorism in the struggle against the Czars as well as the notion that bombings and assassinations were, in themselves, noble acts which elevated both the perpetrators and their cause. Abraham Stern, a Biblical scholar and founder of a terrorist group which took his name, was much impressed by what he saw of Italian Fascism and dreamt of a Jewish Empire in the Middle East.

Stern and his followers continued to fight the British throughout the war and beyond. Their dramatic assassinations, like that of Lord Moyne and his chauffeur in Cairo in 1944, did nothing to assist the creation of Israel and much to embarrass the moderate Jewish leadership, which disowned Stern and his works. *Irgun Zvai Leumi* (National Military Organization) had been divided by the war with its leader, David Raziel, losing his life whilst on an undercover operation for the British army in Iraq. Menachim Begin, who escaped from Poland to Palestine in 1942, had no doubts that Britain was the enemy. He stood rigidly by his faith in Israel as a land given by God to the Jews, and that the British with their mandate stood in the way not only of Jewish destiny but of the will of God. He became the mainstay of *Irgun*, and later set down in his memoirs, *The Revolt*, a bleak record of intolerance, violence and casuistical self-justification. 'We fight, therefore we are' was Begin's rallying cry, which at times grated harshly on the ears of his fellow Jews who wondered what sort of country could grow out of such a slogan. It would take them forty years to find out.

Begin was a resourceful commander. *Irgun* possessed a High Command, staff, special 'assault' forces, a revolutionary army and a propaganda directorate. The aim of *Irgun* was to terminate the mandate and prepare the way for a Jewish take-over of Palestine, meaning in effect, a war first against Britain and then the native Arab population. In terms of numbers and training, *Irgun* and its sympathizers could not engage the British police and army in an open war. Its operations were therefore designed to have the maximum nuisance value so that thousands of men would be needed to hold down a province scarcely larger than Wales, and the British Government would have to shed blood and expend money and resources. Targets in this war were government offices, lines of communication, oil installations, army and air force bases, and anyone associated with the government.

This campaign, which began during 1944-5, intensified at the end of the second year. This was because the end of the war in Europe had re-opened the Palestinian question as an international issue. There were thought to be over a million Jewish refugees in Europe, nearly all of whom wanted to leave the countries where they had suffered and escape to Palestine. Palestine therefore faced a demographic revolution which, if successful, would have guaranteed a Jewish majority and assured the foundation of Israel. Standing in the way of this influx of Jewish refugees was the British Government which, through the Royal Navy, attempted a blockade of the Palestinian coast. British policy, under the direction of Ernest Bevin, looked for a peaceful, negotiated settlement, in which a Jewish enclave might be allowed to exist within a federal Arab state. If this proved impossible and the cost of policing the turbulent province was too high, then Britain would have to cut and run, leaving the Jews and the Arabs to their civil war.

Britain would fight, but not for long. As it was, 100,000 men were stationed in the province between 1945 and 1948 at great cost. Just as the Imperial will was sapped, so too were the Imperial coffers after six years of global war. An impoverished Britain had to turn to the United States for the wherewithal to keep going and, since October 1944, its creditor had openly sided with the Palestinian Jews. 'We favour the opening of Palestine to unrestricted Jewish immigration and colonization', announced Roosevelt, and in August 1945, his successor, President Truman, was badgering the new British Prime Minister, Clement Attlee, to issue 100,000 immigration permits to Jews from Europe. There were several reasons for this intervention. American Jews had been busy working for the Zionist cause for years and, as a well-organized lobby, they possessed considerable clout which presidents would have been foolhardy to ignore. Truman cheerfully admitted that he had no Arab voters to bother about, when he dismissed his State Department's warnings about antagonizing the Arab states in the Middle East. Nor did the Americans seem much worried about General Glubb's prophecy that support for the Jews might push Iraq and Syria towards the Soviet Union.

Britain therefore had to devise a Palestinian policy under pressure from an American President who favoured the establishment of a Jewish state. This line was not dictated by sentiment alone or by anxieties about the voting patterns of the American Jewish community. Support for Zionism might pay political dividends in the future, as Roosevelt recognized when he justified his own stance on the matter of Palestine. By helping the Jews, 'we should have increased the hope of finding a friend, an ally, if we need one somewhere in the Eastern Mediterranean or the Middle East'. Jewish Palestine, once fondly thought to be a prop for British Imperial interests, was well on the way to becoming a bastion of America's unofficial empire.

The United States gave more than rhetoric and diplomacy in support of the Jews. Money and arms flowed from the fund-raising organized by Jewish groups, which found some sympathy amongst Irish communities where rancorous memories of British Imperialism were still strong. During July 1946, when Congress was debating a $3,750 million loan to Britain, a few speakers raised the issue of Palestine, although many American Jews were ashamed at this crude tactic. The Palestine Resistance Fund could, however, touch deeper chords in the American consciousness, for a newspaper advertisement in 1947 contained the claim that, 'the Hebrew Underground is fighting a war for national independence. It is 1776 in Palestine today!' One of the Fund's committee members, Ben Hecht, who wrote film scripts, boasted that there was a song in his heart each time he heard that a British soldier had been killed.

He had much joy during 1946. During that year *Irgun* stepped up its attacks and British servicemen became a target. In April seven were murdered in a Tel Aviv car park and, on 22 July 1946, two *Irgun* bombs demolished most of the King David Hotel, killing ninety-one of the staff of the High Commission and Army Secretariat who were housed there. A two-minute warning was given but its wording gave no clear indication of the terror to come. In the second half of the year, *Irgun* turned its attentions to 'reprisals' for punishments inflicted on its members. A Major and three NCOs were beaten in retaliation for the flogging of two Jewish youths found guilty of terrorist offences. *Irgun* warned British servicemen that they might be victims if any more of its men were flogged. On one of the admonitory posters a soldier added: 'Don't forget my sergeant major!'. The execution of Dov Gruner, for his part in an armed raid, and several other terrorists in July 1947 led to the kidnapping of two intelligence sergeants from Nathanya. They were held for over a fortnight and then hanged from trees in an olive grove, one of the bodies being booby-trapped. The bomb exploded and blinded an officer.

Such crimes, in 1947 at least, still shocked. The wider Jewish population and its political leadership, the Jewish Agency, maintained an ambivalence towards such outrages. Support for *Irgun* and other terror groups was not universal, but it was strong enough to enable many leading 'wanted' men, like Begin, to move undetected and to find a hiding place when required. The enforcement of the ban on immigration had seemed inhuman in Jewish eyes and did much to provide sympathy for the terrorists. When the Jewish Agency and some of its offshoots were raided by police and troops in June 1946 there was considerable fury. Among the many slogans which followed was a wonderful mixture of ancient Judaic and modern history — 'Out with the unclean sons of Titus from our Holy Land! Down with the Nazi-British Empire in *our country*!' [My italics].[50] The King David Hotel bombing disturbed many Jews and the Jewish Agency deliberately distanced itself from the incident and its perpetrators. Yet the Agency and *Haganah* offered little help in the search for those responsible for the murder of the two British sergeants, although the people of Nathanya were horrified by what had happened.[51]

To defeat terrorism (and there were officers who believed that a victory could be secured), the army had to isolate the Jewish activists, and their sympathizers. It had also to maintain a vigilance against assassins and bombers, guarding possible targets. For the soldiers involved it was an unwelcome duty which was hard to understand. The soldier who had been fighting for the liberation of Western Europe 'was asking himself what had he been fighting for during the past five years'. Sympathy felt for the Jews by fighting men who had seen something of their miseries under the Nazis evaporated during the time they spent in Palestine. There was ignorance about the precise political situation and often men felt themselves the hapless victims of political expediency which was a 'cause of the greatest frustration to all ranks'. There was bitterness, too, that no punitive measures were taken against the Jewish community which had given succour to the murderers of British soldiers. The Arabs, who knew a bit about punitive measures after their revolt, were bewildered and could not understand why nothing was done after the King David Hotel bombing.[52] There were, officially, some misgivings about employing methods against the Jews which would have been used against Arabs. In March 1944, when the Middle East Command was toying with the idea of introducing tear-gas for use in Jewish disturbances, Field Marshall Dill agreed with a subordinate's comment that since the Jews were 'a semi-European' race, they should not be controlled by gas although its use was all right for Indians; and, anyway, German propaganda might exploit the gassing of Jewish demonstrators.[53] It would be hard to generalize from this but, at least from the standpoint of the Arabs, the suppression of the Jewish revolt appeared to be undertaken with kid gloves.

In 1945, the armed forces were better organized to meet the Jewish revolt than they had been nine years before. Palestine was split into three regions. The Defence Emergency Regulations gave the GOC powers equivalent to those which obtained under martial law and these were devolved on the three local commanders. In the field, officers could supersede civilian district commissioners and did not need continual appeals to their superiors before an operation was sanctioned. There was continuous close co-operation with the Palestine police. The armed forces' major duties were the passive maintenance of the civil government, the guarding of its property and communications, and the active pursuit of terrorists through cordon and search operations.

From the end of 1945, the largest proportion of troops in Palestine were concerned with guarding and keeping open lines of communication. This involved the creation of mobile columns, guarding railway lines, manning armoured railway carriages and protecting the Haifa oil refinery. Between 1945 and 1947 there were fifty cases of railway sabotage but no line was shut for more than two days. The news of immigration restrictions and the seizure of refugee ships provoked a series of riots and strikes in ports and inland towns in which the army had to support the police. In November 1945 the 3rd Parachute Regiment occupied Tel Aviv for five days and patrols suffered heavy stoning by mobs. Amritsar had not been forgotten, so officers and men were issued with limited rounds and were warned not to fire. Under a particularly severe pelting, one unit opened fire.

Active operations involved tracking down terrorists and depriving them of their supplies of arms, explosives and popular assistance. It was a thankless and souring task. Then, in November 1943, troops and police searched the settlement at Ha Horesh for terrorists and Polish deserters, they were set upon by the inhabitants who shouted, 'Gestapo Fascists', 'Hitlerite Dirty Englishmen' and 'English Swine'. The women were the most ferocious, going into action with pots, pans and containers of boiling water 'like vicious, demented wild beasts', according to the commander of a Sikh detachment who had never seen such fanaticism, even in Ireland! One Jew died in the fracas. Police with tracker dogs who followed suspected terrorists to the villages of Givat Haiyam and Hogla in November 1945 were similarly berated and belaboured, this time with stones and cudgels. Their assailants called up reinforcements from settlements close by and the police fell back, bruised and outnumbered. The next day troops were sent in and when their cordon was in danger of being broken, they opened fire. Six Jews were killed, including a ringleader who rode a horse and wielded a whip.[54]

Mishaps like this did the army no good. As the struggle deepened and the outrages multiplied, careful procedures were devised to govern these operations which offered the only change of catching the terrorists and their accomplices. It was essential that an area was cordoned tightly and secretly, so six hours' preparation was needed to collect enough men and there had to be a total radio and telephone blackout. All Jewish civilians were deemed untrustworthy and with good reason, for the resistance had developed a good intelligence network. Cordon and search operations, together with the deployment of large numbers of soldiers as guards over government buildings, oil refineries, airfields and communications, forced the numbers of the Palestine garrison up to 100,000. In strategic terms, this was farcical. Forces that were, in theory, guarding the Canal in accordance with the still-current notion that its safety was vital to the Empire, were in fact tied down keeping the peace in a province where the population was either openly hostile or malevolently neutral.

By December 1946 the Labour Cabinet had had enough. Britain's precarious financial situation forced the issue, and the Government made public its intention of withdrawing servicemen from Greece, where they had been helping frustrate a Communist *coup*, and giving notice that the future of Palestine would be passed to the United Nations. All the United Nations could come up with was a rehash of the scheme for partition which had been bandied about for the past ten years. This was an invitation to an Arab–Jewish civil war which became a certainty when, on 29 November 1947, the Cabinet announced that it would pull out British troops during the next seven months.

Jewish terrorism had won the war of attrition. As an armed camp, held down by a permanent garrison in a state of siege, Palestine was strategically worthless and Ernest Bevin, who was no Zionist, realized that the Palestine war was hurting Britain's relations with the surrounding Arab states who repeatedly accused Britain of being pro-Jewish. As it was, the debacle of the evacuation and the subsequent first Arab–Israeli War of 1948–9 only added to Arab resentment.

In Palestine itself, the news of the coming end of the mandate marked the beginning of a civil war between Jews and Arabs for control of the country. From December 1947 until 15 May 1948, when the mandate finished, British forces had to do what they could to keep some kind of order and many units found themselves drawn into the fighting. The situation was passing from their control as *Haganah* came into the open and *Irgun* turned its guns on the Arabs. The Arab population was left in no doubt that resistance to the establishment of a Jewish state was hopeless; on 1 January 1948 Jewish forces attacked Balad es Sheik, killing ten women and children, and worse followed on 9 April, when *Irgun* killed 250, including many women and children, at Dir Yassim. Afterwards *Irgun*'s commanders announced, 'We intend to attack, conquer and keep on until we have the whole of Palestine and Transjordan in a greater Jewish state . . . we have to improve our methods in the future and to make it possible to spare women and children'.[55] The Arabs were not convinced and over 300,000 fled into neighbouring states. From here, during the spring of 1948, the Arab Liberation Army was formed and became involved in clashes with British forces on the Syrian border and in and around Haifa, from where a quarter of the Arab population was expelled. The Arab irregulars were followed, once the mandate had ended, by the armies and air forces of Egypt,

An Empire Founded upon Sand: The Middle East

Transjordan and Syria. The civil war became an international conflict which has continued to flare up intermittently ever since.

The last efforts by the British army to prop up the mandate in Palestine were matched by those of the Royal Navy to enforce the immigration quotas of Jews. From 1945 until 1 January 1948, men-o'-war from the Mediterranean Fleet patrolled the coastal waters of Palestine, intercepted ships carrying illegal immigrants from Central and Eastern Europe, boarded them, and then took the passengers to Famagusta as prisoners and thence to detention camps. In the opinion of the Chiefs of Staff, an 'open door' to Jewish immigrants would have started a Jewish–Arab civil war, which the land forces would have been unable to contain.

The naval blockade presented the navy and the Foreign Office with enormous problems.[56] In October 1946, naval intelligence put the numbers of potential immigrants at over 40,000, most of them waiting for shipment from various ports in the Mediterranean and Black Sea. There was little help or sympathy from other countries; French officials assisted the refugees by providing trains to take them to southern ports and in Italy, Jewish emigrants were helped by the Italian authorities and by Americans serving with the Italian Control Commission. There were thought to be over about 100 ships ready in various ports to run the blockade, including a number of former Canadian navy corvettes.

Sir John Cunningham, the naval commander in the Mediterranean, was worried about the legality of stopping ships on the high seas, which was a breach of international law. When the Cabinet discussed the matter on 10 December 1946, the Lord Chancellor made it clear that any interception of an immigrant boat would be illegal. The prior agreement of the country of registration would be required, and this was secured from two 'flag of convenience' nations, Panama and Honduras, which, in April 1947, allowed the *Guardian* to be stopped and boarded. The 2,400 refugees on board were taken and put in camps in Cyprus. There was one loophole, as Bevin discovered, for ex-enemy ships and those without flags could be lawfully boarded. In other cases, individual commanders had to contact the Admiralty and the Foreign Office, which, as was pointed out, was not easy at week-ends.

Interception and boarding were legal in Palestinian waters and it was here that most of the immigrant ships were taken. Operations were often risky for the pursuing warship had to catch its victim in three miles, and the skippers of the immigrants boats tended to make a dash for the shore. It was often an awkward business if the immigrant ship was fast, for instance an ex-corvette, and the pursuer had little choice but to fire a shot, if possible at the rudder. As the Senior naval Officer in Haifa warned, this was difficult and might provoke fierce resistance when the ship was boarded. Still, warships involved in these operations were given some gunnery practice in aiming at rudders.

The main difficulty always remained boarding the immigrant ship. In September 1946 Admiral Cunningham was troubled by reports of increasing resistance to the boarding parties which, he feared, might lead to an untoward incident. 'In the present fanatical state of the Jews in general and the illegals in particular, "abandon ship" tactics are by no means unlikely, which would result in great loss of life and consequent propaganda'. The propaganda value of such an incident was exploited by the immigrants. When the destroyer *Childers* intercepted the *Fede* off Tel Aviv on 3 October 1946, a slogan was displayed reading: 'If you want to stop us you will have to sink this ship. Will you do this? Remember we have no lifebelts'. Some on board were getting ready to swim, but they and the rest stayed put and attacked the boarding party. Many of the resisters were women, some of them pregnant and others ill from sea-sickness. For those who took part in these operations, it was a grim experience.[57]

> It was terrible, the boarding of some of the ships. It was a terrible escapade, they [the immigrants] were crowded in, and, in the case of the smaller caiques the crews used to leave their stations and mix in with the Jews because, I think, at the time the Master of one of them had been sentenced to life with hard labour. When you went alongside, they were out of control and you feared that they were going to turn over. You used to get badly attacked, when you went aboard, by the Jewish people. Some of the blokes got knocked on the ground and women put knitting needles into their testicles, so we had pads. They used to bombard us with tins of fruit (the Americans used to supply them) and everybody used to grab them. . . .

As Fred Paice, a wireless operator on the *Brittenden*, recalled, many of the immigrants were desperate, having spent all their money on the passage without knowing that they might be intercepted. Tear-gas was used twice to quell disturbances during February 1947 and at the end of the month, a dozen ratings were injured, some badly, when the *Ullua* was taken near Haifa. There were Jewish casualties as well, including a man killed on board the *Merica* in the same month.

News of such brawls and the interception of immigrant vessels enraged Jewish opinion and led to riots on shore. Yet ashore sailors, who moved in small groups and were unarmed, were cordially treated. There was always a danger of sabotage and so when a ship took on oil at Haifa, most of the crew were taken off; once it had left the harbour, divers inspected the hulls for limpet mines. In October 1946 there was a scare after 500 lb bomb was discovered close to the oiling jetty at Haifa, and for a time all warships were diverted to Port Said. The navy was particularly anxious, since there were not enough police or soldiers to watch the port, and the loss of a warship would have been a tremendous blow to British prestige throughout the Middle East. Even when boarding immigrant ships, there was a fear of sabotage, so when the *Childers* closed with the *Fede* whe fired depth charges as a caution against swimmers armed with limpet mines.[58]

The last immigrant ships to be taken were the steamers, *Pan York* and *Pan Crescent*, which were arrested on 1 January 1948 and found to contain over 15,000 Jews. Both vessels had been tracked by radar and on board the cruiser *Mauritius* Fred Paice remembered taking wireless messages from *Haganah*, acting officially in order to prevent bloodshed. *Haganah* asked that the boarding parties should not wear steel helmets or carry 'coshes' or sidearms. In all, just over 40,000 immigrants were detained, taken from twenty-two ships.

The naval blockade of the Palestinian coastline, and the wider conflict ashore between 1945 and 1948, were direct legacies of the Balfour Declaration and the various pledges made to the local Arabs before and after the First World War. Then it had appeared that a British-dominated, tranquil Palestine would assist the promotion of British interests in the Middle East, and in particular the defence of the Suez Canal. This scheme had been dislocated by the fierce hatred between the Jews and the Arabs and their willingness to wage war for the control of Palestine. The British could not square the circle of contradictory promises, nor could they assuage the antipathies of their subjects. By the end of 1947, the game was becoming too hazardous and costly, and so the British army disengaged, leaving the Jewish immigrants to impose their own partition on the area at the point of a gun. A few months after the last British detachments pulled out of Palestine, India received self-government and was partitioned. The cornerstone had been knocked out of British Imperial policy in the Middle East for the security of communications with the sub-continent were no longer a vital concern for Britain.

Oil and Troubled Waters: Egypt, South Arabia and The Gulf, 1919–70

Before 1947, Britain's relations with the Arab world had been governed by considerations for the protection of India. Afterwards, they were concerned solely with the safety of oil. Of course the change in emphasis was not so sudden: the old obsessions with Imperial security and the desire to uphold global pretentions did not vanish and the old lion did not pass away without a few last roars. Between the evacuation of Palestine and the withdrawal from Egypt, at the end of the Suez adventure of 1956, British governments remained firmly attached to atavistic concepts of military and political paramountcy in the Middle East.

There seemed good reasons for the Labour Government and its Conservative successor, after 1951, to believe that they could behave in a traditional manner, in spite of financial weakness and the growth of local nationalism. In terms of wealth and armed forces, Britain, in 1945, stood well behind the United States and Soviet Union, but then and later British politicians made much of a 'special relationship' with America, though this *rapport* only possessed any substance when it came to squaring up to the Russians. The United States recognized British decrepitude and the gulf between Britain's global ambitions and her capabilities. It was not willing to applaud or

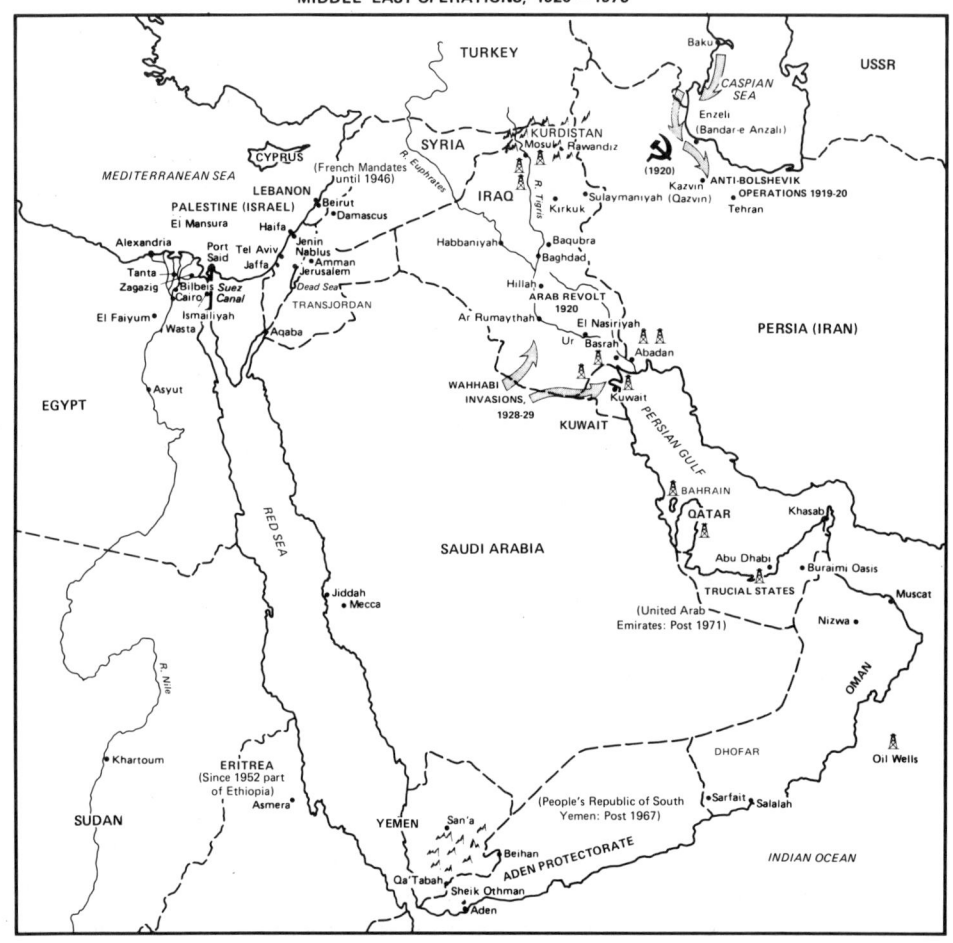

MAP 2 The Middle East

underwrite Palmerstonian flourishes of the kind which Sir Anthony Eden proposed and tried to carry out in 1956 when, in harness with the French, he invaded Egypt. By then, Britain was in the middle of abandoning her Empire, and it seemed to the Americans that the time had arrived for an end to the traditional Imperial stance. Britain was no longer up to her old responsibilities; these ought now to pass to the United States which was better able to handle them. She had the ships, the men and the money too.

Nowhere did Britain cling to its old assumptions more tenaciously than in the Middle East. The motives for British policy in the region were not based entirely upon a wish to keep and, from time to time, employ the old apparatus of paramountcy which had been created to protect India. What was loosely called the 'Communist threat' offered an excellent reason for Britain to maintain bases in the Middle East which also guarded oil wells and pipelines. Many of these were in Kuwait, the Trucial States of the Persian Gulf and the ramshackle Sultanate of Oman, all of which had been bound to Britain by treaties, a legacy of nineteenth century obsessions with Indian security. When, from the 1950s onwards, oil production began in these sheikhdoms, British governments started to take very seriously their diplomatic and military obligations. For their part, the rulers of these petty states were well pleased with British protection and assistance, especially when faced with unrest amongst their own subjects.

The years during which Britain 'hung on' in the Middle East were a period of transformation and political upheaval. The mainspring of change was nationalism, the intense feeling that Arab peoples should choose their own destinies unfettered by external controls. Notice of the new mood was served in Egypt and Iran. In May 1950, the Iranian Prime Minister, Dr Mussadiq, nationalized the Abadan oil refineries of the Anglo-Iranian Oil Company. Given that the Labour government had lately nationalized a third of British industry, its reaction was surprising. The affair was only seen in terms of prestige with Ernest Bevin predicting that if Mussadiq got away scot free, others would copy his example, and British influence in the Middle East would be undermined. The new Foreign Secretary, Herbert Morrison, who had begun his term of office by reading a biography of Palmerston, wanted to reach for a gunboat, and so the cruiser *Mauritius* was ordered to stand by off Abadan Island. In the meantime, the Chiefs of Staff drew up war plans for the taking of the refineries and their future defence, one appropriately code-named 'Buccaneer'. British forces were already committed in Malaya and Korea, and the United States stood strongly out against armed intervention. By the beginning of October, the last British technicians had been evacuated from Abadan, and the *Mauritius* steamed away. Soon after there was a General Election in which Morrison accused the Conservatives of wanting to fight for Abadan; warmongering, he claimed, 'is the background of their mental outlook — the old imperialist outlook'. It was left to the 'new Imperialists' to settle accounts with Mussadiq, who was ousted in a CIA-managed *coup* in 1953 and replaced by Shah Reza Pahlevi, who soon showed himself more in tune with the needs of the United States.

Egyptian nationalism had been a bugbear for Britain ever since her forces had first occupied the country in 1882. Opposition to British domination of the country sprang from two main sources. Egyptian army officers were embittered by the hurdles placed in the way of their promotion by their British counterparts who monopolized the senior posts. Intellectuals resented the way in which British advisers dictated the government's policies. There had been portents of future unrest in 1900, when Egyptian officers serving in Khartum had encouraged a mutiny in the belief that current British difficulties in South Africa might offer Egypt the chance to throw off the Imperial yoke.

The yoke became even more unbearable after 1914, when Britain assumed direct control of Egypt. Pushed unwillingly into Britain's war, the Egyptians discovered that much was demanded of them in terms of men, who were enlisted into the Egyptian Labour Corps for service in France, Palestine and the Suez Canal Zone, and animals and provisions required for Allied forces in the Middle East. There were isolated revolts by Egyptian labourers in France and Palestine in 1917–18 in which the wretched *fellahin* vainly protested that they had been tricked over the terms of their contracts. By the end of the war, the mood of the whole country was sullen. Open unrest broke surface at the beginning of March 1919 after the British authorities had arrested and exiled leaders of the Wafd nationalist party. The disorders began in Cairo and radiated outwards to engulf the towns and villages of the Nile Delta.[59]

The principal actors and the scenario in the tragedy which followed would in time become familiar in other parts of the Empire, although the severity with which the uprising was crushed stands on its own. On 12 March, students from the Islamic college at Tanta massed in the streets and shouted, 'We want our independence and our Ministers to be free', 'Down with the British', and 'Hurrah for Turkey!' The same day, pupils from the Ras-al-Jin school in Alexandria left their classrooms and took to the streets, some canvassing support from other schools and colleges. Their behaviour was attributed to agitators from Cairo, but it was not long before the Alexandrians were exhorting each other with 'wild speeches'. The local British commander was taking no chances, so he ordered two armoured cars to drive slowly through the city's native quarter, a progress which had a calming effect, or so he told his superiors in Cairo.

Sedition was preached in mosques, and on 24 March, HQ in Cairo received disturbing reports that Egyptian troops stationed at Beni Suef had egged on the local population to destroy railway track. Stories in *Mokattam* and *El Ahram* together with students returning from Cairo and Tanta fomented unrest in El Mansura. Here the mob, swelled by 'a great number of roughs', attacked the British vice-consulate. Matters were made worse when some of the rioters asked a Greek café owner for a drink and were dowsed with dirty water. Elsewhere, Greeks, keen to protect their businesses, fired random shots at crowds, recklessness which irritated British officers and infuriated Egyptians.

Disorder spread rapidly during the first fortnight of March, revealing the depth of rancour towards Britain. As authority fell apart, the Beduin who lived close to El Fayum saw their chance to line their own pockets and serve Allah at the same time. Over 3,000 of them attacked the town under religious banners in the belief that the *jihad* against the infidels had begun. Armed with rifles, swords and axes, they challenged the garrison of under 200 men, most of them Punjabi infantry. 'Our men were splendid', reported their commander, Major Ring, who had had to order his men to open fire on the Beduin. 'Great execution was done', and the Beduin retired after having lost 400 dead and wounded. For the next two days the garrison, aided by light armoured cars, brought the local European population to safety. Additional ammunition was dropped by the RAF, and for four days, between 19 and 23 March, many men went without any sleep.

The alacrity with which so many Egyptians took to the streets and the fierceness of the mobs took the authorities by surprise. Martial law had been imposed and the commander in Egypt, General Sir Edward Bulfin, was well supplied with men. Yet many of the available troops were openly disgruntled, because of the slowness of their demobilization, and there had been noisy displays of impatience by British soldiers at the massive depot at Qantara on the Canal. This vexation and a powerful desire to get home was shared by many Australians and New Zealanders who were still kicking their heels in Egypt. Such men, called out to handle the disturbances, vented their frustration on the Egyptians whom they blamed for their unwelcome detention in the country.

Cairo Headquarters was soon alarmed by what seemed an excessive amount of firing into crowds by troops. Orders were issued on 12 March to reduce this practice. Firing was to be confined to pre-selected men from each unit and, where possible, 'the cane [ie *lathi*, hockey stick or cudgel] must be regarded as a more suitable weapon than the rifle'. Such instructions counted for little in the field where many officers commanded their men to fire into crowds when they thought it necessary. Well aware of the fury generated by Press reports that British troops had shot and killed schoolchildren in Cairo, Lieutenant Colonel Hazel, the Political Officer attached to the Wasta punitive column, advised 'great discretion' when it came to shooting civilians. This proved impossible for his own men who, on coming ashore at one point on the Nile, were beset by an angry mob and fired upon. Soon after Hazel was fatally wounded by a sniper. There was good reason for senior officers to worry about the behaviour of their troops, particularly those in isolated detachments. On 15 March, an Egyptian official at El Mansura, watched British soldiers who 'knelt astride the streets in the face of the mob' and, without warning, open fire, killing fifteen and wounding twenty-five.

In terms of overall operations, the first priority for Bulfin's forces was to secure and keep guard over the major centres of rail and telegraph communication, and to prevent the derailment of trains which was a favourite activity of the insurgents. Mobility was essential so that whenever possible infantrymen were carried by lorry (drivers were officially permitted to drive their vehicles at mobs who barred their way) and frequent use was made of Australian and New Zealand mounted troops. Armoured cars came into their own. They patrolled railway lines and scoured open country for signs of restlessness. Their activities and something of the pungent flavour of this campaign is contained in the terse report of Lieutenant Ellis, who was in charge of a two-car patrol along the Benha-Qalub line.

About eight km from Tukh saw a crowd of natives destroying railway property. As they sighted the cars they fled into adjoining fields. Several shots were fired at my patrol by the natives. I dispersed the mob with machine gun fire.

The other workhorse of Bulfin's contingent was the RAF, whose fighter-bombers were used time and again to look for trouble and coerce insurgents.

A dozen two-seaters had been placed on readiness in Upper Egypt on 12 March whilst a new airfield was levelled at Wasta, south of Cairo. The same day the Egyptian Minister of the Interior gave permission for the punitive bombing of Waladieh village and on the same day six bombs were dropped on Abu Matimr, 'scattering a crowd gathered near that station'. Five more bombs fell on Hashsisha and two on Asyut as a warning to looters. The local police were warned to keep off the streets by a telephone message. This kind of operation was sometimes rather ticklish, since machines were unreliable and pilots could be forced down. On 17 March, Second Lieutenants Hartley and Brodie were ordered to fly their Avro as an escort for a mail train. After the engine cut out, they landed in a field alongside El Shen station where the station-master gave them some petrol. As the two airmen repaired the ignition wires, they were watched by a crowd of about 1500 Egyptians which had gathered on the railway embankment, presumably to intercept or derail the mail train. Oddly, they left the airmen alone and some even helped to manhandle the machine on to a road. Suddenly, the temper of the crowd changed; Hartley was seized and dragged to a cutting where his assailants planned to kill him. They wrangled over it, which gave Hartley the chance to run off and gain sanctuary in the house of a local notable, Muhammad Bey Sherif. There he found Brodie, who had also been mauled, but had managed to escape his attackers. Both men were concealed in a cellar, whilst one of Muhammad's servants was sent on horseback to Tanta from where three armoured cars came to rescue the two airmen. Cheated of its prey, the Egyptian mob had turned on the stranded aircraft and set it on fire.

Cairo HQ felt certain the Egyptian official and propertied classes were sympathetic to the British. Praise was given to the Minister for the Interior and local officials who co-operated with the army by giving generously of their local knowledge. This spirit was by no means universal. At Qalub, Egyptian policemen had stood inertly while a mob besieged a trainload of British and Indian soldiers on 15 March. The crowd was only dispersed after some officers had grabbed the policemen's rifles and fired them at the demonstrators. At El Mansura, a British officer took the precaution of disarming the local police and locking up their rifles.

By the beginning of April the unrest in Lower Egypt had petered out, subjugated by a short campaign which must rank as one of the most savage fought by British forces as part of their Imperial duties. Losses amongst the Egyptians must have been over a thousand, perhaps twice that figure. This condign chastisement brought a sour peace, but it was clear that Anglo-

Egyptian relations would have to be placed on a new footing if Britain was to continue to enjoy undisturbed control over the Suez Canal. Soon after the end of the revolt, a new treaty was negotiated in which Egypt was allowed a fuller measure of sovereignty.

Of course Britain kept its garrison of troops in Egypt, now augmented by RAF fighter and bomber squadrons. There was further trouble in 1924 after Britain had rebuffed Egyptian demands for an end to joint rule over the Sudan, and the governor of the province, Sir Lee Stack, was assassinated in Cairo. On 23 November, the Mediterranean Fleet was placed on four hours stand-by, and the following day, the battleships *Iron Duke* and *Malaya* hove to off Alexandria and Port Said. More men-o'war turned up in Egyptian waters, and the Royal Marines occupied the customs house at Alexandria, whose citizens were treated to a display of British power in the form of a parade through their streets by Royal Naval landing parties. The Cairenes were given another object lesson in Imperial power when three infantry battalions paraded on their streets. Such shows were needed since there had been mutinies by Sudanese infantry and a battery of artillery in Khartum and elsewhere in the Sudan.

After 1924, there were no further signs of open discontent within Egypt. Strong-arm methods were adopted in 1936 when the battleship *Barham* anchored off Alexandria during the negotiations for a new Anglo-Egyptian treaty in which Britain kept her rights in the Canal Zone. The mailed gauntlet was needed again in 1942 when King Farouk's ministers showed distressing symptoms of sympathy towards the Axis cause, and seemed too ready to anticipate its success in the Western Desert. The royal palace was ringed by tanks, and the King was forced to sack his wavering advisers and replace them with men more sensitive to Britain's interests.

Nationalist resistance continued in spite of periodic shows of British might and demonstrations of its coercive power. The nationalist cause flourished most strongly among army officers, who were often men from humble, rural backgrounds. Such men were the spearhead of the Egyptian revolution of 1952 in which King Farouk was deposed and a republic declared. Two years later Colonel Nasser became President and pushed ahead with measures of reform and national regeneration. As a reformer and a nationalist, Nasser was admired by the rest of the Arab world, not least because he championed and assisted Arabs fighting for their freedom, notably in Algeria.

Not long before his dethronement, King Farouk had blown the nationalist trumpet when, in October 1951, he denounced the 1936 Anglo-Egyptian treaty which permitted British garrisons in the Canal Zone. This arrangement was due for renegotiation in a few years and the War Office was doubtful about the Zone's strategic value in a war with Russia. It was an obvious target for an atomic bomb attack: for three years the garrison had been subject to terrorist attacks by Egyptian nationalists and in the event of an international crisis the area could be quickly occupied by air- and carrier-borne forces. There were also British bases in Libya and Jordan. In the event, the defence of the Canal was entrusted to the major base and airfields at Cyprus, where forces would be supported by the Royal Navy from its harbour at Valetta. So, in July 1954, the British and Egyptian governments signed an agreement under which British forces left the Canal Zone.

There was much growling in the Press and on the Conservative backbenches. 'A Day of Sorrow, a Day of Shame', grumbled the *Daily Express*, adding for good measure that the evacuation was 'the greatest surrender . . . since the Socialists and Mountbatten engineered the scuttle from India'. It was not that grim; in 1955 Britain was tied to Turkey, Iraq, Iran and Pakistan in the Baghdad Pact which seemed, with United States sponsorship, to form a bastion along Russia's southern boundary. A year later, General Templer could tour the Middle East and be received by a band playing 'Hearts of Oak' at Mosul, inspect the Arab Legion and its British officers at Amman, and shake the hands of Arab kings and ministers who assured him of their own and their country's affection for Britain.[60] Not all Arabs shared this friendship for Britain, for sweeping out of Egypt was the radical wind of Nasserism spelling internal change and an end to unwanted, alien patronage. In Britain, there were many, especially among the Conservative 'old guard', who chafed against what appeared to be a new mood of defiance and non-co-operation in the Middle East and who yearned for the old days when the lion could roar and bite.

The lion's chance came in 1956 when, on 16 July, Nasser announced the nationalization of the Suez Canal, which in effect meant that all ships which passed through the waterway would in future pay tolls to the Egyptian government and not to the Anglo-French Suez Canal Company. Sir Anthony Eden, the British Prime Minister, immediately imagined that he was dealing with a ruthless dictator who would treat concession as irresolution and bully the world for more and more. Eden was convinced that British faintheartedness in 1936 had encouraged Mussolini in his war against Abyssinia, and incidentally shown the Middle East that Britain could not or would not stand up for herself. Eden's resolve to square up to Nasser was unshakeable, as indeed was his virulent personal dislike of the Egyptian ruler. On 2 August, 20,000 reservists were recalled to the colours and in co-operation with the French, the Chiefs of Staff began to plan for a war against Egypt to regain the canal. The French government had old scores to pay off since Nasser had been giving assistance to the nationalist FLN in Algeria. At the same time, the Algerian campaign meant that France could only spare 30,000 men for the invasion of Egypt, leaving Britain to find 50,000.

By 14 August, the Chiefs of Staff and their French collaborators had completed the plan for 'Operation Musketeer' whose objective was a landing south-west of Alexandria, a march to Cairo and the take-over of the canal. The thinking and precedents were closely tied to experiences during the Second World War, and it was no accident that the phrase 'D-Day' was used to mark the moment of the first landings. This was understandable, given the background of the planners, and the fact that during the past two years Egypt had been importing much modern, Russian-built equipment, Her ability to defend herself had to be taken seriously, although many old war-horses were contemptuous of the martial zeal of the Egyptian soldier. What was planned, therefore, looked very much like a conventional Second World War operation with a thirty-six hour prelude of aerial bombardment to destroy the Egyptian air force, followed by a naval shelling of coastal targets near Alexandria and then landings and parachute drops. Eight thousand men would be required, 300 aircraft and an armada of 100 men-o'-war, including five aircraft carriers.

There was no obvious and suitable base for these forces to concentrate. Cyprus had no deep-water harbour, and its garrison was busy hunting down EOKA terrorists who were fighting a hit-and-run campaign to force the British government into delivering the island to Greece. Naval forces and the landing-craft, therefore, had to be based on Valletta, Malta, which meant a five-day sea voyage to the intended landing area. Other hitches occurred in terms of training, the availability of men and supplies and a mutiny by reservists, the details of which the government, then and later, has been chary of releasing. Relations between the military planners, wedded to diligence and all too aware that there was no 'rapid deployment' force available, and the politicians were often dusty. Afterwards, General Templer, anxious to exculpate the forces from charges of dragging their heels and unreadiness, expressed distaste for the politicians: 'The outcome disgusted me with the conduct of public affairs in this country, whether on the Cabinet level or in the House of Commons', he commented. He was none to happy with the restrictions placed on commanders in the field who were forced to accept limitations on 'the amount of bombing and shelling' since too many dead Egyptian civilians would be politically embarrassing.[61] A few, like Lord Mountbatten, were sceptical about the whole operation.

The flaw in the Suez operation lay at its heart. In making preparations which were all too public for a war against Egypt, Eden served notice that Britain meant business and would not be flouted over the canal. What was unclear was the form of the operations, when they would take place and against what targets. The first 'Musketeer' plans assumed that Egypt would be invaded, Cairo taken and then the unblocked canal would fall into Anglo-French hands. Early in September, the politicians had second thoughts and opted for a surgical operation in which air, ground and naval forces would seize the canal, which of course meant beating the Egyptian army and air force. This was more in keeping with the operations undertaken in 1882 when a stealthy *coup de main* by the Royal Navy gave Britain control over the canal in less than twenty-four hours. Later the army landed and beat the Egyptian army at Tel-el-Kebir, opening the way for the annexation of Egypt.

The revised Musketeer plan with its objective as the Canal was adopted on 10 September under pressure from the French. The French were also in favour of a scheme by which the Israelis created a diversion by an invasion southwards across Sinai which would split the Egyptian forces. This stratagem was politically attractive since Anglo-French forces could be publicly presented as 'peace-keepers' who would separate the Egyptian and Israeli forces and rescue the Canal. The Israeli invasion, therefore, gave Britain and France the fig-leaf cover for what otherwise was naked aggression. A plot was furtively hatched by the British Foreign Secretary Selwyn Lloyd, Mollet, the French Prime Minister and Ben Gurion who were closeted together in a house in Sèvres. The plot was simple and fooled only the naive; on 29 October the Israelis made a pre-emptive raid into Sinai, and the next day Britain and France called upon them and the Egyptians to stop fighting. The Israelis complied with the ultimatum but the Egyptians did not, giving Britain and France a reason for attacking.

For its architects, the invasion of Egypt was an operation to keep the peace and protect the Canal. War had been Eden's last resort, resorted to only after diplomacy had failed. Efforts to put pressure on Nasser and enlist international goodwill had come to nothing, although they clearly revealed that the United States was totally opposed to the use of force. Later, senior officers complained that the attempts to reach a negotiated settlement created difficulties for them in the form of postponements and adjustments to their plan. Certainly there was no secrecy about the likelihood of an attack on Egypt, although it might have been possible to interpret the ostentatious mustering of ships, aircraft and fighting men as sabre-rattling.

It was not, and on 31 October the first stage of Musketeer began. Canberra and V-bombers began their bombardment of Egyptian airfields after a delay of a few hours which allowed Americans to be flown out from Cairo. According to the revised plan, there was to be a pause between the extinction of the Egyptian air force and the invasion, a period during which it was hoped that Nasser might come to terms. The French had been unhappy about this delay and so the landings began on the morning of 5 November when over a 1000 paratroopers were dropped on Port Said. On the eve of the assault, General Beaufré reminded the French soldiers of the time when Napoleon's army had landed in Egypt, and exhorted them to 'repeat the exploits of your forebears'. There was no second battle of the Pyramids; by the afternoon of 6 November a ceasefire was agreed. Port Said had been taken and Anglo-French forces had pushed over twenty miles southwards towards Ismailia past a canal blocked by sunken ships. Within ten days some of them had given up their positions to troops collected by the United Nations, and by the end of December the last British soldier had left Egypt.

The invasion of Egypt had managed, amazingly, to unite the United States and the Soviet Union, both of whom condemned the adventure. Bulganin took time off from the ruthless repression of Hungary to menace Britain and France and even fulminated about the use of missiles. Only Australia stood by Britain, with the rest of the world hostile or dismayed. Inside Britain, opinion was divided with the Labour opposition, buoyed up by Aneurin Bevan's rhetoric, denouncing the government inside and outside the Commons. Save for *The*

Guardian, the Press was either supportive or benevolently neutral; and amongst the public there was a widespread conviction that such a campaign was not only necessary but desirable. Imperial nostalgia was still strong so, in Professor Kiernan's words, 'when the drums beat again at Suez there was instant acclaim from a large section of the middle classes, jubilant at the lion still being able to roar when its tail was twisted; also from a good many workers, mostly of the older generation which grew up with the lion's roar in its ears'.[62]

Whilst it may have made many Britishers feel good, the Suez war did nothing to strengthen their country's position in the Middle East; rather it weakened it. The Suez Canal was out of action, many oil pipe-lines were ruptured, and within two years the friendly government in Iraq had been overturned and replaced by an aggressively nationalist regime. Jordan threw out the last British officers with the Arab Legion and everywhere there were demonstrations against Britain. The whole affair enhanced the credentials of Nasser's Egypt as the powerhouse of Arab nationalism and confirmed what many Arabs already sensed, that Britain was an enemy. Eden's health had been broken by the stress, and he was forced to recuperate in the Caribbean before coming back to offer his resignation in January 1957. He had failed wretchedly in an escapade which confirmed that Britain was no longer a global power, free to use force to uphold its interests or get its way. In actual terms of imperial warfare, operations like the Suez landings, conducted against countries which possessed the means to defend themselves, were rare. They had been undertaken by Anglo-French forces in 1859 against China, and against Egypt by Anglo-Indian forces in 1882. More commonly this sort of gunboat intimidation was reserved for states which lacked the means to resist and possessed little or no international goodwill. Moreover such application of force needed some clear moral justification and this seemed lacking at Suez.

As the lion limped away from the Middle East, the eagle arrived. In 1957 President Eisenhower gave notice that the United States would take on the burden of Britain's position as paymaster and policeman in the Middle East while in Britain, successive Conservative and Labour governments adopted new policies for defence based upon an understanding of what could be done, rather than what should be done. There was still a part for Britain and her forces to play, but its stage was confined to the Persian Gulf, where Britain took up in earnest her duties as watchdog over the small coastal states.

This region had been the traditional stamping ground of the Indian administration which had established local British paramountcy through a network of agents backed by gunboats. Both Delhi and London were periodically bothered by the strategic vulnerability of the Gulf and Persia because of the closeness of Russia. The Russian bogey came to life again in 1918 when there were fears that the Bolshevik revolution might spread south from the Caucasus and disturb Persia. Churchill pressed for a forward policy in March 1919 and expressed a wish to annex the Caspian, although he doubted Britain's ability to hold on to it once Russia had revived.[63] As it was, an Anglo-Indian army occupied northern Persia after the Russians took over the port of Enzeli on the southern shores of the Caspian Sea. This area had been a Russian sphere of influence before 1917 and Lord Curzon, the Foreign Secretary, has hoped that it would pass into British control. When General Ironside took over command of 'Norperforce' in September 1920 he found it in good heart ('All seemed to be a very happy party') but with no very clear instructions what to do in the event of Bolshevik aggression. There was some fighting, most of it undertaken by a Cossack brigade in the service of the Shah. British and Indian troops dominated the Menjil Pass and effectively controlled the route which the Bolsheviks and their protegés of the 'Socialist Republic of Gilan' would take if they chose to attack Tehran.

Fortunately for the Anglo-Indian forces, the Bolsheviks in Enzeli were beset by lassitude, although they did attempt a half-hearted push southwards in October 1920 which was halted by British forces. The Shah's Cossacks proved more of a nuisance for they seem to have lost heart and fell back. They were rounded up by Anglo-Indian forces, including Gurkhas in lorries, and put in a camp, from where they were later shipped to Vladivostock. Ironside was glad to be rid of them, but he had noticed one of their officers, a Persian, who 'reminded me of the Mahomedan Rajput gentleman'. Ironside put this officer, Reza Khan, in command of the residue of the Cossacks whom he transformed into an efficient unit. Ironside had been dismayed by the Persian ruling class which he had found to be 'thoroughly effete and rotten', and he privately feared that Persia was 'ripe for Communism' unless a 'strong man' came forward.[64] King-making had not been Ironside's brief, but his preference for Reza Khan, enabled the officer to manage a coup in 1921 and make himself Shah four years later.

The Bolshevik threat to northern Persia proved to be empty and by December 1920 the government was anxious to withdraw forces from the area as an economy. Within six months the Anglo-Indian army had been pulled back, and under the energetic rule of Reza Khan, Persia moved into a period of stability which was what Britain wanted. One novelty of the short Persian campaign was what Ironside called 'a curious unit of specialists', commanded by an engineer, Lieutenant Muntz. These men set up a listening-post to eavesdrop on Bolshevik wireless traffic and pass what they heard to London. It was an easy job at first since the Russians did not usually bother with cipher, and when they did, Muntz had no trouble in breaking it. Suspicions of Persian duplicity led to other sappers tapping telegraph lines and, on one occasion, rescinding a message from the Shah.

By this time Iraq was now in a semblance of order with a pro-British government, and Britain's relations with the smaller Gulf sheikhdoms and sultanates went on in their traditional way. In theory and practice, local rulers were bound to Britain by a sequence of treaties and received cash subsidies as well as naval support when it was needed. Independence of any kind was actively discouraged. When Muhammad bin Sulaiman, Sheikh of Khasab on the Straits of Hormuz, rashly disclaimed the sovereignty of the Sultan of Oman, retribution followed in the customary form. In April 1930, the gunboats *Lupin* and *Cyclamen* (a class of warship specially built for the waters of the Gulf) in company with a ship from the Sultan's navy, hove to off Khasab. After a warning, a creeping barrage enveloped the town and one of the sheikh's dhows was sunk by shellfire. Larger forces could be deployed quickly to meet more formidable challenges to British paramountcy. When Ibn Saud's Wahhabis menaced Kuwait in 1928, an armoured car squadron from Iraq, two squadrons of fighters and the cruisers *Emerald* and *Enterprise* arrived to see off the invaders. All this was enough to make the Wahhabis think twice, for an air reconnaissance on 1 April revealed that they had vanished into the desert. It was, however, prudent to give a public show of what Britain could do to help Kuwait's sheikh, so an exercise was held in which armoured cars, bluejackets with machine-guns and pom-poms, and fighter aircraft combined to demonstrate how Kuwait would be defended. All this did not convince the Wahhabis, for some returned the next year, and had to be scared off by aircraft.[65]

The Second World War and post-war industrial expansion changed the Gulf and Britain's role there. Before the war just over a fifth of Britain's oil came from the Gulf, nearly all of it from Persian wells. Bahrain had started oil production in 1934, Kuwait in 1946, and the smaller sheikhdoms of Qatar, Abu Dhabi and Dubai between 1949 and 1969. The Iranian oil crisis of 1951–3 had shown the value of reliable suppliers with stable, pro-British governments, and so the need to maintain the goodwill of the Arab rulers replaced the security of India as the motive for British political and military commitments in the Gulf. There also remained vestiges of former Imperial communications networks like the naval and RAF base at Bahrain and military airfields at Sharjah and Oman. After the enforced withdrawals from other Middle Eastern bases, these staging posts took on a new strategic importance; the Bahrain base handled the military traffic for operations in Borneo between 1961 and 1965, and from 1967 was the final resting place for the HQ of Middle East Command. An additional justification for British military involvement followed the commercial expansion generated by the spiralling oil revenues. The once backward Arab states became customers for British goods and technical services as they hurried into programmes of modernization. In the 1980s British ministers visiting the Gulf came as negotiators for contracts and fulfilled, in a strange way, Churchill's prediction that after the loss of India, the British in Asia would be no more than 'commercial bag-men'.[66]

From the mid-1950s onwards, British policy in the Gulf had two aims — the tightening of links already forged during the century when the region had been part of the 'unofficial' empire, and the establishment of a military presence to guard British interests and the local rulers who supported them. The task was harder than at any time in the past since Britain no longer possessed the Indian

Army which had hitherto done the donkey work of providing garrisons and expeditionary forces for the Middle East. Before 1963 the shortfall had been made up in part by national servicemen, who had been called upon to act as Imperial watchdogs in Palestine, the Suez Canal Zone, Cyprus and Malaya. The long-term solution was the creation of a surrogate Indian army from local, Arab recruits, equip and train them, and place them under British officers. The Assyrian levies in Iraq and the Arab Legion in the Transjordan served as prototypes for the new troops raised in the Gulf, and after the expulsion of British officers from the Transjordan, there was a steady flow of experienced officers southwards.

There was plenty of work for them to do. Oil companies sending parties into the hinterland found to their cost that brigandage was commonplace, and pressurized the British government to provide efficient armed forces. One answer was the establishment of the Trucial Oman Scouts (TOS) in 1951, a unit which soon found its duties extending beyond the protection of geologists. In 1952 detachments of the TOS were sent to the Buraimi oasis, a hitherto unimportant collection of villages claimed by Oman, Abu Dhabi and Saudi Arabia, each hoping the district possessed oil. The TOS detachment, representing the Sultan of Oman's rights, quickly ran into difficulties after reinforcements recruited in Aden mutinied in October 1953. They proved a wilful crew, were suspected of trafficking in ammunition with the local Arabs, and had made a nuisance of themselves in Sharjah. Two British officers were shot deat and two NCOs wounded.[67] The enforcement of discipline and soldierly habits was an exasperating, uphill struggle for the British officers involved. 'We had many sit-down strikes', one recalled, 'and most of these were caused by the inability of the British officer to comprehend what the problem was, or by his bad Arabic being misinterpreted by the soldiers he was talking to'. Similar problems of indiscipline troubled other local units and the Hadrami Beduin Legion, which operated in Eastern Aden, was bedevilled by the violent reactions of troopers who felt that they lost face if they were corrected. An alarming and not uncommon reaction was for the man who had been slighted to murder the officer or NCO responsible.[68]

Such volatile units had their uses. The TOS carried out the *coup de main* in November 1955 by which the Buraimi oasis was occupied and the Saudis ejected, much to the initial annoyance of their patron, the United States. More serious crises could not be handled by local forces unaided. The revolt against Sultan Taimur bin Said of Oman and Muscat in 1957 proved too much for the TOS and other local units. In consequence reinforcements, including RAF fighters, had to be brought in from Kenya and Aden. The uprising took the form of a challenge to the Sultan's authority by the Imam Muhammad, Sulaiman bin Himyar, and Isa al-Haitha who wished to assert the independence of the interior tribes. The rebels were backed by Saudi Arabia, which supplied them with arms, many of them imported from the United States. The Sultan's forces were unable to cope with the revolt, and by July

1957 they had been almost wiped out. Immediate British intervention saved the day for Sultan Said and the rebels were pushed back to the highland fastnesses of the Green Mountain by August. RAF Hunters from Bahrain and Sharjah bombed Tanuf, Suleiman bin Himyar's headquarters, and left it in ruins. On the ground three companies of Cameronians, Ferret scout cars of the 15th/19th Hussars, two squadrons of the TOS and detachments of the SAS, homeward bound from Malaya, tipped the balance, and by January 1959 the rebellion had been broken.

It was clear that Britain was prepared to keep the Sultan on his throne and ensure that what he claimed as his historic authority was exerted over Oman and, of course, its oil. Julian Amery, then Under-Secretary at the Colonial Office, visited Oman in 1958 and set in motion the processes for building up the Sultanate's armed forces. The Sultan, Taimur bin-Said was in all respects a traditional client of Britain — he had been educated at the College of Princes at Ajimar in India during the 1920s — and his attitudes were rooted in an even more distant past. He accepted the innovation of oil wells, which began production in 1967 and within three years were yielding Oman £70 million annually, but he distrusted all other forms of modernity, especially 'dangerous thoughts'. He kept slaves, governed as a feudal autocrat with a court of British advisors, and did all he could to keep the twentieth century at bay. It was embarrassing for the British, as one officer in his service recollected. 'I respect the old man's motives and am not so appalled as some by the cruelty and viciousness of his methods. These should not be judged by Western standards; indeed I often found myself trying to explain to foreign journalists that many aspects of life in the country which were anathema to them were accepted as normal by the inhabitants'.[69]

The Sultan's Dhofari subjects were, in 1965, showing signs of exasperation with hidebound Islamic traditionalism, poverty and backwardness. On 9 June, the Dhofar Liberation Front was formed and declared war on the Sultan with the acclamation and support of the governments of the Yemen, Iraq and Egypt. In September 1968 the socialist revolutionaries took the new name, Popular Front for the Liberation of the Arabian Gulf, which was changed again, six years later, to the People's Front for the Liberation of Oman. By this time it was receiving assistance from China and the USSR. The rebellion was concentrated in the southern province of Oman which consists of the forty miles coastal littoral of rain forest, cut by deep *wadis*, and a barren, upland belt which passes into the Arabian desert. To the south was Aden Protectorate, which, after the British evacuation in 1967, became the People's Democratic Republic of Yemen (PDRY) and an armoury, storehouse and sanctuary for the Dhofari guerrillas.

The uprising began with isolated attacks on patrols of the Sultan's army and, in April 1966, a spectacular attempted assassination of the Sultan by Dhofar soldiers whom he was inspecting at a parade in Salala. For the next three years, the guerrilla army grew and made so much headway that much of western

Dhofar came under their control, allowing them the freedom to recruit and move supplies from Yemen. Omani resistance was left to the Sultan's forces which, as the struggle intensified, were being stiffened by more and more British officers who, in 1977, totalled 650. Jordanian engineers appeared in Dhofar and played an important part in the construction of the Damavand line which was finished in August 1974. A year earlier, Shah Reza Pahlevi had sent over a thousand men of the Imperial Iranian Battlegroup to Oman with their American equipment. What was, in effect, Britain's last campaign in the Middle East was fought with new allies who shared a common concern for stability. For the British officers seconded to the Sultan's forces, theirs was not an Imperial campaign. 'Britain's own nationalist interest in maintaining both stability in the Gulf and the free flow of oil', together with checking Communist subversion, was one officer's justification for his part in the war.[70]

It seemed different from the other side of the firing line. One British journalist with the rebels encountered a Dhofari woman who, 'asked why the Labour Government which called itself socialist, was killing the peasants of Dhofar'.[71] Other Dhofar peasants who were unimpressed with socialism also found themselves being killed by local socialists. Inside Britain, the exact nature of the government's intervention in the Oman campaign was kept deliberately obscure by Harold Wilson's government, although in April 1975, the Minister for Defence, Roy Mason, made a visit to forces in the field.

Britain was committed to support the Oman government in what was an ideological conflict as well as a guerrilla war. Military victory was, however, impossible without deep changes within Omani society and the first and most important of these was the dethronement of Sultan Said in a palace coup in July 1970. He was sent into exile at the Dorchester Hotel, London, whilst his Sandhurst-educated son, Qabus, took over the government and began a programme of reform. The sum of £6 million was earmarked for Dhofar so that as the Government army pressed into rebel areas, they were followed by civilians responsible for setting up clinics, schools, shops and mosques. A radio-station at Salala broadcast government propaganda which included pledges of pardon for insurgents who surrendered. The flow of fugitives increased from 1970 and many of them enlisted in the Sultan's forces, where they were formed into irregular units. By 1974 there were 1,400 of these irregulars, known as *firquats*, who were trained and led by British SAS instructors. One party was shown the film *Zulu*, presumably to boost their morale, and its members quickly identified themselves with the Imperial warriors holding Rorke's Drift. Some were so excited by the fighting that they fired their own rifles at the screen as the Zulus charged![72]

The palace revolution which ushered out the Middle Ages in Oman marked not only the spread of enlightenment but a change in the course of the war. Hitherto, the rebels had had the initiative. They had taken over western Dhofar, captured several towns, harassed communications and forced the Sultan's forces on to the defensive. Most important, they had obtained the

PLATE 1 TRADITIONAL IMPERIAL SOLDIERING: Showing the flag; dismounted Kent Yeomanry with band, Egypt, c. 1918. © Dr. Charles Kightly.

PLATE 2 TRADITIONAL CHORES: Digging latrine trenches, Egypt, c. 1918. © Dr. Charles Kightly.

PLATE 3 FRONTIER POST: Razmak, Waziristan, *c.* 1925. After the continuous restlessness among the Wazirs after 1917, this forward camp was established and became one of the major bases in the area and one of the centres for operations against the Faqir of Ipi during the late 1930s. From time to time Wazir snipers would fire on the camp from the surrounding hills. © National Army Museum.

PLATE 4 TRADITIONAL WARFARE: Column of Indian Infantry with mules marching along a military road in Waziristan, *c.* 1925. An armoured car keeps watch from the road on the opposite side of the valley. © National Army Museum.

PLATE 5 TECHNICAL HITCH: An officer emerges from an armoured car whch may have developed a fault, Waziristan, *c.* 1925 © National Army Museum.

PLATE 6   THE NEW CUTTING EDGE OF EMPIRE: BE2c aircraft about to take off for a bombing or reconnaissance mission from a newly levelled airstrip, North-West Frontier, 1917.
© Imperial War Museum.

PLATE 7   RIOT: Peshawar, 22 April 1930. In the centre is His Majesty's Armoured Car 'Bethuane', which has been set on fire by nationalist rioters and, slightly to the left, the charred body of a motor-cycle outrider who had been attacked and killed. Further up the street are detachments of the KOYLI and other armoured cars. The rioters had been driven off by machine-gun fire from another armoured car, but their stones and bricks still litter the street. © National Army Museum.

PLATE 8   WINGS OVER EGYPT: Westland Wapiti bombers of No. 6 Squadron fly in formation over the Nile Delta, an impressive reminder of British power in the Middle East and of Britain's will to defend her authority there. © Commanding Officer, No. 6 Squadron RAF.

PLATE 9 IMPERIAL CHASTISEMENT: RAF bombers attack Ghabaish, a village on the Tigris Delta, December 1924. In the centre is the burning reed house of the Shaik Salim al Khyim, which was the target for the sortie. Other buildings have been hit and set on fire and in the top left corner is a bomber which has just finished its attack run. © Controller of HM Stationery Office.

PLATE 10 GROUND SUPPORT: RAF Rolls Royce Armoured Car squadron on parade at Amman, Jordan, 1940. © Commanding Officer, No.6 Squadron RAF.

PLATE 11 GUERRILLAS: Captured photograph of Arab nationalist commanders in Palestine, c. 1938; the one in the centre is armed with traditional scimitar and a Mauser automatic.
© Commanding Officer, No. 6 Squadron RAF.

PLATE 12 MANDATE IN RUINS: Survivors are carried from the rubble of the Hotel David, Jerusalem, after its destruction by a bomb planted by Menachem Begin's Irgun terrorists, 1946.
© Imperial War Museum.

PLATE 13 THE TUANS ARE BACK: Two youthful Indonesians are questioned about their nationalist sympathies and activities by a Dutch Intelligence officer; British Paratrooper officers look on, Java, 1945. © Imperial War Museum.

PLATE 14 THE EYES OF EMPIRE: Aerial view of pirate junks [centre] anchored on a creek of the Yangtse Delta, 1934. The photo was taken by a Swordfish pilot from HMS *Ark Royal* after the pirates had kidnapped Europeans from a steamer. © Controller of HM Stationery Office.

PLATE 15 TERRORIST HUNTERS: An Aborigine tracker in gala dress poses in front of a light transport aircraft, Northern Malaya, 1954. © Imperial War Museum.

PLATE 16 THE EMPIRE HELPS OUT: Askaris of the King's African Rifles patrol the jungle in search of Communist guerrillas, 1950. © Imperial War Museum.

PLATE 17   AMBUSH: A patrol rests after a successful attack on a Mau Mau bush camp, Kenya, 1953. © Imperial War Museum.

PLATE 18   THE BRITISH ARE BACK: Landing craft and helicopters converge on Port Said during the Suez campaign, November 1956. Within two months British forces would leave Egypt for the last time. © Imperial War Museum.

PLATE 19 SUSPECTS: British infantrymen stand guard over a batch of suspected IRA members rounded up in the Southern Irish countryside. The sergeant and one private [*far left and right*] wear medal ribbons of the First World War and were no doubt used to fighting an enemy which could be recognised. Their prisoners would be turned over to the police, Auxillarite, or 'Black and Tans' for close interrogation. © Imperial War Museum.

PLATE 20 OPERATIONAL DELAY: A motorised infantry patrol held up after the mining of a bridge by the IRA, Southern Ireland, 1921. © Imperial War Museum.

PLATE 21 THE TROUBLES: A 40 Commando Royal Marine on night duty in Bessbrook, South Armagh, Northern Ireland, May 1983. © Alistair Campbell.

PLATE 22 THE EXCLUSION ZONE: Within the 150-mile limit around the Falklands, two Royal Navy Sea Harriers are about to land on a British aircraft carrier. In the background, a Royal Navy Sea King, helicopter prepares to land on the flight-deck of a Royal Fleet Auxiliary vessel. The Harrier played a crucial role in the regaining of the islands. © British Aerospace Plc.

PLATE 23   CAPTURED: Argentinian soldiers taken prisoner at Goose Green, East Falkland, on 2 June 1982 are guarded by a Royal Marine as they await transit out of the area. © Crown Copyright.

PLATE 24 REGAINED FOR BRITAIN: Royal Marine Commandos raising the Union Flag over the Falklands again, after British troops established a firm bridgehead, 22 May 1982. © Crown Copyright.

means to secure supplies of arms and ammunition from Yemen. After 1970 the pattern of fighting changed as the Sultan's forces, their Iranian reinforcements and British assistants took the offensive. Two new Omani regiments were raised, more British officers were seconded, and the Omani air force was expanded with three squadrons of Strikemasters (Provost trainers converted for anti-guerrilla work), Hunters (from the Jordanian air force) and assault and transport helicopters. Salala air base was fortified and in 1973 received an electronic surveillance system for perimeter defence. A year before, the airfield had been hit by a 122mm Katyushka rocket fired from nearly seven miles away which had forced the Sultan's forces to station picquets in the foothills.

The campaign had two objectives; the first was to engage the rebels and push them out of the areas they occupied, and the second was to cut them off from their supplies of arms. The latter was made possible by the building of two cross-country lines, known as the Hornbeam and Damavand Lines which were barbed wire fences surrounded by land mines. Each was regularly patrolled on foot and from the air. Sarfait, close to the Yemeni border, was retaken by air in April 1972 and successfully held, thanks to air drops. Elsewhere the war consisted of engagements with guerrilla groups which were frequently hard-fought since the insurgents often displayed 'skill, courage and impressive determination in the face of superior firepower'.[73] This was inevitably the firepower of the attack aircraft which could be summoned in pairs by ground forces. Still, the insurgents were not without bite, thanks to their Russian and Chinese training and a powerful arsenal which included Kalashnikov rifles, light mortars and mobile rocket-launchers; one of these, a SAM, brought down a helicopter in 1975.

Such a victory meant little by this time for the Dhofar rebellion was on its last legs. Supply lines from the Yemen had been severed and the bands of guerrillas were isolated and on the defensive after a sequence of defeats in small but gruelling engagements. The Omani victory was a triumph for professionalism and political good sense, both of which had been provided by the detached British officers and NCOs loaned over ten years. They had been able to offer technology, expertise, training and leadership and in return had gained experience of, and insight into, what was known as 'counter-insurgency' warfare, although many of its features if not its technical novelties had been around for many years.

Curtain Call, Aden, 1962–7

Success in Oman was a welcome consolation prize for Britain after twenty years of setback and disengagement in the Middle East. After Suez, the successive governments of Macmillan and Wilson remained obsessed with the need to sustain what was called a 'presence' in the region, although the enthusiasm of Wilson's Government was far less than that of its predecessor. This policy of hanging on sometimes seemed at odds with both governments' determination to withdraw from Asia, Africa and the Caribbean, but anxiety about oil and fears that Russia or her catspaws might take advantage of Britain's decampment was sufficient motive for continued activity in the Middle East. It was also difficult for Britain to disentangle itself from the mesh of earlier obligations to various local rulers; nor did it wish to rid itself of these responsibilities since many of the Gulf potentates now presided over oil resources and their new wealth offered opportunities for commerce.

Britain had to tread warily in its dealings with its former clients since local and world opinion was always suspicious of any form of relationship which could be labelled 'colonialist'. To shake off the image of the former Imperial puppet-master, Britain allowed the Gulf states to become 'independent'. Kuwait, Qatar, Bahrain and the Gulf sheikhdoms (herded together as the United Arab Emirates) all assumed the status of independent nations, but with the assurance of British military assistance in the event of any external threat. This was readily available after 1957 when the Defence White Paper announced that Aden would become the headquarters of Middle East Command and the site for a military, naval and air base. The new centre of British power was soon in action, for as soon as Kuwait achieved independence in July 1961 it was menaced by President Qasim of Iraq. He publicly announced the revival of a historic claim to Kuwait and its frightened Ruler appealed to Britain for assistance. Lord Home, the Foreign Secretary, responded in the traditional way, and within two weeks a formidable expeditionary force had been shipped and flown to Kuwait from Aden, Kenya, Cyprus, Britain and West Germany. Iraq backed down, murmuring about 'colonialism', and shortly afterwards the British contingent left. Kuwait's integrity had been preserved, but its future was to be underwritten by its neighbours Iran and Saudi Arabia, both clients of the United States.

The flourish which had preserved Kuwait seemed to vindicate Britain's desire to maintain a position of strength in the Middle East and demonstrated to friendly and unfriendly nations an ability to act effectively. Yet if Britain still wished to throw her weight around, it was vital that Aden was secure. In making the decision to turn Aden into Britain's centre of operations in the Middle East, the planners had been blind to the growth of Nasserite nationalism — or else had hoped that it might be contained. This refusal to recognize historic forces in the Middle East was a grave mistake. The armed forces sent to Aden found themselves having to contend for every inch of the town and its hinterland against a ruthless guerrilla force, the National Liberation Front (NLF).

The scenario for the Aden campaign of 1963—7 was a hitherto-backward colony consisting of a modern port and a hinterland of sheikhdoms and sultanates. These had remained largely untouched by British influence for their rulers had been left to their own devices, in spite of valiant efforts by colonial administrators to construct a system of inter-tribal truces. Deeply-rooted habits of reiving, feuding and preying on camel-trains which passed along the trading routes were not easily eradicated, and efforts to check them were sporadic and ineffective. After 1928 the security of Aden and its protectorates had been the responsibility of the RAF whose aircraft were supported by armoured cars and the Aden Protectorate Levies, an armed camelry under RAF officers.

Air control in Aden had had mixed fortunes. The persistent irredentism of the Imam Yahya of Yemen led to his meddling with the border tribes, and it required a series of air raids in 1928–9 to 'bring him to his senses' in the plain words of Lord Trenchard. Yemeni claims to Aden were never wholly forgotten and formed a powerful element in the nationalist insurgency during the 1960s. Tribal disorder was never fully suppressed. 'Old men, women and children' were warned to get out of two remote villages in January 1929 which were subsequently flattened by two days of bombing.[74] Soon afterwards the miscreant tribes promised to mend their ways, but such pledges were easily broken. The Queteiba tribe had customarily supplemented their sparse living from the land by plundering or taking tolls from convoys which travelled along the Aden to Adh Dhala track, much to the vexation of the Government. In 1934 the exasperated authorities subjected their villages to the astringencies of air control and twenty-eight tons of bombs were dropped over two months. The Queteibi were unchastened, and in 1940 their recidivism earned them a four-month bombardment in which 133 tons of bombs were dropped. This did not provide the final answer, for in July 1947 they were the objects of another spate of bombing, this time by Lincoln bombers and Tempests armed with rockets. According to the AOC in Aden, Air Marshal Sir Harold Lydford, 'the tribesmen were bewildered to see the accuracy of the bombing and the rocket attacks', and the operations 'had a calming influence' throughout the Western protectorate.[75]

It was always British policy to uphold local rulers who, when needed, could obtain the formidable backing of the RAF against their more unruly subjects. When a treaty chief had been deposed by his kinsman, rocket attacks on the usurper's adherents in February 1947 paved the way for the restoration of the former Ruler. An uprising by the Bal Harithis against their overlord, the *Sharif* of Beihan, prompted even more forceful intervention during 1948. Six Lincoln bombers and rocket-firing Tempests delivered two waves of attacks on Bal Harithi villages with the usual forewarning. There was a deliberate intermission between the air-raids during which it was hoped the tribesmen would submit. They did, but only after the second bombardment, and then they chose to humble themselves to the government rather than the *Sharif*.[76] Their villages had been slighted, their crops partially destroyed and many camels killed. Ten years later the region was disturbed by a tribal uprising which received aid from neighbouring Yemen.

There had always been a contrast between the feudal and impoverished agrarian sheikhdoms and sultanates of the interior and the port of Aden. This gap widened during the 1950s with the building of the BP oil refinery at Little Aden, the expansion of Aden as a bunkering port and the construction of the facilities for the British base. One consequence was the creation of a large Arab working-class, many of whom were Yemeni migrant workers, and the corresponding growth of trade unionism. Industrial grievances went hand-in-hand with nationalist fervour and both contributed to strikes during 1956 when there was much open support for Nasser. Aden could not be quarantined from the wider Arab world, nor could its inhabitants be isolated from the wave of nationalism sweeping through the Middle East. In December 1947 the news of the partition of Palestine and the plight of the Arabs there had provoked rioting during which local Jews and their property were attacked. Controlling the disorders was beyond the power of the local police and so the Aden Protectorate Levies were called in, which made matters worse. 'Recruited from up-country', they were, in the opinion of Air Marshal Lydford, 'A wild, savage lot' who shared the sentiments of the rioters. Over one hundred casualties were suffered, two-thirds of them Jewish, before calm was restored. What Lydford described as 'stern repressive measures' were needed, together with landing parties from two destroyers and a battalion of the North Staffords hurriedly flown in from the Canal Zone.[77]

With the resurgence of anti-British, Arab nationalism after Suez, it was clear that the security of the new base at Aden rested on brittle glass. Egyptian influence in the region increased after September 1962, when a Nasserite *coup* overthrew the Imam of Yemen and began an eight-year civil war between the republicans and royalists. Egypt backed the republicans and poured soldiers and aircraft into the Yemen (Egyptian air control included the use of poison gas) and King Feisal of Saudi Arabia lent help to the royalists. The conflict spilled over into Aden. The republicans were eager to promote old claims to the colony, support the insurgents there with arms, offer them sanctuary and, most importantly, step up the flow of anti-British propaganda. Nearly every Adeni possessed a transistor radio, from which he heard a flood of anti-British vitriol broadcast from Cairo and Taiz. In the view of one commander, this technical novelty tipped the balance against Britain during the five years of the guerrilla war.[78]

When the decision had been made to site the base in Aden in 1957, no-one had foreseen that the colony would become a battlefield with the garrison engaged in fighting rural and urban guerrillas. To forestall the emergence on the base's doorstep of a Nasserite, revolutionary movement, the Colonial Office had planned to create a South Arabian Federation in which the port of Aden would be joined with the petty states of the interior. The begettors of this hybrid hoped that it would promote a stable hinterland for the base and that the political radicalism of the Adenis would be balanced by the conservatism of the tribal interior. The idea belonged to that never-never land of post-Imperial thinking which was based on the belief that radical nationalists could be made to see reason and would accept compromise. In 1962 a White Paper declared that after six years the new Federation would come of age and be granted independence.

The Federation scheme became not the key to Aden's future as a biddable state but the focus for all political and armed opposition to British rule. This might have been anticipated, for local Arab trade unions had already rejected the Federation and there were scant signs of enthusiasm elsewhere. In spite of these unpromising signals, the local administration and its political masters in London pressed ahead to make the Federation work, for without the stability it promised the British base would be untenable. Inside Aden and its surrounding protectorates, the NLF and its temporary ally, the Front for the Liberation of South Yemen (FLOSY), worked for the subversion of the Federation. They aimed to make the area ungovernable and thereby discountenance both Britain and the new Federal authorities. Britain would be forced to drop the idea for the base and, once deprived of the prospect of future British support, the Federation would crumble away and Aden would succumb to a popular revolution.

The NLF and FLOSY waged war in two ways. The first was to secure the allegiance or benevolent neutrality of the majority of Adenis who were to be convinced that the Federation was a mask for British control and that the future lay with the revolutionaries. A further propaganda war was fought to win over international opinion to the view that Aden was the victim of British Imperialism and where possible to discredit British forces as cruel oppressors. On the ground, the NLF fought a terrorist campaign against British forces and Britain's supporters and infiltrated their adherents into the Federal administration, education services and police force. In this war the NLF were assisted by the Wilson Government which in the Defence White Paper of February 1966 announced that the British base was to abandon once the South Arabian Federation received its independence in 1968. By this time the struggle to keep order in Aden had been going on for three years without any indication of eventual success. There were many residual political reasons why the Labour Government did not wish to fulfil its predecessor's obligations. Many Labour party members were uneasy about the morality of giving support to what appeared to be backward rulers of feudal states, there were misgivings about the costs of maintaining Aden and waging a war there, and a party which had promoted itself as symbolizing modernity was embarrassed by entanglement in an old-style colonial war. Above all the intensity of opposition to the British presence in Aden suggested that the original decision to place a base there had been a miscalculation. The announcement that the base would go was a triumph for the NLF and made its last task, the destruction of the Federation, that much easier.

The decision to pull British forces out of Aden changed the war which, after February 1966, became an eighteen-month exercise in keeping the lid down on unrest and preserving some semblance of order in the thin hope that the Federation might somehow survive Britain's military withdrawal. Before, the war had been a straightforward struggle against rural and urban insurgents. It had started in the countryside with operations against tribesmen in the Radfan district during 1963–4, followed by a campaign against urban terrorism inside Aden. This lasted from 1964 until the final evacuation in November 1967.

Urban and rural armed resistance began simultaneously in December 1966 with an attempt to assassinate the British High Commissioner at Aden airport. For some time the situation in the Radfan region had been deteriorating with signs of unrest from the Queteibi who were hankering after the old days and the exaction of tolls from traffic along the Dhala road. Then and later, those at war with the Federation and the British relied on supplies of arms from across the border and for their part the Yemeni republicans were attempting to subvert border chiefs. This interference included a MIG attack on Beihan, where the *Sharif* was resolutely pro-British (he had been delighted with the news of Suez) and this affront was countered by a RAF raid on Harib in the Yemen soon afterwards.

The initial task of bringing the tribesmen of the Radfan to heel fell to Federal forces with RAF backing, but their efforts to penetrate the mountainous region were disappointing. While 'Operation Nutcracker' in January 1964 proved that government forces could enter the region, it was less easy to keep permanent forces there. In a terrain which closely resembled the North-West Frontier of India, fighting techniques used in those wars were reintroduced and updated. As with the earlier frontier campaigns, the Government forces faced opponents who were not willing to concentrate their forces or hold lines or areas. The Guerrillas fought a war designed to harass and wear down the detachments sent after them in the hope that culminative losses and frustration would lead to an abandonment of the campaign. By April 1964 it was clear that the Government had to demonstrate its will and show conclusively that its forces could enter the Radfan and occupy it unchallenged.

To prove its point, the Government began an air control exercise in April in which aerial bombardment wrecked the Radfanis' spring sowing and forced many to evacuate their villages and flee into the Yemen. This was followed by a widespread penetration of the region by a force of about 3,000 British troops, supported by the RAF. Much of the movement to the area and across it was facilitated by Belvedere helicopters which proved invaluable in saving time. Even so, the forces involved were hampered by a lack of precise knowledge about the region, its inhabitants and the numbers of guerrillas opposed to them. Some information was provided by SAS patrols who went ahead of the main detachments, but even their covert activities could not compensate for the lack of information from local sources. On one occasion an SAS patrol was discovered by a shepherd who immediately alerted guerrillas in the vicinity. The operations were, however, finally successful in that British forces were able to move deep into the Radfan, establish posts there, and so control strategic points. Many involved likened the campaign to others fought on the North-West Frontier of India and some of the methods of the earlier opera-

An Empire Founded upon Sand: The Middle East 123

tions were copied, in particular the absolute necessity to occupy high ground. There were many novelties; small patrols escaped from tricky situations through their ability to invoke close and accurate artillery and air support, and supply difficulties were overcome by the use of helicopters. These proved most helpful although there never seemed to be enough of them. Another innovation were the SAS patrols which slipped into hostile territory, lay low and watched for guerrilla bands whose movements they radioed to the gunners and the RAF. The gains of the campaign were short-lived for when the news was announced that all British forces would pull out, the authority of the local rulers crumbled and the way was open for the NLF to take over.

During the Radfan campaign, the soldiers on the spot had to grapple with the unwelcome task of accommodating journalists and TV camera crews anxious to report the war in this remote region. In some quarters in Britain there were misgivings about the justice of a war fought on behalf of the feudal sheikhs and the asperities of air control provoked criticism. Denis Healey complained in the House of Commons after the local commander had publicly announced that the guerrillas had cut the heads from the bodies of two dead British soldiers and had them displayed in Sana. This grisly tale turned out to be true, and when the rumpus had died down some servicemen felt sore about the treatment they seemed to be getting from the Labour Opposition and some sections of the Press.

Similar feelings were generated during the urban conflict in Aden although here resentment was directed towards the local civil authorities. From the declaration of a State of Emergency in December 1963 until February 1967, the colonial bureaucracy decreed that all security operations were to be undertaken on the assumption that too much toughness would alienate the local population. It was a classic dilemma; the army wanted vigorous measures but the civil powers shrank from their adoption on the grounds that they would lead to long-term resentment. The outcome was that the Arab population soon realized that the military lacked the means to protect them from NLF intimidation, and so they either gave covert assistance to the guerrillas or else adopted an attitude of benevolent neutrality. This was a triumph for the NLF, which could claim widespread popular support, and a setback for the security forces who found themselves deprived of intelligence from the Adeni population. Close identification with the security forces was extremely risky and once it was known that the British were pulling out, suicidal.

For the men who had to patrol the streets of the Arab quarters, stand guard at checkpoints and man observation posts, the official policy of 'minimum force' was always bewildering and sometimes irritating. Soldiers were forbidden to enter mosques and Arab cemeteries, they could not shoot unless they were fired on at first, and they were ever aware than an error of judgement could lead to awkward consequences. A miscalculation made in a moment would have 'world-wide publicity and possibly political repercussions that can extend to the United Nations' commented one officer. This knowledge placed an enormous burden on junior officers, NCOs and other ranks and it was made worse by an awareness that the terrorists considered that the 9,000 wives and children of servicemen, living in local quarters, were targets for assassination.

Until 1967, when military commanders were placed in direct charge of operations, the campaign had been run by a cumbersome, quadripartite body which included the military, the High Commissioner (who represented the British government), the Federal authorities, and the pro-nationalist Aden State Government which was dissolved in September 1965. Its chief minister, Abdul Makawi, was a socialist who included one suspect terrorist in his Cabinet and later joined the FLOSY government-in-exile. His presence in the executive which directed counter-terrorist activities was a puzzle to some officers. Equally troublesome was the lack of intelligence, a deficiency created by the murder of all members of the local Special Branch and the NLF's ability to coerce the local population. The army attempted to make up for this shortcoming by the creation of intelligence branches attached to field units and belatedly the formation of a Directorate of Intelligence.

Effective intelligence might have balanced the disadvantages suffered by the army in Aden in having to operate using 'minimum force' in the middle of an indifferent or hostile population. Technical superiority, which enabled the situation in the countryside to be controlled, could not be brought into play in the major concentrations of Arab population, Crater and Sheikh Othman. Here the war was a routine of surveillance and snap raids against a background of more and more frequent terrorist attacks, mostly undertaken by bomb-throwers. When the British government gave notice of the withdrawal of all service personnel, the war became clearly unwinnable at least in terms of its original objectives. The 'honour of his Regiment of Corps' became the soldier's sole motive for holding down the lid on the colony, and so for the next eighteen months the army and the RAF went on, driven by a sense of professional pride.[79]

For the Adenis, the final days of British government were marked by a necessary switch of loyalties to the NLF who were obviously the successors to the Federation. In June 1967, five months before the final evacuation, there was a mutiny by police and Federal troops in Crater which was both unexpected and savage. Its immediate consequence was the British abandonment of Crater which passed into NLF hands. From the high ground above the town, British troops 'saw NLF flags flying over some of the buildings', and 'terrorists strolled openly and defiantly in the streets, carrying their weapons and enjoying their moment of victory'. This was galling and frightening since rebel-occupied Crater was within mortar range of Khormaksar airport, vital for the approaching final evacuation. On 3–4 July, the town was retaken by the Argyll and Sutherland Highlanders under Lieutenant Colonel Mitchell, an officer whose temper and spirit seemed to belong to a more distant Imperial past. Echoes of that past were heard when his troops began their advance to the sound of the pipes.

The insurrection in Crater sounded the death-knell of the Federation whose soldiers and policemen had shown themselves ready for a wholesale defection to the nationalists. *Cairo Radio* was jubilant. 'Britain will not remain in the south. The darkness of the bitterest enemy of Arabism and Islam will lift from the south of the Arabian peninsula, the land of Muhammad, may the blessings of God be upon him'.[80] The now confident inheritors of Aden had, however, fallen out, so the final months of British rule were marked by a civil war between the NLF and FLOSY. The NLF came out on top and on 29 November 1967 declared the birth of the People's Republic of South Yemen just as the last British detachments withdrew to the waiting flotilla of warships anchored off Aden.

At the moment when the British High Commissioner, Sir Humphrey Trevelyan, boarded his plane for England, a Royal Marine band played 'Fings Aint Wot They Used to Be', much as another band had played 'The World Turned Upside Down' when General Cornwallis surrendered to the Americans at Yorktown in 1780. Both Lyrics were appropriate for the last hours of Britain's occupation of Aden, and indeed the disappearance of the last vestige of British paramountcy in the Middle East. A combination of local nationalism and an inability to match pretensions to resources had brought about the extinction of British military power. It was extraordinary that just three years before the withdrawal from Aden, Harold Wilson had proclaimed, 'We are a world power and a world influence, or we are nothing'. Five years later, in 1969, Denis Healey was predicting, with equal confidence, 'Britain's transformation from a world power to a European power'. The collapse had been as sudden as it was unavoidable. The month which saw the British departure from Aden also saw a financial crisis which had led to the devaluation of the pound and the start of a period of stringent Government economies. One quick result of this was the announcement in January 1968 that all military and naval facilities east of Suez would be shut down within three years. This termination of global pretensions was confirmed two years later in the Defence White Paper which affirmed 'the broad direction of our defence policy . . . will be a European policy based on NATO'.

In one sense this final abdication of old ties was an appreciation of reality. As a world power Britain's recent record had been dismal, a sequence of meddle and muddle which merely exposed failing influence everywhere. Rhodesia's Unilateral Declaration of Independence, the loss of Aden and the failure of the South Arabian Federation, and the inability of Britain to influence, let alone settle, the Nigerian civil war, the Indo-Pakistan war and the war in South-East Asia were all tokens of impotence. Ironically, one international success comprised the bloodless occupation of a tiny but wayward Caribbean island, Anguilla, in 1967. The Americans had, since 1961, tried to turn Britain away from old yearnings towards global flourishes and push it instead towards Europe. With differing degrees of enthusiasm, Labour and Conservative Governments sought membership of the EEC and with it public admission of the end of world power. Not that Britain possessed the means to play the world power: flagging national productivity could no longer sustain the demands made by a growing military budget. Nor was the Labour Party, already pledged to an expensive programme of modernization and radical social reform, particularly keen to let the armed forces have a bigger slice of the cake. Committed to NATO and the maintenance of Britain's nuclear arsenal, the Labour Government was willing to sacrifice what was left of Britain's presence in the Middle East; the base at Bahrain was accordingly abandoned.

In 1918, when Britain was poised to assume political and military paramountcy in the Middle East, the *fellahin* of Egypt lamented:[81]

> Woe on us Wingate*
> Who has carried off corn,
> Carried off cotton,
> Carried off camels,
> Carried off children,
> Leaving only our lives.
> For the love of Allah, now let us alone.

Britain was not willing to leave the Middle East or its people alone. They occupied a region astride the route to India, and it possessed oil. The end of Turkey produced a political vacuum which Britain had no choice but to fill, regardless of the wishes of the inhabitants. In 1919–20 Britain was able to defeat and contain local nationalist insurgency and consequently impose a political settlement conducive to its interests.

This victory had not been easily won. Commitments elsewhere and dwindling resources meant that control over the Middle East had to be exerted indirectly through friendly governments which depended for their survival on British military assistance. Air control offered the means to help out co-operative regimes at little cost to Britain in terms of cash if not goodwill. The legend of British invincibility was never universally believed in the Middle East thanks to memories of Gallipoli, Kut and the humiliation at Chanak in 1922, when British forces stepped down in the face of Turkish threats. Defiant local rulers and nationalists periodically challenged Britain. Revolts in Iraq in 1920 and 1941, intermittent uprisings in Kurdistan, the rebellion in Palestine, the disturbances in Egypt in 1919 and 1952–4 demanded military action which both placed a strain on already overstretched resources and showed that, in the end, British power rested on an ability to coerce. Rural insurgency was inevitably broken because of technical superiority and air power, but urban

---

*Sir Reginald Wingate, Governor-General of the Sudan and Sirdar of the Egyptian army. The rest of the chant refers to the exactions of material and men for the Egyptian Labour Corps during the First World War.

terrorism in Palestine, the Canal Zone and Aden proved irresistible. In each case, political considerations militated against the kind of military ruthlessness which might have produced results, and even this might not have tipped the balance, as the French found out in Algeria.

There were other practical restrictions on military action in the Middle East. After 1936 the British government had its hands full with troubles in Europe and the Far East and could not afford to offend the Arabs. This was appreciated by both Italy and Germany which, like Russia after 1945, exploited British colonial embarrassments. In 1936 Italy made open her sympathies for the Arabs in Palestine who were also receiving friendly approaches from German agents.[82] After 1945 Britain's Arab adversaries began to turn to Russia for assistance and in particular supplies of arms; after the 1967 Arab-Israeli War, Egypt, Syria and Iraq relied heavily on Russian equipment. By this time Britain's pretensions in the Middle East looked threadbare. The Palestine debacle in 1948, the humiliation at the hands of Mussadiq and the withdrawal from Egypt all added up to evidence that British power was crumbling. The Suez fiasco was an attempt to give the lie to this, a desperate and panicky measure designed to recover lost prestige as well as the Suez Canal. The outcome confirmed Britain as the belligerent opponent of Arab nationalism and made it even harder for it to preserve what was left of its interests elsewhere in the Middle East.

It became harder and harder to justify clinging to remnants of former Imperial influence. Indian independence in 1947 had ended Britain's need to worry about lines of communication. Nevertheless, anxieties about communications persisted, even though Britain was less able to do anything about them since she could no longer call on the Indian Army. In 1919 half the troops in Iraq were Indian, as were a third of those in Palestine. Smaller contingents garrisoned Aden and the Gulf sheikhdoms, much to the annoyance of public opinion in India which, until 1930, had to foot the bill. As late as 1944 there were Indian troops in Palestine and Indian divisions had played a significant part in the Western Desert Campaign where the overriding military objective had been to keep the Germans and the Italians out of Egypt and away from the Canal. Fortunately, residual obligations to the principalities of the Gulf could be honoured without the maintenance of large, permanent garrisons. Air and sea transport saved Kuwait and Oman was preserved by loans of specialists, together with assistance from non-radical states such as Jordan and Iran. But old strategic thinking, like old warriors, faded away slowly, and so from 1963 until 1967 the British army was called upon to wage a war against local insurgents who menaced the security of the base at Aden. It was a thankless task, undertaken valiantly, although one officer later remarked that he and his men were fighting for 'political aims' which were 'confused and uninspiring'.[83]

Confused thought often appeared to be the hallmark of British political aims in the Middle East. Soldiers were called upon to fight campaigns to impose Britain's political will on the people of the region when that will often represented a hotchpotch of contradictions. As a benevolent Imperial power, dedicated to the promotion of humane and civilized values, Britain held the Arabs in tutelage until such time as they could safely manage their own affairs. Even when many Arabs felt convinced that the time for self-sufficiency had arrived, Britain insisted on the maintenance of ties for strategic reasons. When local interests or aspirations clashed with Britain's, the latter prevailed. Nationalists were tolerated so long as their programmes and activities did not endanger British interests. When they did they were dismissed as agents of foreign subversion. The officials and professional experts who conducted relations with the Arabs or advised their governments sometimes mistook the goodwill of ruling elites (often, as in India, educated in Britain) for popular friendship towards Britain. Like nanny, Britain always knew what was best for her charges. Nowhere were the contradictions of British policy more obvious than in Palestine which after the war became the focus of much Arab radical nationalist indignation. At one and the same time Britain adhered to the principle of the Jewish national homeland, outlined vaguely in 1917, and acknowledged the rights of the Arabs already living in Palestine. As this policy proved more and more unworkable, Britain wobbled, first in its assurance to the Arabs and then to the Jews. Neither was placated and both turned from Britain to find new friends. In the end British paramountcy rested on the ability to coerce. Coercion had worked in 1919–20 when Arab revolts were broken in Egypt and Iraq, and again in 1939 when Palestine was pacified. After 1945 it failed.

As British power and influence in the Middle East dwindled, the United States stepped in. The Americans still listened to British politicians and diplomats but, as in the Jordanian crisis in 1970, what really mattered was the US Mediterranean Fleet and its ability to give close support to King Hussein. After the death of Nasser in 1970 and the subsequent expulsion from Egypt of the 15,000 Russian military 'advisors', Anwar el-Sadat turned to America in search of co-operation, cash and equipment. The United States copied its predecessor's behaviour in handling the problems of the region. Iran and Israel offered themselves as stable and well-armed clients and, when required, there were formidable shows of intimidatory strength in the Mediterranean and the Gulf. Air strikes were used to frighten the racalcitrant and defiant, much as they had been in the 1930s. Like Britain, America has learned the limitations of the use of force. Since 1979 she has discovered the power of Muslim passion, expressed by mullahs and other messianic holy men, features of a Middle Eastern landscape familiar enough to the British army fifty to a hundred years ago.

4
Wars of the Jungle: The Far East

Prelude: Old Empires for New, The Far East, 1945-46

The people of Malaya suffered three wars of liberation within less than a decade. The first began on 9 December 1941 when a Japanese army landed on the colony's north-eastern shore and marched southwards through the jungle to capture the fortress base of Singapore just over ten weeks later. Japan's propagandists proclaimed that the Emperor's armies were waging war to free the native populations of South-East Asia from their European oppressors. The new era of 'Asia for the Asiatics' did not last long. In August 1945 mainland Japan surrendered, its empire of conquest fell to pieces and the old rulers returned. Malaya was freed at the end of August when an Anglo-Indian army landed unopposed and restored British colonial government. The last and longest war of liberation was started in June 1948 by the Malayan Communist Party which launched a campaign of terrorism against the government. Its immediate aim was to cause widespread disruption which would open the way for a popular revolution.

The first two Malayan campaigns were the prelude to the third. They had both been part of the Second World War and marked the beginning and end of Japan's endeavour to secure military and economic mastery in South-East Asia. To fulfil their ambition the Japanese had first to defeat and humiliate the hitherto-dominant colonial powers, Britain, France and the Netherlands. In 1941, none was capable of much more than a desultory resistance; the French and Dutch homelands were in German hands and Britain was deeply involved in the struggle to hold the Middle East and the Mediterranean. There were few forces to spare for Malaya. 'We could not protect our interests in the Yellow Sea from Japanese attack', admitted Churchill, though he and many others placed a vain faith in the ability of Singapore to hold out for six months. In fact the war in Malaya had already been lost before the Japanese invaded. The 1922 Washington Naval Treaty and the abandonment of the twenty-year-old alliance with Japan had left Britain dependent upon the fleet and goodwill of the United States for the protection of colonies in the Far East and Pacific.

The full extent of British vulnerability and impotence was first apparent soon after the outbreak of the Sino-Japanese War in 1937. Two gunboats on routine patrol on the Yangtze, HMS *Bee* and *Ladybird*, were shelled by the

Japanese, and elsewhere Japanese troops committed outrages against British subjects and their property. Hong Kong was soon enveloped by Japanese-occupied territory and was recognized as indefensible long before it fell in 1941. All that Britain could offer was empty protests since a strong line, backed by force, was out of the question. The sequence of European crises during the 1930s compelled the government to keep troops, ships and aircraft concentrated in Britain and the Middle East to counter the ambitions of Germany and Italy. The Abyssinian crisis of 1935–6 forced the Admiralty to recall men-o'-war from Far Eastern waters; then and later the Royal Navy could not stand up to Italy in the Mediterranean at the same time as facing up to Japan. There was belated flourish when the ill-protected *Repulse* and *Prince of Wales* were despatched to Singapore, but this ended in disaster when they were sunk by Japanese aircraft in December 1941.

'We didn't really know what we were up against and just passed them off as slant-eyed so-and-so's', was the comment on his Japanese adversaries made by one member of the *Repulse*'s crew. Such contempt for the Japanese was endemic amongst Europeans in the Far East, London and Washington on the eve of Pearl Harbour, and it was a prejudice which united statesmen, diplomats and commanders. Racial arrogance towards Asians was common, and then and later it drove leaders in Britain and the United States to dismiss out of hand the ability of 'yellow men' to fight successfully against Europeans. The folly of European assumptions of racial superiority was brutally revealed during the twelve months after December 1941 when the Japanese over-ran Malaya, the Dutch East Indies, the Philippines, Burma and much of New Guinea. At the same time they gained temporary naval mastery in the Indian and Pacific Oceans. European prestige had been swept away, and in some areas the Japanese were welcomed by the native population. For all the characteristic pitilessness of their military government, the Japanese went some way towards the accommodation of nationalist aspirations and encouraged the setting up of compliant local regimes.

After four years the Japanese *imperium* was in ruins. This reversal of fortune had not been achieved by the efforts of the former colonial powers alone. The destruction of the Japanese new order in South-East Asia had been accomplished principally by the war effort of the United States which had taken the front line to Japan itself and shown its rulers the hopelessness of further resistance. This military fact alone ensured that future paramountcy in South-East Asia and the Pacific would lie with America. As the new power-broker, it fell to the United States to decide whether the old empires would be restored and on what terms. Like Britain, the United States had been at war for the preservation and extension of the freedoms already enjoyed by their peoples. The Four Freedoms and the Atlantic Charter were ideals that questioned both the justification for and continuation of the old order of European empires. Allied propaganda promoted Allied war aims and its drift was quickly understood by the former colonial peoples of South-East Asia. Among the slogans which greeted Anglo-Indian troops when they landed at Batavia (Jakarta) was 'Atlantic Charter means freedom from Dutch Imperialism'. The Viet Minh nationalist declaration of independence for Indo-China, drawn up in September 1945, called to mind the by now embarrassing fact 'that the Allies ... have recognized the principles of equality at the conferences at Tehran and San Francisco'.[1]

The Indo-Chinese consciously adapted the language of 1776 in their declaration and there were many in the United States who were troubled about the future of the former colonies, returned to their old rulers by American blood and money. The *Chicago Tribune* spoke for many in February 1945 when it asked whether America had spent lives and gold just to return the former subjects of the Netherlands, Britain and France to what it called colonial 'slavery'.

Practical problems ruled out any moral alternative based upon ideals of freedom. For the United States the resuscitation of the imperial *ancien regimes* of South-East Asia was the only answer to the immediate difficulties of the region. After four years of turmoil the urgent need in 1945 was the restoration of stable governments which would impose tranquillity. Only the old Imperial powers could achieve this stability and so the United States passed to Britain the responsibility for rebuilding South-East Asia, a task which first required the return of its former rulers. It was a cautious policy which assumed that at some later date, after the imposition of order, the time would be ripe for moves towards self-government. The burden of putting this policy into practice fell upon Lord Mountbatten's South-East Asia Command. It was empowered to reoccupy Malaya (which it did without trouble) and set up makeshift administrations in Indo-China and the Dutch East Indies to prepare the way for the arrival of administrators and soldiers from France and the Netherlands. Since Mountbatten and his local commanders took for granted the return of the former colonial governments, their plans inevitably led to clashes with Vietnamese and Indonesian nationalists. As a consequence Anglo-Indian forces found themselves drawn, unwillingly, into the strangest of Imperial wars, fought not for Britain but for her fellow colonial powers.

The Dutch East Indies created the worst problems. Here an ill-organized Communist uprising in 1926–7 had given the Netherlands the excuse to stifle all political activity. Political life was resuscitated under Japanese direction during the occupation, so that on 18 August 1945 an Indonesian Republic was declared under President Sukarno. Two weeks later, Anglo-Indian forces disembarked at Batavia with orders to keep the peace until Dutch contingents, then at sea, arrived, and to rescue Allied POWs who with Dutch and Eurasian internees, were still held in Japanese concentration camps. When the first British and Indian soldiers came ashore they were faced with republican, anti-Dutch graffiti daubed on walls, and hordes of local nationalists, many armed with captured Japanese weapons.

South-East Asia Command was in a tricky position since official British policy backed the reimposition of Dutch colonial rule, which the Indonesians almost universally rejected. In fact, during the war the Dutch Government in exile had broadcast an undertaking that Indonesia should become independent when the Japanese had been defeated. The Dutch now wanted their empire back, and insisted that British officers disregard Sukarno and his ministers, whom they considered to be collaborators, and temporarily occupy the territory to prepare the way for reimposition of the old regime, regardless of the wishes of the local population. This was nothing more than bluster; the Dutch had fewer than 2,000 fighting men in the Indies and substantial reinforcements did not appear until the early spring of 1946. By this time the Anglo-Indian contingent had spent six months fighting against the nationalists who had come to see them as catspaws of Dutch Imperialism.

British forces did their duty gallantly in a war which was not of their making. A summary of morale among men of the 1st Seaforth Highlanders, who were stationed at Bandung in April 1946, suggested that many soldiers considered the Dutch churlish ingrates. 'The general attitude towards the Dutch is not one of great friendliness. This may be due partly to a lack of understanding of what the majority of Dutchmen out here have been through during the last three years, but is greatly influenced by the often rude and hostile attitude of the Dutch themselves'. Evidence for this was plentiful. Highlanders were told that they were a 'nuisance', that Britain wanted the Netherlands Indies for itself, and one group was ordered out of a cafe by a party of Dutch *colons*. It was hardly surprising that most of the Scotsmen held the view 'that we shouldn't be doing the dirty work of the Dutch'. Several months of doing this 'dirty work', even for mannerless Dutchmen, had expunged the sympathies which the Seaforths had had for the local nationalists and nearly all the men of the battalion were keen 'to have a "go" at any armed Indonesians'. For the Indonesians, their sometime liberators had become an army of occupation, keeping the bed warm for troops from a colonial power which, ironically, had itself not long been liberated from German rule. Still, a nationalist propaganda leaflet, discovered close to the Seaforth's lines in March 1946, claimed that the Indonesians had no quarrel with Britain, which was true, and that their real foes were the Dutch. For men under intermittent mortar and sniper fire, this knowledge could have been of little comfort.

During the first days of the Anglo-Indian occupation of Batavia, local commanders had had no choice but to do business with the local nationalists, who were, after all, in possession of the town, and with some authority over their followers. By late October, relations between the British and the nationalists were breaking down. The insolence of the local Dutch added to the tension and efforts by patrols to uncover arms dumps and disarm nationalists led to clashes. Civil order was precariously maintained within Batavia, but beyond the Indonesians were bracing themselves for a war of resistance.

Serious fighting broke out at Surabaya on 25 October. When the 4,000-

Wars of the Jungle: The Far East

strong 49th Brigade came ashore, they discovered that the former Dutch naval base was in the hands of local nationalists. Three days later there was a mass uprising in which the Indian troops, heavily outnumbered and scattered in isolated detachments, were beset from all sides. Savage street-fighting in which neither side gave quarter lasted for several days. On the night of 28–29 October, the Indonesians deployed captured Japanese light tanks and armoured cars, and a day later, the British responded by sending a squadron of Thunderbolts (specially fitted with long-range fuel tanks) to overfly Surabaya. The insurgents were not cowed, for four of the machines were hit by rifle fire. The treacherous assassination of the local commander, Brigadier Mallaby, during cease-fire talks, was the final straw. His superior, General Alexander Christison, had run out of patience. On 30 October he broadcast a warning to the Surabayans:

> I intend to bring the whole weight of my sea, land and air forces and all the weapons of modern war against them until they are crushed. If in this process innocent Indonesians are killed and wounded, the sole responsibility will rest with those Indonesians who have committed the crime [Mallaby's murder][2]

Shelling began on 10 November and during the next two weeks ground forces penetrated the town and overcame resistance. Losses were heavy with over 220 Anglo-Indian troops killed or missing, more than half the casualties for the entire campaign.

Stubborn resistance was met in other parts of Java. On 31 October, Thunderbolts went into action to help an isolated Ghurka unit at Maglang, and later they were used, in conjunction with artillery, to dislodge nationalists from Abbarawa gaol. At Semarang, where 130 Japanese POWs had been massacred in the local prison, forces sent inland to rescue internees found themselves and their charges under frequent vengeful attacks. The local commander, Brigadier Bethell, had to call up assistance from the heavy cruiser *Sussex*, which had steamed up the coast from Surabaya. On 25 and 27 November, her 8" guns fired over 100 rounds against targets ten miles inland.

In the midst of the struggle to keep the upper hand, forces in Java had to do their best to find, rescue, and care for the thousands of European and Eurasians who had been held in Japanese camps. They were commonly the objects of fierce nationalist hatred and their guards had to fight off attacks from vengeful mobs. Racial antagonisms were unleashed against the Chinese community. During fighting for control of Bandung in March 1946, a British officer noted that the Indonesians 'were pretty ruthless to the Chinese, burning their homes and in some cases the people inside, or shooting them as they came out'.[3] Many of the defenders of Bandung were 14-year-olds, whose fanaticism, like that of other young nationalists, was officially put down to the effectiveness of earlier Japanese indoctrination and training. The 'unexpected sense of discipline and control' shown by nationalist forces had taken some British commanders by surprise. There were plenty of former Japanese servicemen available to instruct the Indonesians, especially around Bandung, where they also fomented anti-British sentiments amongst the local Chinese. Japanese POWs in British hands had been drawn into the war from the start for they provided a useful source of labour; in February 1946 over 4,000 of them were repairing roads around Batavia. Some of these men still wanted to fight the British and deserted to the rebels, including some officers and NCOs who were reported to be training Indonesians in Bandung during March 1946. One, a sergeant major, was shot dead while commanding a nationalist demolition gang.

Pan-Asian political ideas may have moved many Japanese to fight alongside the Indonesians. The Indonesians themselves made direct appeals to Indian soldiers who made up a substantial part of the British forces. They were appealed to on religious grounds, since many were Muslims like the Javanese, and as Asians, called upon to fight an imperialist war on behalf of Europeans. Information about this kind of subversion was provided by a Ghurka deserter who had fled to the nationalists in Bandung. He was asked to return to his lines and persuade others to desert, but thought better of it and rejoined his unit. Nationalists inside India felt strongly about Britain's use of Indian forces to suppress another Asian nationalist movement and this led to protests. It was the last time that Indians were ordered to fight for Britain, even though the objective of the campaign was the preservation of the Dutch rather than the British Empire.

By the spring of 1946, the British forces in Java had fulfilled their Government's obligation to the Dutch. Major centres were occupied by forces which maintained patrols, searches for arms and shows of force, although control over the countryside was precarious. The last detachments of this army had left Java by November, leaving the reinforced Dutch to continue the war Dutch mulishness, which had been responsible for the war, lasted until 1949, when the strain of holding down the Indonesians proved too much. A compromise was agreed and in the following year, Indonesia became independent.

Like the Dutch, the recently liberated French were keen to get back their old possessions. The retrieval of Indo-China depended upon the goodwill of the Americans who also had to take into account the ambitions of the Chinese nationalists. De Gaulle badgered the Americans for the recognition of what he regarded as France's historic rights in Indo-China and after threats that France, if denied, might slip into the Communist orbit, was given a free hand. British forces, under South-East Asia Command, were already on the spot in Saigon by September 1945, and Britain had no intention of ditching her former ally. With an eye to future French friendship, the British Government approved the suppression of local nationalists opposed to the revival of French Imperial government. To assuage doubts in Britain, the Foreign Secretary,

Ernest Bevin, assured the House of Commons that France was pledged to offer a 'wide measure of autonomy' to her Indo-Chinese subjects.

The small British mission which reached Saigon at the end of August, found the city, like the rest of the country, in a muddle. From mid-1941 to March 1945, the pro-Vichy colonial administration in Indo-China had worked hand-in-hand with the Japanese, who abruptly terminated the unequal partnership by taking direct control through a puppet Emperor. This regime crumbled after Japan surrendered, leaving the way open for a nationalist *coup*. In the northern part of the country, Ho Chi Minh's Communist Viet Minh movement seized power whilst in Saigon his followers joined the local Annamite nationalists and declared independence. Neither government was acknowledged by Major-General Gracey, the local British commander, who, with his staff, refused to have anything to do with the nationalists who were written off as 'quislings' or collaborators.

Gracey's mission was substantially reinforced by the 26th Indian Division which occupied Saigon and its hinterland in readiness for the arrival of large French forces. The maintenance of civil order rested in the hands of a ragbag British army which included Indians, rearmed French POWs, and men from the former Japanese garrison. Gracey had ordered Japanese troops to hold on to their arms and be prepared to handle any trouble from the Annamites. If any Japanese soldier had doubts about where his duties lay, they were swept away by his Commander in Chief, Field Marshal Count Terauchi, who warned that anyone who refused to fight for the British would be branded a traitor to his Emperor. Not that many had second thoughts; one Japanese officer led his men in a surprise raid on the Annamite HQ outside Saigon and killed 10 nationalists. Conduct of this kind won the approval of British HQ, which, at the end of the campaign, praised the valour and resourcefulness of the Japanese.

Not everyone was so delighted. The Chinese nationalists officially complained to Mountbatten in October 1945, and General MacArthur was incensed. 'If there is anything that makes my blood boil', he exclaimed, 'it is to see our allies in Indochina and Java employing Japanese troops to reconquer the little people we promised to liberate'. It was too late for protests, at least for the 'little people' of Saigon. On 23 September, Gracey's polyglot forces had thrown their weight behind a French *coup de main* in Saigon which toppled the nationalist government. Fighting went on for a week, but the nationalists were unable to retake the city. More and more French troops disembarked and by the end of October were engaging the nationalists with armoured cars and tanks. The outcome was no longer in doubt even though SEAC's assessment of the situation was pessimistic. 'The first taste of modern warfare, having proved discouraging to the Annamites, they may well intend to avoid open fighting and fall back on guerrilla warfare', was the prophetic summary of operations during October. Just before they finally withdrew from Saigon, the British contingent had its first taste of the kind of warfare which would bedevil Indo-

China for the next thirty years. However, they had done their job and helped the French back into the saddle.

The two wars fought in Java and Indo-China during 1945 and 1946 were amongst the strangest undertaken by British forces. They entered both countries as liberators, but with orders to bring back discredited and detested regimes. Yet the alternative to the revival of Dutch and French colonial governments appeared at the time to be disruption and in its wake, the spread of Communism, a phenomenon which was already ringing alarm bells in Washington. So, for the time being, the old order in South-East Asia was brought out of mothballs. In the long term, Britain and the United States hoped that stable colonial government would provide the period of tranquillity during which its peoples could be prepared for responsible government with power in the hands of rulers who could be trusted.

Tuans and Terrorists: The Malayan Campaign, 1948–60

The return of the British to Malaya was a straightforward affair for there was no tradition of organized opposition to colonial rule. The Japanese occupation had been accepted by the native Malays, who made up just over half of the country's five million inhabitants. The other big racial group, the immigrant Chinese, were less tolerant of Japanese rule and had been persecuted accordingly. They provided the rank-and-file of the anti-Japanese resistance which coalesced around the pre-war Malayan Communist Party. This largely Chinese party gave up its internal wranglings after Hitler's invasion of Russia and threw in its lot with the colonial government. Members took courses with Colonel Spencer-Chapman's jungle warfare training school and just before the fall of Singapore, many slipped into the jungle in readiness for the underground war against the Japanese.

Over ten years of clandestine activities against the British had given the Malayan Communists the experience and organization needed to wage a guerrilla war. Limited supplies of arms and some training were offered by the British through the Special Operations Executive, although until the closing stages of the war, the guerrillas were more-or-less on their own. In three years they learned the arcane skills of concealment and jungle fighting and created an underground network, the Anti-Japanese Union, in the towns and countryside. A few months before Japan surrendered, Malaya came within flying range of British aircraft based in Burma, which enabled a body of British officers to be dropped into the jungle to guide the guerrillas. Rearmed and with British liaison officers, the Communist fighters proved a valuable asset when the time came for liberation, particularly in the detection of jungle POW camps, many of which were unknown to the British army.

Peace meant that the Communist army had to be disbanded. Chin Peng, the future Secretary-General of the Malayan Communist Party, who had been, according to Spencer-Chapman, 'Britain's most trusted guerrilla', was given an OBE. His brothers-in-arms each got a £45 bounty, considered by some to be derisory, surrendered their arms, and returned to everyday life. Former connections were not broken, and in the postwar years the guerrillas banded together into Old Comrades Associations. This apparent disbandment of the underground network was, in the circumstances, quite remarkable, given that elsewhere in South-East Asia anti-Japanese forces turned their guns against the returning colonial armies. Some Malayan Communists sensed later that they had missed a chance in 1945 to put themselves forward as a patriotic nationalist front ready to take power from the discredited colonial regime the moment it reappeared.

Even though the Malayan Communist Party (MCP) was not thinking in terms of an armed struggle in August 1945, many ex-guerrillas chose to stay in the jungle and support themselves as they had for the past three years. Their survival there depended heavily on the goodwill of the scattered communities of Chinese squatters and the inertia of the colonial authorities. Pre-war slump and wartime dislocation had pushed half-a-million jobless Chinese into the fringes of the jungle, where they had cleared land, built hutments, and begun subsistence farming. The official position of the Chinese in Malaya had always been marginal ever since they had first been welcomed as migrant workers during the tin and rubber booms. They were liable to deportation on the slightest pretext and as squatters they frequently came up against the local police, whose efforts to control them led to violence.

Chinese alienation was soon obvious once Imperial government had been restored in 1945. Rice shortages led to looting by armed bands which also attacked Malay policemen, tainted with collaboration. A mob of 5,000 Chinese atacked the British officers' residence at Sungei Siput on 21 October 1945 and were dispersed by firing. There were further attacks on British forces at Ipoh where three rioters were shot dead.[3] Early in 1946, Major Marshall, the Forestry Officer in Perak state, found that the Chinese squatters 'were and still are "anti" army control or restriction of their rights to make the best they can for themselves'. He predicted that they would make natural allies for the Communists with whom they already had close links. Marshall also came across repeated acts of defiance, including the murders of Malay forestry officials, which were symptomatic of the violence endemic throughout Malaya in the years immediately after the reintroduction of British rule. The sporadic disorders between 1945 and 1948 were unco-ordinated which made it simple for the colonial authorities to dismiss them as just 'banditry', that convenient word with which officials glossed over lawlessness in areas where their writ failed to run unchallenged. Whether in fact the restored government of Malaya was ever in full control of the colony during these years is open to question. The debacle of 1942 had undermined the British and their administration and wartime losses deprived the Government of experienced men, leaving postwar Malaya with more than its normal share of novices in the police and government departments. Acute racial divisions, the alienation of a segment of the

Chinese population, disruption, banditry and an inexperienced administration were all grist to the Communists' mill.

Much of the post-war 'banditry' which the British had to face had its roots in the war. There was a good deal of settling old scores against collaborators in which Communist former guerrillas played a major part. During 1945–6, Perak experienced a small-scale civil war in which collaborators, often Malays, were identified and murdered. Official policy in this complicated area was to bring to justice those whose collaboration involved torture and killing and leave minor offenders alone. This was not satisfactory to the Chinese, who had suffered most at the hands of the Japanese, and the underground in particular. The 'terror' of this time not only indicated the weakness of government control; it served as a prelude for the campaign of intimidation waged by the Communists after 1948. Memories of the death squads of 1945–6 must still have been fresh two or three years later, and served to remind the faltering of just how far the Communists would go to enforce co-operation.

Communist policy during this period was indecisive. Allowed to flourish openly, the MCP turned to the subversion of the colony's trade unions. It was successful, for just before the declaration of the emergency, military intelligence believed that 65–75% of organized labour was under MCP control. Through the unions, the Communists fomented unrest and disruption which led to a rash of strikes during 1947 and 1948. In a sense, the Communists were engaging the Government on its own ground, for the code of colonial law contained plenty of regulations against trade unions and strikes. Countermeasures such as deportation of Chinese back to China and the arrest of strike leaders, together with the adequacy of the security forces, gave the Government the upper hand. Moreover the MCP and its union adherents were hindered by the old bugbear of a limited racial appeal. Relying heavily on Chinese support, the Communists made little headway with the Malays and the Indians.

Between March and June 1948 the Malayan Communist Party met in two plenary sessions and examined critically its past and future plans. The outcome was an appeal for an 'armed struggle' which in effect was a declaration of war on the British authorities and their supporters. The efforts of the past two-and-a-half years had not borne much fruit, and isolated attacks on white rubber planters during 1947 suggest that some groups within the party were turning to the 'armed struggle' in frustration. Malayan Communist representatives had attended a South-East Asia Communist Conference at Calcutta at the end of 1947 (it masqueraded as an 'International Youth' gathering) where there was some nudging towards the opening of armed fronts by the Russian delegate. Obviously the opening of a war for control of Malaya was attractive in terms of global strategy, given the importance of Malayan rubber, but then and later there was no hard evidence that the MCP was waging a struggle for Moscow as part of a world-wide effort to injure the West.

When it issued a declaration of war through *Min Sheng Pao*, the party's

Wars of the Jungle: The Far East

journal, on 15 June 1948, the MCP justified itself in defensive terms tied to local conditions.[4]

> Imperialism declared trade unionism to be illegal . . . Imperialism wants to arrest the leaders of the workers and the responsible members of the people's organizations. . . . Imperialism orders its running dogs and their followers to oppress us: then we will use the same methods against them. All in all, for the sake of our lives, we cannot procrastinate any more . . . Today the British Imperialists' cruel fascist countenance has been completely exposed. Imperialism is fascism and their violence and outrages are the same as those of the Japanese. The people of Malaya can never forget the bloody role of the Japanese fascists. At the same time they will remember the methods used against the fascists.

Three years after the 'liberation' by the British army, the Malayan Communists had taken on themselves the patriotic, nationalist mantle and, wearing it, claimed to speak for all the Malayan people. At the same time they admitted that the pressure from the colonial Government had become unbearable; in other words, the authorities were in the process of checkmating them and their 'open' campaign. The armed struggle proposed by the Party's Central Committee was naturally presented as a defensive war. The circumstances of 1948 suggest that this was not just propaganda rhetoric.

If in political terms, the Communist campaign was defensive, its military strategy was offensive. 'Reactionary village chiefs, corrupt officials, running dogs, local bullies (including reactionary gangsters) in rural areas' were in the firing line from small parties of guerrillas. The overall strategy, conceived by Chin Peng, the Party Secretary-General, was to sabotage the economy, drive out the Europeans who directed it, and disrupt the administration by the murder of its officials and their supporters. In the wake of this campaign, areas of the country would become unmanageable as the Government withdrew. The Communists would then step into the vacuum and establish an alternative government in the 'liberated' areas. The Communist areas would become the springboards for guerrilla campaigns designed to deal the final blows to the tottering administration and take over the urban centres. This pattern of rural revolution derived from Mao Tse-tung and for its success demanded mass following for the revolutionaries, who would emerge as a credible government long before that of the British had withered away. It was a flawed plan which ignored too many realities, underestimated the response of the British, and was over-confident about the creation of a mass following. From the start, the MCP could not have won, even though it possessed the ability to fight with determination to the point where its adversaries began to think that they could not win outright.

As the Communists admitted at the start, victory would depend upon which way the masses jumped. This was not only so in the long term, but also in the immediate future, for the units of the MCP guerrilla army (the *Lau Tong Tui*) depended upon the sympathies and assistance of large numbers of the population, both Chinese and Malay. As the war progressed, Government intelligence assessed the total active support for the Communist guerrilla groups at between 50,000–60,000. Nearly all were Chinese, either squatters on the periphery of the jungle or the inhabitants of the villages close to the rubber plantations and tin mines where most of the Chinese worked. These villages had between 500 and 2,000 inhabitants, of whom less than twenty might be Communists. They were members of the *Min Yuen*, the non-combatant, political organization without which the fighting units could not operate. In structure the *Min Yuen* was the successor to the wartime anti-Japanese front and its members' duties were much the same. They served as both the commissariat and intelligence network for the guerrillas which involved the extortion of money, collecting and delivering food, making uniforms, and obtaining information about the security forces, their plans and sympathizers. *Min Yuen* members were in frequent contact with bands of guerrillas on whose behalf they manipulated the local Chinese, often through terror. In Perak, early in 1950, a simple code had been worked out by which squatters alerted guerrillas to the activities of police and army patrols. Lights were turned off in the squatter settlement when the security forces came near at night; in daylight, their approach was signalled by a man making three strikes with his hoe, pausing and then making three more. Blankets laid out and a voice calling chickens to be fed indicated an ambush.[5]

Such stratagems assisted the guerrillas. In 1948 their strength was estimated at 4,000–5,000, of whom about two thirds were fighters and the rest undertook political and ancillary duties. They contained a powerful element which had fought against the Japanese, both guerrillas who had gone back to everyday life and those who had stayed in the jungle. Active service units were between five and 200-strong and the whole army was split into eight regional units, sometimes called 'regiments' by their adversaries. Each guerrilla was given 30 Malay dollars* a month and was subjected to a strict regime of discipline and political instruction. All units were mobile, moving between temporary camps, although there were larger bases deep in the jungle which served as headquarters and rest-camps where food was grown in plantations which had been specially laid out. Command flowed through an elaborate structure. At its apex was the Central Political Committee or Politburo and below was a chain of regional and district committees and finally the Party branches and field units. Messages and instructions passed by couriers who commonly followed routes first plotted in the war against the Japanese. Radio communication was impossible, for the fighting units possessed few sets and fewer spare parts. Very often it was difficult for orders to be passed quickly, the more so after the security forces stepped up the harassment of the *Min Yuen* and field support

* A Malay dollar was worth about fourteen pence.

groups. A Politburo directive of October 1951 only reached some units in the jungle five months later.

The fighting units moved in the jungle which covers four-fifths of Malaya. Their weaponry was limited to small arms and mortars, which had either come from the British during the war or had been left behind by the Japanese. Communist Chinese officers appeared in 1949 at the Politburo's meeting to suggest ways in which the guerrilla detachments could be reorganized, but there is little evidence that China supplied arms to the Malayan Communists. In terms of fighting, the guerrillas were tied to Mao's dictum which called for withdrawal when opposed, and this inevitably led to lost opportunities. In July 1948 a guerrilla force overran a police station at Batu Arang and began to sabotage the coal mine there. News that Government forces were coming made the guerrillas withdraw immediately, without even bothering to discover the size of the force that had been sent against them. This was a time when, in terms of numbers, the guerrillas had a brief parity with the security forces. It was never exploited, and so while service units were able to destroy police stations and occupy villages, they always withdrew at the first hint of a counter-attack.

Misfortune also dogged the guerrillas at the onset of their campaign for on 16 July, their overall commander, Lau Yew, was shot dead by the police who had discovered him after a tip-off from an informer. There were other disappointments during 1948, the chief being the fact that the assassinations of police, officials and European planters and engineers had not disrupted the administration or the economy as Chin Peng had anticipated. Indeed the campaign against the British planters, their plantations and the tin mines had flopped; the Malayan economy continued to function and actually prospered.

In terms of losses, the guerrillas paid a heavy price. In 1948 they lost 500 dead and in 1949 the number rose to 1,200. This wastage was made up with recruits from the *Min Yuen*, although as time went on their quality in terms of fervour and fighting skills deteriorated. The strengths of fighting units fell and it became impossible by 1952 to field detachments of more than twenty or thirty. The annual wastage in terms of casualties and deserters continued to increase so that by mid-1955 the guerrilla army stood at 3,000. Seven hundred were lost in that year alone and the shortfall could not be made up. In this war of numerical attrition, the Communists were ready to take big losses which, they hoped, would always be compensated for by recruits. But there was a corresponding weakening of the *Min Yuen*, due in large part to the Government's measures against it.

By the beginning of 1949 there were no 'liberated' areas, although the MCP would draw strength and encouragement from the news of the Chinese Communist successes against the *Kuomintang*. A Central Committee meeting, under Chin Peng's direction, drew up a political programme which promised an elected government for the future 'People's Democracy' and a parcel of welfare measures to attract the masses who had hitherto not been drawn into the Communists' camp. At the same time, the guerrillas were renamed the Malayan Races Liberation Army, a fiction since only one of the large regional units was Malay. A new name and a belated political manifesto could not offset the lack of success of the guerrillas' campaign. Efforts to create a 'liberated' area in the predominantly Malay state of Pahang failed because of local opposition. By the end of 1950 the Johore Communists were under growing pressure after their local support groups had crumbled away. The disruption of supplies, the erosion of the *Min Yuen* and the unending harassment of bases and field units all suggested that the 'armed struggle' was hopeless. In September 1951 the Central Committee was forced to reconsider its strategy, and agreed in a directive that in future the emphasis of the campaign would be shifted towards winning over the masses. Military action was to be limited to attacks on the security forces and officials which, it was hoped, would not imperil the rest of the community or disrupt its daily life.

After just over three years of guerrilla warfare, the Malayan Communists were still far from achieving their first objective. The change of policy owed much to the inherent weakness of their position in 1948. No areas of Malaya had passed into their control during the war and for many Malayans, both Malays and Chinese, the Communists offered little more than barbarous coercion; nearly all their victims were civilians and many were tortured and killed for failing to co-operate. The Communist political programme of social reform remained for most Malayans a distant prospect, at odds with the reality of the Communist campaign which brought death and hardship. Perhaps the greatest miscalculation of the Communist Central Committee had been its underestimation of the will and ability of the Government to fight not only the guerrillas, but their ideology. The problems which bedevilled the Politburo and its fighting detachments had, for the most part, been created by the government's counter-insurgency operations.

For the rulers of Malaya, the British public and those called upon to resist the Communists, the war was known as the 'Emergency'. This was announced by the High Commissioner, Sir Edward Gent, on 17–18 June 1948 after some days of consultations and official fumbling. Gent, according to his critics, had faltered when presented with evidence for an impending crisis. In fairness, whilst the information about future trouble was abundant and well known to military and police intelligence, it contained little precise detail about the nature of the Communist plans. Given that the Communists themselves were not entirely clear about their tactics, this was not surprising. Gent himself was not popular with the veteran officials, survivors from pre-war days who were always claiming an arcane knowledge of Malaya and its peoples' minds, based on the length of their service. *Tuans* (literally 'masters') of the European rubber planter and commercial community were also suspicious of Gent for, as a reformist, they thought he showed too much interest in and sympathy for the poorer, non-European classes.

The Malayan European plantocracy was to play an important part in the

Emergency. On one hand they were capable of an unpleasant arrogance which, in 1945, expressed itself in disdain for British soldiers serving in Malaya, and on the other, they were capable of fortitude and steadfastness. Their determination to remain on their rubber plantations and, when necessary, fight back upset the Communists' plans to dislocate the economy. Type and attitude can be summed up by the reaction of one, described by Noel Barber.[6]

'Puck' — an ex-RAF officer who had shot five elephants at Jenderak in a matter of months — loved the estate, which abounded in game. But he was determined to be 'British' with a capital 'B' and as the CTs [Communist terrorists] stepped up their attacks he decided it was time to show the flag — literally. Every evening at sundown he lined up his squad of home-trained guards beside the flagstaff. Ceremoniously, the Union Jack was hauled down for the night while 'Puck' blew his own home-made trumpet.

Men of this sort were in the front line and from the early days pressed for stern measures and the means to fight back. 'Govern or Get Out' was the headline of the *Straits Times*'s warning to the High Commissioner on 17 June 1948. Under pressure from Malcolm MacDonald, the Commissioner-General for South-East Asia, Gent agreed to the imposition of a State of Emergency. Shortly afterwards, he was killed in an air crash.

Gent had armed the Malayan authorities with a powerful range of weapons with which to combat the guerrillas. The regulations insisted that all Malayans over twelve years of age possessed identity cards with fingerprints and photographs; detention for two years without trial was permitted and the local authorities could restrict civilian movement and impose curfews. Persons and property could be searched at will, and anyone found with guns or ammunition was liable to execution. At a local level, this coercive machinery could make life uncomfortable, even intolerable, for communities suspected of helping the Communists. After a long sequence of murder and sabotage in the region, the village of Tanjong Malim suffered what amounted to proscription during March 1952. The High Commissioner, General Templer, called the villagers together and recited the many outrages committed locally over the past months. 'None of this would have happened if the inhabitants of this part of the country had had any courage', he observed. 'You want everything done for you but you are not prepared to assume the responsibility of citizenship. I want law and order, so that I can get on with many things which are good for this country'. Having shown the carrot, he then wielded the stick and the village lost its status as a provincial capital: it was placed under a 22-hour curfew, the school was closed, the rice ration halved, and the inhabitants were not allowed to travel. The people of Tanjong Malim were allowed to expiate their sins by secretly submitting written evidence of Communist activities and revealing names of Communist sympathizers and activists; many did so. Forty suspects were detained. Templer was pleased and used the incident as an example with which to warn other recalcitrant areas.[7]

Templer had served in Palestine in 1936 where he had no doubt seen similar procedures during the Arab revolt. Other older precedents were introduced to Malaya, including the burning down of houses of men known to have helped the rebels. At Kachau in Selangor in November 1948 matters got out of hand when the flames from one miscreant's house set the whole village on fire. The inhabitants were known to have supported the Communists (they had played an important part in anti-Japanese resistance) and a local staff officer later commented: 'This hard blow has had a most determined effect on this area and is generally felt by the lower classes up there to be a lesson for their disinclination to help the government'.[8]

Such actions were designed to make Malayans more scared of the Government than the Communists, but matching one kind of fear by another was not enough although there were some who thought that it might win the war. A confidential police report from Perak described the attitude of one newly-arrived officer who was prepared to use 'fire and slaughter' to settle the trouble. 'He has been in India and assumes that Chinese react in a similar way to the Indian'.[9] Such attitudes did exist, but they never came to dominate military thinking.

During and after the war, the struggle against the Malayan Communists was described as a contest for 'the hearts and minds' of the local population. This of course did not exclude coercive measures, which were readily available throughout the campaign, but it did characterize the policy evolved from autumn 1948 onwards. In essence military and political objectives were merged to secure a victory which would combine the defeat of the guerrillas and independence for the people of Malaya. The architects of this policy were Sir Henry Gurney (High Commissioner from September 1948 until his assassination three years later), Lieutenant General Sir Harold Briggs (Director of Operations from April 1950) and General Sir Gerald Templar, his successor from February 1952 and also High Commissioner. Each realized that the British were fighting a political as well as a military campaign in which it was vital to enlist the goodwill and co-operation of the great majority of Malayans.

Most important of all was the need to gain the support and help of the Chinese community which had hitherto been either wavering or in the Communist camp. At first the authorities turned to the old device of deportation and, in 1949, 10,000 Chinese, most of them first generation immigrants, were shipped back to China. Ths policy became unworkable by the end of that year after the compliant Nationalist government of Chiang Kai-shek was ousted by Mao's Communists. Deportation was ruled out because the new regime would not co-operate, and the government, therefore, had to come to terms with the fact that in future the Chinese would remain a part of the Malayan population. Not only would the Chinese population have to stay, but demographic changes meant that it would increase in numbers. As matters stood, a large number of the Chinese remained outside Malayan society and doubtful of the government's ability to overcome the Communists. A tin miner in Perak spoke for many when he remarked, in February 1950:[10]

> The government is getting weaker and weaker — Communism, which is to liberate us all, is triumphant in China and will shortly be the same in Siam and then here. Russia has the biggest and best bomb. The government is terrified and has recognized Communism in China.

The last comment referred to the recent official recognition of the Communist government in China. This gesture by a British Labour Government enraged the planters, who never cared for the Socialists and saw this as the first step towards betrayal.

As an alternative to deportation, the state government of Perak had introduced a scheme for the resettlement of Chinese squatters in October 1948. It had initially been dismissed by the Federal authorities and the GOC Singapore predicted that the new villages for the ex-squatters would become hotbeds of sedition. Gurney and later Briggs were impressed, and, at their direction, the scheme was extended to the whole of Malaya in June 1950. There were many problems. First, land had to be obtained, which meant that Gurney had to approach the Malay Sultans for their co-operation. This involved more than just selling off suitable agricultural land; it meant obtaining Malay acquiescence to a programme which would integrate the Chinese as equal citizens in the future Malayan nation. Something along these lines had been put forward in 1946, but had been opposed by the Malayan Union, a political organization of Malays who were unwilling to extend the suffrage to Chinese. In 1949-50 circumstances had changed, and the Malay Sultans agreed to the scheme which was better than leaving nearly half the country's population alienated and therefore recruiting material for the Communists.

The resettlement scheme was masterminded by Briggs, a veteran of the Burma jungle war, whom a visiting American officer found to be 'a real individualist, a man of bold and unorthodox military thinking'. His ideas were indeed bold, but they were carefully contrived as a means of cutting off the guerrillas from their potentially most valuable supporters, the marginal squatter communities which had hitherto been all but impossible to control. Mass resettlement as a method of severing guerrillas from their supporters was not a novelty though; it had been used by Lord Kitchener in South Africa in 1900, and in another brutal form by Graziani in Libya in the 1930s. In both cases the results were a crop of mass prison camps. What was new about the Malayan 'new villages' was that they were purpose-built communities where the inhabitants could be supervised as they started fresh lives. Each family was given land on which to grow crops and graze pigs, accommodation and cash, and there were schools and clinics to help them adjust to their new lives. In time, the resettled Chinese were officially encouraged to elect their own councillors and take a hand in running their own affairs.

At the time the resettlement programme started, the war in Malaya had been going badly for the Government. The monthly death tolls for civilians and police during 1949 had been about 200; Communist losses were about 100 a month and the flow of new recruits appeared promising. As yet there were no 'liberated' areas but the guerrillas were finding it easy to frighten the population. Outwardly it appeared the Government was no longer able to protect its subjects who were left with no choice but to work with the Communists and their forces. Briggs intended to reverse this process and by so doing demonstrate clearly that the British Government did not intend to abandon the Malayans. At the same time a blow would be struck at the *Min Yuen* which would no longer be able to flourish undetected.

The mechanics of uprooting the squatters were simple. A cordon of British troops was thrown around a selected area at dawn and soldiers, with police and civilian officials, closed in. A truck would be allocated to each Chinese family who were told to gather up their possessions and permitted livestock and be ready to be driven to the new village. The process was distressing and, for those involved, sometimes distasteful but the soldiers behaved with even-handedness and good humour. In their new villages, the Chinese would be surrounded by barbed wire perimeter fencing (later changed to the less emotive chain-link fencing) and were subject to close, official supervision. Resettlement did not always mean a break with old ways and the Communists were anxious not only to keep open old supply channels, but to obstruct as far as possible the development of the new communities. Men and women passing to and from the villages were searched for food and spare clothing, and strict controls were placed on the sale and cooking of rice. Smuggling continued; amongst the receptacles for contraband rice were brassières, buckets of pig-swill, bicycle frames and bicycle pumps. Yet the scheme was soon showing signs of success, closing down many old links between the squatters and the Communists, and forcing the guerrillas to seek ways of becoming self-sufficient.

The wider purpose of the resettlement plan was to bring the Chinese more closely into the Malayan community, to change them from immigrants living on the margins of society into citizens with a stake in a new state. The future of that state had already been outlined by Attlee in 1950 when he anticipated Malayan independence within the Commonwealth. A time-limit had been set to British rule, and it was Templer's duty to supervise the timetable. His predecessor, Gurney, had intended to hold local government elections by 1952, state government elections by 1954 and national elections by 1955. Templer kept to this schedule which was completed in 1957 when total independence was achieved. As Malaya proceeded along this path the Communists, their party illegal and at war with the Government, were isolated from political life. Moreover, they could no longer claim to be fighting against 'imperialism' on behalf of the people, who were being encouraged to look elsewhere for their political future. One feature of this political change was the emergence of the Malayan Chinese Association which gained 100,000 members and received powerful backing from the local Chinese business community.

By the end of 1952, 462,000 Chinese squatters had been transferred to over 500 new villages at a cost of £11 million, leaving a further 100,000 still living on the fringes of the jungle. The upheaval had been considerable and had only been possible because of the solvency of the Malayan government. When the Communist insurgency started, Malaya was on the verge of a period of unprecedented boom. The Cold War between the West and the Soviet Union was at its height and the outbreak of the Korean War in 1950 forced the American Government to concentrate on stockpiling raw material. The price of rubber jumped from £578 a ton to £1,200 and production soared to 700,000 tons in 1950. The tin trade also prospered, for the Communists made no very serious attempts to hinder mining; there were, in fact, less than 100 attacks on the colony's 700 mines. During the 1950s Malaya's Gross National Product rose annually some 3%–4%, enabling the authorities to foot the bill for many of the war's costs, including the resettlement scheme. In 1948 the war was costing Malaya 14 million dollars, a charge which rose to over 250 million within five years; for its part, Britain settled the accounts for its own forces and their equipment which averaged £500 million a year.

Malaya was worth fighting for and its wealth made possible the ambitious schemes designed to convince its population that their future lay in a plural, self-governing nation. The policy was successful in that the Malayan Communist Party never emerged as a mass movement. Indeed after 1951, its fighting units were more and more isolated and thrown on to the defensive.

The Government's campaign to separate the guerrillas from those sections of the Chinese community on which they relied and at the same time convince that community that its future lay in a self-governing Malaya was vital for the defeat of the insurgents. This was not, however, enough — the guerrillas had to be eliminated. To do this, the civil and military authorities had to mobilize and augment the police, create local volunteer units, and call upon the help of regular British and Commonwealth forces.

In 1948 the regular Malayan Police Force comprised 10,000 men under a cadre of officers most of whom had enrolled after 1945. At the onset of the Emergency auxiliaries were enlisted, mostly from the Malay population. After six months these totalled 12,000, and by 1951 there were 100,000. With the creation of the 'new' villages, a force of Chinese Home Guard was raised who, with Templer's encouragement, were armed. British forces, at first thought sufficient to crush the uprising, were also reinforced so that in 1952 they numbered 35,000, of whom 10,000 were Ghurkas. Commonwealth and Imperial troops were drafted in, 15,000 in all, including seven battalions of the Malay Regiment, Fijians, King's African Rifles, trackers from Borneo and Sarawak, and units from Australia and New Zealand. By the time the tide turned against them, the guerrillas were outnumbered 30 to 1 by over 150,000 men.

Command over this growing army rested with the Police Commissioner, Colonel Nicol Gray, a former commando who had served with the Palestinian Police. His first task was to augment the regular Police force which he did by bringing in former Palestinian colleagues and later men from the old Shanghai Police Contingent, whose duties had been terminated by the Communist victory in 1949. The newcomers were not welcomed and feeling against them was sharpened by resentment against Gray's open preferment of former Palestine men. Gray's judgement was sometimes flawed. He urged aggressive tactics on his men, but early attempts to penetrate the jungle and engage the guerrillas were often disappointing. One reason was Gray's disdain for the widespread use of armoured vehicles which he believed would encourage his men to stay on the defensive. This was dangerous nonsense leading directly to the deaths of sixteen policemen travelling in unarmoured vehicles, who were ambushed near Helebu in December 1949. Fortunately, the guerrillas did not often ambush convoys, but when they did, they sometimes used techniques learned from British instructors at the end of the war which involved setting a separate ambuscade to trap relief forces.

Misfortunes like this added to Gray's unpopularity and impaired police morale. Briggs was unhappy about Gray's methods and his advice, together with the evidence of mismanagement he discovered during his visit to Malaya in November 1951, convinced the Colonial Secretary, Oliver Lyttelton, to dismiss Gray. He also removed the head of police intelligence which was inadequate and mishandled. Gray's successor, Colonel A. E. Young, who had been Commissioner for Police for the City of London, immediately reversed Gray's policies. The police were re-armed, supplied with over 800 armoured vehicles and instructed to regard themselves as essentially a civilian rather than a military force.

Lyttleton's descent on Malaya came at a difficult time, soon after Gurney's death and Briggs's departure. In spite of their joint efforts, Lyttleton found much evidence of inertia and moribund administration which led to a minor purge of the Government. He recognized that the dual functions of Director of Operations and High Commissioner needed to be merged. General Sir Gerald Templer was the man, who, with Churchill's approval, was given the task of directing the war effort and conducting Malaya towards self-government and self-reliance. The appointment was resented in some quarters; MacDonald, a casualty of the purge, grumbled about a military dictatorship and this view was echoed both in Britain and Malaya.

When he left Malaya in 1954, Templer had come to be regarded as the man who had won the war and beaten the Communists, and like all architects of victory he was honoured accordingly. In fact he inherited a favourable situation. The gloom and demoralization which marked the interregnum after Gurney's death was deceptive. No one then knew that a deeper despair was infecting the Communists, who were coming to terms with failure and adjusting their plans. Briggs and Gurney had created a war machine which was basically sound and had laid the foundations of the policy which aimed towards self-government. This, in essence, was the policy which Templer would accelerate and bring to fruition. In 1950 Briggs had tackled the problem of diffuseness of command and pulled together the different agencies involved in operations by the creation of the equivalent of a national war Cabinet which met weekly to share ideas and shape strategy. This executive was copied at a state level and, in spite of all manner of hitches, managed to work well.

Templer's main task was to provide enthusiasm and generate motive power so that the machinery would work efficiently. He commenced by sweeping out those officials whose ossified Imperial ideas or incompetence would hinder his plans. The plantocracy and bureaucracy were slated for clinging to antique notions of racial superiority which effectively excluded non-whites from their clubs. (Such behaviour may have prompted Noel Coward's pre-war description of Malaya as 'a first-rate country for second-rate people'.) At times, planters were warned that niggardly wages would drive their workers towards the Communists. Templer was invariably brusque and sometimes testy. A redundant senior police officer of the old colonial species was told: 'you've been a difficult and awkward bugger, but you've been a man. Goodbye'.[11]

Templer worked with a small staff and was always on the move, meeting the men who were actually fighting the guerrillas and listening to what they had to say. They, after all, knew what their business was, as Templer said in his own justification. Always he was on the look-out for ways in which the war in the field could be waged more effectively, and at the same time, he was looking for means by which the Chinese could be drawn into the war and shown that it was being fought for their own best interests. His tours, inspections, exhortations and investigations were conducted with energy and zest. In many ways they resembled Montgomery's progresses around the 8th Army, and certainly their purpose was similar. Like Montgomery, Templer possessed the means to win; what he hoped to whip up was the will for victory.

When the campaign had begun in 1948, the successive army commanders, Major Generals Wade and Boucher, both underestimated their adversaries and overestimated the ability of their own forces to win swiftly. 'Just the job for the army' asserted Boucher, who was dismissive of any help from the police. 'A bunch of coppers . . . telling the Generals what to do' was out of the question.[12] His answer, between 1948 and 1950, was a series of ponderous operations in which large bodies of troops cordoned areas of jungle and closed in to trap guerrillas. Such plans were ambitious and owed much to previous experiences in the open country of the North-West Frontier and Palestine. In the rain forest the results of these manoeuvres were discouraging, at least in terms of casualties inflicted on the enemy. Still it was claimed, with some justification, that the larger concentrations of guerrillas were broken up, kept on the move, and sometimes driven into the deep jungle. They were by no means beaten, even though, in smaller parties, they had to seek less prestigious targets for attack. There were drawbacks for the Government for such massive concentrations of troops meant that some districts were stripped of forces, which was exactly what the Communists needed if they were to extend control over 'liberated' areas, This nearly happened in Pahang during October 1948.

Cordons were not abandoned by the security forces. In July 1954 a variation on the old procedure was tried when small SAS units were parachuted into the jungle where they lay low, watching. Bigger forces fanned and beat through the jungle in the hope that the guerrillas would be caught in ambushes as they moved along the tracks. Only fifteen were killed. Yet on another occasion a smaller cordon worked well. Four battalions of Gurkhas surrounded ten Chinese villages in November 1956 and the subsequent combing flushed out over 200 suspects, all of whom were detained. Given the nature of the jungle and the smallness of the guerrilla bands, grandiose operations were inevitably destined to yield small gains. Even if the guerrillas were unaware of the approaching sweep, they could sidestep the beaters with ease, for even the best trained men could not approach silently through the foliage. Experiences of this kind led to a new pattern of jungle operations where small patrols went in search of guerrillas and their camps.

Success in hunting guerrillas depended upon intelligence about their whereabouts and movements. Since 1951, there had been a directorate of intelligence which aimed to co-ordinate information from the police and service agencies. When he arrived Templer, realizing that intelligence was the key to victory, appointed a new director for gathering information, John Morton. Procedures were tightened, especially those for the assessment of intelligence and its dispersal.

Basic Special Branch intelligence came from local informers. All kinds of men and women offered information for a wide range of motives. Cash offers were made for the elimination of terrorists (a Communist Party district official was worth 4,000 dollars) and victims of the guerrillas were often glad to pay off old scores against their tormentors. There were ways of exerting pressure, particularly on those, willing and unwilling, who supplied the guerrillas with food and clothing. If apprehended, they could be offered the choice between arrest and imprisonment or turning informer. In return for revealing details which could lead to ambushes or the arrest of other sympathizers, these informers gained immunity from prosecution and even the wherewithal to start a new life in Thailand, Hong Kong or Sarawak. Propaganda was directed towards guerrillas in the jungle in the hope that they would surrender. Most of this type of persuasion was in the form of leaflets dropped by aircraft, the contents of which owed much to the experience gained in the psychological warfare campaign against Japanese forces in the Burmese jungle. The pitiable life of the lean, hungry guerrilla, vexed by leech and insect bites, was contrasted with that of the defector, now sleek and well-fed; some handbills portrayed a photograph of a defector with wife or girl friend. Like the Japanese

Wars of the Jungle: The Far East   **151**

warrior, the guerrilla was an enforced celibate, but this restriction did not extend to their leaders and these leaflets stirred up sexual jealousies by reminding the rank-and-file what they were missing. The Communist Party was worried about this sort of propaganda and one Politburo directive stated with wonderful pomposity, 'many of our comrades, not abiding by our organization discipline about love-making, are doing it without the knowledge of the Party. Such improper occurrences are frequent and must be corrected'. One Party commissar who was not moved by this command openly stated that 'the only way to liberate women is to loosen their trouser belts'. Artistic efforts by the propagandists luridly to illustrate this comment were banned.[13] The propaganda war was not always so light-hearted; guerrillas executed men who showed signs of wishing to give up and some defectors led troops back to their former comrades. Defectors helped in other ways; some made tape-recordings, exhorting others to follow their example, and these were broadcast over the jungle from low-flying aircraft — a technique first used in Iraq thirty years before.

About 50,000 leaflets were dropped for every guerrilla. The man who threw in the towel was always offered immunity from punishment, a favour which was constantly reiterated in all forms of propaganda. In retaliation, Communists warned that absconders would be tortured. They were not, and in many cases were very willing to offer information, sometimes out of private malice against their former comrades. Some were 'turned' and went back to the jungle to fight alongside the security forces. Small units of ex-guerrillas were formed under Major Kitson who had recently devised techniques for working with former Mau Mau guerrillas in Kenya.

The flow of information grew into a flood after 1952. Its increase was a sign that more and more Malayans were coming to appreciate that they could and would be protected by the Government and its forces. In safety they could tell what they knew, often with some relief, for the extirpation of local guerrilla bands often meant that the population was freed from the burden of exactions. In terms of fighting and killing guerrillas, the abundance of intelligence meant that patrols went about their business knowing where to look and sometimes for whom. From the first days of the war there had been no shortage of experienced jungle-fighters, men who had served in the three-year campaign in Burma. In a former lunatic asylum at Tampoi, a jungle training school was established through which new arrivals passed. In the early days one of the instructors, Lieutenant General Walker, helped to form small units of policemen, civilians and soldiers called 'Ferret' groups. Like their namesakes, these parties hunted down their quarry in its natural environment, the jungle.

The jungle patrol formed the basis of soldiering for the mass of the servicemen on active duty during the Malayan campaign. There was no exact pattern of individual experience for like so many other similar colonial campaigns in which small units worked alone, each operation was different. All who took part, fought in an environment which was unkind and unsuited to the support of human existence; bloodsuckers and insects plagued the body and clothing disintegrated quickly. The enemy was unseen and often very cunning in concealing himself. Looking for a member of a group of guerrillas one patrol moved through the undergrowth:[14]

> Shoulder to shoulder we moved forward. Carefully we swept the area — nothing. Not long after a *Min Yuen* member was captured or gave himself up. Yes, he had been in that grassy patch. We couldn't believe it. The jungle boot of one of our soldiers had stepped on his head.

Those involved believed that they were fighting for right against wrong, in so far as they had political views. Old traditions died hard and some senior officers discouraged an interest in the subject. One told a journalist, 'You see, my young officers don't know much about politics — no reason why they should — and if they tried to spout this stuff, some bright spark is sure to ask: "What about Syngman Rhee?" "Syngman Rhee", the men whisper, "Got him there" — and it's bad for discipline'. In Malaya, soldiers 'did not lose sight of the fact that they [the guerrillas] were human beings. Sometimes, as British soldiers do, they nicknamed their enemy "Gooks" or "Nignogs" or such like. In this case we sometimes called them "Jiggerboos" . . . Somehow it seemed less likely that one would be killed by "Jiggerboos breaking cover" than by Communist terrorists making a counter-attack'.[15] In official language the adversaries were CTs (Communist terrorists) or, devoid of any cause, just 'bandits'. Once this professional detachment appears to have vanished when twenty-five Chinese suspects were shot dead by a unit of the Scots Guards at Betang Kali. The shady circumstances came to light in February 1970 during the rumpus which followed revelations of a massacre of Vietnamese villages by an American unit whose commander, a conscript subaltern, was later court-martialled.* There are an 'awful lot of spectres in our cupboard' remarked George Brown, the Foreign Secretary, a mixed metaphor which led some of the soldiers present at Betang Kali to make a series of despositions for the *People* newspaper. In sum, these suggested that the official explanation of the killing as the consequence of an ambush and panic was inaccurate. The matter was looked into by the police who passed their dossier to the Director of Public Prosecutions, but the matter was subsequently dropped. Whatever the precise truth, the incident was exceptional.[16]

Engagements in the jungle were brief and sometimes confused. One, recalled by Major Gibb, may serve for many others, at least in some of its details.[17]

> I had just come from the demonstration platoon at a jungle warfare school. I followed the prescribed tactics exactly . . . First man in the patrol, a Chinese

---

* Lieutenant Calley: his death sentence was not confirmed by President Nixon.

guide — I never liked this idea and fought it unsuccessfully at the school. Next in the patrol our leading scout, another man with an automatic then me. Two other Chinese on this day were on my coat tails. We were on a track. I was wary, but not over-concerned. We had only been back a single day with the battalion and had entered the jungle on vague information. We had entered the jungle this morning only an hour ago. Contact didn't seem too probable, but you never know. We rounded a bend, so my platoon was L shaped on the ground. Then we walked head on into the opposition. Or rather my Chinese guide did. He gave a piercing yell, sprinted back along the track grabbing the rifle of my number two. He was followed by a hail of bandit fire; my two Chinese companions were loosing off their automatics in my ear. The tail end of my platoon was shooting us up the backside. I couldn't see anything. I couldn't hear much. I was deafened. I remember suddenly noticing the twigs over the head of my scout being knocked off closer and closer to his head. I fired straight along the line back at his unseen opponent. I could suddenly hear my opposite number yelling out his instructions in Chinese — I came to with a jolt. The jungle school said immediate charge. I didn't always follow the jungle school, but this time I did. It was no good, it was too late. The bandits scattered and bolted. One khaki hat with a Communist red star lay on the track amongst the spent cases of ammunition. I had failed. Never again did I have anyone but a good soldier in the lead.

Head-hunters from Borneo and Sarawak proved more adept at leading patrols and tracking their quarry. Later in the war, aborigines from the deep jungle were enlisted as auxiliaries and guides and were formed into a regiment which undertook some of the final operations against scattered bands of guerrillas on the Siamese border.

From the onset of the war, ground forces had been supported by aircraft. No doubt with his experiences of the coercive effect of air strikes and air control in Palestine, Police Commissioner Gray hoped to repeat the pattern in Malaya. So from 1948 onwards suspected camps were bombed and strafed with rockets. Between 1952 and 1953, 7,500 tons of bombs were dropped, but the results were hard to judge accurately. During the week beginning 27 January 1950 (at the end of the official 'Anti-Bandit Month') just over 100 sorties were flown by Spitfires, Tempests, Beaufighters, Brigands, Harvards and Dakotas, but the weekly RAF report indicated no definite casualties. There were also flights over jungle tracks 'to show the flag', and four Tempests enabled a patrol of Green Howards to withdraw from an ambush on 18 February 1950.[18] Close ground support like this could be a double-edged weapon when the men on foot lacked radio contact with the pilots, as Major Gibb recalled.[19]

From time to time we had air support. This was often rather dangerous and more than once we were caught in our own bombs. On one occasion a small group with their Company Commander moved into an exposed place in an open patch. There were five or six bombers with rockets. They thought this group was the enemy. I last saw them through a haze of exploding rice fields as the rockets struck. I thought they were all dead. They were only 50 yards in front of us as we lay at the edge of some young rubber trees. Furthermore they had the only wireless set. The planes turned on us. We had to retreat in extended line through the rubber. I called for each soldier to keep his five paces apart.

The string of men suffered some cannon and incendiary machine-gun fire, and in extremity, Gibb remembered that he had a Verey pistol with which he fired a warning flare. The spotter aircraft saw this and the attack was at once stopped. Amazingly, no one was killed or wounded.

Gibb concluded from this and other experiences that 'bombing was not very effective, but supply dropping was'. Like every other unit in the jungle, Gibb's force depended on supplies of food and clothing dropped by parachute. This vital assistance could be summoned up at twenty-four hours notice and made it possible for forces to operate deep into the interior of the rain forests. A novel form of aerial technology made its first appearance in Malaya in May 1950, the helicopter. These soon proved their value and became a mainstay of logistical support; in 1953, 14,000 helicopter airlifts occurred. The value of the helicopter was enormous for it overcame what had been the bugbear of colonial campaigns for over two hundred years. Helicopters moved troops swiftly to positions deep in remote and inhospitable country close to their enemies, which removed for ever the need for long, easily observed and debilitating cross-country marches. At the same time troops in inaccessible regions were not hampered by the need to carry supplies or attend the sick and wounded. Both were now handled by the ubiquitous helicopter.

The navy's part in the war was limited by its nature. Men-o'-war patrolled the Malayan coastline to ensure that no seaborne supplies reached the guerrillas. On one occasion in 1952, the frigate *Amethyst* steamed twenty miles up the Perak River to shell a guerrilla camp which had previously been pinpointed. An even more formidable bombardment of a camp was undertaken by the light cruiser *Newfoundland* using six-inch guns. As with bombing from the air shelling, to be effective, needed accurate identification of the target. Once an electronic homing device was left in a camp which was later attacked at night by aircraft guided by its signals.

Aerial photographs were vital for the discovery of camps and they also served as useful substitutes for maps in regions which had been ill-charted. Pictures taken from the air often showed the clearings made by guerrillas for the planting of crops. This self-sufficiency had been forced on them as a consequence of the displacement of the Chinese 'squatters' and of official measures to disrupt the flow of food supplies. At first the guerrilla cultivators had planted their crops in regular patterns, unlike the aborigines, and so they showed up clearly on photographs. The RAF was called upon to destroy the guerrillas' crops as part of the wider campaign to starve them out.

The means for this operation were readily available. Since 1944, when the British government had been toying with the sinister idea of using chemicals dropped from the air as a means of eliminating their enemy's agriculture, the official mind had turned to the employment of such weapons 'for the destruction of food supplies of dissident tribes in order to control an area'.[20] In Malaya, trichlorophenoxyacetic acid, also known as 245T, was sprayed from Sikorski helicopters and light aircraft on the guerrillas' crops. Participants in the war have remained rather shy about the results of this spraying, although one remarked that since the substance involved was just 'weedkiller', it only ruined leaves and not roots. Not that this mattered much for tomatoes, rice, maize, cucumbers and sugar were rendered uneatable. Herbicides were also used to strip jungle cover, but according to Richard Clutterbuck, its employment was confined to roadsides and the chemicals were sprayed by hand.[21]* Reticence about this feature of the war is understandable, given the shameful and sombre sequel to the experiment. The results of the crop destruction and defoliation were passed on to grateful US scientists who found them helpful in their own chemical warfare research. The outcome was a grotesque armoury of chemicals which were showered on the jungles of Vietnam during the 1960s. One of the most deadly, known as Agent Orange, contained 245T, which itself included tiny amounts of the virulently toxic dioxin. There were awful consequences of this saturation of the jungles which included miscarriages and horribly malformed children. Fortunately, perhaps, not much 245T was used in Malaya since the guerrillas quickly learned to disguise their plantations so that from the air they resembled those of the aborigines, and so were left untouched.

By the middle of 1953 the war in the jungle was clearly being won. There were still, however, 5,500 guerrillas still at large and fighting. Two years later there were less than 1,500, and in July 1960, when the Malayan Government proclaimed an end to the Emergency, the guerrilla army was believed to number no more than 500 dispirited men and women, lurking on the Thai border. In September 1955 an offer of an amnesty had been made which at first tempted only a few defectors. After Malayan independence in July 1957, the flow increased and included a number of high-ranking officials and group commanders. Surrender with the assurance of immunity from prosecution was increasingly more attractive than continued, futile resistance. The war was no longer against the Imperialists, for the instruments of colonial control had been removed, although the British political, commercial and military presence was still formidable. But in political terms, the proscribed Communist Party was isolated and therefore unable to play any part in Malayan life. Chin Peng vainly sought its readmission in December 1955 when he arranged negotiations with

---

* 245T destroys foliage and is toxic if consumed: its use in Britain is curtailed by the Ministry of Agriculture because of its cumulative effect. Its use in Malaya not surprisingly is rarely mentioned.

Tunku Abdul Rahman, the leader of the Malayan Alliance Party and the future Prime Minister. Chin Peng offered to dissolve his guerrilla army in return for legality and with it the right to join in political life. In effect he wanted to turn the clock back to June 1948, but memories of Communist activities in the three years before the start of the rebellion made Rahman cautious. He refused the bargain.

Chin Peng's tentative approaches to the future ruler of Malaya were an admission that the 'armed struggle' had been a political as well as military failure. No liberated areas had been formed, his forces were depleted and had not dislocated Malayan life. In the meantime the Communist Party had exiled itself from the mainstream of political life which had been transformed during the seven year struggle. When the Emergency began the political future of Malaya had looked bleak, for local allegiances were by-and-large dictated by race. The Communists had at first profited from this, for they had been able to offer themselves as the natural conduit for the aspirations of the ambitious Chinese community. Time and time again members of the Security Forces had been impressed by the intelligence of the guerrillas whom they had taken prisoner, and the *Min Yuen* had found particular support among Chinese students. This was a direct consequence of a widespread feeling amongst the educated Chinese that Malaya offered little or no outlet for their talents. For their part, the traditionalist, Muslim Malaya were anxious that their country did not become dominated by the Chinese.

Such misgivings encouraged racial politics in which the Malays laid emphasis on long periods of 'qualification' as the passport by which the Chinese obtained political rights. This pattern broke up in 1952 with the Alliance between the predominantly Malay party of Rahman and the Malayan Chinese Association (MCA). Both groups were conservative and concerned about the survival of Malayan capitalism, considerations which outweighed racial loyalties. The Alliance prospered and through it the Chinese commercial community, who were amongst its adherents, used their influence to win over the Chinese in the camps and plantation villages. Templer appreciated this need to draw the Chinese into the political future of Malaya and helped the MCA. At independence, the Alliance became the ruling party, and in the 1959 general election obtained a substantial majority in the Malayan Parliament with just over half of the popular vote. By contrast the Chinese Socialist Party received 13% of the votes and eight seats.

The development of a plural society, western-style politics and independence did not mean an end to the Emergency. In October 1957 Britain signed a treaty of alliance with Malaya in which the new state was promised armed help in an emergency and the Commonwealth Division remained stationed in the country to back up the 9,000 strong local forces. Even after the end of the Emergency in 1960, British forces, in the shape of the Ghurka Division, stayed in Malaya.

For the rump of the guerrilla army, the 'armed struggle' finished with a retreat across the Thai border. Here was sanctuary and the chance to reconsider the events and mistakes of the past twelve years; it was not an unconditional surrender, but a breathing space. In 1967 there was a recrudescence of terrorism, including the murder of Special Branch officers, and in 1976 Chin Peng was still contemplating a renewed assault on Malaya. His flight from Malaya and the cessation of terrorism was a victory for the British armed forces on two counts. They had prevented the achievement of even the Communists' most basic objective, the proliferation of 'liberated' districts free from government control. There were lucky bonuses for the British. The Chinese Communists had missed the chance to exploit their patriotic part in the resistance against the Japanese and so after 1945 the Malayan Communist Party never assumed the appearance of a broadly-based nationalist movement. It was a sectional party, based on the Chinese community and without significant Malay support. Against this background, the 'hearts and minds' campaign stood a chance of success. In the end, a substantial number of Chinese were convinced that their future lay in a non-Communist Malayan state. This Government-inspired integration can, however, be exaggerated for in May 1969 race riots in Kuala Lumpur were a reminder that frictions had not been eliminated for good. The 'hearts and minds' campaign was not just a device to cut the Chinese off from the Communists, nor was it only created to secure racial harmony. It ensured that, in 1957, when independence was reached the Government was passed into the trustworthy hands of local nationalists who had been coaxed and coached by the British, and who would not jeopardize British strategic and commercial interests.

The Last Frontier: Brunei, Sarawak and North Borneo, 1963–66

The defeat of the Communists in Malaya and the resignation of its Government to co-operative local nationalists like Tunku Abdul Rahman to some extent redeemed the loss of British prestige suffered when Singapore surrendered. In the wider context of British involvement in the affairs of the Middle East, it was part of a process of gradual disentanglement of Imperial pledges and responsibilities. It was also an acknowledgement of the fact that old Imperial Government could not be maintained effectively in the teeth of local, nationalist opposition. When such a situation came about, world opinion was intolerant, and there were plenty of people in Britain who were vociferous in their support for 'small nations' struggling for freedom. After 1945, successive British Governments paid lip service at least to principles of internationalism, which meant that the opinions voiced in the United Nations were taken seriously. As a colonial power in a period when colonialism was widely resented, British governments felt the need to tread carefully and where possible cover their actions with a cloak of legalism.

Even if Britain was prepared to make concessions to nationalism, she had also to maintain her obligations, particularly to fragile states which depended upon her armed assistance, either against local insurgents or overbearing neighbours. Malaya had, in October 1957, signed a defence agreement with Britain by which Britain kept bases and in return provided the Malayan government with military help. Four years later, the British Government proposed that Malaya should be buttressed by the addition of Singapore (where the emergence of a left-wing government was feared) and the by now embarrassing colonies of North Borneo and Sarawak. These were Imperial oddities, for until 1941 North Borneo had been run by a private company, and Sarawak was more-or-less the private estate of the Brooke family, whose ancestor 'Rajah' James Brooke had carved out a fief there in the 1840s. By the early 1960s the region was on the verge of an economic revolution with the discovery of off-shore oil and its future security became a matter of some importance. The Sultan of Brunei, which was a British protectorate, declined to join the federation which was to become Malaysia, but Sarawak and North Borneo voted to join.

The will of the local population was sought and clearly shown, with United Nations observers present to see that no colonialist tricks were played. Opposition to amalgamation into Malaysia was expressed by the *Parti Ra'ayat*, a socialist, nationalist group. In Brunei, this party won the first general election in September 1962 after a campaign in which they had opposed the continued rule of the Sultan, an autocrat who had reluctantly permitted constitutional government under British pressure. Azahari, the leader of the *Parti Ra'ayat*, planned a *coup* in which he and his followers hoped to depose the Sultan, declare a republic, and begin a wider movement for the liberation of Sarawak and North Borneo, which would together form North Kalimantan. With 150 armed men and 4,000 ancillaries, most of whom were ill-armed, Azahari led an insurrection in December 1962 which, after some initial success, failed. The authorities had wind of the plot and forces were flown in from Singapore. They were more than a match for Azahari's *Tentera Nasional Kalimantan Utara* (North Kalimantan National Army) whose members were either captured or forced to take refuge in the jungle. There were some tense moments when Shell employees and their families were taken prisoner at Seria and had to be rescued by men from the Queen's Own Highlanders.

Azahari fled to Manila and then to Jakarta, where he was warmly welcomed and permitted to set up a North Kalimantan government-in-exile. The advent of Malaysia had displeased President Sukarno who, since his introduction of 'guided democracy' in 1959, had increasingly flirted with Indonesian Communists and taken an implacably anti-Western stance. He had been promoting a form of national identity which fused revolutionary zeal with expansionism. between 1961 and 1963 his armed forces, in spite of a shabby showing, had occupied Dutch New Guinea and he then turned his own and his adherents' nationalist zealotry, towards North Kalimantan. In his view, Malaysia represented neo-colonialism because it harboured British bases, was guarded

Wars of the Jungle: The Far East

S. E. ASIA OPERATIONS, 1945 – 1963

Map 3 South East Asia

by British forces and seemed to serve the interests of Western capitalism. Sukarno therefore threw his weight behind Azahari and his North Kalimantan Liberation Army, and called for volunteers to free Brunei, Sarawak and North Borneo — in one characteristic flight of fancy he demanded twenty million! Sukarno had more than rhodomontade to offer, for since 1961 he had been receiving considerable supplies of weaponry, ships and aircraft from the Soviet Union which were later augmented with arms from China.

In theory Sukarno's blusterings posed a grave threat to Malaysia. It had not been too difficult, thanks to air transport and improvised landing craft, to frustrate the *coup* in 1962. Experienced British and Ghurka forces were able to hold the scattered nationalists at bay in the jungle whilst police forces detained their sympathizers in the towns and villages. The Indonesian 'volunteers' who crossed the 1,000-mile border in groups of up to 200 were less easy to handle for they included units from the regular army. There was also the possibility that all or part of the re-armed Indonesian forces might be committed by Sukarno and this became a distinct possibility after the declaration of the birth of the new Malaysian state in October 1963. Plans were drawn up in the event of an all-out war, in which RAF planes were detailed to excise the Indonesian air and sea forces. This was expected to take twenty-four hours, after which a blockade would be imposed on the Indonesian islands.[22]

The immediate difficulty of Indonesian infiltrators was met in different ways, most of them learned from previous jungle campaigns in Malaya. Three-man SAS patrols were air-lifted into the jungle, where with a month's rations, they waited in ambush for interlopers. Later, the local commander, General Sir Walter Walker, sent groups over the border into Indonesian territory where they acted as a tripwire to catch intruders before they could enter Malaysian territories. These were covert operations; the troops involved were not to be taken or found dead, they carried no identifying papers and could not summon air support if they got into trouble. By 1965, over 27,000 British servicemen had been drawn into the war, either in Borneo, Sarawak and Brunei or in support in Malaya.

In so far as these forces were better trained and able to survive in the jungle, they always overcame the parties which they encountered. Final success, however, was the consequence of events within Indonesia. Sukarno's closeness with the local Communist Party had distanced him from his own army, which was less than enthusiastic about what Sukarno called the 'confrontation' and definitely hostile towards any direct clash with Britain. Given that Azahari had established close links with the Indonesian Communists, the 'war' seemed to have a Communist rather than a nationalist inspiration. As so often with aggressive nationalism in newly independent countries, Sukarno's public posturings were an effort to distract public attention from domestic problems in Indonesia. Inflation was out of control, economic growth was sluggish, and there were deep internal divisions between the army and the conservative Muslim community, and the Left. Late in 1965 there was a bungled Communist *coup*, which alerted the army and the anti-Communists who responded by edging Sukarno from power. Control of the country passed into the hands of Major General Suharto in the following spring and the debut of the new, less radical regime was marked by a massacre of Communists in which the death toll was over 100,000.

Suharto was keen to end a conflict which the armed forces had not wanted and which had been waged on behalf of their political opponents. A peace was agreed in August 1966 and thereafter Malaysia and Indonesia began to find common ground. Their new relationship was expressed in 1971 by a joint declaration of control over the Straits of Malacca. By this time, the Labour Government in Britain had made clear its intention to pull out of defence commitments in the Far East as part of the wider programme, announced in 1968, of ending all 'East of Suez' deployment of bases and forces. The incoming Conservatives, for all their public adherence to finding a new role for Britain in Europe, still hankered after old global pretensions, so in 1970 they reserved the Labour decision. An arrangement was patched together by which Britain maintained training facilities and an airfield in Malaya. Three battalions a year passed through the jungle training school at Johore and during 1970 an exercise was held in north-eastern Malaya when British forces were flown in to train alongside units from New Zealand and Australia. This showed how quickly Britain could get troops to Malaya, but whether it impressed the demoralized rump of the guerrillas still dwelling in the remote jungle or the Indonesians is not known. Not long after the new regional power-broker, the United States, moved a powerful fleet through the Straits of Malacca to forestall Soviet intervention in the Indian-Pakistani War and warn India of the perils of making a direct attack on East Pakistan.

The campaign in Malaya and the subsequent defence of the outlying provinces of Malaysia were overshadowed by the larger war being waged in Vietnam which ended with the US evacuation of Saigon in 1973. During and after this war, many military and political comparisons were made between the two campaigns. On one level much of this comparative literature concerned the recondite subject of jungle survival and counter-insurgency methods. Here the British were happy to put their experiences at the disposal of the United States which sent men for training in British establishments in Malaysia.

The war against Japan had given both the British and the US armies first hand experience of waging war in tropical rain forests, but the US had little knowledge of fighting colonial wars against local insurgents. America had, during the nineteenth century, suppressed the resistance of the Plains Indians, and in the 1900s overcame Filipino nationalists in a guerrilla war. Thereafter American experiences of this kind of war were confined to small expeditionary forces sent to coerce Central American governments during the 1920s and 1930s. By contrast, the British army had a long tradition of colonial warfare. Some of the men who fought in Malaya, like Major General Walker, had served their apprenticeship on the North-West Frontier and others had fought in

Palestine. The British army had always been a colonial police force. 'Today it is Korea, Malaya, Egypt; tomorrow Sarawak or heaven knows where', a recruit told a journalist visiting Catterick Camp in 1952.[23] For his father it would have been a choice of India, Palestine or Iraq, and for his grandfather, South Africa, the Sudan or Afghanistan. (Shortly after her Coronation in 1953, the Queen inspected Chelsea Pensioners who included veterans of the Ashanti and Zulu campaigns of the 1870s). One consequence of this continuity of Imperial soldiering was what the British public was used to colonial wars. It had been brought up with them and took them for granted. Long after the era of flag-waving jingoism which ended in 1914, the British considered colonial campaigns as a duty which went with possession of an Empire. During the 1920s and 1930s remote wars in colourful places were invested with a new glamour by the cinema and movies were still appearing in the 1950s and 1960s which told tales of imperial derring-do. *North-West Frontier* and *Zulu* were two of the last and they were well received.

For Americans, colonial wars were a novelty. For many they were an unwelcome aspect of the new US global power, since the concept of fighting people who seemed to be fighting for their freedom caused moral unease. After all, the Americans had once been on the other side of a colonial war fighting for ideals which had much in common with those cherished by other fighters against colonialism. Yet in 1963 the American public had faced up to what seemed a disagreeable duty. Five years later the mood had changed dramatically. Mass protests emerged, conscripts refused to enlist, and there was a rash of mutinies during 1968–9. Americans had had the opportunity to watch the combat at first hand thanks to television coverage. Casualty lists lengthened, the horrors of technological and chemical war waged against civilians as well as guerrillas repelled them, and the apparent inability of US forces to secure victory galled them.

What disillusioned and embittered Americans was a war of far greater scale than the one fought in Malaya. Over half-a-million US troops, many of them national servicemen, supported 800,000 locally-recruited South Vietnamese forces at the beginning of 1969. They were there in fulfilment of a traditional colonial policy, the rendering of assistance to an embattled client state faced with internal insurgency and external aggression. This was not all, for the US government had come to understand that success as a global power required universal paramountcy. 'Displays of American impotence in one part of the world such as Asia or Africa', argued Dr Kissinger, 'would immediately erode our credibility in other parts of the world, such as the Middle East'. Prestige was therefore at stake.

The assertion of US prestige proved impossible. Indeed, soon after he took office, President Nixon pledged the evacuation of American troops and so demonstrated to his adversaries that there was a limit to her people's will to fight. The Viet Cong were very different from the Malayan Communists. The history of Communist resistance to colonial government in Indo-China

Wars of the Jungle: The Far East 163

stretched back to the 1930s and immediately after the war the Viet Minh gained a nationalist credibility for their efforts to frustrate the reimposition of French colonial government. Unlike the British in Malaya, the French never reasserted control over their former colony whilst their adversaries gained more and more popular support. By 1954 the guerrilla army controlled whole regions of the colony and were able to emerge into the open and engage the French armed forces in pitched battles. North Vietnam, a Communist republic supported by both the USSR and China, was one result of the French defeat, and in the subsequent war proved a valuable base for the Viet Cong in their war with the United States and her allies. No such facility existed for the Malayan Communists nor did they ever secure the right to speak as nationalists with broad, deeply rooted local support.

In terms of fighting, the US lacked a clear strategy. Until 1968 the emphasis had been on the offensive, but later a new commander, General Abrams, concentrated his forces on urban defence, virtually offering the guerrillas the countryside. Throughout the war there was a high reliance on aerial bombardment at levels of intensity which had not been seen since the Allied offensive against Germany in 1944–5. It was not decisive; nor were chemical weapons which included defoliants and CS gas, though they were used on a scale which had not been witnessed since the Italian invasion of Abyssinia. There, as in Vietnam, they were weapons reached for by frustrated Generals. Yet unlike Mussolini's Italy, America was not waging war as a conqueror. It was fighting for the South Vietnamese people. They, unlike the Malayans, gradually came to see that a US victory was impossible and that their chances of future happiness, such as they were, lay with America's enemies.

5

Winds of Change and Storms of War: Africa

Chariots in the Sky: Somaliland and the Sudan

I am a pilgrim and a holy fighter, and have no wish to gain power and greatness in the world. I am a Dervish hoping for God's mercy and consent and forgiveness and guidance, and I desire that all the country and the Muslims may be victorious by God's grace.

Sayyid Muhammad Ibn Abdullah Hassan.

This letter is sent by the British governer of the Somalis to the Dervishes of the Mullah, Muhammad Ibn Abdullah Hassan. It is carried by British officers, who, like birds of the air, fly far and fast. Their journey from me to you will occupy but one hour. Now listen to my words. The day of destruction of the Mullah and his power is at hand. . . . The arm of the British government is long.

Official leaflet, dropped from aircraft on Medishe, 1920.

By 1914 nearly every part of British Africa had been pacified. It had been the creation of forty years of intermittent war in which local opposition had been ruthlessly crushed. Yet in many areas, British authority was still precarious, liable to challenge from native peoples who resented the deracination of old customs and the imposition of such novelties as hut taxes. The first years of the century had therefore seen outbreaks of unrest in East, West and Central Africa, all of which were suppressed by small punitive columns of troops and police, commanded by British officers. Only in Somaliland did these 'local difficulties' prove insurmountable.

Somaliland lay across the Red Sea from the vital Imperial staging post of Aden and for that reason it had been annexed in 1884. Its nomadic Muslim tribesmen felt little affection for the British Government and its unwelcome innovations. The defence of Islam fell to a messianic holy man, Sayyid Muhammad Ibn Abdulla Hassan, a widely-respected teacher and apostle of the fiercely ascetic Salihipa sect. Not long before he declared a *jihad* against the British administration in 1899, Sayyid Muhammad had been affronted by the setting up of a French Roman Catholic school and orphanage in Berbera. It seemed to him a wedge that would eventually weaken and split the faith of the Somalis. Only by a war against the interlopers could the Somalis save their faith and customs, and within three years Sayyid Muhammad had rallied over 30,000 to his cause.

A series of expeditions was sent against Sayyid Muhammad, now known to the British as 'the Mad Mullah', but he skilfully avoided pitched battles and drew the Imperial armies deep into the arid Somali hinterland. By 1904 he had captured three machine-guns, won a few skirmishes, and compelled his opponents to withdraw to the coast. For the next sixteen years, the Mad Mullah was unchallenged in southern and eastern Somaliland, where he built stone keeps as a sign that he controlled the land. There were limits to his power, imposed by a chain of British fortresses which barred the way to the coast and by the fact that his support was confined to his own people, the Darod tribe. In his dealings with the British, the Mullah was anxious to reach some kind of accommodation, even though he repeatedly claimed that they had given too much credence to the slanders made against him by his tribal foes. In April 1916 he even offered to mediate between the British and the Turkish Sultan ('He will accept my words') in return for being left in peace with an open trade route to the coast.[1] Sayyid Muhammad was, however, hedging his bets. The previous August he had received an embassy from Abdullah Sadiq, a Turkish agent in Harrar, who had sent him nine boxes of cartridges, and by way of return, his own emissaries had carried one of the Maxim guns taken from the British to the Ethiopian Emperor, Lij Yasu.[2] As a consequence of this flirtation with Turco-German interests, Sayyid Muhammad received the services of a German armourer to look after his arsenal of smuggled modern weaponry.[3]

Intelligence reports of the Mullah's dealings with the Turco-German clique in Harrar stiffened British determination to overthrow him. It was no easy matter though. The distressful experiences of earlier campaigns had shown that Imperial columns, operating in remote, waterless regions, needed a vast logistical apparatus. In 1903 over 13,000 camels had been required by one column alone. A cumbersome baggage train was a brake on swift movement which was necessary to catch and trap the Mullah's forces. Moreover, Somaliland was an impoverished protectorate unable to foot the bill for a large-scale campaign, which was why, in 1906, the British Government had restricted operations against the Mullah. By 1914, however, the outlook was more cheering for the advocates of an aggressive policy towards the Mullah. Encouraging reports of the bombing of Sanusi tribesmen by Italian airships in Libya during the 1911–12 campaign made Churchill propose the use of aircraft and an airship in Somaliland.[4] The French had also pointed the way forward by their use of bombers in Morocco and British airmen had flown machines from Cairo to Khartum.

The outbreak of the First World War in August 1914 diverted attention from the Mullah, and the plans for aerial action against him were shelved. They were revived at the end of 1919 when the Commander in Chief in East Africa, Major General Sir Reginald Hoskins, visited Berbera at the request of the governor, Sir Geoffrey Archer. What was at stake was prestige. What Archer described as the 'continued immunity of the Mullah' was an affront to British authority, the more so since over the past four years he had raided his tribal enemies and set up his castles across the border on Ethiopian soil. 'Mentally active and virile', according to intelligence reports, the Mullah possessed 6,000 rifles and could quickly muster a field army of 2,000 warriors.[5] To overcome him, the British would require an expeditionary force of three African and two Indian battalions, motor transport and an arsenal of modern weaponry, including mortars. Even so, argued Hoskins, the Mullah could still evade engagement, thanks to his efficient intelligence service which had always given him at least four weeks advance notice of what the government in Berbera was planning. Aircraft alone could give the element of surprise which was so vital. Hoskins therefore concluded that the 'main effort will be produced by aeroplanes dispersing his forces by bombing and by wireless telegraphy, affording co-operation' with the ground units.

The proposals pleased Churchill, the Secretary for War, and were warmly supported by Lord Trenchard for whom they were a heaven-sent opportunity to prove the value of the RAF. On 9 October 1919, the Cabinet gave its approval for the campaign, the last of its kind to be fought by the British in Africa. Men and material were already being mustered at Berbera, for an operation in which the RAF would provide the cutting edge. The ground forces involved were far less than those originally thought necessary to trap the Mullah and his followers. They were split into two contingents. A battalion of the King's African Rifles was stationed at Las Khorai to prevent any attempt by the Somalis to flee eastwards. The main pursuit force comprised 700 men from the Somaliland Camel Corps and a small Indian infantry unit, equipped with mortars and a dozen machine-guns. Its quarry was to be kept on the move by a squadron of six DH 9 bombers based at a newly-levelled airfield at Eil Dur Elan. The machines, dismantled and crated, were brought from Egypt by the aircraft carrier *Ark Royal*, along with their pilots and ground crews.

In an unsuccessful attempt to fox the Mullah, the unloading of the aircraft and the laying of the airfield were explained officially as preparations for oil-prospecting. It is doubtful whether Sayyid Muhammad was fooled; Somalis who had sought work in Egypt knew something about aircraft, but all speculation about their purpose ended on 20 January 1920 when they flew over the Mullah's fort at Medishe and dropped leaflets. It was later rumoured that the more credulous of the Mullah's supporters believed that the strange machines were chariots, sent from heaven by Allah to carry away the Mullah. Those who could read discovered that deserters would be pardoned by the Government, save the Mullah and his immediate retinue, for whom head money was offered.

On 21 January bombing raids began. Six aircraft left Eil Dur Elan; one suffered engine trouble and made an emergency landing at Las Khorai, four found and bombed a fort at Jidalli, and one made its way to Medishe where its bombs killed ten people. Raids continued during the day with forty casualties at Medishe, where one incendiary killed Sayyid Muhammand's uncle and singed his own robes. At the same time the Camel Corps column moved into action after a pause to level a landing-strip at Al Afweina. Guided by RAF reconnaissance reports, their aim was catch or kill the Mullah, but information about his whereabouts was scanty and confusing. A deserter reported on 30 January that he and his party were heading southwards after the destruction of Medishe and raids on Jidali. Contact was made on 3 February when a camel patrol encountered a convoy of pack camels and ponies, whose well-armed guards attacked the troopers. 'While extricating themselves, they noticed a knot of men rally round a stout man and hustle him off a mule', a circumstance which led the commander to believe that he had at last come across the Mullah. Wounded prisoners denied this.

As the mobile patrols fanned out across a landscape where the grazing was thin or non-existent, camels and ponies were weakened. Still, the columns pressed on gamely, exhilarated by the chase. Their spirit is described in the unpublished narrative of the operation, written for the Camel Corps.[6]

> The ponymen came up with their quarry, and resolutely hunted them down, killing eight and capturing two prisoners . . . All ranks of the column worked excellently, the handful of ponymen especially distinguishing themselves by their contempt of Dervish fire and their relentless determination in independent pursuit.

This bravado was matched by the RAF pilots who kept the fleeing Somalis under a constant pressure of strafing and bombing raids. Such punishment produced 'severe casualties to the Mullah's Dervish following and their stocks and hutments'. The Royal Navy gave a hand as well. A landing party, armed with Lewis guns and hand grenades, came ashore on 8 February and stormed the Mullah's coastal castle at Galbaribur. The war also presented an opportunity for those tribes which had always rejected the Mullah's leadership. They formed the backbone of the 3,000 tribal irregulars who joined in the pursuit with an eye to getting their hands on captured camels.

Yet the Mullah escaped. Its mobility impaired by losses of camels and ponies, Colonel Hastings Ismay's column reluctantly pulled back. They had, however, captured fifty-five of the Mullah's kinsmen and women, including six sons, four daughters and five sons.[7] It was assumed that Sayyid Muhammad had 'sacrificed his family to save his skin', although at the same time none of his adherents offered his pursuers any information as to his whereabouts or destination. He died, it was presumed, in December 1920, somewhere over the border in southern Ethiopia; he was aged about 50, and when Somalia obtained independence he was lionized as a proto-nationalist, resistance leader.

While the Mullah himself escaped Imperial retribution, his power in Somaliland had been broken forever. The RAF was well satisfied with its part in the operations. Its six machines had dropped bombs which had severely damaged the Mullah's castles and turned his supporters into scattered refugees. The overthrow of the Mullah was 'primarily due to the Royal Air Force', asserted Sir Geoffrey Archer, who stressed that the bombing, 'exercised an immediate moral effect over the Dervishes, who in the ordinary course are good fighting men'.[8] The British officers of the Somaliland Camel Corps took issue with this conclusion. When one of their detachments stormed the recently-bombed fort of Jidalli, its defenders were heard singing and shouting insults, suggesting they were far from unnerved. The camelry resented the way in which the RAF had taken all the credit for the operation's success and relegated its role to mopping-up. There were probably deeper reasons for this acrimony since the Camel Corps officer stood firmly for traditions of imperial service, as one remembered:

> In general, our mode of life was, I suppose, fairly rough and tough. Of creature comforts there were few, but the climate inland was good even if, at times, a trifle hot, and we had plenty of physical exercise to keep us fit and hard. Our games, chiefly polo, were played 'all out' . . .[9]

Such *beaux-sabreurs* of Empire did not take kindly to being up-staged by technology and its operatives, especially when they boasted that they had played the decisive part in the defeat of a man against whom local forces, like their own, had had such paltry success.

The departure and death of Sayyid Muhammad did not bring immediate tranquillity to Somaliland, where tribal feuding, stock-rustling, and defiance of the government continued. Internal security rested on the Camel Corps together with the Governor's ability to summon by wireless aircraft based 150 miles away at Aden. A dozen landing strips had been prepared in different parts of the country in readiness for an emergency. One occurred in February 1922, when Captain Gibb, who had commanded the irregulars in the campaign against the Mullah, was murdered by rioters during a protest against taxation at Burao. Governor Archer immediately called for aircraft which were at Burao within two days. The inhabitants of the native township were turned out of their houses, and the entire area was razed by a combination of bombing, machine-gun fire and burning.[10] Aircraft again appeared over Somali skies in 1927 after the flight of the Sultan of Mijjertem from Italian Somaliland. He showed no inclination for a tussle with the British after aircraft had been summoned. 'Bombs were seen on the machines when they landed at Erivago', reported the Governor, Sir Harold Kittermaster, and 'within twenty-four hours the news had been conveyed to the Sultan by his spies, and he surrendered precipitately'.[11]

Kittermaster was impressed and, full of praise for the RAF, he concluded that 'the Somali is an unconquerable bushman, but he cannot compete with the resources of science'. His memory did, however, need prompting and so, during the 1920s and 1930s, the RAF squadron from Aden periodically overflew the colony. Such shows of force may have reminded Somalis of the fate of the Mullah, but they did not force them to abandon their hostility towards British rule and its novelties. During 1935–6, riots greeted the announcement that the administration planned to set up secular schools, and so intense was the opposition that the plan was dropped. Only in 1942 did Somaliland get its first non-Quranic schools which were introduced by the temporary military government which ran the colony after its reconquest from the Italians. Even the military administration trod warily, so that Somali girls had to wait until 1949 before they were afforded education. Public order remained shaky. A brawl over a girl in the streets of Hargeisa in November 1947 triggered a full-scale tribal war in which revolvers and a sub-machine gun were used and hundreds were killed or wounded.[12] Worse was anticipated two years later, when the Somalis heard the news that neighbouring Somalia would be returned to the Italian government. The local military authorities feared an uprising, and laid plans for the quick evacuation of all the dependants of British and African servicemen from British as well as Italian territory.

Within the vast compass of the Sudan, as in Somaliland, there were regions inhabited by peoples ill-disposed towards the Government. Kitchener's army had conquered the country in 1898, but total control over its outlying provinces proved hard to achieve. Darfur, in the west, was only subjugated in 1916 after its semi-independent Sultan, Ali Dinar, had thrown in his lot with Turkey and rebelled against the Anglo-Egyptian Government. Further south, in the Sud, over a quarter of a million Nilotic tribesmen remained more-or-less ignorant about the government and its laws. This situation was intolerable to the administration in Khartum which was determined not only to extend its influence into the most remote regions, but to stamp out the cattle-rustling and inter-tribal warfare which persisted there.

To achieve this, a series of small expeditions was sent into the region during the 1920s, ostensibly to squash sporadic outbreaks of unrest among the Nuer tribesmen, but in fact to show them that Imperial authority was irresistible. What made the luckless Nuers into toads under the Imperial harrow was their adherence to their *kujurs*, preachers who claimed possession of magical powers. In the official mind, *kujurs* were no more than witch doctors whose activities fomented disruption and subversion. The extirpation of their influence was the first aim of the small punitive expeditions sent against the Nuers during the 1920s. Assistance was asked of and willingly given by the RAF. Aircraft possessed what was considered an awesome magic, far superior to anything which the *kujurs* could invoke, and they had great practical value for tracking down semi-nomadic tribesmen in a remote area.

Aircraft first appeared over the Upper Nile in January 1920, after there had been restlessness amongst the Garjak Nuers as a result of the activities of a *kujur*, Mut Dung. In response to a request from Khartum, two DH 9s, with spares for four months, were created and transported from Egypt to a site at Nasir. It took a few days to level an airfield and a few days more for the twenty-eight airmen to repair their machines which had been damaged during the journey. On 31 January, both machines took off, dropped mail to the ground forces and scoured the grassland for Nuers. When they did not appear, incendiaries were dropped to set the long grass alight and flush out the tribesmen. Ten days later, news that parties of Nuers had been sighted by troops led to a sortie in which they were 'bombed and machine-gunned with good effect'. Technical hitches, which included a crash landing, a fire in the camp, and a wait for spare parts, held up operations during much of February. There were further air raids at the end of the month and at the beginning of March, in which the Nuer's herds of cattle were targets. By now the Nuers had learned something about aircraft, and either took to caves when they were heard approaching, or else cowered in their huts. 'It was sometimes found necessary, in order to discover if a village were occupied, to drop a bomb, when the occupants would run out and scatter', reported one pilot. The Nuers appear to have been given some warning from local officials as to what was in store, but their sense of wonder when they first saw the aircraft was not as great as had been hoped. The official summary of the operation concluded:[13]

> It is characteristic of those and probably all natives that they seldom believe what is told them, but must have ocular proof. The vast majority of the fighting men therefore showed no signs of having been profoundly impressed.

They did, however, learn to keep themselves hidden when the aircraft were about.

The Sudanese administration was uncomfortable about the use of aircraft against tribesmen, and so no further air operations were undertaken until December 1927. The previous July, the Committee for Imperial Defence had suggested that 'the efficacy of air forces in relation to the defence of the Sudan' should be given a one-year test, and the Cabinet had concurred. The decision was regarded with disfavour in some quarters in Khartum, where the Civil Secretary found the whole business 'highly unwelcome and inopportune'.[14] There was something distasteful about reports which read, 'the Nuer when frightened invariably attempts to merge himself into the landscape, clasping any natural object such as a tree or large ant hill'. Reservations based on information of this kind, together with a feeling that such methods did not assist the extension of civilization, even to what one official called 'The Monkeydom of Nations', made the Sudanese administrators reluctant to unleash the full rigours of 'air control' over the Nuers.

Doubts about the employment of aircraft to coerce were evident throughout operations during 1928 and 1929.[15] The punitive expeditions followed a sequence of delinquencies, which included the murder of a British official and inter-tribal raiding. *Kujurs* and their activities again attracted special attention, in particular a sixty-foot sacred pyramid which one, Guek Woudring, had had made at Dengkurs. It was a target for a number of unsuccessful bombing raids, but was blown up by sappers after the village had been taken by Sudanese mounted infantry. During the last week of January 1928, a number of sorties were flown against tribesmen and their stock, which included an attack on those concentrated on the Bahr-al-Jabul islands in which it was estimated at least 200 were killed.[16] There were further operations in this region during the following year. District officers accompanied pilots in operations designed to coax tribesmen who had dispersed to concentrate with their cattle at the government's command.[17] Several times during March 1929 bombs were dropped, but it was a method of persuasion that made local civilian officials uneasy.

RAF officers chafed against the restrictions placed on them. Flight Lieutenant Crofton, who commanded the flight based at Khartum, believed that 'natives generally are quite ignorant of the power of aircraft', and that, 'in their ignorance they have no fear of aircraft'.[18] Efforts to teach them otherwise during the operations in the spring of 1929 had ended with squabbles between RAF officers and civilian administrators. The officers wanted to keep up the hammering as the only way to make the obstinate Nuers come to heel, whilst the administrators favoured sporadic raids. The civilians won and the raids were temporarily cancelled. The unlooked-for upshot was a bonus for one *kujur* who, after a severe raid, told the frightened Nuers to take what for them was a rare step and sacrifice some cattle. No aircraft appeared the next day which no doubt increased the Nuers' respect for the supernatural powers of the *kujur* and diminished their fear of aircraft. In any case they were learning how to conceal themselves and one had fired back at a machine during the attempts to destroy the Dengkurs pyramid and wounded a pilot in the thigh.[19]

The Government's objections to bombing were based on the way it killed indiscriminately, although apologists for the RAF pointed out that in 1898 women and children had been killed by Kitchener's shelling of Atbara and Omdurman.[20] Kitchener had never been regarded as an advocate of humanity towards the foes of empire nor, for that matter, were the officers who commanded the ground columns which the RAF was helping. Nuer tribesmen, confronted by these forces in 1929, 'would not even wait and see what they had to say, but would run off into swamps'.[21] Since the troops in the columns were burning Nuer huts and slaughtering Nuer cattle, this shyness was hardly surprising. Such corrective chastisement, delivered by ground forces, continued to be favoured by the Sudan administration. Aircraft were used from time to time during the 1930s, but to impress rather than bomb tribesmen.

While the administrators of the Sudan were rather cool towards the use of aircraft against tribesmen, the Chief of Air Staff, Marshal of the Royal Air Force Sir John Salmond, was highly enthusiastic. In 1929, he outlined the value of the RAF in the Sudan where its presence was an insurance against the revival of Mahdism and a means of underwriting the loyalty of the Sudan Defence Force, which had been convulsed by a pro-Egyptian mutiny in 1925, and the means to crush 'occasional sporadic outbreaks among the savages of the south'.[22] There was, he alleged, further scope for 'air control' elsewhere in British Africa. Squadrons could be based at airfields along the newly-opened civil air route from the Mediterranean to East and Central Africa, where they would replace the King's African Rifles as the local defence force. The white settlers in Kenya already had their own flying club and their kin in Southern Rhodesia were anxious to have their own volunteer unit. Opposition from colonial governments and other services checked the scheme which, given the outward tranquillity of the colonies involved, hardly seemed necessary.

The employment of aircraft in Somaliland and the Sudan was overshadowed by their use in Iraq and the North-West Frontier, and by the French, Italians, and Spanish in their African campaigns. South Africa was also quick to realize the value of aerial policing; bombers supported ground forces in 1922 when the Government broke the miners' strike on the Rand, and later they were used for dealing with black unrest. Here, as elsewhere, the victims were not completely browbeaten or awestruck. In 1930, adherents of Chief Wellington Buthelezi believed that they would be aided by aircraft piloted by American blacks who would come to rescue the Bantu. The lessons of air power were soon well understood throughout Africa. Ethiopia, which suffered grievously at the hands of the Italian Air Force in 1935–6, gained victory in its war with Somalia in the 1970s thanks to superiority in the air.

Black Terror: Kenya and the Mau Mau, 1952–63

His Majesty's Government record their considered opinion that the interests of the African natives must be paramount, and that if and when those interests and those of the immigrant races should conflict, the former should prevail.
       The Duke of Devonshire, Colonial Secretary, 1923.

I speak the truth and vow before our God
And by this Batuni *oath of our movement*
Which is called the movement of fighting,
That if I am called on to kill for our soil
If I am called on to shed my blood for it
I shall obey and I shall never surrender,
And if I fail to go
       May this oath kill me,
       May this he-goat kill me,

May this seven kill me,
May this meat kill me.

I speak the truth and vow before our God
And before our people of Africa
That I shall never betray our country,
That I shall never betray anybody of this movement to the enemy
Whether the enemy be European or African,
And if I do this
   May this oath kill me, etc.
                                            Mau Mau Warrior's Oath.

Mau Mau means 'greedy eating' in the Kikuyu language.[23] Through a process of mistranslation and misunderstanding, the words were transformed into the name given to a clandestine Kikuyu organization whose members called themselves *Uiguano wa Muingi* [The Unity of the Community] or *Muma wa Uiguano* [Oath of Unity]. Other words and phrases were sometimes used but their import was always the same. The Mau Mau was a secret fellowship, its members bound together by the magic of powerful oaths in which they swore to help each other, regain their land and overcome the enemies of their people. Those enemies were the Europeans who ruled Kenya and monopolized its more fertile lands, and for them the words Mau Mau came to have a special terror. The sorcery, the grisly rites of initiation, the mutilations and murders seemed to raise the phantasm of a distant, barbaric African past.

Whilst the oath-swearing ceremonies were rooted in a pre-colonial African past, the peculiar circumstances which gave rise to Mau Mau were very much the product of Kenya's recent history. This was apparent when information about the illicit administration of oaths began to filter through the authorities during 1950. One Kikuyu postulant, who later turned informer, told how he had been taken with others to a darkened hut, and told: 'We want you young men to join us in the struggle for freedom and the return of our stolen land'. He swore that he would unhesitatingly assist the organization and his fellow members at any time, help raise money, and never reveal what he knew to the Government or outsiders. After each pledge he repeated, 'And if I fail to do so, may this oath kill me'. In his hand the oath-taker held a 'damp ball of soil against his stomach', which symbolized 'his willingness to do everything in his power to assist the association in regaining and protecting the land belonging to the Kikuyu people'.[24] Other rituals were performed which involved the insides of a lately slaughtered goat and making the mark of a cross in blood and grain on the oath-taker's forehead. The ceremony, with its paraphernalia of an arch of plaited banana stalks, hung with parts of a goat and plants, and the incantations which promised future terrors for the perjurer, was dramatic and awesome. There were variations. Josiah Mwangi Kariuki, who took the oath in December 1953, chanted:[25]

*I speak the truth and vow before God
And before this movement,
The movement of Unity,
The Unity which is put to the test
The Unity that is mocked with the name of 'Mau Mau',
That I shall go forward to fight for the land,
The lands of Kirinyaga that we cultivated,
The lands which were taken by the Europeans.*

The oath administered to Karari Njama in September 1952 pledged him never to sell land to a European or an Asian, never to drink European beer, smoke European cigarettes or obey a strike call, and be willing to hide firearms and ammunition.[26] He also promised that he would 'never help the missionaries in their Christian faith to ruin our traditional and cultural customs', one of which he would preserve by insisting that his daughters underwent customary circumcision [removal of the clitoris]. The common theme of fighting 'for our soil' was central to the *batuni* vows by which the ordinary Mau Mau member was inducted into the movement's fighting units. [*batuni* was a corruption of platoon]. It was a fearsome oath, which was accompanied by the performance of a sexual aberration, a thing usually repugnant to the Kikuyu, but which added great supernatural force to the vow. What happened was described by Kariuku.[27]

I took off my trousers and squatted facing Biniathi. He told me to take the thorax of the goat which had been skinned, to put my penis through a hole that had been made in it and to hold the rest of it in my left hand in front of me. Before me on the ground were two small wooden stakes between which the thorax of the goat was suspended and fastened. By my right hand on the floor of the hut were seven small sticks each about four inches long. Biniathi told me to take the sticks one at a time, to put them into the thorax and slowly rub them in it while repeating after him these seven vows, one for each stick. (After each promise I was able to bite the meat and throw the stick on to the ground on my left side.)

Oath-taking such as this was at the heart of the Mau Mau. The general oath of initiation for the warriors which they swore before a raid, exercised a powerful hold over the Kikuyu imagination. It made the swearers part of a brotherhood in which would-be dissemblers lived under a dual threat of supernatural and physical retribution. The magical element was so compelling that the Government, before and during the war against the Mau Mau, had to devise an 'official' cleansing ceremony in which oath-takers were purged of their bewitchment. Oath-taking was the cement which bound together the local cells whose members recruited, collected funds, and carried out chores to help the fighting men. Each cell chose representatives to higher committees at

Winds of Change and Storms of War: Africa 175

EAST AFRICA OPERATIONS, 1919 – 1960

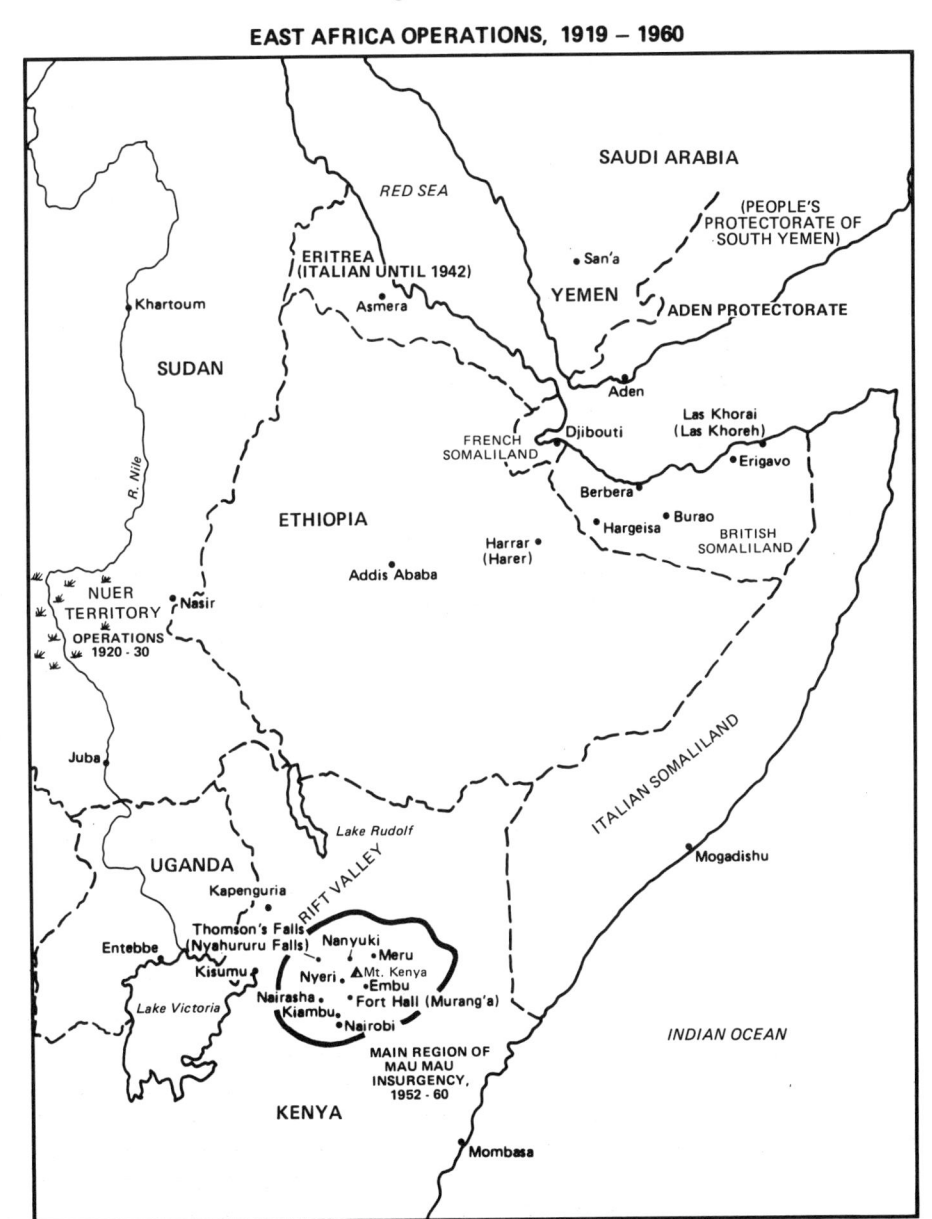

Map 4   East Africa

district level, who in turn sent delegates to the Central Committee which directed the movement.

From the start, Mau Mau members were committed by their oaths to join a struggle for the repossession of land taken from the Kikuyu by European settlers. The disputed lands were the White Highlands, a region of 6½ million acres of fertile land which had been set aside for white farmers by a series of official ordinances since the turn of the century. By 1952, most, but not all of this acreage was cultivated by 9,000 European farmers. They, and in some cases their fathers and grandfathers, had come to Kenya over the past fifty years with the encouragement of the colonial government which had, in 1919 and 1945, set out to attract ex-officers as settlers in a country where crops grew, labour was cheap, and the climate agreeable. There were some Boers from South Africa amongst the colonists, but most came from those groups within British society which believed themselves predestined to give orders to others. As in Southern Rhodesia and Palestine (and for that matter eighteenth century America), settler loyalty to the colonial government was conditional upon its willingness to rule in their interests. There was an abundance of good land and cheap, biddable labour to work it.

Faced with the need to balance the interests of the settlers with those of the native population, the Colonial Office had, in 1923, affirmed the principle that when the two clashed, native advancement would always come first. This was wormwood to the settlers. In 1946 they vainly tried to secure the removal of Colonial Office control from Kenya, and five years later, in a memorandum to the Government, they threatened to 'take matters into their own hands' unless there was an official undertaking not to follow any policy which aimed at majority government in Kenya.[28] This was an empty boast; there was little the settlers could do and anyway, within twelve months, they had become totally dependent upon the Government and its resources in the struggle with Mau Mau. There was much else for which the settlers had reason to be grateful. Since 1900, the colonial government's regulations had given them a monopoly of the best land in the country, and when necessary had facilitated the eviction of its original Kikuyu and Masai occupants. All Africans were made tenants-at-will of the Government and were denied deeds to what they occupied; this of course made official ejection easy. Taxation forced many to seek work on white farms for cash wages. In justification of their advantages, the colonist farmers claimed that they alone were the mainspring of the development of Kenya and the creators of its wealth.

The introduction of the land-hungry settler economy led to major upheavals within African society which created the conditions in which Mau Mau flourished. Just before the declaration of a State of Emergency in 1952, the total population of Kenya was about 5,250,000, of whom about 1.75 million were Kikuyu. Most were subsistence farmers on reservations, where an expanding birth-rate led to the fragmentation of plots, over-intensive farming and its consequence, soil erosion. By 1948, a quarter of the Kikuyu population had succumbed to economic pressures and left the reservations to seek their fortunes outside. Many were migrant labourers, others permanent farm workers or domestic servants. Some took their families with them and became squatters on European-owned farms, where they were allowed to stay on a smallholding for up to three years in return for up to 270 days labour on the farm. In a system reminiscent of medieval manorial feudalism, the squatter had to seek his landlord's permission before moving on. Since 1920 native mobility had been controlled by the *kipande*, a combination of work permit and identity card which was marked with the owner's fingerprint.

Considerable numbers of rootless Kikuyu drifted towards Nairobi. There were at least 50,000 living there in 1948, many of whom eked out a marginal existence with forays into petty crime. Street gangs flourished and at night controlled certain districts.[29] Vagrants and hoodlums with little to lose were attracted to the Mau Mau, which by 1952 had picked up a substantial following within the city where its organization was deeply-rooted and strong. Mau Mau also drew support from Nairobi's urban workers and two trade union leaders, prominent in the 1950 general strike, Fred Kubai and Bildad Kaggia, were also members of the local Mau Mau committee.

At the same time as the Kikuyu were being alienated from their land and edged into a form of helotry by the demands of the settler economy, their political consciousness was developing. Since the foundation of the young Kikuyu Association in 1921, Africans had worked together to gain some say in the running of Kenya and through it the means to reverse the legal processes which seemed designed to reduce them to landless serfs. The Kikuyu Central Association (KCA) started in 1924, went further and rallied to the defence of native customs and culture which were under attack, especially by missionaries. The KCA championed polygamy, female circumcision, and pagan songs and dances and, discovering that the Old Testament sometimes favoured polygamy and had nothing to say about female circumcision, developed independent African churches which by 1939 had their own schools and a training college. Behind this movement lay the fundamental question of African identity. Education was the means by which the African could advance himself within Kenyan society, but this key to self-improvement was invariably held by the missions. Attachment to Christianity forced the convert to turn his back on many tribal customs and by this process of rejection, cut himself off from his people.

There were hurdles to African advancement within Kenyan society. The colony's 120,000 Asian immigrants controlled much of the day-to-day business life and competed with Africans for junior clerical posts in commerce and the administration. A colour-bar was exercised by white society, many of whose members felt challenged by the educated African. Fear, as often happens, was masked by contempt:[30]

During this time the mission boy had learned to talk like a leading article in the *New Statesman*: the well-proportioned tribesman of the early photograph he liked so much had degenerated into a heavy-bellied hedonist with blood-flecked eyes; the inner resentments had spread like a cancer; arrogance and vanity had begun to move towards megalomania.

The time in question was the seven years which separated the end of the Second World War and the declaration of the Emergency in 1952. One man dominated this period, Jomo Kenyatta. Before the war, Kenyatta had been in the vanguard of the struggles of the KCA; he had travelled abroad extensively, spent much time in Britain, and had close contacts with other African nationalist leaders. In 1946 he had returned to Kenya where his reputation and prestige were immense. A year later he became president of the Kenya African Union (KAU), the recently-formed political movement which now channelled the growing African political consciousness. For the 100,000 members of the KAU and many others, Kenyatta was a charismatic leader who gave voice to their feelings and held out the chance of a new and better Kenya. It was a voice of persuasive reason:[31]

> He said he did not want the Europeans to leave the country, but it was time that they started to behave like guests in our house. They had come as strangers to us and we have accommodated them and now they claimed that our house belonged to them . . . They should not forget that the land they tread on is ours. Under an African governmnent Europeans would have nothing to fear in the same way as he, Kenyatta, an African, had not feared while in Europe under a European government. During the last war we sent our young men to sacrifice their lives in helping the British people to fight and conquer Germany. The white officers had been rewarded with farms on which to settle in our land and loans with which to stock them. The African soldiers had been rewarded with the colour bar, unemployment and the *Kipande*. There had been no colour bar to prevent us dying for Britain in the war.

The battle lines had been set. Directed by the settlers' needs, Kenya could follow the path taken by Southern Rhodesia, where the white community dominated the administration and shaped its policy, or it could progress towards African majority rule and with it a redistribution of land. The admission of four Africans, chosen by the Governor, to the advisory Legislative Council in 1944 suggested the latter course, but that body also contained eleven Europeans, elected by the settlers. Kenyatta favoured gradualism. He was prepared to tolerate the presence of settlers within an African rule Kenya, and was willing to co-operate with the colonial authorities. For two years he served as a member of the African Land Settlement and Utilization Board. His popular following seemed large and dedicated; at meetings they sang 'May Kenyatta be victorious' to the tune of 'God Save the King'. But Kenyatta's moderation, ambivalence and faith in constitutionalism began to lose him support amongst those who were in a hurry.

The KCA, which had been banned between 1940 and 1944, had been resuscitated after the war and flourished in a small way under the shadow of the KAU. Its adherents came from the urban poor of Nairobi and the dispossessed of the countryside. In its early days the KAU had hoped that the Labour Government would sympathize with the extension of political rights to Africans. It was an assumption commonly held in Africa and reinforced by the news that India had been granted independence. In Northern Rhodesia, the Conservative election victory of 1951 was interpreted as the consequence of Labour Colonial Secretaries being too kind to Africans. According to an African trade union leader, Churchill had been placed in charge 'because England was frightened of losing her colonies as she had lost India'.[32] Lack of headway in Kenya was already creating a mood of bitterness and frustration.

Within the KAU, a militant wing became restless and disillusioned with Kenyatta's leadership, which, by 1952, was under increasing criticism. The KCA benefited from growing disappointment, not only amongst the Kikuyu of the overcrowded reserves and Nairobi, but amongst the educated Africans who saw their people's chance of freedom fading.[33] The KCA had already anticipated a violent struggle and had tried to draw former askaris into its fold. They had had their horizons widened by war service, felt discontented with the authority of their elders and chiefs, and had often suffered setbacks in setting up businesses with their gratuities.[34] Yet while their knowledge of fighting made them attractive recruits to a militant movement, the askaris also understood only too well the military power which the government had at its command, which made them reluctant to join the KCA or the Mau Mau. 'Normal political methods through KAU seemed to be getting nowhere. The young men of the tribe saw that a time of crisis was approaching when great suffering might be necessary to achieve what they believed in', was how Josiah Kariuki recalled the temper of his people in 1952.[35]

His flight from the ways of the KAU to Mau Mau was a path trodden by many other Kikuyu after 1950. Oaths similar to those taken by Mau Mau postulants had been taken by Kikuyu since 1944, but six years later the movement was spreading rapidly despite an official ban in August 1950. The binding by oath was popular not only amongst those driven by economic forces to the margins of society, but by men of education and ambition. Many pledged themselves just to keep in with their neighbours, or as the result of pressure from friends and kinsmen. By November 1952, the Commissioner of Police, M. S. O'Rourke, believed that the Mau Mau membership was about 200,000.[36]

O'Rourke's estimate had been made in the month after the Governor of Kenya, Sir Evelyn Baring, had, with the Colonial Secretary's permission, declared a State of Emergency. O'Rourke predicted a hard struggle to suppress the Mau Mau on the grounds that 'the predeliction of the Kikuyu for gangster crime, his savage cruelty, his cunning and ability to plan crime make him a most dangerous enemy'.[37] During the past year, there had been mounting evidence that the Mau Mau was heading for some kind of trial of strength with the colonial government. Not only were its numbers growing, but there were indications that it might be making a bid for totality of support amongst the Kikuyu. Mission schools were losing pupils; 3,000 had abandoned their classes in the Nyeri district alone, and congregations were dwindling. Those who ignored pressure to withdraw from mission life were the victims of intimidation.[38] Intelligence reports suggested that Mau Mau oath administrators were moving into new districts. The assassination on 7 October 1952 of Senior Chief Waruhui on the streets of Nairobi presaged a campaign of open violence against the government.

Kenya was facing a major crisis by the autumn of 1952. Reports of Mau Mau oath-taking and intimidation flooded in, and after a tour of the disaffected districts, Sir Evelyn Baring realized that he had no choice but to seek permission for the declaration of a State of Emergency. 'I think that the position is very serious', he confided to Oliver Lyttelton, on 9 October.[39] It appeared that Mau Mau was extending its influence into new regions by the exploitation of 'grievances' which had 'much force' among the Kikuyu. The settlers had been alarmed by this development and Baring feared 'there would come a moment when the more hot-headed would undoubtedly take the law into their own hands', especially if Europeans became the targets of Mau Mau attacks.[40] The Government had to be seen to be in control and not flinch from taking the necessary remedial measures. 'I hope you will not think that I have been carried away by panic on the part of excitable Europeans here. I have reached my conclusions very unwillingly and fully realize that the strong action I recommend will cause you much political trouble', Baring concluded. Delay in checking a 'formidable organization of violence' would make matters worse, and lead to the kind of bloodshed which might create the legacy of racial rancour that existed in South Africa. The Cabinet approved Baring's request and the State of Emergency was declared on 20 October.

Baring and his Secretariat had become convinced that Kenyatta was inextricably mixed up with Mau Mau. 'The instigators of the Mau Mau movement and the planners of the movement are leaders of the Kenyan African Union', Baring had warned Lyttleton. His first move was the arrest of Kenyatta and his 'henchmen' who were flown to exile in the distant northern frontier province.[41] This was a sop to the settlers and to those within the administration who were convinced that Kenyatta's several public denunciations of Mau Mau had been deliberately fraudulent. The Kenya Police Special Branch, which had monitored the Kenyan African Union, were sceptical since they were well aware that Kenyatta was losing ground within the movement in the face of criticism from its more militant members, whom he was no longer able to control.[42] His detention, trial, and imprisonment for seven years were, in fact, a considerable personal fillip since they transformed him into a martyr for the Kenyan national cause and his standing rose throughout the country. When he was released and began to bargain with the British Government, his nationalist credentials were impeccable. Within the Mau Mau he became a legendary, fellow victim of Government oppression.[43]

Kenyatta and six others stood trial at Kapenguria (well away from Nairobi) between November 1952 and April 1953. He was charged with having masterminded the Mau Mau, but the evidence against him did not add up to much. He had never been a member of the Mau Mau Central Committee which, during 1952, had been alarmed by the impact of Kenyatta's condemnation of the movement to mass meetings. (After discussions with Mau Mau leaders Kenyatta called off further such assemblies.)[44] Kenyatta's conviction was a valuable display of government determination and strength. According to police intelligence, news of his imprisonment reduced general tension among the Kikuyu and boosted the Home Guard and resistance movement within Nairobi.[45]

The arrest of Kenyatta and other activists during the early hours of 21 October appears to have taken the Mau Mau by surprise. This is what Baring had wanted, for earlier he had written to Lyttelton, 'we hope to move the moment the psychological effect of the arrival of the first British troops is felt'.[46] The sudden appearance of British soldiers (called 'Johnnies' by the Mau Mau), who had been flown in from Egypt took the movement unawares. It was certainly unready for a prolonged war with the Government. Karari Njama, who was to become 'Brigadier General' within the Mau Mau army, recalled that the creation of field units through the swearing of the *batuni* oath was hardly underway when the Emergency started.[47] Not only did the movement lack adequate forces, but efforts to entice non-Kikuyu into the Mau Mau had not been very successful. The quick arrest and detention of leading Africans, including the 'educated leadership' of the Mau Mau, left it headless and in disarray.[48]

In terms of the structure of the Movement, this Government move virtually wiped out both the Central Province and 'Central' Committees and, in so doing, the key institutions linking the various rural and urban district councils. Decision-making powers thus necessarily devolved to intermediate councils, comprised largely of semi-educated or uneducated leaders.

This was a considerable bonus for the Government's forces. Yet it is doubtful whether a well-informed leadership would have perpetuated the struggle. As Njama later admitted, 'the fear born out of knowledge caused many educated men to seek security in the white men. On the other hand, the ignorance of the illiterate peasants of the enemy's power was our warrior's strength and courage'.[49] Such a man, after enduring aerial attack, may have been the author of a note discovered in April 1954 at the edge of a forest which threatened the government's forces with 'airoplanes' and 'strong bombs'.[50]

There were others who turned to the sort of spells which had failed when the white men had first come to Kenya, and claimed powers which would turn bullets to water.[51]

Such hocus pocus was often all that Mau Mau gangs had to rely on, since few possessed many modern weapons. Men at an oath-taking ceremony near Thomson's Falls, which was attacked by the police at the beginning of December 1952, were all armed with *pangas* and *simis* [Kikuyu swords].[52] Half the men operating with Karari Njama in the summer of 1953 were likewise equipped with bladed weapons, and many of the rest had home-made firearms, From the very beginning of the war, Mau Mau units had to keep up what were often costly attacks on European farms, police stations and defended villages to get hold of firearms and grenades. Success was variable. What the police called 'a well-planned' attack carried out with swift efficiency on Naivasha police station at the end of March 1953 was the Mau Mau's most telling *coup*, devised, it was thought, by Dedan Kimaithi, its most able commander.[53] Over fifty rifles and carbines together with 3,000 rounds of ammunition were stolen and 170 prisoners were released. This success was never repeated; modern guns and ammunition trickled through to Mau Mau units so that throughout the campaign more than half its fighters had to make do with bladed weapons or improvised firearms.

Even if it had managed to secure a more formidable arsenal, there is little reason to believe that the Mau Mau could ever have forced Britain to pull out of Kenya prematurely. 'Overall strategy and long-range aims were either absent or very confused' during the early stages of the campaign, regretted Njama. His record of his own and his brothers-in-arms' experiences between 1953 and 1955 suggest that much of their energy was channelled into keeping alive rather than waging guerrilla offensives against the Government and its forces. The major, active Mau Mau groups in Nairobi, the Kikuyu Reserves, the Rift Valley and the forests of the Aberdares and Mount Kenya were never able to maintain permanent contact with each other. The concentration of groups which had fled to the foothills of Mount Kenya and the Aberdares were usually cut off from each other, in spite of the efforts of commanders like Kimaithi and Stanley Mathenge to set up a chain of command and impose some form of co-ordination. Kimaithi did succeed in the establishment of a command structure in which officers took to themselves ranks such as 'General' and 'Field Marshal'. He was also instrumental in the creation of what was called the 'Kenya Parliament'. This Mau Mau assembly first gathered in February 1954, when its members attempted to shape an overall military and political strategy for the whole movement. Its subsequent history was far from happy; simmering rivalries ended with a serious schism in the spring of 1955, when Mathenge formed his own Kenya *Riigi* (council). The consequence was a feud between Kimaithi's and Mahenge's factions which further hampered the Mau Mau's war effort. By then the numbers of fighters still at large had dwindled to 5,000.

There had been no system of recruitment or training for the Mau Mau fighting forces. The *intungati* were the 'professional' warriors, oath-bound, disciplined and part of a recognizable military structure. They looked askance at the *komerera*, the men and women driven by hunger and hopelessness into the forests who had formed themselves into fissiparous bands. They were Kikuyu, Meru and Embu who had been driven out of Nairobi, fugitives from the Reserves, or refugees from the Rift Valley or settlements on the edges of the forest which had been razed by Government forces. Landless and homeless, the *komereras* had nothing to lose, so they joined the struggle to get back at the forces responsible for their misfortunes. They never became fully integrated into the warrior units with whom they were often at loggerheads. Unruly and loosely led, the *komereras* preyed on each other as well as their enemies.

Neither kind of Mau Mau were ever, after the summer of 1953, able to establish permanent bases, thanks to aerial surveillance, bombing, and the pressure from ground patrols which were beginning to penetrate the forests. Groups were under continuous pressure and had to keep on the move. Women toiled and fought alongside men, although their duties, as laid down in Mau Mau field ordinances, were confined to carrying supplies, preparing meals and caring for the wounded. In Mathenge's unit, they were accorded the full status of warriors and in Kimaithi's they were given ranks just like the men. A strict code of sexual morality was set down which outlawed promiscuity and insisted on formal marriages between *intungatis* and women warriors. Women joined in raids. Four were killed when a gang was ambushed in March 1953, and a month before, a patrol took fifteen prisoner after trapping a gang of twenty-eight.[54] During the first days of the Emergency, the authorities were aware of the value of women to the Mau Mau, and steps were taken to discourage them from joining. In December 1952 a number of leading Kikuyu women in the Nyeri district were sent to all the women's markets where they exhorted all who would listen to remain loyal to the government.[55]

The prime concern of both the men and women actively serving with the Mau Mau was survival, which meant getting food and keeping out of the way of patrols which always had the edge in any skirmish because of their greater firepower. As the war went on, it became increasingly more difficult for the Mau Mau to replenish their stocks of food. The Government had deliberately uprooted Kikuyu communities around the fringes of the forest as a way of severing the Mau Mau from a conveniently-placed larder. The Mau Mau had therefore to rely more and more on plundering the cattle of loyalist Kikuyu, a task which became harder once the beasts had been penned and placed under watch by the local Home Guard units. As in the contemporary war against the Communists in Malaya, one major thrust of the Government's strategy was to cut off the Mau Mau guerrillas from their local sympathizers or, as they were officially known, the 'passive' wing of the movement.

At the start of the Emergency, the Mau Mau lacked full support from all Kikuyu and its following amongst neighbouring tribes was thin. Once the Government resolved to create a counterbalance to the Mau Mau in the shape of a body of 'loyal' Kikuyu, the movement responded with an effort to assert and extend its authority. The result was a civil war within the Kikuyu. In this struggle, which was central to the war, both sides turned swiftly to terror. For some time before the Emergency, the Mau Mau had been using strongarm methods to discourage waverers and scare its opponents. This campaign of menace and revenge continued, with Kikuyu men and women who disavowed Mau Mau and supported the Government as targets. Victims were usually beheaded and corpses were often vilely mutilated. One wretched example may stand for many; during Operation Thunderbolt in September 1954, a King's African Rifle patrol discovered the headless corpse of a girl of about ten years, whose fingernails had been torn out.[56] According to Njama, genuine Mau Mau warriors would have had no part in such brutalities and blame for many outrages was attributed to the *komereras*. Whoever was culpable, evidence of such atrocities provoked a mood of vengefulness amongst Kenyan whites and the Kikuyu who were serving with the Government.

The most notorious incident of this kind was the Lari massacre of 26 March 1953. The police believed that a force of about 300 Mau Mau carried out a carefully co-ordinated series of attacks on Kikuyu in a group of small villages scattered over an area of thirty square miles north of Nairobi. The operation had two objectives, the assassination of the pro-government Chief Luka and his family and to scare the local population into support for the movement. After the raids, the police discovered ninety-seven bodies and forty-six wounded; a further twenty-nine tribesmen were reported missing. Immediate newspaper reaction in Britain was hysterical with reports of at least 400 dead. According to police intelligence the massacre had 'struck deep terror into the hearts of the Kikuyu in the Kiambu reserve' which made it difficult to get evidence as to who had been responsible. There was also understandable 'anger and bitterness' amongst many Kikuyu whom it was 'very difficult to restrain' from taking vengeance.[57] Later some within the Mau Mau tried to exculpate the movement from guilt for most of the killings alleging that government forces had been responsible in spite of photographs which showed women and small children slain by spears, swords and *pangas*, all common Mau Mau weapons. The Lari massacre and the Naivasha police station raid occurred on the same day and each was a clear fulfilment of current Mau Mau policy, the creation of an arsenal of modern weapons and the obtainment of total support among the Kikuyu.

The Lari massacre hardened the attitudes of those resisting the Mau Mau, many of whom became convinced that they were fighting an inhuman foe who showed no pity and deserved none. In consequence, incidents occurred which suggest a powerful spirit of vengefulness, which was especially, and understandably, strong amongst some of those from the local white community who served as volunteer policemen and soldiers. Similar feelings enflamed many of the Kikuyu who sided with the Government and who suffered the brunt of Mau Mau intimidation and vengeance.

The declaration of the State of Emergency and subsequent decrees created an awesome machinery of coercion, backed by condign punishments for anyone whose behaviour or actions suggested that they were hostile to the Government or its aims. The regulations gave the police the power to arrest and intern anyone suspected of having taken a Mau Mau oath. By December 1953, when the Emergency regulations had been in force for thirteen months, over 150,000 had been arrested and nearly 120,000 convicted Mau Mau were in gaol.[58] Since the beginning of the year there had been massive deportations of Kikuyu from the Rift Valley from where they were moved either to the tribal reserves or newly-built villages. Operations followed the pattern established in Palestine and Malaya; areas were cordoned by troops and then combed by police. In April 1953, three companies of the Devons with police and armoured cars surrounded the Nakura reservation at dawn. Speaking through loudhailers, the police ordered those who would normally be going to work to proceed to checkpoints for screening, whilst the rest stayed in their homes. Searches revealed pieces of firearms and out of 5,000 questioned, 1,000 were detained.[59] The round-up and screening of 70,000 in Nairobi during April 1954 led to the detention of 50,000 suspects and the virtual end of effective Mau Mau power within the city. Where there was evidence of collusion between local Kikuyu and the Mau Mau, collective fines, usually of farm stock, were imposed on the district. This harsh measure proved doubly effective. Covert Mau Mau members, fearing detection or internment, broke cover and fled to the forest, while in some districts underground Mau Mau cells became nervous about co-operating too closely with the fighters for fear of bringing down official retribution on their neighbours.

The Kikuyu became aware of the dangers of association with the Mau Mau. The movement, which from its genesis had endeavoured to create an unseen but binding unity amongst all Kikuyu, was in fact dividing the tribe and turning it against itself. Many within the Kikuyu, particularly the traditional upholders of authority, the Chiefs, were wooed by the Government. They were also targets of the Mau Mau and so from the start of the Emergency they were given guards, often imported Somalis and Turkana, who had little love for the Kikuyu. The next stage in the Government's programme to create a loyalist faction within the Kikuyu was the creation of the Home Guards, a special corps which guarded villages and their stock and assisted police and army patrols. At first they were armed with spears but later they were issued with rifles. Imperilled villages were encircled by barbed wire (which hindered Mau Mau sympathizers from making nocturnal trips into the forest with supplies) and sandbagged blockhouses were built. The work of fortification was often carried out by Kikuyu forced labour, another of the official penalties imposed on a district where there had been too much evidence of Mau Mau activity.

The Mau Mau loathed the Home Guard, whom they often considered their principal adversaries. Tales were spread of Home Guard brutality in which the volunteers misused their authority within a village to denounce rivals and sequester their property and wives. Obviously the Mau Mau were anxious to discredit those who stood in the way of total Kikuyu dominance, but the nature of the war made it very easy for those who had taken Government service to use it for private advantage. A war of this kind offered unexpected opportunities to many who were quick to embrace them. Josiah Kariuku came across some of these beneficiaries in 1954, when suspects rounded up in Nairobi were brought to his detention camp.[60]

> All the prisoners were then brought in front of Special Branch agents who were dressed in huge hoods with eye-holes, and who became known as 'Little Sacks', or *Gakunia*. The agents were a mixed lot. Some were ordinary 'spivs' who became professional betrayers because this gave them a steadier income than they had known before: as the tempo of the Emergency increased so did the demand for such people and the supply never seemed in danger of drying up. But there were also those whom we called *Tai Tai* because they came from the class of educated young men who wore ties. Many of these were unemployed and became agents to earn money, while others were simply cowards and did it to escape arrest. All these groups originally had the same ardent desire for freedom that we had but the essence had been diluted by their own personal needs and fears. It was the illiterate people who throughout remained strongest in the struggle.

Ingenuousness presumably prevented them from identifying the probable winning side or recognizing the chances for personal profit. What mattered was that the colonial authorities never faced a shortage of Kikuyu who were willing, for whatever reason, to resist the Mau Mau.

The creation of the Home Guard and Tribal Police units freed the army and the police from the chores of static defence of villages and guarding the detention camps which proliferated across Kenya during 1953 and 1954. They were free to concentrate on their first task, the isolation of the active Mau Mau from its passive supporters within the Kikuyu. Once the job of deportations and mass arrests was underway, plans were put in hand for offensive operations in the forest regions where the Mau Mau would be harassed, tracked down and eliminated. Draconian restrictions were placed on the movement of natives. The Kikuyu reserves were designated 'Special Areas' where a strict curfew was enforced and anyone who failed to stop when ordered could be shot. The Aberdare Range and Mount Kenya district were 'Prohibited Areas' where any unauthorized person could be shot on sight. Illicit possession of firearms and ammunition was punishable by death and illegal oath-taking by up to fifteen years imprisonment.

The arrival in June 1953 of General Sir Geoffrey Erskine as Commander of forces in Kenya marked the start of continuous operations in the forest regions where the Mau Mau fighting units were gathered. Royal Engineers using Kikuyu labour opened tracks into the region and built operational bases around the edges of the forests. Two brigades of British Infantry, the Northumberland Fusiliers, and five battalions of the King's African Rifles were available for deployment in the forests, supported by the Kenya Regiment of white territorials, the police, and tribal ancillaries. In all 50,000 men were available, of whom over 20,000 were police, and the conduct of sweeps, cordons and patrols was closely based on Malayan experience.

Beyond the day-to-day discomforts of traversing bamboo forest or upland bush, there was no universal pattern of experience in the campaign against the Mau Mau gangs. The records of one unit, C Company of the 3rd battalion of the King's African Rifles, may stand for many others and give some impression of what it was like to hunt the Mau Mau.[61] It was part of a non-Kikuyu battalion made up of Nandi, Kipsigis, Akamba, Turkana, Samburu, Somalis, and Rendille, which from December 1953 was stationed in the Aberdare region, where each company had been allocated a special area. This enabled contacts to be developed between the unit and the local police and loyalists. Skirmishes with the Mau Mau were commonly the result of intelligence provided by informers. At the end of January 1954 two suspects were arrested and identified as Mau Mau members by a local informer. In April another informer, previously a Mau Mau fighter, (they were officially called SEPs, Surrendered Enemy Personnel) led a patrol to a camp where it came across three guerrillas, of whom one was killed, ten home-made guns, and a makeshift field hospital. A week later, on St George's Day, a patrol was taken by an informer to a camp believed to contain 150 Mau Mau. 'Troops [were] unable to approach into [the] camp as 1 Mau Mau, probably inspecting sentries had to be shot'. The Mau Mau, alerted, bolted, but later a SEP reported that four had been killed and fifteen wounded. Amongst the haul of captured weapons was a Martini-Henry rifle, the kind which had once been used by British forces against the Zulus. There were, however, reports that the gang which had fled possessed a Sten sub-machine gun and a Bren. Called *Nakombora* [the destroyer] by the Mau Mau, the Bren was greatly prized and feared.

It was often difficult, even with the help of informants, to get close to a Mau Mau camp. Women's shouts warned Mau Mau of the approach of a patrol during Operation Octopus in the Kianjege region during July 1954. The alarm calls of birds and monkeys often alerted Mau Mau, who considered them allies, but the rhinocerous was malignantly neutral in a war which disturbed his habitat. C Company's only fatality was Sergeant Mkori, fatally wounded by a rhinocerous in July 1955. Testy rhinos also accounted for Mau Mau warriors, who nicknamed them 'Home Guards' on account of their ferocity.

Apart from following up intelligence gained from informers, C Company took part in a number of larger operations, either cordons of villages and townships, or joining with other troops for 'sweeps' across wide areas of forests. In September 1954, C Company took part in Operation Thunderbolt, backed up by Kikuyu Home Guard and a Land Rover for prisoners. As its commander, Major Stockwell, later commented, the preparations for the operation had forewarned the Mau Mau who cleared out of the area as quickly as they could. His own unit was beset by ill-luck, which included being accidentally strafed by an aircraft and pursued by an angry elephant. In twenty-two months of active service, in which it suffered one casualty, C Company killed 112 Mau Mau, wounded nineteen, and captured forty-three. By the official end of the campaign, in December 1956, 11,503 Mau Mau had been killed and over 2,500 taken prisoner. Government forces lost just over 2,000 dead, of whom 1,920 were Africans. In terms of fighting, it had been a war of attrition in which better armed and better trained forces wore down loosely commanded units scattered through the forests.

Aircraft had been extensively used throughout the campaign for reconnaissance, bombing and later 'sky-shouting'. Much of the work was undertaken by Havards, including some from the Rhodesian Air Force, but in June 1953 a squadron of Lincoln bombers was deployed for bombing the forests. These were called *Nyagi-Kongi* [protruding navel] by the Mau Mau who noticed the small pod under their fuselages. Their appearance aroused much terror and their 1,000 pounders were believed to be atomic bombs.[62] The Mau Mau attempted to decoy the aircraft by such stratagems as lighting fires to indicate camps and draw fire, but the presence of 'planes overhead meant that all large camp sites had to be abandoned. It was extremely unusual for the Mau Mau to shoot back at aircraft, although one unknown warrior scored a hit on a spotter plane in February 1952 and punctured one of its tyres.[63] Air-to-ground liaison was fraught with snags which led to occasional mischances. A platoon from C Company of the 3rd King's African Rifles was fired on by Havards, whose pilots mistook it for a band of Mau Mau and ignored desperate smoke signals. When the matter was thrashed out later over beers, the RAF liaison officer claimed that the fliers believed green smoke signals indicated 'continue firing' and they were unaware that any Government forces were in the area.[64] Towards the end of the campaign 'sky-shouting' was used to tell Mau Mau fugitives where in the forest they could find letters giving details of the Government's amnesty terms.

Victory in the field had been made possible by the Government's swingeing security measures, which many in Britain believed amounted to ruthlessness. In the early months of 1953, when the Mau Mau appeared to be making a frightening headway, there were signs of despondency amongst the European community. The Ruck murders, in which a farmer, his wife and six-year-old son were slain by Mau Mau armed with *pangas* and swords brought about an eruption of purblind fury. Soon after, Sir Evelyn Baring was faced by vengeful demonstrators who gathered outside his office in Nairobi. After an exchange with two 'well-known leaders of the extreme European movement named Vigar and Thornton', Baring said that he would not speak to demonstrators of any race. This did not please the settlers and there were scuffles with police.[65]

As the struggle in the countryside intensified, the mood of those holding the

Mau Mau at bay became more and more remorseless. Two days after the Ruck murders, reserve police officers arrested a dozen oath-takers near the scene of the crime. Four were shot dead after they attacked the policemen in a car.[66] During February 1953 a further six suspects were shot as they tried to escape from cars in what seemed an odd frenzy of rashness.[67] Even more reckless was a Mau Mau suspect turned informer who had promised to lead a King's African Rifles patrol to a gang, but took his own life by throwing himself into a burning hut.[68] Between the start of the Emergency and 20 April 1953, 430 arrested men had been shot dead as they tried to escape.[69] Some killed in this way had been 'positively identified as wanted for murder', according to the police. The plain statement of the figures stirred up disquiet in Britain and led to a series of awkward questions to Oliver Lyttelton, the Colonial Secretary.

Before the Emergency, a group of Labour MPs had actively supported and encouraged Kenyan nationalism, in particular Fenner Brockway. Just before the declaration of the State of Emergency, Baring had asked Lyttelton to prevent Brockway from coming to Kenya on the grounds that 'most of his friends [his hosts, the Kenyan African Union] will probably by then be in gaol and we might find it difficult to protect him from the Europeans'.[70] Brockway, with another Labour MP, did arrive on 29 October 1952 and met various local nationalists, promising to put their case before Parliament. As allegations of brutality by the security forces began to filter back to Britain, other Labour MPs took up the cudgels for the Kikuyu. There was a censure motion in July 1953 which drew attention to the high casualties, and in December an inquiry was made as to how many dead escapees had been shot in the back. The forensic evidence was not available.[71] There had been twenty-four official complaints about maltreatment of which eight were unsubstantiated, five were proven and the rest were still being investigated.

There was evidence that some amongst the security forces were descending to torture. Reserve Police Officer Keates and Sergeant Ruben (of the Kenya Regiment) were fined £100 and £50 and bound over for twelve months for the manslaughter of Elijah Gideon, who had once been a Missionary Society teacher. An informer had told the Embu police intelligence that a Mau Mau unit had hidden firearms locally, and put the finger on Gideon as one who had aided the gang. He denied this. Then, 'a unanimous decision was taken by all concerned that so urgent was it to find the firearms that Elijah must be beaten to make him disclose their whereabouts'. Askaris were ordered to carry out the thrashing and Gideon, a hunchback who had been a consumptive, died from shock and multiple injuries. Soon after, Keates and Ruben were questioned by a local magistrate who discovered that both believed that Gideon was a Mau Mau member (which appears later to have been confirmed), and that his torture was justified because they believed that they were fighting a war.[72] Justice Geoffrey Rudd who heard their case eight months later in October 1953, seems to have shared this view that Kenya's State of Emergency was a war, and therefore the rules of human conduct could be radically changed. He explained the comparative leniency of his sentences by drawing attention to 'the heavy responsibilities' that had fallen on the shoulders of that 'small section of the community' from which Keates and Ruben had come.[73] Ruben's and Keates's methods were only revealed because of Gideon's death, so it would be impossible to say for certain whether they were common of time and place. General Erskine was clearly unhappy about the prevalence of such behaviour for soon after his arrival in Kenya, he issued a memorandum on 23 June 1953 which warned men under his command against 'beating up' natives, behaviour which would damage the forces' reputation and make their task harder.[74] For their part, the Mau Mau continually attributed acts of brutality to their adversaries, in particular local Kikuyu and white forces. The Kenya Regiment was specially dreaded. According to Njama, 'the difference between the Devons and the Kenya Regiment was that the latter wanted to kill us while the Devons wanted to capture us'.[75]

A stream of complaints about rough usage and torture flowed from the detention camps. The most infamous was at Hola where ten internees died in March 1959.[76] The Press was immediately told that all had perished from poisoning 'after they had drunk water from a water cart'. Autopsies revealed that they had died from repeated blows to the head and body, and a later official inquiry proved that these had been dealt by camp guards. Each of the dead men had been officially categorized as 'hard core' Mau Mau, a designation based on their behaviour. They were implacably hostile towards the camp authorities and deliberately obstructive on every possible occasion. Just before the fatal cudgelling, they had been among a party commanded to work on an irrigation scheme. When marching to the work site they had set up Mau Mau howls and hurled themselves into a human pyramid. The African warder in charge of the detail had been told by the Camp Commandant: 'If people make trouble you will hit them, but you will only hit them on the legs', a form of chastisement which seems to have been commonly used on would-be escapees, violent men and idlers.

Such treatment was not unusual for those deemed incorrigible. Moved from camp to camp during 1957–9, Josiah Kariuki recalled a sequence of rough-handling which was the reward of his refusal to abjure the Mau Mau. His attempts to write letters to outside sympathizers, such as John Stonehouse and Barbara Castle, were vigorously discouraged. He came across vindictive sadists, but also white and black men who treated him with equity and kindness. He was able to earn money and, like other internees who suffered unduly at the hands of the brutal, he was not without the means of bringing knowledge of his mistreatment to the notice of the authorities. At the tough Manyani camp he had been able to speak in Kikuyu to a visiting churchman for whom he outlined his and fellow inmates' grievances. The atmosphere within Kenya during the Emergency was one in which fear and fury alternated and sometimes merged. When it became clear that Mau Mau was a spent force, incapable of seriously damaging, let alone overturning, the Government there remained the problem of what to do with those Mau Mau members who, whilst locked up, still clung to their oaths. From the first days of the Emergency, Mau Mau adherents had been officially foresworn in ceremonies conducted either by pagan or Christian clerics. In November 1952, 4,000 Africans were 'cleansed' at a mass ceremony at Molo, and a month later 400 Kikuyu, all in Government service, publicly denounced the Mau Mau and took an oath of allegiance to the Queen at Nyeri.[77] Denunciation of the Mau Mau and the purgation of oaths were the ways by which detainees secured their release from camps, but there remained an irreclaimable minority. Their stubbornness exasperated the authorities and in various camps, such as Hola, led to gross maltreatment. Much may have passed unnoticed, but even had they wished to do so, camp administrators could not have thrown codes of humane conduct to the wind. The colonial authorities in Nairobi were responsible to London where the Government had to answer to the House of Commons.

The Mau Mau always considered themselves as political nationalists and as the struggle developed, they claimed, amongst other things, that they were fighting for Kenyan freedom as well as the return to the Kikuyu of land taken from them by white settlers. Soon after the beginning of the Emergency, intelligence investigations were set in hand to discover whether the movement was Communist-inspired or aided. The Cold War had been underway for several years and Western governments were well aware that the USSR was willing to exploit colonial liberation movements, even non-Communist ones. The Foreign Office was interested in Kenyatta's 1929 visit to Moscow, but the British Embassy there stated that he had not been given any special honour.[78] Former Senior Chief Peter Koinange, who had come to Britain in 1951 to plead for Kikuyu land rights and who was suspected of complicity in the Mau Mau, had been spotted in British Communist circles, but he and his colleagues were not taken 'much into their confidence'.[79]

Within Kenya, the activities of the left-wing MP, D. N. Pritt QC, who defended Kenyatta, aroused great police interest. Considered 'dangerous', he left on 5 March 1953, claiming that Kenyatta was innocent and his departure caused 'general relief'.[80] Another lawyer attracted the interest of Nairobi's Special Branch. He was an Irishman, Peter Evans, who was suspected of Communist Party membership, and was deported from Kenya 'after indulging in dangerous conduct' which included association with F. W. Odede, an official of the Kenya African Union who was detained as a Mau Mau suspect. Evans was later reported to be in India, where he was canvassing support for the Mau Mau.[81] Another Indian connection which concerned British Intelligence was Muhammad Rahman, a suspected Russian agent, who had been appointed First Secretary to the Indian High Commission at Nairobi in August 1952. It was known that the Kenya African Union and Mau Mau had been seeking his advice and that he had offered money to meet the costs of Kenyatta's defence.[82] Rahman's wife was also suspected as a Russian agent.[83] According to her colourful file, she had been born to Russian and Dutch parents in the Dutch East Indies, had been 'intimate with one of the chiefs of Kempetei [Japanese Military Intelligence]' to whom she had betrayed her first husband. After the war, she had married an Indian diplomat and travelled with him to postings in Eastern Europe and Bonn. Like him she was thought to have had contacts with Mau Mau and other African nationalists.

The precise details of the Rahmans's activities remain obscure, although, strangely for a Soviet agent, he spoke in favour of the proposed Central Africa Federation to an African audience at Kitwe, Northern Rhodesia, in January 1953.[84] The lessons of the Indian national struggle were naturally of great interest to Africans embarked on the same course, and the administration in Nairobi was anxious that Kenya's 120,000 Asians stayed loyal. Politically-active Indians were therefore kept under surveillance.[85] During the first stage of the Emergency, there was good reason for the authorities to feel nervous about the way which Indians might jump since there had been a nasty fracas between Indians and Europeans during a cricket match in December 1952. The trouble started after some Indians moved in on a stand reserved for Europeans. Like Africans, Asians found themselves the victims of the local colour bar.[86] Yet Mau Mau had nothing to offer the Asians, although some of their leaders were well disposed towards African nationalism, even though the Kenya African Union had spurned an alliance in 1950. By March 1953, the Asians were seen to be aligning themselves with the Government.[87]

Intelligence analysis in Nairobi were extremely worried about the possibility of the Mau Mau receiving arms from Communist sources. In November 1952, there was a scare in Nairobi which followed reports that Italian Communists had arranged for the shipment of pistols from Somalia to Zanzibar for delivery to the Mau Mau.[88] Enquiries by the British Consul in Mogadishu drew a blank and the pistols never appeared. Another will-o'-the-wisp was the tale that the Russian embassy in Addis Ababa with a reputed staff of 400 was sending help to the Mau Mau.[89] This *canard* went the rounds of Nairobi and found its way into *Time* magazine in December 1952, where it was attributed to the Director-General of MI5, Sir Percy Sillitoe. The rumour was pooh-poohed by the British Ambassador to Ethiopia who found no evidence of either an enlarged Russian embassy or covert help to the Mau Mau. The Ethiopians were highly indignant about the suggestion.

The flimsiness of the evidence linking Mau Mau with Russian efforts to exploit Britain's colonial misfortunes did not hinder the Foreign Office from an attempt to make a connection. Still, there was useful political mileage in any hints that what was essentially an African peasant *jacquerie* could be tied in with Communist world conspiracy. As a political movement, the Mau Mau had little chance of success. The sudden declaration of the Emergency and the immediate arrests of its leadership caught the Mau Mau unawares. It lacked full support from the Kikuyu, had few adherents outside that tribe, and was unprepared to fight the forces ranged against it. By the end of 1956, there were only a few diehards, like Dedan Kemaithi, still at large to be hunted down by small units, some of which included former Mau Mau, who had surrendered and sold their forest skills to the security forces. Some assisted in the final entrapment of Kemaithi, who was caught and hanged in 1957.

By the time the Mau Mau 'last ditchers' were being hunted down, the British Government was considering the timetable for Kenyan independence. Political life had been revived in Kenya in 1957, but as in the years leading up to the Emergency, it was dominated by Kenyatta, who was then still in prison. African nationalists repeatedly demanded his release and the new nationalist party, the Kenyan African National Union, campaigned under the slogan *Uhuru na Kenyatta* [Freedom with Kenyatta]. The British Government was pressed for his release during the Lancaster Gate conference in 1961, and soon afterwards Macmillan and Ian MacLeod, the Colonial Secretary, agreed. Kenyatta left prison in August 1961 as president of KANU. A year before, Macmillan had made a tour of Africa, then and now remembered for his 'winds of change' speech in which he acknowledged African nationalism as a historic force which it would be folly to block. He took a Whiggish view that Britain was faced with a movement which was not without moral force and certainly was unstoppable. Unbending opposition to change would be politically fruitless and likely to lead to a series of colonial rearguard actions which would drive African nationalists into the arms of the Soviet Union or China. On the other hand, if the British Government came to terms with the new forces in Africa, the result would benefit everyone.

This was also Kenyatta's view. A conservative, he saw his task as the imposition of national unity, which included calming the European population whose view was that African self-rule would bring catastrophe and chaos. 'If you cannot obey the present laws how will you be able to obey our own laws when we have them?', he asked those who wanted to seize independence forcibly. Of the whites he said, 'the Kenya Government will not deprive them of the right of owning property which they own at present'. Mau Mau belonged to a past which had to be forgotten otherwise it would remain a stumbling block to racial and tribal unity. His appeal worked and the past was buried, by both Mau Mau and loyalists. 'The spirit of revenge', claimed Kariuki, would not 'help us to harvest the real fruits of Independence, which will be gathered in a spirit of tolerance, restraint and co-operation'. Kenya received its independence in 1963 and, thanks to the extraordinary charisma of Kenyatta, the passions generated by the Mau Mau campaign were buried.

On the eve of the Mau Mau Emergency, many white settlers in Kenya were convinced that their's was a 'white man's country'. They were unable to convince the British Government and so the Colonial Office was able to continue its policy of African advancement. They ordered matters differently in Southern Rhodesia where, from 1923 onwards, the European settlers asserted a decisive influence over the colony's development. As in Kenya, the white community was at loggerheads with the black over the issue of who owned what lands. Arguing that their efficient farming was the backbone of the

Rhodesian economy, the settlers had occupied the most productive lands which they worked with African labour. Inextricably linked with the land question was contention over the pace at which Africans were to be admitted to political rights. The settlers naturally wished to forestall African majority rule which once achieved would open the way for a redistribution of land. African impatience was beginning to show in 1961 when Southern Rhodesia faced a campaign of terrorism and intimidation by black nationalists. The pattern followed closely that of Kenya in 1952, with those Africans who supported the Government as the main victims. Across the border in Angola there were chilling portents of the future in the shape of a savage uprising against the European community and its African allies.

Anarchy and massacres of Europeans in Angola and the Congo suggested to white Rhodesians that African majority rule was a recipe for chaos. They came to believe that, left to their own devices, they could overcome pressure from local nationalists and their backers elsewhere in Africa. In 1963, Britain had passed control of the local armed forces to the Rhodesian parliament, in spite of Ghanaian opposition in the United Nations. By 1965, Rhodesia was, next to South Africa, the best armed state in southern Africa. She possessed three battalions of regular infantry and eight of territorials with a further four being formed. The Royal Rhodesian Air Force had one squadron of Canberra bombers, and one each of Hunters, Vampires and Provosts. There was also a squadron of Alouette helicopters and 34,000 police of whom two-thirds were reservists. Rhodesia was therefore well able to cope with internal insurgency and any threat from her neighbours, Zambia and Malawi.

When he declared Rhodesia independent of British control on 11 November 1965, its Prime Minister, Ian Smith, did so from a position of considerable military strength. Although it was shocking at the time (the Queen had sent a personal message asking Smith to reconsider what he was about to do), the declaration of independence was little more than a statement of political fact. During three years of intermittent negotiations, the Rhodesians had not moved on basic constitutional issues, and there had been little which the British Government had been able to do to make them change their minds. Harold Wilson, the Prime Minister, was in an awkward position. He was faced with a rebellion from what had been, at least in terms of absolute legality, a British colony. The governor had not asked for British forces and contacts with local Rhodesian commanders revealed that they would obey Smith. Wilson faced mutiny as well as rebellion. African Commonwealth states expected a traditional response. Presidents Kaunda of Zambia and Kenyatta of Kenya wanted British troops to occupy the Kariba Dam to guard it and with it the source of electric power for Zambia's copper industry, which then supplied 40% of the world's copper. 'Stern measures' against Rhodesia were expected from Uganda, and the Prime Minister of Nigeria, Sir Abubakar, insisted that 'the only way to handle him [Ian Smith] is to deal with him savagely'.

In Britain, there were those who favoured armed intervention; Jeremy

Winds of Change and Storms of War: Africa

Thorpe, at that time leader of the Liberal Party, demanded that most illiberal form of colonial intimidation, bombing. War fever was not endemic. The *Daily Mirror* cautioned against war with the Rhodesians and elsewhere in the country there was open sympathy for Ian Smith. There were also dark tales that service chiefs had confided to Wilson their reluctance and that of many of their men to undertake operations designed to reinstate direct colonial rule in Rhodesia. Wilson chose a cautious path by which he hoped that he could avoid an unpopular war to bring a wayward colony to heel. On 2 December he announced that Britain would deploy her forces if Rhodesia attacked Zambia and that Britain 'would not stand idly by' if the Kariba Dam was endangered. Kaunda had already asked for help, specifically to safeguard the Kariba Dam. Wilson was worried about Zambian copper, but he was also perturbed by the possibility that states of the Organization for African Unity might be involved. Kaunda was offered a flight of RAF Javelins at Lusaka conditional on the airport staying under British control, and forces from other African states, especially Egypt, the Congo, and Ethiopia, being kept out of Zambia. Zambian integrity was preserved and Britain was spared being drawn into a racial war in southern Africa. As a token of concern, Wilson and his successor, Edward Heath, maintained naval patrols off Beira to check Rhodesian oil imports. Since most of these passed through South Africa, the gesture did not add up to much.

War did break out in Rhodesia, which from 1966, faced a struggle with African guerrillas fighting under the banners of Robert Mugabe's ZANU and Joshua Nkomo's ZAPU. Auguries for Rhodesian survival were few. In 1974, the new revolutionary government of Portugal sounded the retreat from Angola and Mozambique, which left Rhodesia more and more dependent upon South Africa for help. By January 1979, the strain of the bush war in Rhodesia was becoming unbearable, and the Government was forced to take the step of imposing conscription on the black community. Before the year was out, Smith capitulated in the face of pressure from the newly-elected Conservative Government of Mrs Thatcher and South Africa. Both wanted stability and as the Rhodesian war increased in intensity so did the chances that Russia and her Cuban catspaws, already active in Angola, might eventually become embroiled. Mugabe was not a Marxist and his Government was assured of US cash. Those whites who stayed behind have not suffered, unlike ZAPU supporters. A thousand British troops were sent to Rhodesia where they supervised the surrender of ZANU and ZAPU guerrillas and the administration of a general election. It was their last imperial duty in Africa just a hundred years after the Zulu War.

6

John Bull's Other Wars: Ireland

The Rattle of a Thompson Gun: 1919–22

Another martyr for old Ireland,
Another murder for the crown,
Whose brutal laws may kill the Irish,
But can't keep their spirits down
Lads like Barry are no cowards,
From the foe they will not fly;
Lads like Barry will free Ireland
For her sake they'll live and die.
                                    Kevin Barry.

Come all ye young rebels and list while I sing
For the love of one's country is a terrible thing
It banishes fear like the spread of a flame
and makes us all part of the Patriot Game.
                        Brendan Behan, *The Patriot Game.*

At the beginning of 1919, Irishmen were full of fight. Across the southern counties, the Irish Republican Army (IRA) gathered weapons, formed battalions, drilled, trained, laid ambushes and launched sorties against police barracks and army patrols. The IRA waged war by stealth since it never had enough men to take on the British army in open battle, and anyway the Irish had learned by experience that even the most determined and brave rebels stood little chance against well-armed and disciplined regulars. The IRA's soldiers were not, however, lacking in courage and resourcefulness although their enemies, cheated of the kind of fighting they were best at, considered them craven and murderous. Their objective was to make Ireland ungovernable and so leave the British authorities no choice but to pull out so that a government chosen by Irishmen could take control of the whole country. Not all Irishmen wanted a united Ireland, free of Britain. The prospect was unthinkable for the Protestants in the six northern counties, so they got ready to fight the local IRA and make certain that their Catholic neighbours remained docile.

The motives for this belligerency were complex and rooted in the distant and not so distant past. The Irish were no strangers to the paraphernalia of secret societies, covert conspiracies, intimidation and guerrilla warfare which their rulers called terrorism. The preparations before and during 1919 were a continuation of nearly 800 years of conquest, resistance and subjugation. This history of spasmodic political violence marked out Ireland from the rest of Britain to which it had been reluctantly attached by the Act of Union in 1800. In Britain the next 100 years had seen the decline of political violence and the triumph of those liberal ideals which made men place their faith in reasoned discussion, negotiation and compromise. Ireland had benefited from the transformation of British political life which gave its inhabitants greater rights than they had ever known before. The majority of the Gaelic, Catholic Irish used their new liberties to campaign for an Irish parliament which they believed would best suit Ireland's needs. The Home Rule Party convinced Gladstone, who, in 1886 proposed the restoration of the Dublin parliament.

Violence had not been banished from Irish political life. Many Irishmen believed that the half-hearted rebellion of 1848 and the more threatening Fenian conspiracies of the 1860s had forced an otherwise indifferent British Government to take heed of Ireland and offer concessions to its people. The agricultural slump which began in 1879 was followed by an upsurge in unrest and the reappearance of an underground resistance movement. Rural guerrillas waged nocturnal war against landlords, the police and farmers who dared to take over the holdings of evicted tenants. Gladstone's conversion to Home Rule brought threats of violence from a new quarter, the Protestants of Ulster, who dreaded that in a self-governing Ireland they would be overwhelmed by the Catholic majority. Their combativeness was actively encouraged by the Tory opportunist, Lord Randolph Churchill who first vaunted the slogan, 'Ulster will fight and Ulster will be right'.

Conservatives and Liberal Imperialists imagined that Irish Home Rule would be the first stage of the disintegration of the British Empire, and for this reason they fought tooth-and-claw to prevent it. Once it was clear that Home Rule was inevitable, the teeth and the claws were publicly bared. The third Home Rule Act was passed by a far from enthusiastic Liberal administration in 1912 in return for Irish backing in the Commons but, thanks to the delay imposed by the overwhelmingly Tory House of Lords, the introduction of Irish self-government was postponed until the autumn of 1914. This gave the northern Protestants the chance to work up a head of steam, pledge themselves to fight Home Rule and muster an army. By the end of May 1914, the Ulster Volunteer Force (UVF) numbered 85,000 and was believed to have an arsenal of over 50,000 rifles and a few machine-guns which had been smuggled from abroad.[1] The UVF drilled, exercised and fired publicly at targets, and their activities were applauded by Conservative and Unionist leaders in Britain. Not only had the old tradition of Irish political violence reasserted itself, but it appeared to have taken over the minds of British politicians.

In the past, insurrection or the threat of it in Ireland had been firmly met by the police, backed by the garrison of British troops. As recently as the 1880s and 1890s the full machinery of coercion had been applied to root out the underground Land League. Yet in 1913–14, the British government shrank from taking the customary measures against Irish insubordination since it was troubled by misgivings about the loyalty of its own armed forces. Not only did the rebels of Ulster have the blessings of the Conservative Party, but there were signs that many army and navy officers were not disposed to taking part in operations to disarm them. There were murmurings amongst officers on board the squadron anchored off Lamlash with which Churchill had hoped to menace Belfast. A number of cavalry officers, stationed at the Curragh Camp near Dublin, stated that they might resign their commissions rather than obey orders to proceed against the Volunteers. A lack of steadfastness was apparent elsewhere. Many officers were well aware that arms were hidden in Ulster country houses where they stayed as guests. A cache of rifles was accidentally uncovered by an officer who had gone in search of croquet mallets, but 'being a man of great discretion, doubtless he decided that the matter was not one that came exactly within his province'.[2]

While the UVF imported Mauser rifles from Germany and British officers wobbled, supporters of Home Rule began to raise their own army. Enlistment of the Irish Volunteers started in November 1913 and within twelve months 180,000 Irishmen signed on. Their efforts to equip themselves were less successful than those of the UVF. The benevolent neutrality of the police and the army to the Ulster gun-runners was not extended to their counterparts in the south. On 26 July 1914 police, backed by a detachment of the Scottish Borderers, thwarted the unloading of a shipment of rifles at Howth, near Dublin. They in turn were intercepted by an angry crowd, and three civilians were shot dead before the soldiers could extricate themselves.

Britain's entry into the European war on 4 August 1914 prevented the conflict from deepening since, by the common consent of a thankful British government and John Redmond, leader of the Home Rule party, all decisions about Ireland's future were postponed until the end of the war. The UVF backed the war and many of its members gave proof of Ulster's attachment to Britain by flocking to Kitchener's army. In the south, enthusiasm for Britiain's continental war was muted despite Redmond's efforts to encourage recruiting. The nationalist volunteer movement split into National Volunteers, who stuck by Redmond, and Irish Volunteers who came increasingly under the influence of Sinn Fein. With the old Home Rule Party compromised, Sinn Fein was able to put itself forward as bearing the banner of Irish nationalism. Since its foundation a few years before, Sinn Fein had pressed for an Irish Republic totally severed from Britain and created by the patriotic will of the Irish people. Irish freedom lay at the end of the hard road of armed struggle rather than the serpentine track of British constitutionalism. The European war was a valuable boost for Sinn Fein for it offered a fresh chance to employ the old Irish stratagem of making the most of Britain's temporary distraction. But in 1916, as in 1798 and the 1590s, this device failed.

The Easter Rebellion of 1916 caught the local military authorities off their guard, but Sinn Fein lacked popular support and manpower. Once they had recovered from their initial confusion, the Government had more than enough troops to overwhelm the rebels. The aftermath of the rising witnessed army commanders taking full advantage of martial law and doctrines of massive coercion which had always prevailed whenever the Irish took up arms against their rulers. Fifteen leading rebels were shot after summary courts martial, 140 others were gaoled, and a further 1200 were locked up without trial. By the end of the year, the British Government repudiated the sternness of its agents in Dublin, and the bulk of the imprisoned rebels were freed and, in some cases, allowed to return to Ireland. Many of the men who survived, like Michael Collins who in 1919 became Director of the IRA, continued to work for Sinn Fein.

Sinn Fein had scored a victory in 1916 even if it had failed to beat the British army. Its ideals offered Irish nationalists the best chance of getting separation from Britain on their own terms and the lion-hearted 'martyrs' who had died during and after the fighting in Dublin set a pattern for heroism in the Irish cause. The extent of Sinn Fein's hold over the country was revealed in the general election of December 1918 when seventy-six Sinn Fein MPs were elected, taking three-quarters of all the Irish seats. Nearly half of them, including Eamonn de Valera, were still in British gaols. The new MPs disdained to cross the sea to Westminster, and instead remained in Dublin, where, on 15 January 1919 they issued a declaration of independence. The founding fathers of the Irish Republic called on Britain and all her soldiers and civil servants to get out of Ireland and insisted that Ulster, which had returned twenty-six Unionist MPs, was to be an inseparable part of the new state. 'We are now done with England', asserted Cathal Brugha, Chief of Staff of the Irish Volunteers, and his verdict was confirmed a year later when Irish voters placed Sinn Fein councillors in charge of seventy-two local authorities.

There were, at the beginning of 1919, two governments in Ireland. One, under the Chief Secretary for Ireland at Westminster and the Viceroy, Lord French of Ypres, said that it ruled in Britain's name, even though its judiciary soon ceased to function and its policemen and civil servants could not collect taxes; soon they were going in fear of their lives. The other government, the Irish Parliament of *Dáil*, raised its own taxes and foreign loans and with the help of its Sinn Fein supporters ran its own police and courts. Its Finance Minister, Michael Collins, at the beginning of 1919 appealed for men for the Irish Republican Army which would resist the armed forces of the British authorities.

Just how the British authorities would react was still, in the early months of 1919, far from clear. Two days after the *Dáil* had proclaimed Irish independence, the Viceroy asked the War Office for men and equipment. The

Chief of the Imperial General Staff, Sir Henry Wilson, sent French what he wanted in the way of men, armoured cars, tanks and machine-guns and by May there were 53,000 British troops in Ireland. Wilson was an Ulsterman with an ancestral loathing for Gaelic nationalism and he was an Imperialist who shared with many others in the Cabinet the dread that if Sinn Fein was allowed to get away with rebellion a mortal blow would have been struck against the Empire. It was the old Unionist line that Irish self-government would irreparably weaken Imperial ties. There was a new twist to this argument since concessions to Irish rebels would undoubtedly have encouraged nationalists in Egypt and India who were taking considerable interest in events in Ireland. Churchill, the Secretary for War, recognized the Imperial dimension which he described in a heady speech in November 1920. What he called the 'Irish murder gang' was part of 'a world-wide conspiracy against our country' which if unchecked in Ireland, India and Egypt would damage the Empire.[3] Political rodomontade was plentiful throughout 1919 and 1920 and it did much to obscure the Cabinet's confusion and indecision about Ireland's future. Lloyd-George realized that some kind of self-government would have to be conceded to Ireland and that the peculiar interests of the Ulster Protestants would have to be accommodated even if that meant partition. At the same time he could not tolerate the methods of Sinn Fein, let alone their insistence on a unified Ireland under republican government. His Home Rule Bull of February 1920 (the fourth in less than forty years) envisaged extensive British control over Irish affairs, including agricultural policy, and the subsequent Government of Ireland Act of 1921 acknowledged Ulster's separate identity.

There was nothing here for Sinn Fein, nor was there meant to be. In August 1920 Lloyd-George excluded their representatives from negotiations about Ireland's future and, like Churchill, he made many public avowals that he would never do business with murderers. For all this bluster, Lloyd-George and the Cabinet shrank from declaring war on Sinn Fein, although it had been outlawed by Lord French in September 1919. This left the British garrison in Ireland in an awkward position. 'The rebels were at war with us and we were at peace with them' noted a vexed and bewildered Sir Henry Wilson in June 1920.[4] 'We were fighting with one hand behind our backs, this being the usual English custom in civil strife', recalled an officer of the Worcesters, one of the many who had to enforce what passed for the Government's will.[5] 'What a hole to be in' was the candid comment of a private soldier in the Lancashires.[6]

Both of these remarks were made during the winter of 1920–1 in the middle of a violent struggle between the IRA and the British armed forces. The drift into war had been slow. Since January 1919, when the IRA began to collect men, train them and acquire arms, Sinn Fein had expected the British to take the offensive. In fact French had been instructed not to open hostilites but to wait until the IRA made the first aggressive move. There were probably no more than 15,000 volunteers in the IRA and from the start they were short of guns and ammunition. Both commodities were available in abundance at police stations and so, during the spring and summer of 1919, a number of raids were made on the isolated Royal Irish Constabulary barracks which existed in every small town and village. Random murders of policemen also occurred and by the end of the year nineteen members of the security forces had been killed.

The two sides in the growing conflict appeared unevenly matched. The IRA, which had been drawing in recruits since soon after the declaration of the republic, was organized on a regional basis and directed from General Headquarters in Dublin. Its shortage of arms and ammunition to a certain extent dictated its strategy of sorties against police stations and small units of police and soldiers. In the summer of 1920, Cork No 3 Brigade possessed thirty-five rifles, each with thirty rounds, and twenty pistols, each with ten rounds.[7] Raids in June and July on a coastguard station gained it a further twenty-five rifles and 20,000 rounds. The need for replenishment of stocks remained throughout the campaign; scrap iron was melted down for grenade cases, mortars were improvised and spent cartridges were kept for refilling.[8] At a meeting of senior regional commanders in Dublin in the autumn of 1921, there was great pessimism about supplies of guns and ammunition. Their tenor irritated Ernie O'Malley who saw fit to remind all present that it was deeds rather than words that mattered.[9]

> 'Lack of rifles and ammunition is due to officers in each area', I said. 'We get little supplies from the Quartermaster General. Our main source of supply is the enemy. It is not a question of arms or ammunition. I have never yet met a keen, good officer or volunteer who did not by hook or crook obtain arms and stuff.'

Arms were by then coming from abroad, including Thompson sub-machine guns bought by American Irish sympathizers which were easy to conceal and therefore well suited for close-quarter street fighting. O'Malley was himself able to cross to England and buy wireless sets, prismatic compasses, Sam Browne belts and the like from war-surplus sales. Bribery of staff in chemical works opened the way for the procurement of explosives which were shipped back to Ireland.

Service in the IRA offered excitement in an honourable cause and for many the chance to display manly panache like that of a volunteer encountered by Lieutenant Barton when he was off duty and in mufti in Dublin.[10]

> One day, Twining . . . and I were on the top of a tram when one of a bunch of four young men produced a revolver and declared that he was a Shinner and cared naught for no one. However, he got suspicious of us and started off down the stairway, we followed after him, but his companions made a block on the stairway, and delayed us and we lost him up a side street.

This sort of bravado was risky, the more so during 1920 when discovery and capture could lead to torture or summary shooting. The IRA commanders saw themselves as men apart, single-minded and guided by a deep love of a country which they saw imperilled. They considered themselves soldiers, held to the martial virtues and demanded and got discipline from their men. Like all soldiers they constantly had to concentrate on survival in the face of an enemy which was better armed and more numerous. Their camouflage was a population which, whilst it did not always approve of their murders and arson, sympathized with their patriotism and was not a little scared of the retribution which they visited on informers, real and imaginary. The IRA soldier wore no uniform and his arms were concealed about his person or hidden in secret dumps.

Without any distinguishing features the IRA fighter mingled with the crowds, one moment a civilian, the next an armed ambusher. His ability to pass undetected through towns and countryside was frustrating for his adversaries who found themselves fighting will-o'-the-wisps. When Sir Henry Wilson voiced his own and the army's impatience with a Government which would not declare war on Sinn Fein and the IRA, Churchill responded by asking how a war could be waged against an unseen foe.[11]

> It is no use, for instance, answering the question, 'What would you do in Ireland', by saying 'I should shoot', or 'I would shoot without hesitation', or 'I would shoot without mercy'. The enquiry immediately arises, 'Whom do you shoot?' And shortly after that, 'Where are they?' 'How are you going to recognize them?'

In a final sally, Churchill concluded that he did not think the present situation in Ireland would be improved by the adoption of 'the kind of methods the Prussians adopted in Belgium'.

So, as long as he kept out of sight of the police and the army, the IRA fighter possessed a considerable advantage. A few IRA men, like the Cork commander, Tomas Barry, had previous experience of soldiering in the British army, but most were apprentices at war who learned their skills on the job. Watchfulness, fieldcraft, stealth, and such arcane arts as recognizing the difference between the engine noise of the Crossley tender (much favoured by the Auxiliary police and the Black and Tans) and other British army vehicles were usually learned on active service. Local knowledge and local assistance, including that of vigilant children and the Sinn Fein women's organization, the *Cumann na nBan* gave the IRA an edge in intelligence, but civilian cooperation ws increasingly risky as the authorities adopted more and more fiercesome reprisals against those suspected of helping the guerrillas.

British soldiers had to wage war on a phantom army whose soldiers dressed like civilians and could appear anywhere, attack and then vanish. It was a new kind of war made worse by the fact that officers and men alike were uncertain just what they were supposed to be doing. In March 1920, the Cabinet turned

John Bull's Other Wars: Ireland

to a man who seemed like a specialist, General Sir Nevil Macready, the son of a celebrated Victorian actor, who had commanded the special detachments of police and troops during the South Wales coal strike in 1910 (the Tonypandy riots of industrial folklore). In 1914 Macready had been given the tricky task of commanding forces in Belfast and in 1918 had been employed by the Cabinet to deal with the police 'strikes' in London. When he reached Ireland, he immediately asked for substantial reinforcements, a big intelligence staff, and supplies of wireless sets and lorries. Sir Henry Wilson was worried about pouring men into Ireland as it would drain the numbers available for handling unrest in India and Egypt as well as industrial trouble in Britain. Even so, by July 1921, there were 80,000 regular troops in Ireland.

One answer to the shortage of manpower was the creation of special units of *gendarmerie* which would assist the police and army. In the spring of 1919 the Government had created volunteer brigades for service in North Russia after it had become clear that British conscripts fighting there wanted to get out. The men who came forward were ex-soldiers, often officers, who were tempted by the pay and the promise of action. The same sort of man volunteered for the proposed Irish formations, the Royal Irish Constabulary (RIC) reinforcements known from their khaki breeches and dark green jackets as the Black and Tans [a pack of Tipperary foxhounds] and the Auxiliary Police Division, who were known as 'cadets' or 'Auxies'. Both were well paid, the Tans got ten shillings a day and the Auxies £1. Hallowed legend has it that both were brought up to strength with gaolbirds, but in fact the average recruit was a former frontline officer, hardened by the war and unable to adjust easily to the tempo of civilian life. Typical was a former Royal Marine Major who had been decorated for gallantry, but had been cashiered in October 1919 on charges of cowardice after his unit had been ambushed in North Russia. There were also some men like Major Bruce DSO, MC, (who had lost an arm during the war) who found service in Ireland provided opportunities for lawlessness. His repeated rough-handling of 'respectable Irish people' led to his dismissal, whereupon he formed his own gang which borrowed a police car and carried out a number of armed robberies.[12]

The Tans first arrived in Ireland during January 1920 and were followed by the Auxiliaries who took up their duties in the summer. In theory both forces were extensions of the RIC under their own commanders and paid for from police funds, although their duties were solely to seek out and engage the IRA. Both were very hard to control. Command of these forces was in the hands of Major-General Sir Henry Tudor whom a colleague described as 'a good sportsman, a champion boxer, a famous amateur jockey', for whom service in Ireland was somewhat disconcerting since he 'had to associate with people not of his sort; one expects the British Empire to be run by gentlemen, and Ireland, in those days, certainly expected to be ruled on gentlemanly — not genteel — lines'.[13] There was little either gentlemanly or genteel about the Tans and the Auxies.

'The show has gone to the dogs' admitted Major General Tudor in January 1921 after a year in which the Tans and late the Auxies had committed numerous outrages, which included sundry murders of suspects, random shootings, looting, and arson.[14] Brigadier General Crozier, an Auxie officer, found that most of his men were out of control and furiously resentful of any effort by him or anyone else to discipline them. After two Auxies had reported their colleagues' looting at Trim, they were blackguarded, and five men accused in the case publicly threatened to expose the government's collusion with the 'official' terror.[15] While the scandal of the outrages buzzed across Britain, Private Swindlehurst of the Lancashire Fusiliers stood guard at Jury's Hotel in Dublin. He could hear the sounds of beatings administered by the Tans and watched suspects hustled out 'about all in, covered in blood, minus teeth, and with numerous other injuries'.[16]

There is some evidence that the army resented the methods of the Tans and the Auxies for Swindlehurst noted that the Tans did not shoot suspects when soldiers were present. From the beginning of the disturbances, the main job of the army had been to assist the police which meant that soldiers escorted police patrols in the town and countryside, investigated reports of IRA activity, enforced curfews, searched houses, scoured the countryside and guarded government buildings. It was dull, thankless and dangerous work for which few had been trained.[17]

> Raids for information or wanted men were usually made at night. We moved off towards midnight in a lorry; sometimes, though rarely, we were accompanied by a cumbersome armoured car. Our first call would be at the police station of the district we would be raiding in, here we would meet the constable who would be coming out with us. . . . We would plan out in what order we would raid the places, and glean information from the police that would have any bearing on the raid. We would stop the lorry some distance from the house to be raided, send a few men round the back and then knock and gain entrance. Pickets were left at the front and back doors while the searching was done by one or two officers helped by a senior NCO. It was not a pleasant job and was not improved by the stale air in most houses; this staleness was largely caused by the fumes from little red-globed oil lamps burning before a highly coloured picture of the Blessed Virgin Mary. Most bedrooms had these lamps burning all night, and with the windows tightly shut and chamber pots under the beds it was not at all a bed of roses. Sometimes we had to raid the tenements on the north side of the river; these were big, crumbling Georgian houses, with a family in each room. On entering these rooms the first thing to do would be to dash across to the window and try to open it. On going into one of these rooms once I found a blanket on a line nailed across a corner; behind this a woman was giving birth to a child.

On such duties, men were met with indifference or abuse. Private Swindlehurst and men from the Lancashire Fusiliers were spat on when they were searching houses in the poorer quarter of Dublin and taunted with remarks like 'that didn't hurt' and 'rubber footed murderers' in a street where a child had been killed in crossfire.[18] All the time there was the threat of ambush by concealed snipers or grenade throwers against whom there was little protection save chicken-wire stretched over the open lorries. Even then bombs did pass through the gaps. If a patrol was able to retaliate its assailants ran off and could not be detected amongst the civilians about their daily business. Off-duty soldiers were always in danger. Private Swindlehurst, walking down Sackville Street, was prodded in the back by a gun. An Irish voice said, 'Stick your hands up', and then he was asked: 'How long are you going to be here?' After answering, Swindlehurst hurried back to his barracks; a sergeant who grappled with his interrogators had been shot in the stomach.[19]

It was warfare which was trying on the nerves and generated a purblind anger amongst British troops, a great number of whom were under twenty years old and recent recruits. They were professional fighting men engaged in what seemed an unequal contest against amateurs who killed without pity. The temptation to hit back and take revenge against those closest at hand was very great, especially if they seemed tainted with sympathy for the IRA. To start with, what were soon to be called 'reprisals' were random and personal acts of vengeance undertaken on the initiative of junior officers or men. A man stopped by a patrol and found him in possession of a bag of shirts which were the spoils from a hold-up of some off-duty soldiers was given 'two jabs from a bayonet to make him see reason' before he was arrested.[20] When, in September 1919, the Fermoy coroner's court refused to find a verdict of murder after a soldier from the Shropshires had been shot, his comrades spontaneously entered the town and took apart the houses of the jurymen. As the pace of the war quickened and the number of outrages increased, so did such private retaliation. On 15 November 1920 four Staff Officers were kidnapped and assumed murdered; two days later houses were burned and three men killed by the Tans in Cork; and on the night of 20–21 November fourteen British officers were murdered in their hotel rooms and homes in Dublin. Some had been killed in front of their wives, and it was rumoured in barrack rooms and messes that one of the women had been driven mad by her ordeal. Revenge was in the air.[21]

The troops were burning to get out and take affairs into their own hands. In fact the men of one regiment, which had lost two officers in the murders, paraded on their own with no higher ranks that Corporal with the intention of marching out of barracks. They were stopped in time.

The IRA, with its penchant for self-dramatization made much of such incidents which seemed to offer some justification for the ruthlessness of some of its own men. The men who ran the British army were also concerned on the grounds that the unchecked proliferation of private vengeance suggested the decay of traditional discipline. 'The human endurance of the troops is rapidly reaching a point where restraint will be impossible', warned Macready in September 1919. He was also anxious about the Tans and the Auxies for whom such conduct had become normal. Churchill sympathized with the troops whose actions stemmed from provocation, and he went so far as to insist that all sentences on soldiers who had taken private revenge were to be passed to him at the War Ministry before being confirmed by Macready.

What Macready and his commanders wanted was to reassert their right to command by persuading the Government to sanction reprisals. Wild destruction, plundering and drunken assaults would be replaced by bureaucratic retribution, approved and undertaken by the army under strict orders. Instead, Macready got martial law in Cork, Kilkenny, Kerry and Limerick which was proclaimed at the end of December 1920.

Macready's request for martial law to be extended to more counties was not based on weakness but a strong feeling, shared with his divisional commanders, that the British army was on the verge of turning the tide. There was some evidence for this optimism. During 1920, the security forces had suffered 230 dead, whilst losses for the IRA were considerably less. Between January and April 1921, the IRA lost 317 dead and 285 wounded, against 174 of the security forces killed. New field tactics were swinging the balance a little more evenly, in particular the replacement of regular patrols, whose movements were known to their opponents, with ones which came and went to no fixed timetable. The lightly equipped and mobile IRA 'Flying Columns' were matched by similar groups from the British army which often moved across country by night. Small police and army patrols disappeared and were replaced by bigger units which offered less tempting targets for ambush.

With more forces at their disposal, British commanders could undertake large-scale cordons and 'sweeps' of the countryside where IRA units were known to be sheltering. For troopers of the Royal Dragoons, stationed in Connemara, the sweeps were reminiscent of operations on the South African veldt twenty years before. A triangular area was sealed by posts manned by infantry and police on two sides whilst the cavalry advanced from the remaining side and 'beat' the ground, taking all men between fifteen and fifty, who were later screened by the RIC. Those driven by the beaters thought it wisest to keep on the move. Michael Brennan's Clare forces broke up and escaped as best they could rather than recklessly engage their more numerous hunters and risk attack by aircraft and armoured cars.[22] What Macready hoped for was a situation in which the IRA, compelled to keep on the move, would lost its grip on the local population, which in time would swing behind the Dublin administration. This possibility worried the IRA which stepped up its killings of informers.

By the beginning of 1921, the Irish campaign was entering its third year, and there was much public distress about the way it was being waged. During 1920

John Bull's Other Wars: Ireland

revelations about the misdemeanours of the Tans and the Auxies had aroused widespread Press and parliamentary criticism which extended to the Government's refusal to negotiate. This, in fact, was more apparent than real since from the beginning of 1921 feelers had surreptitiously been extended towards Sinn Fein's leaders. There was no Damascene conversion by the Cabinet which, at the end of May 1921, was discussing plans for further Irish counties to come under martial law and a proposal that the country be placed under colonial administration. King George V's speech inaugurating the new parliament in Belfast was a suitable pretext for direct talks with Sinn Fein and on 11 July a truce was agreed. Negotiations followed and in December the Irish Treaty was signed. During the exchanges with the Irish delegates, both Churchill and Lloyd-George emphasized that Britain would willingly continue the war relentlessly if no agreement was reached.

The treaty was signed and approved by a majority of seven votes in the *Dáil* on 8 January 1922. Southern Ireland, shorn of Ulster, became a Free State enjoying Dominion status. These terms fractured the nationalist movement; one faction under de Valera continued to press for a republic of all Ireland, whilst the other accepted the Free State. A subsequent general election confirmed a margin of popular support for the treaty within the country, but did not prevent the outbreak of a civil war. Britain was deeply concerned at the outcome of the struggle and in May Churchill warned that the Government would intervene directly and occupy Dublin if the republicans won. As it was, General Macready had been given permission to loan the Free State Government 18 pounders to bombard the Four Court buildings in Dublin which had been held since 14 April by IRA units. On 29 June the Free State also approached the British Government for aeroplanes and pilots for a bombing attack on the buildings, and Churchill acceded to the request. He did, however, suggest that they were painted in Free State colours, which displeased Trenchard.[23] They were not needed, as the Four Courts fell to conventional shelling and assault which was fortunate since the appearance of RAF bombers over Dublin would have discredited the Free State Government and boosted the republicans. The war continued for several months and ended with victory for the Free Staters.

Who had won the Irish war? The British armed forces had not been able to defeat the IRA in the conventional sense for, although under growing pressure in the first months of 1921, it had not been broken and its members still showed plenty of fight. 'A real war — not mere bushranging' was in store for Ireland if its delegates did not sign the treaty, or so Churchill warned. Field commanders were asking for martial law to be extended to more areas, and in March 1921 Macready had been permitted to use aircraft armed with bombs and machine-guns. There had been aircraft in Ireland for over a year, but their use had been confined to reconnaissance flights even though, in July 1920, Churchill had suggested bombing and strafing raids against identifiable IRA units training in the open.[24] No doubt such tactics would have fallen into the category of 'real war' and, as such, would have been immediately recognizable to enemies of the Empire in India and the Middle East. Trenchard disliked the idea of importing to the British Isles methods which were becoming common enough in remote regions and the terms of engagement considered for Ireland demanded sanction in writing from the most senior level.[25] No targets close to towns could be attacked.

In the event the Irish struggle did not see the introduction of 'aerial policing', a wise decision given the possible emotional reaction it might have provoked in a Britian which had not long since suffered German air-raids on its own towns and cities. Given the Government's willingness to 'lend' bombers to the Free State for use against the Four Courts it seems likely that restraint in such matters might have disappeared had the treaty not been signed. It would, of course, have been very hard for many Irishmen to discern any hints of 'restraint' in the behaviour of the forces of the Crown during 1920 and 1921. Their methods had stirred up widespread disquiet in Britain and criticism from abroad which did much to convince the coalition that the time had come to seek a settlement. Within the higher ranks of the army there were fears that discipline was cracking up as officers and men indulged in private acts of vengeance. Far away in northern India, there was a mutiny amongst ranks of the Connaught Rangers, who included Sinn Fein supporters, provoked by news of the 'terror' in their own homeland. This upheaval in July 1920 threw into doubt the loyalty of other southern Irish regiments where the mutineers claimed there was a similar mood of anger. There were no grounds for this belief; in 1921 the Leinsters took part uncomplainingly in punitive actions against the Mopilah tribesmen of western India which more than matched in savagery anything that was going on in Ireland.[26]

A double-standard existed which was why Ireland was spared the type of repressive measures undertaken against nationalists in Egypt, India and Iraq. How-long this immunity would have lasted is uncertain and the possibility that it might end did much to convince the Irish delegates that they must accept the treaty. The treaty enabled the British Government to salvage something from the campaign in the shape of a truncated Ireland which, on paper at least, was still attached to the British Empire. These Imperial ties were illusory; in 1939 the Government of Eire — the Irish Free State — remained neutral when the rest of the Dominions declared war on Germany and in 1949 Eire became a republic outside the Commonwealth.

The Old Cause: Northern Ireland, 1969–

In County Tyrone near the town of Dungannon
There was many a ruction meself had a hand in.
Bob Williams who lived there, a weaver trade,
And all of us thought him a stout Orange blade.

*On the twelfth of July as it yearly did come
Bob played on his flute to the sound of a drum.
You make talk of your harp, your piano and lute,
But nothing can sound like the old Orange flute.*

*But this cunning old bugger he took us all in,
And married a Papist called Bridget MaGinn,
Turned Papist himself and forsook the old Cause
That gave us our freedom, religion and laws.
Now the boys in the townland made noise upon it,
And Bob had to fly to the Province of Connaught.
He fled with his wife and his fixings to boot
And along with the others went the old Orange flute.*

The Old Orange Flute

The 'Old Cause' for which Bob Williams and others like him played flutes and beat drums was that of the Protestant ascendancy in the six counties of Northern Ireland. Scottish Presbyterian settlers of all classes had arrived in the region at the beginning of the seventeenth century and, like their counterparts in the New World, they brought with them a frontier spirit and a determination to subdue the natives. Like the Indians of North America, the Gaelic Catholics resisted and the subsequent conflicts became embedded in the ancestral memories of both groups. The turning point in the struggle came in 1690 when the Catholic Irish, who had backed the dethroned James II, were defeated at the Battle of the Boyne by William of Orange. The Catholics have never been allowed to forget this trouncing for the annual anniversary of the battle on 12 July became a day of clamorous Protestant celebration.

The Orange Lodges, so called after King William, had much to rejoice about since the victory assured their dominance over the Catholics. When it was threatened in 1886 and 1912 by the possibility of Home Rule, the Ulstermen got ready to take on the rest of Ireland and the British Government. In the end their intransigence paid off for the 1921 Government of Ireland Act gave them their own parliament at Stormont Castle as well as MPs at Westminster. Protestants outnumbered Catholics by two to one in the six counties, which ensured that henceforward the Protestant Unionist Party would have an immovable majority.

Irish nationalists in the south had always rejected partition and in 1920–22, the IRA waged a brief war in the six northern counties. This guerrilla war was a further reminder to the Ulster Protestants that the Catholics were their enemies, a disruptive minority which needed to be kept on a tight leash just as they always had been. The temporary 1922 Special Powers Act provided the means for the Stormont Government to handle any signs of restlessness from the Catholics; it was made permanent in 1933 on the grounds of its value in the event of trouble from the IRA. Ulster's Minister of Home Affairs could suspend the Habeas Corpus Act and grant the police extensive powers of search and interrogation in an emergency.

British political parties put down no roots in Northern Ireland, where political life stagnated. One party, the Unionists, enjoyed a permanent supremacy, perpetuating dominance which suited its rank-and-file supporters. They had their own schools, traditions which gave them a powerful sense of historic identity and, in return for their loyalty to Unionism, the lion's share of government patronage in the form of jobs and housing. The Unionist establishment had little to offer the Catholics, who also stayed in their own areas, were educated in their own schools, and stayed loyal to their own customs, which for many included a seemingly futile adherence to wider Irish nationalism.

It was not, however, nationalism that sparked off the crisis in Northern Ireland in 1969. For several years there had been indications that the Catholic community was no longer willing to accept a system in which the dice were perpetually weighted against their interests. The beginnings of agitation coincided with a period in which the Ulster Prime Minister, Captain Terence O'Neill, was beating a new type of Ulster drum which sounded notes of reassurance for would-be investors in Northern Irish industry. O'Neill wanted an injection of British cash, which he hoped would finance new manufacturing industry and introduce new growth to the province. Investors needed affirmation of Ulster's stability, and so O'Neill publicly promised reforms designed to remove long-standing local grievances. 'Comments equating the lot of the Ulster Catholic with that of the American Negro are absurd hyperbole', O'Neill assured *The Times* in April 1967. Catholics in Ulster did not agree, nor were they convinced that O'Neill was sincerely prepared to redress the imbalances against them.

Comparison between the American Negro and the Ulster Catholic was not accidental for in the United States the 'Civil Rights' movement was making great headway. A similar movement had grown up in Ulster which aimed to extend full rights of citizenship to Catholics by the dismantlement of the machinery of the Unionist Protestant ascendancy. This movement wanted to end electoral chicanery, the 'B' Special police reserve, the repeal of the Special Powers Act and the establishment of an impartial system for the allocation of local government housing. For these purposes the Northern Ireland Civil Rights Association (NICRA) was formed in 1967 and later the 'People's Democracy' which veered towards socialism.

The emergence of Catholic groups seeking changes in Ulster's old order soon provoked a fiercesome Protestant reaction. Since the troubles in the early 1920s all Catholics had been indelibly stamped as disloyal and any concessions to their interests appeared to most Unionists tantamount to treason. Unionism had always found sectarian antipathies electorally advantageous and had done little to dispel them. Captain O'Neill's reform pledges made at the end of 1968 looked dangerously like surrender to men like Ian Paisley, a Presbyterian pastor whose fundamentalism and dogmatic anti-Catholicism were common features of Ulster Protestantism and won him a wide following. Signs that the Catholics were stirring triggered a traditional response which took the form of a sequence of attacks on NICRA marches and Catholic districts. The Belfast to Londonderry march on 1 January 1969 was ambushed by Protestants, the assailants including 'B' Special police reservists in mufti. The predominantly Protestant Royal Ulster Constabulary (RUC) left no doubt about their feelings when it came to intervention in the brawling, and in April detachments terrorized the Catholic slum area of the Bogside in Londonderry.

Disorders of this kind were not unusual in Northern Ireland where their baleful history stretched back at least as far as the 1880s. On 12 August 1913 (the anniversary of an incident in the siege of Londonderry when a party of apprentices closed the city's gates which had been opened to a Catholic army by the faint-hearted) the traditional Apprentice Boys parade was attended by hundreds armed with revolvers. Shots were fired during a series of scrimmages and a policeman was killed. In the same year, a gang of about sixty attacked a party of girls and young women who were passing through a Protestant district on their way to a Catholic bazaar.[27] What was novel about the riots during 1969 was that they were seen in Britain and the rest of the world on television. Eyes were suddenly opened to the grotesque antics and attitudes of men and women who proudly called themselves loyal British subjects and lived in the United Kingdom.

Worse was seen by television audiences during August. Following custom, the Apprentice Boys marched around the walls of Londonderry on 12 August, some hurling pennies at the Catholics of the Bogside, a gesture which reminded them not only of high local unemployment, but also that their place was at the bottom of the pile. This insolence was too much, especially since Catholic parades had been banned by Stormont, and the Bogsiders replied with a barrage of their own which invited retaliation by the RUC. To meet the police, the Bogsiders built barricades, which they defended with stones, bricks and petrol bombs against the police who attacked with batons and tear gas. Under the inspiration of Bernadette Devlin, who had lately been elected to the Parliament in Westminster, the Bogside called itself 'Free Derry' and prepared for a siege. The new Ulster Prime Minister, Major Chichester-Clark, mobilized the 'B' Specials whilst Protestant extremists, affronted by the challenge to their position, launched sorties against Catholic districts in Belfast. Their mood and behaviour was celebrated in song.[28]

On the 15th of August we took a little trip,
Up along Bombay Street and burned out all the shit,
We took a little petrol and we took a little gun,
And we fought the bloody Fenians till we had them on the run

Ancient malice was breaking the surface all over the province. Police stations were attacked by petrol bombs, mobs clashed, and scared Catholics gathered up what they could and hurried over the border into Eire. The Unionist government was no longer able to control Ulster and was forced, reluctantly, to turn to Westminster for assistance in the shape of the British army. Two weeks before the upheavals of 12–15 August, Sir Anthony Peacocke, the Inspector-General of the RUC had asked for army help, but the Unionist Cabinet shrank from making a decision. A request for intervention was an admission that the Unionists could no longer keep order in Ulster without the resources of the central government which, while it could not withold assistance, would expect a price to be paid in the form of close involvement in decisions about the future governance of the province. Spreading anarchy, religious pogroms and the possibility that Eire might intervene (its forces had contingency orders to move up to the border) forced the hand of the Stormont Government. On 15 August the Home Secretary, James Callaghan, informed the Commons that the GOC Northern Ireland had received instructions 'to take all necessary steps, acting impartially between citizen and citizen, to restore law and order' in Northern Ireland. He ended his statement with an affirmation of previous governments' pledges which assured the people of Northern Ireland that they could stay in the United Kingdom as long as this was the wish of the majority.

The British army's 'campaign' in Northern Ireland began and eighteen years later there is no sign that it will end. The war of ambushes, patrols and searches has been the longest Imperial campaign undertaken by Britain's armed forces apart from the operations on the North-West Frontier, where at least there had been respites when the tribesmen had been comparatively calm. When forces from the 2,500 regular Ulster garrison first appeared on the streets of Londonderry and Belfast, they received a guarded welcome from people who thought them deliverers from further Protestant wrath. Bernadette Devlin did not share this reaction. 'They have not come here to help us', she warned her adherents and reminded them about British Imperialism in Aden and Cyprus.[29]

This was not just political rhetoric. On one level the conflict in Ulster followed classic lines of other Imperial problems which the armed forces had been called in to solve. The 'frontier mentality', and with it the need to maintain paramountcy over the Catholic minority, permeated Protestant and 'loyalist' political thought. In its extreme forms, as propagated by Dr Ian Paisley, such ideology embraced doctrines of an 'elect', a chosen, Godly people favoured by Providence, and possessed of such moral virtues as addiction to sobriety and hard work which set them apart from their adversaries. European settlers in America, their kin in southern Africa and the Jewish colonists in Palestine would have recognized this portrait of themselves. When the interests of colonists clashed with those of the indigenous population, it was the unenviable task of the army to guard the settlers and sometimes push forward their claims. This had been the case during the Kaffir and Maori wars of the nineteenth century and more recently the campaigns in Palestine. In these wars the settlers often represented themselves as 'loyalist' but, as in Rhodesia, loyalty was conditional upon the British Government's willingness to give them a free hand in dealing with the local population.

Faced with the Ulster can of worms, successive British Governments have acted like their predecessors in the belief that Ireland's difficulties can be solved politically. The role of the armed forces has been to keep the peace in cooperation with the local police agencies until the sources of communal disharmony had been removed. From the start, British policy was based on the assumption that conciliation was possible in Northern Ireland, and that by careful adjustments to local institutions, the wishes of every faction could be accommodated. The first casualty of British policy was the old Unionist Party which, by 1971, had begun to splinter. The Stormont Parliament went down next in March 1972 when it was superseded by 'direct rule' from Westminster. The vacuum was to be filled by a Northern Ireland Executive with four Catholics among its ten members. It was regarded as the first stage in 'power-sharing', a political arrangement which, its advocates hoped, would unite the two religious groups in the province. Plans were also in hand for a Council of Ireland which would include representatives from Eire. The Protestants were unimpressed with these replacements for their old Assembly and considered them the thin end of a wedge which would shatter for ever their position of political dominance and even prepare the way for Ulster's absorption into Eire. These misgivings led to a mass Protestant response which was as formidable as that to Home Rule sixty years before. The working class mobilized and paralyzed Northern Ireland with a series of strikes during May 1974, of which those in the power supply industries were the most devastating. Harold Wilson chose not to deploy troops against the Protestants or countenance the arrest of their ringleaders, the most prominent of whom were Ian Paisley and William Craig. The army was disappointed, but pusillanimity had spared it a war on two fronts which, given the bloody experience of Protestant riots after the abolition of the 'B' Specials in the autumn of 1969, might have worsened an already bad situation. Subsequent efforts to devise a new local constitution and invite the assistance of Southern Irish politicians and administrators in dealing with Ulster's difficulties have not come to much.

By the first decade of the next century, Catholics will outnumber Protestants in Northern Ireland unless there is a change in the local birth-rate or a radical revision of Rome's dogma on contraception. Whether this demographic change will lead to a united Ireland is uncertain. For the time being, the Unionist majority wishes to keep its connection with Britain and is ready to go on the warpath whenever this appears endangered. Within the rest of the United Kingdom, the convolutions and vagaries of Irish politics provoke boredom, irritation and frustration, and for British politicians are a costly distraction which they could do without. At the beginning of 1987, an opinion poll in the *Daily Express* suggested that as many as three out of five people wanted British forces to be withdrawn from Northern Ireland, even though it was unclear whether they understood what the consequences might be.

In the summer of 1969, the army had been ordered on to the streets of Northern Ireland at a time when it seemed possible that the Catholics might be driven from their homes and even killed in large numbers. Their traditional defenders, the IRA, was taken by surprise by the events in Londonderry and Belfast and its leadership was in disarray. Membership in Ulster had dwindled since the end of the last, fruitless campaign in 1962, and the movement's leaders had their time taken up with internal, ideological wrangles. One, Séan Macstiofáin, recalled the faltering response to the upheavals in August. 'What hit us all was that we had long been waiting for an opportunity for the IRA to prove itself, to grab the opening and then expand it to achieve the national aims of the movement. Now, when the opportunity had been handed to us on a plate, the organization had not been up to it'. This seems to have been a view shared by some northern Catholics for Macstiofáin noted with shame the graffito 'IRA = I RAN AWAY' scrawled on a Belfast wall.

The IRA had developed connections with the NICRA before 1969, but not to the extent to justify the Unionist argument that the political movements were a mask for republican subversives. Furthermore the IRA was short of arms, ammunition and field equipment, and so they had to scour the south for supplies to be sent to cells in the north. There was no agreement as to whether a military response was the most efficacious policy, the issue which divided the movement at a meeting in December 1969. What emerged from the row was an 'Official' IRA, whose followers wanted to fight a political campaign on behalf of Sinn Fein, making the fullest use of existing democratic institutions in Eire and Northern Ireland. This was not to the liking of the 'Provisional' IRA which saw itself as the unswerving successor to the rebels of 1916 and the true cause of Sinn Fein, a united, republican Ireland torn from Britain's grasp. Further fragmentation of the armed nationalists followed in 1974, when the Irish Republican Socialist Party came into being after a row within the 'Official' IRA. Its fighting cell, the Irish National Liberation Army, [INLA] became a fiercesome terrorist group responsible for a number of sorties which included the assassination of Airey Neave in 1979. At the end of 1986 this minute faction was sundered by violent internal disputes.

From its genesis in January 1970, the Provisional IRA has waged the most deadly campaign of terrorism in Northern Ireland and, from 1972, in Britain. It was and is the army's major adversary. Its gunmen, bomb-makers and passive helpers regard themselves as heirs of past generations of Irishmen and women who had fought against the 'Imperial' army of occupation. Their task was 'to fight the massive British occupation forces and bring home to the British people the hard price that must be paid for the foolishness of propping up a colonial system which could not survive'.[30] Like their forefathers in 1919, today's IRA lacks the men and weaponry to engage the British army on equal terms and its fighting men have revived the tradition of stealth and surprise and waged a war of ambuscade, assassination and sabotage. At the outset, in 1970, the IRA command had hoped that by killing thirty-six British soldiers, the same number that had been killed in the lately-ended Aden war, it would force the British government to do in Ulster what it had done in Aden — retire. The Provisionals also believed that they could so disrupt life in Northern Ireland that the province would become ungovernable and the British Government, its will broken by the culminative effect of bombings and murders, would drop its opposition to a united Ireland. At the same time, the Provisionals had to convince the Catholic population that they were 'its army', a force to be reckoned with, and the only channel for nationalist aspirations. From time to time they have reminded the world of their presence and temerity with spectacular *coups* like the murder of Lord Mountbatten and several members of his family in August 1979 and the ambush the same day of an army patrol at Warrenpoint in which eighteen paratroopers were killed.

There has been a macabre historical undertone to such outrages. The murder of twenty-one people by explosions in Birmingham public houses on 24 November 1974 was timed to occur on the anniversary of 'Bloody Sunday' in 1920. Then British officers had been murdered and the security forces retaliated by shooting down a dozen or so spectators at a hurley match in Dublin. Likewise, the Warrenpoint ambush was presented as an act of revenge against the regiment which had opened fire on 'Bloody Sunday' in Belfast in January 1972.

To survive, the Provisional IRA and the INLA rely upon the active co-operation or benevolent neutrality of sections of Northern Ireland's Catholic community. As in the 1919–21 war, the IRA quickly reverts to coercion of people who step out of line or render assistance to the security forces. The creation of what were known as 'No Go' areas in Belfast and Londonderry after the 1969 disturbances was a bonus to the IRA for it was able to put down roots and enlist help without interference from the police or army. It possesses youth wings (school-children act as scouts and sometimes decoys) and a women's wing. The latter were responsible for a particularly vile murder in 1973 when a gang of women surrounded a soldier, took his rifle, and held him until an assassin arrived who shot him dead. IRA recruits are drawn from the unemployed Catholic working-class for whom membership provides a chance for bravado and an opportunity for self-dramatization, while giving them a standing within the community. Family traditions of republicanism play their part so many young men followed in the footsteps of their fathers or brothers. Members of units receive £20–£40 a week from the IRA's warchest. This is topped up by the proceeds of bank and post office robberies, racketeering, voluntary contributions and the generosity of the American-based NORAID. NORAID raises funds from American Irish, ostensibly for the relief of civilian victims of the war, but the British Government has insisted that much of the cash has gone direct to the IRA. Since the US Government has taken a bullish stance towards terrorism, NORAID has been a source of embarrassment and efforts have been made to restrict its activities.

Since 1969, the British army has faced a bewildering number of duties in Northern Ireland in the face of a volatile and seldom grateful population. It left its barracks first to guard the local Catholics and within a year found itself fighting an extended war against a ruthless and often sophisticated enemy, the IRA. Until 1974, when the decision was taken to start the reintroduction of normal policing throughout Ulster, the army was often the only source of authority within an area. Its duties commonly involved facing and overcoming bodies of rioters who could act as decoys for IRA gunmen; a crowd might suddenly open to reveal a rifleman who would fire and then the mob would close ranks. After 1974 the nature of the war began to change, albeit slowly, and soldiers found themselves with more familiar duties which included covert operations devised to trap terrorists and restrict their movements. Numbers needed for operations increased steadily until 1972 when 22,000 men were deployed in Ulster, but the total has fallen considerably since, not least because of anxiety that such a heavy concentration reduced the forces available to fulfil obligations to NATO.

Two major problems faced British soldiers in Northern Ireland. The first was the tactical difficulty of finding and fighting guerrillas who dressed as civilians and passed to and fro amongst a sympathetic or disinterested Catholic population. There was nothing new about this; it had been an experience common to Dublin in 1920, Jerusalem in 1946 and Aden in the early 1960s. There was not much that was new about the army's more complex difficulty, that of the definition of exactly what it was supposed to be doing. An extension of this was the vexed question of who controlled operations and how far soldiers could go to overcome their adversaries. To this was added the dimension of Press and television coverage; the 'firm line' approach which might have been taken with comparative impunity in the Kenya Highlands or the Arab quarter of Crater looked too much like outright brutality to at least some of the soldiers' fellow countrymen who watched or read about it. Furthermore, there were no blanket 'Emergency' rules which could be invoked to justify tough measures.

The RUC had been widely discredited after the autumn and summer upheavals of 1969, and in Catholic areas distaste for its members was so intense that everyday policing activities were stopped. Its auxiliaries, the 'B' Specials, were disbanded in the autumn of 1969, a sop to Catholic opinion which worried some commanders who wondered whether dismantling the Unionist police and intelligence structure was wise in the face of growing IRA activity. Control through Stormont was resented and the advent of direct rule in 1972 was welcomed. One candid officer remarked of the Unionist leaders, 'they just wanted to smash the Catholics', presumably with army assistance. As it was, the army found itself in an auxiliary position to an unpopular police force which was unable to perform its function in many areas. Help came with the introduction of internment in August 1971 and the Emergency Powers Act of 1973 which permitted soldiers to make arrests.

Where the complexities of who was responsible for what mattered most was on the streets. Here units had the tasks of mounting patrols, enforcing curfews, searching houses for suspects and arms dumps, and quelling disorders. Such training as had been given was with traditional Imperial policing in mind.[31] On Long Kesh airfield men learned how to form the equivalent of a *testudo* to meet a bombardment of brickbats and stones, getting a magistrate to read a Riot Act and opening banners which read 'Halt or we open fire'. It was described as the 'shoot one round at the big black bugger in the red turban' school of training, and when one banner was unravelled it turned out to inscribed in Arabic. What if anything the IRA made of this Imperial relic is not known. By 1973 all this had changed. In Britain and West Germany, special training areas had been built where men practised in locations made to resemble those where they would be stationed, and instruction was given about the IRA, its methods, organization and thinking. Officers, men and NCOs learned the right techniques for searches and, most importantly, how to recognize an imminent ambush. Urban counter-insurgency joined the novices' curriculum of basic training.

Other skills were picked up on the job. Units drafted to an area picked up information from the men they relieved about the inhabitants and their behaviour, and in turn passed on this lore to their successors. This had not been so at the beginning, when one officer remembered having to discover everything from scratch in 1972 after his unit took over a position in a Catholic enclave in Belfast.[32] It was a 'bloody grotty' area of working-class housing, but since the soldiers kept the Protestant Tartan gangs at bay, they were welcome. Still, customary Tam o'Shanters were discreetly replaced as headgear so as not to arouse old memories of the Black and Tans who were remembered from fifty or so years earlier. Like other units, this one was only too well aware of the need to do everything possible to 'win hearts and minds', and its Catholic officers went to a Christmas Mass in the local church. Despite the suspected presence of the IRA, the men went unarmed save for a cautious officer who concealed an automatic pistol on him. It fell out at the altar rail, but the celebrant seemed unperturbed.

No police went into this area so the soldiers escorted gas men, social services staff, helped in emergencies like a chimney fire, and kept an eye out for such tell-tale signs as an extra milk bottle on a doorstep or additional washing on a line. These could reveal the presence of a bird of passage who could easily be a gunman. Intelligence co-ordination was chaotic since the gathering and assessment agencies were riven with jealousies and addicted to hoarding information. The RUC, the RUC Special Branch, the RUC CID, the British CID, the British Special Branch, MI5 and army intelligence units all worked side by side, but not in harness. When an infantry detachment caught an IRA Quartermaster, its intelligence officer accompanied the prisoner to the Belfast Prison Handling Centre, where, under threat of the 'black bag' treatment, he revealed what he knew about arms dumps. Knowing well that police intelligence might keep such knowledge to themselves or, more likely, use it to their own advantage, the officer returned to his unit, which after clearance from Brigade HQ set out to get the weapons.[33] Too often separate pieces of a jigsaw were deliberately kept apart. Even more irritating were undercover intelligence men in mufti who turned up and were arrested by men from a unit which had been told nothing about their presence. This has changed, especially since 1979, and the introduction of computers has banished self-contained stacks of index cards which had been the backbone of intelligence work at the beginning of the campaign.

The officer who gave me these details recollected that, in 1971–2, his men felt a 'genuine sympathy and humanity' towards the community to which they were attached even though Catholic attitudes were hardening elsewhere. His own men from a line regiment were, he thought, temperamentally better suited to facing up to foul-mouthed abuse and pelting, often from teenage hooligans, than the so-called 'elite' units, notably the paratroopers. What were, in effect, battle units trained to warrior aggression, who cherished a hard, steely image, tended to lose their tempers. He also noticed that their officers liked to show that they were as tough as their men, and therefore put themselves in the forefront rather than keeping back and giving orders. This too was the view of one of these officers.[34]

> We have something far more valuable than a flak jacket or rifle. Our reputation; the myth that surrounds the 'Paras', the image of supermen in smocks and denims. A load of rubbish, of course, we are just as vulnerable as everyone else, it's just that we don't seem to have the hang-ups about using force of the most vicious kind whenever possible. You can't train people to the ultimate in death-dealing and expect them to sit down and do nothing.

The same writer gives many indications of this attitude of mind translated into action; one example, taken from a description of riots on the Shankill Road in January 1973 will serve for others:[35]

> The driver throws the Pig [personnel carrier] sideways, nearly tipping over, and within moments toms [paratroopers] are spilling out into the street, batons flailing and whooping with aggression. The noise is deafening, screams from the women, threatening yells from the men. Identify the troublemakers and scatter the rest, then deal with smaller groups. The initial charge has worked and we have a good position having opened the road and pressed people back against the walls, but they are growing braver again as more people flood in from neighbouring streets, alleyways and spill out of clubs, bringing crates of empty bottles to hurl.
> 'Fucking Army bastards.'
> 'Paras out Paras out.'
> The same chants over and over again, a scream goes up as a snatch squad

leaps into the crowd and drags a man out by his hair, batons beating at his knees and kidneys. They're doing a good job diving into the seething mass and pulling out the ringleaders, slowly forcing back the turmoil, preventing any upsurge, killing it before it has a chance.

The question of how much force was permissible was one which troubled both soldiers and politicians. Veterans of campaigns in Aden and Malaya found the restraints imposed in Ireland inexplicable and outsiders often wondered whether the army was being too 'soft' with its opponents. The experience of Aden made some commander wonder whether the Labour Government would repeat its policy there in Northern Ireland and publicly decree a date for withdrawal which would boost the IRA's morale. A firmer line was expected from the Tories after Edward Heath's election victory in June 1970, but the comments of the new Home Secretary, Reginald Maudling, about an 'acceptable level of violence' as his objective for the province was hardly a token of resolution. (Maudling later had the misfortune to be set upon by Bernadette Devlin, who had been unable to contain herself during a Commons debate.)

Defining just how much force the army could use rested on a precise official revelation of its purpose in Northern Ireland. Brigadier Kitson, who took command of 39 Brigade in Belfast during September 1970, had clear ideas on this subject which he attempted to put into action. Kitson had a long record of Imperial campaigns; he had served in Malaya and Kenya where he had developed his own brand of counter-insurgency warfare. This was based upon the 'turning' of former guerrillas into government irregulars who formed 'gangs' under British officers and used their old skills against their sometime comrades. Of course for Malayan Communists and Mau Mau warriors service with the British was an attractive alternative to imprisonment or in some cases execution. Similar irregular units had been recruited from the Pushtun of the North-West Frontier since the early 1900s, but their constancy was variable. Kitson did not propose using ex-IRA men, but he did favour close army and police co-operation and argued that civil administration should be reshaped along colonial lines. He also considered that undercover efforts were needed to divide the IRA which would be disconcerted by a sustained propaganda campaign.

In essence, Kitson, like many others, wanted the army to be free of the shackles of the police, and contest control of the streets with the IRA in an undercover war. Ponderous army patrols presented targets for the IRA and the troops lacked an effective way of hitting back. From 1972 SAS units have been active in country areas like South Armagh where IRA activity has been common, and, in particular, have scouted for terrorists passing to and fro across the border with Eire. In the streets soldiers have been given powers of arrest and since August 1971 the Government has had the authority to intern IRA suspects without trial. Offences connected with terrorism have been tried by special courts with no juries in which judges assess evidence and deliver sentences.

Internment was shortly followed by charges that British forces had employed torture to intimidate suspects and these allegations were duly examined by a Committee of Enquiry during the autumn of 1971. The most interesting finding of the Committee was that the methods applied to detainees had evolved directly from those employed in earlier 'conflicts' in Malaya, Kenya and Aden. They included the placing of thick hoods over suspects' heads, subjecting them to distressful noise, making them lean against walls supported only by their fingertips, and various forms of rough-handling. How far, if at all, the mass of the British public was troubled by these revelations is not known, although opinion polls at the time suggested a general inclination towards 'tough' measures in Northern Ireland. There was predictable indignation from some quarters, most of it along the lines set out by Graham Greene in a letter to *The Times*, where he drew attention to the double standards of the British Government which seemed to tolerate ill-usage of suspects in Ireland at the same time as condemning torture in other countries. More recently there has been newspaper criticism of what has been called a 'shoot to kill policy' used by the RUC since 1982, although it is hard to understand just what alternative there is for men faced with terrorists who are usually armed.

By 1982 the RUC was becoming more and more prominent in Northern Ireland as a consequence of the policy to restore as much normal policing to the province as was possible. Reorganized and skilled in counter-terrorist operations, the RUC has taken on more and more of the everyday security work, permitting a reduction in the British garrison which stands at about 7,000 men, backed by the Ulster Defence Regiment (UDR) with a strength of 8,000, two-thirds of whom are part-timers. The Provisional IRA has continued with its war of assassination against the police, the UDR and the army as well as bomb attacks in Britain. There has been a shift away from 'economic sabotage', a euphemism for bomb attacks on plant and businesses in Ulster, and the adoption of a policy which involves utilization of the local political machinery. By its own admission, Sinn Fein now wants to fight with both ballot box and Armalite victory, but so far results have not been encouraging. For their part, the Protestants still cling to the British connection and have greeted political efforts towards greater involvement of the Eire government with suspicion and rancour.

As yet, there has been no clear outcome to the campaign in Northern Ireland which means that a balanced assessment of the army's role there is impossible to obtain. Certain points do stand out. In 1969 British soldiers checked a possible pogrom against Roman Catholics before it got completely out-of-hand. Three years later it eliminated the No-Go areas, products of the sectarian riots, which were enclaves where the Provisionals could govern, convert and recruit. When, in July 1972, military plans for the re-occupation of 'Free Derry' and other pockets were completed, permission to put them into effect had to be sought from the Cabinet. During the discussions, Edward Heath asked the operational commander, Major General Ford, for an estimate of the likely casualties and was told that they might total 100. 'I think that up to 100 casualties is politically acceptable', he remarked. Throughout the campaign in Northern Ireland, British politicians have had to keep looking over their shoulders for signs of public reaction and accordingly have developed a recondite skill of being able to sense what the public would accept and what it might reject in terms of military operations. Such exercises in prediction were puzzling and sometimes frustrating for soldiers. As it was, the retaking of the No-Go areas, code-named Operation Motorman, was a relatively bloodless affair. The IRA had been forewarned and wisely decided to cut and run rather than risk a stand-up fight in which they would be outnumbered and outgunned. They did, however, draw some satisfaction from comparing the British use of armoured vehicles to sweep aside barricades and the deployment of tanks by the Russians to quash unrest in Czechoslovakia in 1968.

The elimination of the No-Go districts ended the bizarre situation in which parts of the United Kingdom enjoyed what was tantamount to independence. Thereafter Britain's writ ran throughout Ulster, even if it was continuously challenged by the IRA. History cannot be written in the subjunctive, so it would be fruitless to wonder what would have happened in Ulster if British forces had not been committed there in 1969. The expanding conflict in the early 1970s drove Protestants and Catholics into the safety of their own areas and since then they have continued to kill each other, often in a random manner, in what are called 'sectarian' murders. If the British army withdrew precipitately it is highly likely that the pace of this assassination campaign would accelerate. There is clearly plenty of fight still left in Ulstermen, significant numbers of whom, both Protestant and Catholic, continue to think and speak in terms of 'victory', 'defeat', and 'no surrender'. They mean as much now as they did sixty, a hundred or even three hundred years ago.

7

With Moore to Port Stanley, or Regained for Britain: The Falklands War

The whole scene of the departure of three leading elements of the assault troops of the British Falkland Land Force resembled a newsreel of forty years before. The patriotism, the red, white and blue, was a little self-conscious, the boast and swagger of a nation that had not needed to prepare for this kind of conflict for a generation.

Robert Fox, *Eyewitness Falklands.*

The dockside scenes in the first week of April 1982 summoned more to mind than the departure of any modern expeditionary force. They evoked *Illustrated London News* pictures of red-coated infantrymen setting out to rescue Gordon from Khartum a hundred years before, or early flickering cinematograph images of flag-waving crowds cheering the embarkation of the Imperial Yeomanry for Cape Town in 1900. The scenario of the Falklands war belonged to a distant age, and even now reads like a plot devised by G. A. Henty or Percy Westerman. A remote island, peopled by loyal, hard-working folk of British stock, is seized by a blustering South American dictator and placed under the heel of one of his henchmen, rumoured to be a torturer of women. To the rescue come the Royal Navy's men-o'-war with such names as *Fearless*, *Ardent* and *Alacrity*, manned by sturdy bluejackets and gallant marines. After many perilous moments, British pluck triumphs. Most of the craven invaders throw down their arms, whilst their Generals slink away to face the wrath of their own people whom they have misled and plundered. Even a few Argentinians appeared to see the war in these terms. One of their commanders expressed his amazement that an expeditionary force was on its way to the Falklands and wondered if the British believed that his countrymen were Zulus to be overawed by old fashioned Imperial *force majeure*.

This analogy was in part false; unlike the Argentinians, the Zulus were brave warriors fighting for their own country. Yet for patriotic Argentinians, the Falklands and their scattered, unpopulated dependencies were part of the national homeland which had been occupied by Britain in 1833 and held ever since. Argentinian irredentism has flared up periodically but Britain has firmly rejected the Argentine's claims. British rights to the islands were upheld on legal grounds (which Argentina considered invalid), their occupation by British settlers who wished to stay under colonial government and strategic necessity. In the early days, the islands had been a naval base with coaling facilities and a wireless station which was conveniently close to the major shipping lanes out of the Plate River estuary. From here, the navy's cruisers could keep an eye on Britain's extensive investments in Chile, Uruguay and Argentina, and guard them against damage during the political upheavals which were endemic in the region. By 1982 the Falklands appeared an Imperial anachronism, celebrated only for its handsome postage stamps, but no longer useful, since Britain no longer possessed a South Atlantic squadron.

This is how it appeared to the praetorian government of Argentina, a *junta* of army, navy and air force officers which had taken power in 1976. In six years this cabal had become a byword for repression, corruption and economic mismanagement, and by 1982 its position looked increasingly fragile. A foreign adventure offered the means for the *junta* to retrieve some prestige even though, as its senior member, General Leopoldo Galtieri, admitted, its armed forces were unready for a war with Britain. There can be little doubt that the invasion of the Falklands was a gambler's last throw in which the odds were determined by the belief that Britain would not fight for their recovery. Just when the die was cast is far from clear. Between 25 and 31 March, Argentinian naval units with amphibious assault forces were at sea close to the Falklands, and a number of reconnaissance forays were made on their shoreline to discover suitable landing places. Actual invasion took place on 2 April, so it must be assumed that the final decision to attack had been made some time during the previous week, perhaps even a few hours before the invasion.

In Britain recriminations abounded once it was realized that the Foreign Office had been taken by surprise and that a rational interpretation of available intelligence might have led to the conclusion that Argentinian forces were poised to attack. Certainly the Government was aware of the concentration of Argentinian warships, but it was assumed that they were taking part in an exercise designed only to intimidate. By 31 March, the evidence of decoded messages which had been passing between the ships suggested that an amphibious attack was in the offing. Inside Argentina there were no signs of mobilization which, at the time, seemed to support the contention that the fleet exercises were no more than a show of force.

Subsequent events have been exhaustively covered by narratives of war correspondents who, like their Victorian forbears, rushed into print to satisfy a public which wanted to read about the campaign, and the officers and men who took part. All that is needed here is a brief outline of the main events. Britain's response to the invasion was swift once the Cabinet had resolved to regain the islands; RAF transport aircraft began to gather at Wideawake Field on Ascension Island on 3 April, and the first ships of the task force set sail from

Britain and Gibraltar two days later. As the armada steamed southwards, the Argentinian Government was given a series of warnings. On 12 April a 200-mile exclusion zone was declared around the Falklands; eleven days later it was announced that any Argentinian warships or warplanes which threatened the task force would be attacked, and on 30 April what was described as a total exclusion zone came into force. Just over a week later, Britain served notice that it would attack any Argentinian men-o'-war or aircraft which ventured within twelve miles of the mainland. Together these pronouncements added up to a statement that Britain meant business and would not flinch from fighting. It was also clear what Britain was fighting for; on 3 April the UN Security Council had passed a resolution which called on Argentina to withdraw its forces from the Falklands, a step-down the *junta* could never afford to take if it wished to retain it authority within the country.

Fighting began on 25 April when British units recaptured South Georgia and crippled an Argentinian submarine, the *Santa Fe*. The Falklands themselves became a target for naval gunfire and aerial bombardment on 1 May, when a number of Argentinian warplanes were shot down. By this time, small SAS and Special Boat Squadron parties had been put ashore on the islands for reconnaissance and sabotage. A day later, the heavy cruiser, *General Belgrano*, was sunk by torpedoes fired from the nuclear submarine, HMS *Conqueror*. Two days later an Argentinian Super Etendard aircraft launched an Exocet missile which disabled the radar picket frigate *Sheffield*.

The first attack on the Falklands themselves came on the night of 14–15 May when Special Forces landed on Pebble Island and destroyed eleven Argentinian aircraft on the ground in an action designed to remove a threat to the main amphibious assault on the other side of the Falkland Sound. Six days later, 3 Commando Brigade came ashore at San Carlos where a bridgehead was speedily established. It now fell to the Argentinian Air Force to make sorties against the naval and land forces concentrated in the area and make the bridgehead untenable. The islands were 400 miles from the mainland Argentinian air bases and so were just within the maximum, unrefuelled ranges of her Mirage [625 miles], Skyhawk [575 miles] and Super Etendard [450 miles] fighters, but the time available for the pilots to make their attacks and engage in dog-fights with Britain's Harriers was limited. This factor, together with the skill of the Harrier pilots, the ground-launched Rapier missiles and the improvization of old-fashioned machine-gun anti-aircraft batteries, prevented the Argentinian aircraft from gaining mastery of the air. It was a close run thing; between 21 and 25 May, fifty-one Argentinian 'planes were destroyed for the loss of HMS *Ardent*, *Antelope* and *Coventry*. Another casualty was the transport ship, *Atlantic Conveyor* which was hit by an Exocet on 25 May and sank three days later, with a number of much-needed helicopters still on board.

Despite the gallant pertinacity of the Argentinian pilots, the air raids failed to force a withdrawal or hinder a break-out from the bridgehead. Between 28–30 May, British forces advanced across country and took Darwin, Goose

Green, Douglas and Teal Inlet. A second landing at Fitzroy on 8 June ran into trouble from the Argentinian Air Force which mounted a final, fierce sortie in which the fleet auxiliaries, *Sir Galahad* and *Sir Tristram* were badly damaged and the Welsh Guards suffered severe casualties. Ten Argentinian aircraft were shot down in what was their final intervention in the war. By 11 June, British forces were encircling the main concentration of Argentinian infantry at Port Stanley, the island's capital. Driven back by a series of determined assaults and under shellfire, the Argentinian soldiers, most of whom were young conscripts, had become a panic stricken rabble, in many cases infected with dysentery and by mutiny born of despair. After the surrender there were a handful of attacks on Argentinian officers who pleaded for pistols to be reissued to them so that they could defend themselves against their own men. The disintegration of the Argentinian forces around Port Stanley left the islands' commander, General Menendez, with no choice but to seek terms, and on 14 June he agreed to unconditional surrender.

Official regulations covering the release of documents and the absence to date of memoirs from members of Mrs Thatcher's Cabinet mean that many details of the political and military decisions of the campaign are still unknown. This has in no way hampered speculation, especially about the attack on the *General Belgrano*. The root of this controversy lies in the political brouhaha which immediately followed Mrs Thatcher's decision to retake the islands. Many on the Left faced a dilemma, since they shared a natural loathing for the Argentinian *junta* which embodied all the reprehensible features of an antique South American dictatorship of the extreme Right, not only in its Draconian persecution of opponents, but in its adherence to monetarism. Nevertheless, the pacifist wing of the Labour Party and 'peace' groups within Britain denounced the war for its own sake and as an expression of Imperial atavism which they hoped that Britain had outgrown. Opponents of the war placed their hopes on an accord being agreed before the fighting began, and were therefore dismayed when the *General Belgrano* was sunk, on the grounds that its destruction and the loss of over 300 Argentinian sailors effectively ended any chance of a compromise being reached. Furthermore the cruiser was steaming outside the exclusion zone when it was hit, so it appeared to be a breach of the rules Britain itself had imposed. Whether or not it was a case of the Marquess of Queensberry hitting below the belt, the commander of the *General Belgrano* has not protested that his ship was unfairly attacked.

Efforts to discover just what happened and why have entered the murky world of intelligence which may explain the Government's guardedness in offering a complete explanation of the considerations which led to the issue of orders. Throughout the war, Britain was able to monitor and decipher Argentinian signals thanks in part to assistance from the United States and Chile, although the precise nature of their help remains unknown. From various sources it was known that the *General Belgrano*, a formidable, if old, warship with fifteen 6" guns and an Exocet missile-mounting, and her powerful escorts, were one wing of an Argentinian flotilla which had put to sea to engage the task force. The other wing was spearheaded by the ageing aircraft carrier, *Vintecinco de Maio* which was not up to the job because of its faulty engines, and had to pull back. Its misfortunes made it necessary for the Argentinian naval command to revise its plan. Their reaction appears to have been muddled and irresolute. As a result, the *General Belgrano*'s captain was not clear whether he should proceed to engage the task force or turn back to port. When attacked, his squadron was zig-zagging, a normal precaution given the suspected presence of submarines, and he was uncertain what his seniors wanted. *Conqueror*'s commander was in contact with the War Cabinet in London which believed, thanks to intercepted Argentinian naval signals, that the *General Belgrano* would take the offensive and could inflict considerable damage. There is, of course, a time lapse between the interception of signals, their deciphering, assessment and delivery to senior commanders, so that it would be quite possible for the decision to sink the cruiser to have been taken before clear evidence had been received that the Argentinian naval command had called off its operation. Even so, this does not take account of the possibility that minds might quickly have changed in Buenos Aires.

The news that the *General Belgrano* had been sunk was greeted with an eruption of gung-ho jingoism in some quarters of the Press. 'GOTCHA' was *The Sun*'s headline, but whilst it may have quickened the blood of saloon bar patriots, it was ill-received by many sailing towards the Falklands. 'Lurid headlines in some papers made us uncomfortable — and some made us angry', especially those which gloated over the enemy's losses.[1] On board the ships, there was keen interest in what was being written and said about the war coupled with irritation about the speculation invited from strategic pundits. In making suggestions as to what might happen next, some of these experts were thought to have placed operations in hazard. As men tensed themselves for action, there were strong hopes that the various diplomatic manoeuvres to avert a fight would come to nothing.[2] Mrs Thatcher's steadfastness won widespread approval from officers and men, but it was not universal. One naval officer, who died when the *Sheffield* was struck, expressed misgivings about the war in letters home which his family subsequently published. In tone and content, they were uncommonly like the material sent back to Britain by officers serving in the Crimea.

In terms of Imperial warfare, nothing like the Falklands had been experienced since the Boer of 1899 when British forces, in pursuit of Imperial policies, engaged a foe who possessed an abundance of modern weaponry which they knew how to use. In wider strategic terms it was a limited war of the eighteenth century type in which political and diplomatic objectives were first clearly laid down, and once they had been achieved, the fighting ended. To forestall a further Argentinian *coup de main* against the islands, which remains a possibility since Britain and the Argentine have not yet reached any agreement about their future, a large and costly base has been built there. The construction of what its detractors call 'Fortress Falklands' represented a remarkable reversal of British strategic planning, which since 1970 has pared former global commitments to the bone, and concentrated the bulk of land, air and sea forces in Western Europe and the North Atlantic.

In picking up a small part of its former network of world bases, Britain has performed a useful service for her allies. The previous two decades of European withdrawal from colonial empires had been marked by a steady advance of Soviet Russia as a global power. Soviet pretensions in Southern Africa and the South Atlantic were supported by a naval base at Luanda, which was in turn safeguarded by a client regime underpinned by Cuban troops. Western interests in the region were supported by the South African Government which is at present facing an upsurge of internal restlessness. Distasteful features of South Africa's racial policies make it hard for Western nations to back it too openly, and the same has also proved true of the old-style South American warlords who, whatever else they did, cared for American interests and took a strong line with Communism. The time when United States administrations could follow Truman's line of 'maybe he is a bastard, but he's our bastard' is passing. At the same time, America must face the abandonment of control over the Panama Canal which in a nuclear age was always a risky communication link. Whatever else it may be, 'Fortress Falklands' is a strong Western base in the South Atlantic which flanks the Cape Horn route around South America. It remains to be seen whether such considerations influence the development of the Falklands or any settlement of their sovereignty.

By the reconquest and fortification of the Falklands, Britain seems to have embraced policies which appeared to have been abandoned long before the final dismantlement of the Empire. At home, the war was seen as a reassertion of old values and as a psychological regeneration of a country which had been too long caught up in an apologetic retreat from former glory. Victory in war has always been considered as a yardstick of national willpower and moral fibre, so it was not surprising that the Falklands campaign triggered a mood of jaunty congratulation and cocksuredness. The armed forces had much to be proud of, for they had performed with efficiency and courage. Those involved had all been professionals, well-trained and with a high morale, factors which, together with an absence of exposure to heavy artillery bombardment, led to relatively few cases of battleshock. Details of the men's performance and that of their weaponry, all of which was conceived for use in a war against the forces of Russia and her allies, are still being evaluated.

The Falklands enabled Britain's wars of Imperial withdrawal to end with a flourish. Elsewhere there was a harder reality; the garrison in Hong Kong will depart within a decade when the colony passes back to China as the result of an agreement reached in 1984. In the same year the British people had another galling reminder that the old days had passed away when United States forces occupied the former West Indian colony of Grenada to frustrate a Communist takeover.

In 1953, when the new Queen inspected the veterans at the Royal Hospital at Chelsea, she met old soldiers who, as young men, had fought the Empire's wars in Zululand, the Sudan and Burma. Amongst their brothers-in-arms had been survivors of the Indian Mutiny who, like them, had taken the Queen's shilling in the certain knowledge that they might be called upon to fight for the defence and extension of Britain's Empire. Amongst today's Chelsea Pensioners are men who wear medals won in similar wars in India and the Middle East, earned in the campaigns between the wars when there was still a need to chastise the bolder and more persistent breakers of the Imperial peace. There are others, too, who gained their medals in the last Imperial wars fought not to conquer or to punish, but to smooth the way for a withdrawal from the tropical Empire and the Middle East. All, together with sailors and airmen, did their duty according to the traditions of their service and irrespective of their private feelings.

Thanks to their adherence to duty, Britain was able to dissolve the largest Empire which the world has known with relatively little disruption and bloodshed in just over twenty years. The political mainspring for this policy was a Whiggishness which recognized the historical forces of nationalism and worked with, rather than against, them. By bowing to the winds of change, Britain saved herself much heartache and treasure. Other colonial powers were less far-sighted and less fortunate. France fought a long, tenacious war in defence of Algeria against FLN which culminated in a *coup* managed by diehard front line commanders in May 1958. The upshot was the reinstallation of de Gaulle whose realistic willingness to negotiate with the Algerian Arabs prompted a further, unsuccessful military revolt in 1961. Portugal, embroiled in a struggle for her African territories from 1960 onwards, suffered convulsions after fourteen years of war undertaken by a largely conscripted army. The 'Movement of the Armed Forces' unseated President Caetano in April 1974 and paved the way for the evacuation of the empire and the establishment of democratic government. No such traumas accompanied Britain's retreat from Empire.

Notes

1. Introduction

1. Younghusband,
2. Richards, 182.
3. Swindlehurst,
4. Haldane, 401–2.
5. Stockwell, 6, fos. 5, 22, 26, 28 and letter of 19.9.56.
6. Dunsterville, 11.
7. Killingray, 438.
8. See page 119.
9. Adm. 53/125421.
10. CO 123/296 (Report of Belize Riot).
11. Adm 116/3253.
12. CO 968/3/13,95.
13. *Ibid.*, 43.
14. CO 968/17/5.
15. CO 968/13/5,1.
16. Kisch, 138.
17. Thorne, 392.
18. CO 318/350 (16.2.19).
19. Marder, 71 note 2, Adm 116/3476.
20. Air 8/45,2.
21. Green, 14.4.53.
22. Gibb, 96.
23. WO 32/15772,106A.
24. WO 203/4460 (8.1.46).
25. WO 32/11757,23A.
26. *Ibid.*
27. Wavell, 297.
28. WO 106/259 (Memo from Capt. J. E. Phillips, 15.7.17).
29. Collins, 135.
30. CO 1015/463, Report May 1953.
31. Furse, 306.
32. CO 968/3/13, 89 & 99.
33. Allen, 149.
34. Thorne, 392.
35. WO 106/1594C.
36. Nkomo, 80.
37. WO 32/11757, 10A.
38. Dinwiddy, 43.

2. The Raj Under Siege

1. Swindlehurst, 14.2.20.
2. WO 106/3793.162A,167A.

3. Maynard.
4. Smyth, 105.
5. Interview with Mr. Wright.
6. Prendergast, 89–90.
7. Masters, 83.
8. Interview with Mr. Roberts.
9. WO 32/5916; Letter from Mr. Deighton, 22.8.85.
10. *Operations in Waziristan*, 32.
11. Lewis, 21.9.20.
12. WO 106/15A, 17A, 29A, 30A.
13. Air 2/125B/11395.
14. Hauner, *passim*.
15. Lewis, 11.11.19.
16. Quoted in WO 106/1594C.
17. Masters, 195–6.
18. Molesworth, 80.
19. Masters, 198–9.
20. *Operations in Waziristan*, 66–7, 69–70, 71; Lewis, 9.9.19.
21. Gould, 117–21.
22. Letter from Brigadier Hopkinson, 20.10.85.
23. Letter from Mr. Deighton, 22.8.85.
24. Lewis, 29.2.20.
25. Maynard, Letter from Brigadier Hopkinson, 20.10.85.
26. *Operations in Waziristan*, 49, 83.
27. Air 2/125B/11395.
26. *Operations in Waziristan*, 89, 90, 94–6, 117–8; Lewis, 3.12.19; Air 8/72.
29. Air 8/72 (Report of 1926–7 Operations).
30. Air 8/40.
31. Air 8/40, 9.
32. *Ibid*.
33. Townsend, 158.
34. WO 32/3519.
35. WO 106/3793, 81A, 84A.
36. For what follows, letters from Brigadier Hopkinson and Mr. Rainey.
37. WO 106/3793, 43A, 48A.
38. WO 106/3822.
39. Wavell, 179.
40. O'Dwyer, 3.
41. Willcocks, xii.
42. Wavell, 97.
43. WO 32/15772, 72A.
44. WO 106/3723A, 125.
45. Interview with Mr. Roberts.
46. WO 32/3519.
47. Atkinson, 386–7.
48. WO 32/4564.
49. Morgan.
50. *Ibid*.
51. Air 8/46, 9.
52. Morgan.
53. Swindlehurst, 14.2.20; letter from Mr. Simms, 27.9.85; Smyth, 61.
54. *Ibid*., 93–5.
55. Letter from Mr. Simms, 27.9.85.
56. WO 106/3721, 1, 1A.
57. Wavell, 181.
58. Bristow, 163.
59. Wavell, 181.

Notes

3. An Empire Founded Upon Sand

1. A. T. Wilson, 18.
2. WO 32/9614, 4.
3. B. Thomas, 46, 51–2, 57–8.
4. A. T. Wilson, 128.
5. Gilbert, IV, 492.
6. *Ibid.*
7. WO 95/5414 (15th Sikhs War Diary).
8. *Ibid* (E. Yorks Regt., 1–30.10.20).
9. Bousett, 6, 8, 9.10.20.
10. WO 95/5229 (5th Brigade; App. 1, 11–12.12.20).
11. Gilbert, IV, Comp., 1591; WO 32/5191,13A.
12. Gilbert, IV, 649; WO 32/5184.
13. Gilbert, IV, 494; WO 32/5191.
14. WO 32/5749.
15. WO 95/5430 (Staff Diary; Sadleir-Jackson's Brigade, 2.8.19).
16. Gilbert, IV, Comp., 1591.
17. Haldane, 390–2, 401–2.
18. Gilbert, IV, 709.
19. Keith, 18.
20. *Ibid.*, 24–5.
21. Boyle, 390.
22. Adm 116/3190.
23. Air 40/1442, 2.
24. Air 2/269.
25. Air 5/1292 (Operations Diary 1930–32).
26. Keith, 13.
27. Air 5/1292 (Operations summary, 1932).
28. Keith, 7.
29. Air 5/1292 (Operations summary, 1931).
30. Simmons, *passim.*
31. Air 8/40; Air 8/45; Air 8/72 (all contain evidence and arguments for air control).
32. Air 8/45; Townsend, 155.
33. Gilbert, IV, Comp., 1561; Boyle, 389.
34. Gilbert, IV, Comp., 1561.
35. Boyle, 511.
36. CO 968/10/3, 1, 5, 12.
37. Townsend, *passim* for moral debate.
38. WO 106/5708, 2,15, 26.
39. Gilbert, IV, 615; *Ibid.*, Comp., 1450; WO 32/9614, 22.
40. CO 733/311/2, 48.
41. WO 95/4725 (M. P. & Provost-Marshall Lines of Communication, Dec. 1918).
42. WO 32/4562 (HQ Palestine 1938; propaganda).
43. WO 32/4177.
44. Norman, 26.9.36.
45. WO 32/4562, 11–12.
46. CO 733/315/6.
47. *Ibid.*
48. Letter from Mr. Weaver, 19.9.85.
49. Verney, 48.
50. Begin, 205.
51. WO 106/5929.
52. R. D. Wilson, 15, 17–18, 28–8.
53. WO 32/10837, 57A.
54. *Ibid.*, 1B; R. Wilson, 30–3.
55. Bethel, 352, 355.
56. Adm 116/5648 for what follows.

57. Interview with Mr. Paice.
58. Adm 116/5648 (Report of Lt. Comm. E. A. S. Bailey).
59. This account is taken from: WO 95/4455 (General Staff Diary), 1–31.3.19. Details of the use of aircraft, *Ibid.*, 11–12, 16, 24.3.19, App. C (10). Also Brugger, 103–4, 116, 117–8. Details of the 1924 deployment are in Air 9/49, 10.
60. Cloake, 341–2.
61. *Ibid.*, 355.
62. Kiernan, 228–9.
63. Gilbert, IV, 575–6.
64. Ironside, 149, 152–3.
65. Simmons.
66. Wavell, 94–5.
67. WO 32/15497; Lunt, 93.
68. Lunt, 163–4.
69. Akehurst, 13.
70. *Ibid.*, 16.
71. Halliday, 327–8.
72. Akehurst, 43–4.
73. *Ibid.*, 26–8.
74. Air 8/72; Boyle, 570.
75. Lydford (HTL 7: Report of Lydford's period as AOC Aden, 1945–8).
76. *Ibid.*
77. *Ibid.* and HTL 4 and 5.
78. Paget, *Last Post*, 151.
79. *Ibid.*, 170–1.
80. Halliday, 226.
81. Monroe, 56.
82. WO 106/1594C.
83. Paget, *Last Post*, 255.

4. Wars of the Jungle

1. Gentleman, 48.
2. *Ibid.*, 265; The account of operations in Java and Saigon is based upon the following War Diaries: WO 172/1789 (S. E. Asia Command HQ), WO 172/9878 and 102000 (Seaforth Highlanders) and Adm 53/122341 (log, HMS *Sussex*).
3. Marshall, 18.1.46 and Report (15.2.46); WO 172/1789, Intelligence Reports 53 and 63.
4. Short, 60–1.
5. Air 34/1936.
6. Barber, 48–9.
7. Cloake, 221–2.
8. Short, 163–5.
9. *Ibid.*, 153.
10. *Ibid.*
11. Cloake, 234.
12. Barber, 62.
13. *Ibid.*, 121.
14. Gibb, 98.
15. *Ibid.*, 77.
16. Short, 168–9.
17. Gibb, 97.
18. Air 34/1936.
19. Gibb, 96.
20. Harris and Paxman, 100.
21. *Ibid.*, 191–2; Clutterbuck, 160.
22. Adm 116/5752.
23. Pocock, 161.

5. Winds of Change and Storms of War

1. WO 32/5809 (Despatch: 5.4.16).
2. *Ibid.*
3. WO 106/272 (Mss History of Somaliland Camel Corps).
4. Killingray, 429.
5. WO 32/5828.
6. WO 106/272, fo. 107.
7. *Ibid.*
8. Air 8/40.2.
9. Russell.
10. Air 5/1422.
11. *Ibid.*
12. Lydford (HTL, 5 & 6).
13. Air 20/680.
14. Air 20/684, 34.
15. Killingray, 439.
16. Collins, 134.
17. Air 9/49, 13.
18. *Ibid.*, 7.
19. Killingray, 439, Air 20/683, 19, 2 & 3.
20. Air 9/49, 14.
21. Air 20/683, 19, 3.
22. Air 8/45.
23. Kariuki, 23–4, Barnett and Njama, 53–6.
24. Barnett and Njama, 56–9.
25. Kariuki, 29–30.
26. Barnett and Njama, 118–9.
27. Kariuki, 28–9.
28. Arnold, 62.
29. Throup, 419.
30. Arnold, 57.
31. Kariuki, 11–12.
32. CO 1015/463 (Report Nov. 1951).
33. Kariuki, 32.
34. Throup, 411.
35. Kariuki, 22.
36. CO 822/447, 71.
37. *Ibid.*
38. CO 822/444, 5.
39. *Ibid.*, (Baring to Lyttelton, 9.10.52).
40. *Ibid.*, pp. 11 and 13.
41. CO 822/444, 6.
42. Throup, 420.
43. Barnett and Njama, 180–3, 347.
44. Arnold, 120–1.
45. CO 822/454, 124.
46. CO 822/444. 6.
47. Barnett and Njama, 130–1.
48. *Ibid.*, 70.
49. *Ibid.*, 299.
50. Stockwell, 5 (4.4.54).
51. Barnett and Njama, 137.
52. CO 822/854, 229 and 252.
53. *Ibid.*, 141.
54. *Ibid.*, 194.
55. *Ibid.*, 237.
56. Stockwell, 5 (30.8.54).

57. For reports on Lari Massacre and Naivasha Raid, CO 822/447.14., CO 822/454, 141.
58. CO 822/474, 20 (figure for arrests between 20 October 1952 and 15 December 1953; nearly 120,000 'convicted' Mau Mau were in detention).
59. CO 822/454, 119.
60. Kariuki, 60.
61. Stockwell, 5.
62. Barnett and Njama, 203, 267, 309, 410–11.
63. CO 822/454, 194.
64. Stockwell, 5 (Report on Operation Thunderbolt).
65. CO 822/454, 211.
66. *Ibid.*, 201.
67. *Ibid.*, 38, 158, 159, 169, 171, 173 for suspects shot whilst trying to get away during February 1953.
68. *Ibid.*, 179.
69. CO 822/474, 20.
70. CO 822/444 (Baring to Lyttelton, 9.10.52, p. 14).
71. CO 822/474, 20.
72. CO 822/471, 70 and 71 (Report of RA Wilkinson, magistrate).
73. *Ibid.*, 33.
74. CO 822/474, 42.
75. Barnett and Njama, 220.
76. Documents relating to the deaths of eleven Mau Mau detainees at Hola Camp, *passim*.
77. CO 822/454, 247.
78. CO 822/461 (Information from WH Ingrams, 7.7.53).
79. *Ibid.*, 29.
80. CO 822/447, 25.
81. CO 822/461, 29.
82. *Ibid.*, 94, CO 822/447, 58, 67, 71.
83. CO. 822/461, 94.
84. CO 1015/463 (Report, February 1953).
85. CO 822/447.3467.
86. *Ibid.*, 58.
87. *Ibid.*, 14.
88. CO 822/461, 76.
89. *Ibid.*

6. John Bull's Other Wars

1. *Intelligence Notes*, 95, 100, 102.
2. Childs, 109–10.
3. Gilbert, IV, 464.
4. *Ibid.*, 454.
5. Barton, 209.
6. Swindlehurst.
7. Butler, 34.
8. O'Malley, 17.
9. *Ibid.*, 23–4.
10. Barton, 200–1.
11. Gilbert, IV, 455.
12. Crozier, 274.
13. *Ibid.*, 290.
14. *Ibid.*, 255–8.
15. *Ibid.*, 258–9.
16. Swindlehurst, 20.1.21.
17. Barton, 199–200.
18. Swindlehurst, 20.1.21.
19. *Ibid.*, 19.1.21.
20. *Ibid.*

21. Barton, 205.
22. Brenan, 94–6.
23. Air 8/48.
24. Gilbert, IV, 455.
25. Beaumont, 89.
26. Kiernan, 192–3.
27. *Intelligence Notes*, 4. 6–7.
28. Hamill, 18.
29. *Ibid.*, 13.
30. Macstiofáin, 269.
31. Hamill, 23–4.
32. Private Information.
33. *Ibid.*
34. Clarke, 53.
35. *Ibid.*, 59–60.

7. With Moore to Port Stanley

1. Fox, 15.
2. *Ibid.*, 61.

Bibliography

Public Record Office, London

Air [Air Ministry] 2, 4, 5, 8, 9, 20, 34, 40, 48
Adm [Admiralty] 53, 116
CO [Colonial Office] 318, 733, 822, 968, 1015
WO [War Office] 32, 95, 106, 172, 203

* Denotes unpublished material: IWM = Imperial War Museum; NAM = National Army Museum.

Africa Research Bulletin, I (1964) onwards
A. S. Ahmed, *Millenium and Charisma among the Pathans* (Routledge & Kegan Paul, 1976)
J. Akehurst, *We Won a War: Campaign in Oman 1965–75* (Salisbury: M. Russell, 1974)
*W. D. Allen, Papers, IWM
G. Arnold, *Kenyatta and the Politics of Kenya* (Longman, 1974)
*C. T. Atkinson, *A History of the Royal Dragoons* (1934)
N. Barber, *The War of the Running Dogs* (Collins, 1971)
C. Barnett, *Britain and her Army* (Penguin, 1974)
D. J. Barrett & K. Njama, *Mau Mau from Within* (1966)
E. C. Barton, *Let the Boy win his Spurs* (Research Publishing Co., 1976)
M. Begin, *The Revolt* (W. H. Allen, 1979 ed.)
R. A. Beaumont, *A New Lease on Empire: Air Policing, 1919–39, Aerospace Historian*
N. Bethel, *The Palestine Triangle* (Deutsch, 1979)
B. Bond, *British Military Policy between the two World Wars* (Oxford, 1980)
A. Boyle, *Trenchard: Man of Vision* (Collins, 1962)
*E. V. S. Bousett, Diary 1919–20, IWM
M. Brennan, *The War in Clare* (Dublin: Four Courts, 1980)
*R. C. Bristow, *Memories of the Raj* (1974)
S. Brugger, *The Australians in Egypt* (Melbourne University Press, 1980)
*E. Butler, *Barry's Flying Column* (1971)
*W. Childs, *Episodes and Reflections* (1930)
A. F. N. Clarke, *Contact* (Secker & Warburg, 1983)
J. Cloake, *Templar: Tiger of Malaya* (Harrap, 1985)
R. Clutterbuck, *The Long, Long War* (Cassell 1967)
M. J. Cohen, *Palestine: Retreat from Mandate, 1936–45* (Elek, 1978)
D. H. Cole, *Imperial Military Geography* (1929 ed.)
*R. O. Collins, *Shadows in the Grass: Britain and the Southern Sudan, 1918–56* (1983)
*F. P. Crozier, *Impressions and Recollections* (1930)
F. P. Cruikshank, *SOE in the Far East* (Oxford University Press, 1986)
H. Dalton, *Hide Tide and After: Memoirs, 1945–60* (Cape, 1962)
J. Danby, *Conflict in Northern Ireland* (1976)
H. Dinwiddy, The Ugandan Army and Makerere under Obote, 1962–7, *African Affairs*, 82 (1983)
Documents relating to the deaths of eleven Mau Mau detainees in Hola Camp, Kenya (HMSO, 1959)
A. J. Doulton, *The Fighting Cock* (Aldershot, 1951)

Bibliography 237

A. Draper, *The Amritsar Massacre* (Buchan & Enright, 1985 ed.)
L. C. Dunsterville, *The Adventures of Dunsterforce* (1920)
O. D. Edwards, *The Sins of our Fathers* (1970)
G. Fairbarn, *Revolutionary Guerrilla Warfare* (Penguin, 1974)
*H. Forster, An account of service in the Regular Army, 1934–66, IWM.
R. C. G. Foster, *History of the Queen's Regiment, VII (1924–48)* (Aldershot, 1953)
R. Fox, *Eyewitnesses Falklands* (Methuen, 1982)
R. Furse, *Aucuparius* (Oxford University Press, 1962)
J. Gallagher, Crisis of Empire, 1919–22, *Modern Asian Studies*, 15 (1981)
M. F. Gentleman (ed.), *Vietnam* (Penguin, 1965)
*I. S. Gibb, A Walk in the Forest, IWM
M. G. Gilbert, *Winston Churchill* IV, 1916–22, and Companion Volumes I and II (Heinemann, 1975–77)
B. J. Gould, *The Jewel in the Lotus* (1957)
*P. C. A. Green, Letters, 1953–4, IWM
A. Haldane, *A Soldier's Saga* (1948)
F. Halliday, *Arabia Without Sultans* (Penguin, 1974)
D. Hamill, *Pig in the Middle: the Army in Northern Ireland, 1969–84* (Methuen, 1985)
R. Harris & J. Paxman, *A Higher Form of Killing* (Chatto & Windus, 1982)
M. Hauner, One Man Against Empire: the Faqir of Ipi and the British &c., *Journal of Contemporary History*, 16 (1981)
I. Henderson & P. Goodhart, *The Hunt for Dedan Kimaithi* (1962 ed.)
F. Hinsley &c., *British Intelligence in the Second World War*, I (Cambridge University Press, 1979)
Intelligence Notes, 1913–16, ed. B. M. G. Choille (Dublin, 1972)
Ironside, Lord, *High Road to Command: the Diaries of Major-General Sir Edmund Ironside, 1920–22* (1972)
J. M. Kariuki, *Mau Mau Detainee* (Oxford University Press, 1963)
C. H. Keith, *Flying Years* (1937)
V. G. Kiernan, *European Empire from Conquest to Collapse, 1815–1960* (Fontana 1982)
D. Killingray, A Swift Agent of Colonial Government: Air Power in British Colonial Africa, *Journal of African History*, 25 (1984)
C. King, *The Cecil King Diaries, 1965–70* (1972)
R. Kisch, *Days of the Good Soldiers* (Journeyman, 1983)
H. Kissinger, *The White House Years* (Weidenfeld, 1979)
M. Leifer, ed. *Constraints and Adjustments in British Foreign Policy* (Allen & Unwin, 1972)
*H. V. Lewis, Letters and Papers, IWM
J. Lunt, *Imperial Sunset* (MacDonald, 1981)
*H. T. Lydford, Letters and Papers, IWM
S. Macstiofain, *Memoirs of a Revolutionary* (Gordon Gremonesi, 1975)
A. J. Marder, *From the Dardanelles to Oran* (Collins, 1974)
J. Marlowe, *Rebellion in Palestine* (1946)
*C. Marshall, Diary, IWM
P. Mason, *A Matter of Honour* (Penguin, 1976)
J. Masters, *Bugles and a Tiger* (Buchan and Enright, 1987)
*E. H. Maynard, Papers, IWM
G. N. Molesworth, *Afghanistan, 1919* (New York, 1962)
M. Monroe, *Britain's Moment in the Middle East* (1981 ed.)
Moran, Lord, *Winston Churchill: the struggle for survival, 1940–65* (Sphere, 1968 ed.)
*M. H. L. Morgan, The Truth about Amritsar, IWM
J. Nkomo, *The Story of my Life* (Methuen, 1984)
*C. P. Norman, Diary, IWM
M. O'Dwyer, The Truth about the Indian Trouble, *The Daily Mail Blue Book on the Indian Crisis, 1931*
Operations in Waziristan, 1919–20 (Calcutta, 1921)
E. O. O'Malley, *The Singing Flame* (Dublin: Anvil Books, 1979)
F. M. Osanka (ed.), *Modern Guerilla Warfare* (New York, 1961)
J. Paget, *Counter-Insurgency Campaigning* (1967)
——, *Last Post: Aden, 1964–67* (1969)

Bibliography

T. Pocock, *Fighting General* (Collins, 1973)
J. Prendergast, *Prender's Progress* (Cassell, 1979)
L. W. Pye, *Guerrilla Communism in Malaya* (Princetown, 1956)
Report of the Committee to consider in the context of Civil Liberties and Human Rights measures to deal with terrorism in Northern Ireland (HMSO, 1975)
Report of the Enquiry into allegations against the Security Forces of physical brutality in Northern Ireland (HMSO, 1971)
J. Richards, *Visions of Yesterday* (Routledge & Kegan Paul, 1973)
*A. B. Russell, Papers, IWM
A. Seldon, *Churchill's Indian Summer* (Hodder, 1981)
R. Shaye & C. Vermaak, *The Silent War* (Salisbury, Rhodesia, 1971)
A. Short, *The Communist Insurrection in Malaya, 1948–60* (Muller, 1975)
*L. A. Simmons, Diary and Papers, IWM
J. Smyth, *Milestones* (Sidgwick & Jackson, 1979)
*Stockwell Papers &c., NAM
*J. P. Swindlehurst, Diary October 1919–March 1921, IWM
B. Thomas, *Alarms and Excursions in Arabia* (1931)
C. Thorne, *Allies of a Kind* (Oxford University Press, 1978)
D. W. Throup, The Origins of Mau Mau, *African Affairs*, 84 (1985)
C. Townsend, Civilisation and Frightfulness: Air Control in the Middle East between the Wars, *Essays in Honour of A. J. P. Taylor* (1986), pp. 142–59
H. Truman, *Years of Hope and Trial, 1946–53* (Harper & Row, 1956)
F. Tuker, *While Memory Serves* (1986)
J. Verney, *Going to Wars* (Collins, 1955)
P. Warner, *Auchinleck: the Lonely Soldier* (Sphere, 1982 ed.)
Wavell, Lord, *The Viceroy's Diary*, P. Moon (ed.) (Oxford University Press, 1973)
J. Willcocks, *The Romance of Soldiering and Sport* (Cassell, 1925)
A. T. Wilson, *Mesopotamia, 1917–20* (1931)
H. Wilson, *The Labour Government, 1964–70* (Weidenfeld, 1976)
R. D. Wilson, *Cordon and Search* (Aldershot, 1949)
G. Younghusband, *Forty Years a Soldier* (Jenkins, 1922)

Index

Abu Dhabi, 113
Abadan crisis (1951), 103, 113
Aden, 7, 24, 68, 114, 117ff.
  evacuation, 121–5
  riots (1947), 120
Afghanistan, 30, 31, 35, 40–43
Afghan War, 3rd (1919), 40–41, 43, 48, 63
Afridi revolt (1930), 44
Alanbrooke, Field Marshal Lord, 65
Alexander, A.V., 18
Amin, Idi, 22, 27
Amritsar riots (1919), 54, 55, 59–64
Anguilla, 125
Arab Revolt
  (1916–18), 68–69
  (1929), 86–87
  (1936–39), 87–93, 126–7
Ascension Island, 223
Asmara, mutiny (1946), 27
Auchinleck, Field Marshal, 68

B Special Constabulary, 210–11, 213, 214
BBC, 16–17
Bahrain, 113
Balfour Declaration, 69, 54, 86, 101
Baghdad Pact, 25, 108
Baring, Sir Evelyn, 179–80, 181, 189
Begin, M., 93–94
Belize (British Honduras), 8
Ben Gurion, D., 23, 90, 93, 94, 103
Bevin, E., 94, 98, 99
Black and Tans, 13, 86, 203, 206
Bogside, 211
Borneo, 24, 113, 157ff.
Briggs, Lieutenant General Sir Harold, 144, 145, 149
Brunei, 157ff.
Burman, 56

Cairo Conference (1921), 75–76
Central African Federation, 192
Chelmsford, Lord (Viceroy of India), 13
Chemical weapons, 154–5

Chichester-Clarke, Major, 211
Chitral, 31
Christison, General Sir Alexander, 133
Churchill, Sir Winston, 11, 12, 53–54, 74–75, 76, 79, 83–84, 111–12, 129, 202, 206, 207
Cinema and Empire, 2, 5–6, 31–32, 162
Commonwealth, 22
Communist propaganda, 23
Communist subversion, 191–92
Congress Movement, 54–55
Cox, Sir Percy Z., 69, 79, 81
Curragh Incident (1914), 198
Curzon, marquess of, 9, 112
Cyprus, 16, 22, 24, 108, 109

Davidson, S., 17
Dedan Kimaithi, 182, 193
Defence expenditure, 14, 26
Dini ya Msamba cult, 6
Driberg, T., 17
Dutch East Indies (Indonesia), 130
Dyer, Brigadier General, 59

Easter rebellion (1916), 199
EEC, 125
Edelman, M., 17
Egypt, 24, 68, 107, 115, 120, 126
  rebellion (1919), 104–6
Egyptian nationalism, 84, 103–4, 107–8
Emergency Powers Act
  (1920), 59
  Northern Ireland (1973), 216
EOKA, 17
Erskine, General Sir Geoffrey, 186–7

Falkland Islands, 27–28
  war (1982), 222ff.
Faqir of Ipi (Mirza Ali Khan), 16, 37, 38–39, 47–48, 49, 51
Faqir of Swat, 37
FLOSY, 121, 124–5
French, Field Marshal Lord, 200

239

Index

Gandhi, M. K., 18, 55, 59, 64
Gas
  poison, 50, 74–75, 120
  tear, 58, 96, 101
General Belgrano, 224–26
Gent, Sir Edward, 142
Germany, 23
  and subversion on North-West Frontier, 38–39
  and subversion in Iraq, 82–83
  anti-British propaganda, 38, 127
Gray, Colonel Nicol, 148–9, 153

Habaniya (Iraq), 82–83
Haganah, 92–93, 96, 98, 101
Haldane, General Sir Aylmer, 5, 72–74
Heath, E., 195, 219, 222
Hola Camp, 190–91
Hong Kong, 10, 130, 227
  mutiny (1940), 11
Hotel David, 95, 96

Imperial strategy, 5–6, 10–14, 25–26
  India, 29–30, 34–36
  Middle East, 69, 76–77, 101–3, 113–15, 117–18, 121, 125, 127–8
India, 4, 9, Chapter Two *passim*
  nationalist movement, 54ff.
  partition, 65–66
Indian army, 10–11, 27, 33, 113–14
Indo-China campaign (1945), 131, 135–7
Indonesia, 158–9
  see also Dutch East Indies
INLA, 214–15
Irish nationalists in British army, 208
IRA, 196–208, 214ff.
  casualties (1919–22), 206
Iraq, 13, 70ff., 111, 112, 115, 118
Iraq Revolt
  (1920), 72–74
  (1941), 82–88
Ireland, 13, Chapter Six *passim*
Irgun, 93, 95ff.
Israel, collusion with (1956), 109–10

Jamaica, disorders (1919), 13
Japan, 11. 56
  and Asian nationalism, 129, 136–9
Java campaign (1945–46), 10, 11, 131–4, 136
Jerusalem riots (1920), 68–69
Jewish Revolt (1945–47), 95ff.
Jingoism, 15–16

Lari massacre (1953), 184
Lawrence, Colonel T. E., 19, 20, 45, 67, 68, 69, 75–76
Lloyd-George, D., 13, 67, 69, 200, 207
Lyttleton, O., 117, 148, 180, 181, 189

MacCready, General Sir Nevil, 203, 206
Malaya, 16, 19, 21, 24, Chapter Four *passim*
  British reoccupation of, 137–8
  mutiny of Parachute Regiment (1946), 17–18
  riots (1945-46), 137
  subversion in, 136ff.
Malayan Communist Party, 136–7, 138ff.
Mau Mau, 6, 172ff.
  oath-taking, 173–74, 179–80
Mopilah rebellion, (1921), 208
Morocco, Rif campaign, 8
Mosul, 67, 77–78
Motorman, Operation, 220–21
Mountbatten, Admiral Lord, 17, 108, 109, 131, 215
Mufti, the Grand (Haj Amin al-Husseini), 23, 82, 87ff.
Muslim resistance to Empire, 35–36, 39–40

Nasser, Colonel A., 23, 107, 108, 120, 128
NATO, 26, 125, 126
National Servicemen, 16
Native forces, 26–27
Nehru, J., 23, 108
Nkomo, J., 23–24
NLF, 121–2, 124–5
North-West Frontier, campaigns (1919–47), 29–30, Chapter Two *passim*
Neurs, operations against (1920–32), 169–72

O'Dwyer, Sir Michael, 54, 62
Oman, 114–15
  Dhofar campaign (1965–75), 115–17
O'Neill, Captain T., 210

Palestine, 8, 16, 17, 19, 24, 83ff.
  Arab-Jewish communal riots, 86–87
  campaigns (1936–39 and 1945–47) 87ff.
  Jewish immigration, 85–86
  Resistance Fund, 95
Persian Gulf, policing, 67–68, 111, 112–13
Persian oilfields, 67, 103
Persian operations (1919–20), 112
Peshawar riots (1930), 55, 64–65

'Quit India' disturbances (1942), 65

Index

Racial attitudes, 19–21, 129, 130, 117–18
Radfan campaign (1964–66), 122–23
RAF, 1, 3, 14, 76, 80–81, 82–83, 107, 113
  Aden operations (1928–48), 119–20
  Afghan war (1919), 48
  armoured car units, 79–80, 83
  Egypt operations (1919), 106
  Indian operations, 31, 40, 44–45
  Iraq operations (1917–41), 70–71, 74, 76–77, 79–80
  Ireland (1919–22), 207
  Java operations (1945–46), 133
  Kenya operations (1952–56), 188
  Kurdistan operations (1919–32), 71, 77–80
  Kuwait operations (1929–30), 112
  Malayan operations (1948–60), 151, 153, 154–5
  Palestine operations (1936–39), 87, 91–92, 99–100
  Somaliland operations (1920–22), 165–9
  Sudan operations, (1920–36), 170–2
Roosevelt, F.D.R., 21–22
Royal Indian Navy, mutiny (1946), 11, 56
Royal Navy, 2–3, 8, 14, 167
  warships
    Amethyst, 8, 154
    Antelope, 224
    Ardent, 224
    Ark Royal, 166
    Barham, 86, 107
    Brittenden, 100
    Childers, 100
    Conqueror, 224
    Courageous, 86
    Coventry, 224
    Cyclamen, 113
    Cyclops, 91
    Eagle, 8
    Emerald, 113
    Enterprise 113
    Greenfly, 73
    Iron Duke, 107
    Ladybird, 129
    Malaya, 107
    Mauritius, 101, 103
    Newfoundland, 154
    Prince of Wales, 130
    Repulse, 92, 130
    Sheffield, 226
    Sir Galahad, 225
    Sir Tristram, 225
RUC (Royal Ulster Constabulary), 212, 216, 217–18
Russia, 13, 15, 111–12, 115, 127
Russian subversion in India, 35, 38, 160, 191

Salmond, Air Marshal Sir John, 50, 61, 75, 77, 172

Sanussi, 165
Sayyid Muhammad Ibn Abdulla Hassan (known as the 'Mad Mullah'), 164–5
Sarawak, 157ff.
Singapore, surrender of (1942), 12, 52, 129, 130
Sinn Fein, 199, 200, 207, 208, 214
Somaliland Protectorate, operations in, 169–72
South Africa, aerial policing in, 172
South Arabia Federation, 120–1
South Georgia, 224
Southern Rhodesia (Zimbabwe), 22, 26, 125, 193, 193–4
Special Powers Acts (Northern Ireland), 209–10
Stern, A., 93
Sudan, 19, 169–72
Suez Canal, 6, 24, 84, 101, 102, 107, 108–10, 111
Suez campaign (1956), 101, 108–11

Tanganyika (Tanzania), mutiny (1964), 24
Templer, Field Marshal Lord, 108, 109, 143ff.
Thatcher, Mrs M., 225
Transjordan (Jordan), 76, 107, 111, 116–17
Trenchard, Marshal of the RAF Lord, 48, 49–50, 76, 80–81, 207, 208
Turkey
  air war in Kurdistan, 78
  threat of war with, 13, 77

Uganda, mutiny (1964), 27
Ulster Volunteer Force, 197–8
United States, 14, 21–22, 25–26, 101, 103, 111, 125–6, 127–8, 129–30, 130–1, 225, 227
  attitude to Jewish immigration, 94–95
  wars in South-East Asia, 161–2
United States Air Force, aerial policing in Solomon Islands (1943), 81–82

V Bombers, 25, 110
Viet Minh, 135

Washington Naval Treaty (1922), 14, 129
Wavell, Field Marshal Lord, 18, 52, 55–56, 89
Waziristan, 29, 31, 34, 43–45
  1936–39 campaign, 47–48
Wilson, Sir Harold, 9, 116, 117–18, 125, 194–5
Wilson, Field Marshal Sir Henry, 13, 74, 200, 203, 213
World War I, 9, 12, 67–68
  recruiting, 9, 21
World War II, 12, 14–15, 30, 129
  recruiting, 9–10, 20–21

Yemen, 7, 115, 117, 118–19, 120, 123

Zambia (formerly Northern Rhodesia), 194

ZANU, 195
ZAPU, 23, 195
Zetland, Lord, 58
Zionism, 23, 84–85, 93ff.